Contemporary Thought
on Teaching

Contemporary Thought
on Teaching

Edited by

Ronald T. Hyman
Rutgers University

PRENTICE-HALL, INC., *Englewood Cliffs, New Jersey*

Current printing (last number):

10 9 8 7 6 5 4 3 2 1

P–13–170209–2
C–13–170217–3

Library of Congress Catalog Card Number: 73–106150

PRENTICE-HALL INTERNATIONAL, INC.
London
PRENTICE-HALL OF AUSTRALIA, PTY. LTD.
Sydney
PRENTICE-HALL OF CANADA, LTD.
Toronto
PRENTICE-HALL OF INDIA PRIVATE LTD.
New Delhi
PRENTICE-HALL OF JAPAN, INC.
Tokyo

Printed in the United States of America

Dedicated to

Jonathan, Elana, and Rachel
who are proud that I am a teacher

Contents

Foreword

This book is offered as an anthology of contemporary thought on teaching, a topic of utmost importance in this decade or any decade. The growing concern about teaching is a natural outgrowth in an era when people urgently seek ways to understand the social problems facing the nation at large and to work out solutions for the problems. People realize full well that in their attempts to reform a school's curriculum, as one significant response to the social problems youth pose to the nation, they must know about teaching. Curriculum reforms in large measure depend on teaching reforms, which in turn depend on an understanding of teaching. This applies to all levels of teaching from nursery school through doctoral seminars.

The growing concern about teaching also stems from the more general concern of all professionals for the clarification of key concepts and the development of theory in their respective fields. That the concept of teaching is a key concept in education is a truism that needs no explication. Likewise, the need and desire for the development of a theory of teaching are evident from any perusal of educational discussions. Much of the recent research effort of educators can be viewed rightfully as being part of the over-all attempt to develop a theory of teaching.

But whether or not we agree that this concern stems from the two sources mentioned above, it is quite apparent that when discussion begins about *what teaching is,* the topic of *good teaching* soon arises. Equally true is the observation that when people discuss what constitutes *good teaching,* they soon turn to discussing the *concept of teaching* and the *theory of teaching.* Discussion on any one of these three aspects of teaching quickly evokes the other two.

Indeed, to discuss one without giving attention to the other two leaves a feeling of inadequate treatment. This is particularly true with prospective teachers and in-service teachers eager to delve into educational issues.

This book brings together a collection of current written thoughts on these aspects of teaching: the concept of teaching, the theory of teaching, and the evaluation of teaching.[1] Each of these three main parts has been subdivided so as to help the reader see the various points more clearly. For example, it is important to note that whereas one author writes about how to measure and evaluate teaching, another author presents his own notions about what good teaching is. However, both are initially concerned with the evaluation of teaching rather than the development of theory. On the other hand, the reader will note that several articles cut across the various divisions established here. These divisions as conceived by the editor cannot subsume all of each selected article for each was written independently and may well have been structured according to a different framework of organization.

The selections were made with these criteria in mind: (1) contribution of significant thoughts on teaching; (2) readability, primarily for students; (3) pertinence of the material to the three parts of this book; and (4) balance of selections. Obviously, then, this book is not a complete compilation of all the available current material on teaching. No single book could be— nor probably should be—all-inclusive. Certain articles well known to professors are not included since classroom experience has shown that they are difficult and confusing for students though not necessarily so for professors. Those who wish to read further on these aspects of teaching are urged to consult the references listed in the various overviews by the editor and in the articles by the authors.

In the overviews I raise questions for the reader to consider. I do not attempt to present a summary of the ideas in each selection. Rather, the purpose of the overview for me is to set the articles in context, to highlight certain points, to relate the articles to other material, and to evoke critical reading via the posing of questions. If the overviews accomplish this and if the articles provide a springboard for examining teaching, this anthology will achieve its objective.

Finally, I take this opportunity to thank my colleagues and students who guided me in the selection of the articles for this book. Most of all, obviously, I am indebted to the authors and publishers who permitted me to print their works here. I offer this anthology with the expectation that the readers will benefit as I have from the stimulating thoughts on teaching presented by

[1] For a companion volume dealing with the various vantage points for viewing teaching see the anthology, *Teaching: Vantage Points for Study,* ed. Ronald T. Hyman (Philadelphia: J. B. Lippincott Co., 1968). This book includes material from most of the current research on teacher verbal activity in the classroom.

the various authors. The complexity of teaching deserves the serious consideration of every reader.

New Brunswick, N.J.   RONALD T. HYMAN

The Concept
of Teaching

part one

Teaching as It in Fact Occurs:
Overview

This first group of selections focuses on the characteristics of teaching as it is. The articles primarily attempt to get at the heart of teaching by describing teaching as it in fact occurs. Their very titles and first sentences indicate their attempts. Smith and Jackson both give their reasons for concentrating on the "as is" of teaching. Smith claims that knowledge of teaching *as it is* is prerequisite to our efforts to improve teaching, and everyone admits the need for improving teaching. Jackson point out first the lack of success of researchers when they focus on the "good" teacher and second the need to know about an "everyday event" central to human affairs. Both Smith and Jackson are clearly right in their claims and the reader is asked to recall them when he ventures into Part Three of this anthology.

Jackson presents several key ideas, which are particularly heightened when they are considered in light of those in other articles. Jackson claims that to understand what occurs in the interaction between teacher and pupil it is necessary to understand what goes on before and after the "interactive teaching" situation. (To his credit, Jackson does not seem to say that this is sufficient but then *we* must ask what else is needed.) He goes so far as to label the "before" part as *preactive teaching*. The reader must ask himself if the preactive activities of the teacher performed without the pupil, however crucial they are to the activity of teaching, are to be considered "teaching." (Mitchell[1] and others make the point

[1] Frank W. Mitchell, "Some Notes on the Concept of Teaching," *Journal of Teacher Education,* 17 (Summer, 1966), 162–71.

that at least two persons are needed in teaching. Hughes[2] describes teaching as the interaction between teacher and student.) In any case, Jackson's distinction between preactive and interactive teaching serves to point up the need for studying more than the "calm" part of interactive teaching if we are to understand teaching as it is. And, as Jackson points out, the calm part has been studied to the exclusion of the more hectic parts.

Smith in this section does not explicitly characterize teaching as interaction, but he acknowledges the mutual influence of teacher and pupil when he says that the teacher observes the students, diagnoses their interests and feelings, and follows the progress of their understanding. This point is also presented clearly in Smith's second article, appearing in Section Two of this book. In yet another place,[3] Smith characterizes teaching as nonsymmetrical and unidirectional. That is to say, teaching is nonsymmetrical in that the teacher influences the pupil, but the pupil may "sometimes but not always" influence the teacher. Teaching is unidirectional in that the influence is directed at the development of the *student*'s cognitive structures, operations, images, and so on. We ask, then, if Jackson and Smith are in agreement regarding the interplay between teacher and student. Keep in mind Jackson's statement, "For one thing, by the questions, requests and reactions, students, to some extent, control what the teacher does...." Hence, we ask, "Is teaching interactive?"

Smith goes on to treat the role of signs and symbols in teaching and emphasizes the use of language in teaching. According to Smith, the teacher uses language in his attempt to "increase the student's fund of knowledge." Is Smith correct in stating that teaching cannot occur without language? Can teaching be conducted nonverbally?[4] Is the main function of teaching to increase the student's fund of knowledge?

Oakeshott presents four tasks that the teacher performs in teaching. Though Oakeshott spends little time with tasks one and three, the reader is well advised not to underestimate their importance. Oakeshott's question about what part of our inheritance to teach is pedagogical dynamite. The reader is asked to compare Oakeshott's points to Smith's statement that the teacher's task is to direct the pupil's attention to what is to be learned and the activities designed to bring about the desired learning. Oakeshott's question about what we *should* teach is obviously related to the question about what we *can* teach. This latter question also deserves the reader's

[2] Marie Hughes, "Teaching Is Interaction," *Elementary School Journal,* 58 (May, 1958), 457–64.

[3] B. Othanel Smith, "A Conceptual Analysis of Instructional Behavior," *Journal of Teacher Education,* 14 (September, 1963), 294–98.

[4] For an emphasis on nonverbal communication in teaching see the work of Charles Galloway, "Nonverbal Communication in Teaching," in *Teaching: Vantage Points for Study,* ed. Ronald T. Hyman (Philadelphia: J. B. Lippincott Co., 1968), pp. 70–77 and "A Model of Teacher Nonverbal Communication," *Classroom Interaction Newsletter,* 4 (May, 1969), 12–21. The latter work includes an excellent bibliography.

serious consideration and he should carefully read Pincoffs' article in Section Six entitled, "What Can Be Taught?"

In addition, Oakeshott claims that the task of deciding upon the order of presenting information to the student is a central task of teaching. Is Oakeshott's *order* equal to Smith's *method?* Would Oakeshott agree with Smith that method is not strictly a part of teaching, but so closely related to it as to be mistaken for it? Finally, Oakeshott ends his selection with a paragraph recalling Jackson's analogy of the bubble blown by the successful teacher. Is there, indeed, some element in teaching that escapes the eye but that the spirit feels? Are Oakeshott and Jackson hinting at criteria for good teaching?

The reader is asked to consider what, if anything, needs to be added to the points presented in these three articles so as to adequately describe teaching *as it is*. Is there anything the reader wishes to delete from the points presented here?

1.

The Way Teaching Is

PHILIP W. JACKSON

Professor of Education and
Human Development, University of Chicago and
Principal of the University of Chicago Laboratory
Nursery School.

Teaching, characteristically, is a moral enterprise. The teacher, whether he admits it or not, is out to make the world a better place and its inhabitants better people. He may not succeed of course, but his intention, nonetheless, is to benefit others.

Given the teacher's moral stance and the social significance of his work, it is not surprising to find that educational researchers, for years, have focused chiefly on the improvement of teaching —through attempting to identify the characteristics of good teachers or good methods—rather than on a description of the process as it commonly occurs in classrooms.

But the moral cast of educational research—its concern with "good" teachers and "good" methods—seems to be changing slightly. Researchers are becoming increasingly concerned with what actually happens in class-

rooms, and somewhat less concerned with what ought to be happening.

No doubt there are several reasons for the shift, but two deserve special mention. First is the lamentable, but undeniable, fact that our search for the good doesn't seem to have paid off. For example, the few drops of knowledge that can be squeezed out of a half century of research on the personality characteristics of good teachers are so low in intellectual food value that it is almost embarrassing to discuss them.

A second reason for the greater concern with teaching as it is derives from the centrality of teaching in human affairs. Next to the family, the unit comprising the teacher and his students is one of the most pervasive social arrangements in our society. Therefore, anyone who is broadly interested in man and his characteristic activities must sooner or later turn to an examination of teaching. And when he does, he will find that very little is known about this everyday event.

"The Way Teaching Is" by Philip W. Jackson is reprinted with permission from the NEA Journal, 54:10–13, 62, November, 1962.

Thus, the efforts of behavioral scientists to observe and describe what goes on in the classroom without thought of changing things begin to look understandable, perhaps even laudable.

To date, attempts to describe the teaching process have concentrated on what goes on during teaching sessions, when teachers and students are face-to-face. Although an examination of these situations is necessary for our understanding of the educational process, it would be a mistake, conceptually, to view the teacher's behavior during class as representing all that is involved in the complex business of teaching.

Much that the teacher does before and after class, as an instance, must be considered if we are to obtain a complete description of his professional activity. The teacher in an empty classroom may not appear to be a likely object of study, but during these solitary moments he often performs tasks and makes decisions that are vital to his overall effectiveness. We know very little, at present, about this important aspect of his work.

Between the empty classroom and the full one are other gradations that require study. There are many times, for example, when the teacher works individually with a student, with or without the presence of others. Although the teacher's activity during these tête-à-tête sessions differs in several ways from his behavior in front of the entire group, little is known so far about these differences.

Much of the descriptive work to date has been based on observation of "typical" classroom activities. Researchers have avoided particularly eventful sessions, such as the first day of class or the day after an examination. This avoidance has methodological advantages, but they are gained at the cost of working with a very small and very bland sample from the total life history of a class.

The tendency of descriptive research to be focused on relatively calm teaching sessions, when several students are present, is understandable from the standpoint of both theory and practice. It is during periods that classroom events conform to our stereotypic notions of what teaching is all about. Also, at such times teachers are more willing to tolerate observers. Yet we know from personal experience as teachers and from the glimpse occasionally afforded us as observers that things are different during the more private moments of teaching. In the remainder of this article, I would like to speculate on the nature of some of these differences.

Behavior relevant to the teaching task includes many things, such as preparing lesson plans, arranging furniture and equipment within the room, marking papers, studying test reports, reading sections of a textbook, and thinking about the aberrant behavior of a particular student. Indeed, these activities, most of which occur when the teacher is alone, are so crucial to the teacher's performance during regular teaching sessions that they would seem to deserve the label "preactive" teaching. This designation commands our attention and helps us distinguish this class behavior from the "interactive" teaching activities that occur vis-à-vis the students.

One of the chief differences between preactive and interactive teaching behavior seems to be in the quality of the intellectual activity involved. Preactive behavior is more or less deliberative. Teachers, when grading exams, planning a lesson, or deciding what to do about a particularly difficult student, tend to weigh evidence, to hypothesize about the possible outcome of certain action, and so forth. At such times, teaching looks like a highly rational process.

Contrast this with what happens when students enter the room. In the interactive setting, the teacher's behavior is more or less spontaneous. When students are in front of him, the teacher tends to do what he feels or knows is right rather than what he reasons is right. This is not to say that thought is absent when class is in session, but it is thought of quite a different order.

There appear to be two major reasons for this shift. For one thing, by their questions, requests, and reactions, students, to some extent, control what the teacher does, and therefore much that goes on during a teaching session is predictable in only a general way. The specifics must be dealt with as they happen, and many of them do not call for prolonged and involved thought.

Another reason for the difference in cognitive style between preactive and interactive teaching has to do with the rapidity of events in the classroom. Research suggests that things happen rather quickly during a teaching session. For example, my own observations indicate that the elementary teacher may change the focus of his concern as many as 1,000 times daily. Amid all this hustle and bustle, the teacher often has little time to think.

These differences in teacher behavior with and without students have relevance for conceptualizing the teaching task, for justifying certain training requirements, and for identifying the criteria of good teaching.

Lately it has become popular to think of the teacher's activity in terms of problem solving or hypothesis testing. The preactive phase of teaching often fits this description. As the teacher decides what textbook to use or how to group the children for reading or whether to notify Sally's parents of her poor performance in arithmetic, his behavior is at least analyzable in terms that describe the rational problem-solver.

At moments like this, concepts such as evaluation, prediction, and feedback have real meaning for understanding what the teacher is doing. It is doubtful, however, that they have similar meaning in the interactive setting.

Another time at which the distinction between preactive and interactive teaching is helpful is when we attempt to justify certain teacher-preparation requirements. In trying to demonstrate that a compulsory course, such as educational psychology, actually makes a difference in the quality of teaching performance, educators usually search for its effects in the interactive setting.

But this may well be the wrong place to look. The major contribution of courses such as educational psychology may be to increase the wisdom of the teacher's preactive decisions rather than to change the way he actually works with students. Even if the teacher's decisions with respect to the course content or the timing of certain activities are never clearly visible to an observer in the classroom, they are an important part of his work.

Many teachers try to have some time alone with individual students, but the teacher-student dialogue is usually public rather than private. In addition to the public and private settings of teaching, with the latter much less frequent than the former, a "semiprivate" arrangement occurs in many elementary classrooms. In this situation, the teacher works with one student while the others, though present, are expected to be engaged in some other activity.

Little is known about the differences among these three instructional modes —public, semiprivate, and private— although common sense would seem to tell us that the educational environment created by each might differ in important ways from those created by the other two. To give an obvious example: When a teacher is alone with a student, he is not faced with the problems of control and management that frequently absorb a large portion of his energies in a group setting.

In addition to such an obvious difference between public and private teaching, there are others a shade more subtle. For instance, most of the time in the group setting the teacher and his students are face-to-face. In private settings, however, teacher and student usually sit side-by-side, gazing at a common object of study rather than at each other. Because of their proximity, the teacher is likely to speak in lower tones than when addressing the whole class.

Another effect of proximity is that physical contact is more common. In tête-à-tête sessions, the teacher will often pat a child on the head or lay a hand on his shoulder. My impression is that teachers also laugh and smile more frequently when working individually with students. There is, then, a much greater sense of physical and psychological intimacy between teacher and student during these sessions than when the teacher is responding to the class as a group.

The chief difference between private and semiprivate situations seems to be in the number of interruptions that occur in the latter. When a teacher attempts to perform individual instruction with other students present, he often must stop what he is doing to respond to a request from some other student or to deal with some deviation from expected behavior.

The distinctions being drawn here between private, semiprivate, and public instruction are not intended to imply that one form is superior to the others. Rather, the point is that qualitative differences among these three teaching arrangements are worthy of more attention than educational researchers have given them to date.

The differences have a bearing on questions such as what is the best class size. Obviously, we need to know much more than we do at present about what happens as we move in small steps from the single student to the very small group, to the typical class, to the lecture hall.

In this regard, it is interesting to remind ourselves that most of what we call learning theory has been obtained under conditions of private instruction. Rarely if ever does the learning theorist deal with a group—a flock of pigeons, say. He may be justified in concentrating on one creature at a time, but the things he learns by doing this are of limited usefulness to the classroom teacher, one of whom described her job as being "master of a twenty-five-ring circus." Surely we cannot learn all there is to know about teaching by analyzing what happens under conditions of private study.

Another aspect of teaching that deserves more attention than it has received to date concerns the changes that take place in a classroom over a period of time. We researchers usually visit before and after rather than during the events in which we claim to be interested. We don't visit a classroom, for example, until the teacher and his students have come to know each other rather well; until methods of daily organization and operation have become stabilized.

Furthermore, when we arrive, we typically keep our eyes closed or our tape recorder unplugged until the students have settled themselves down to business and the teacher stands up in front of the room with chalk in hand. All the preliminaries are merely background noise, we tell ourselves. But are they? The typical observer's sampling bias makes sense, but it does so at the expense of ignoring the psychological reality of the classroom.

The first day of school, as an instance, is different from all others. It is then that initial impressions are formed and the foundations of enduring attitudes established. During those first few hours in the classroom, students are trying to decide whether their new teacher will be as good or as bad as the last; teachers are trying to decide whether this will be an easy or a difficult class to handle.

Many hours in early September are spent on administrative detail. Rules are defined, expectations are set, overviews are given. During this get-acquainted period, students tend to be on good behavior, and the bench in the principal's office remains empty. Many teachers take advantage of this honeymoon period by attempting to arouse the students' interest to a level that will carry them through some of the more pedestrian sessions that lie ahead.

An example of how interpretation of classroom events can become difficult when observers enter in the middle of the show, as it were, involves a group of college students who visited schools about midway through the year as part of a course in educational psychology. They visited two different classes, one taught by a teacher known for having a well-run classroom, the other taught by a teacher with the opposite reputation.

When the college students arrived, the pupils in the first room were hard at work whereas those in the second room were creating quite a disorder. What mystified the college students was the fact that both teachers seemed to be going about their work in much the same way.

A possibility that the college students did not consider was that the differences in the pupils' behavior in the two rooms resulted not from what the teachers were doing at the time but rather from what they had done at some earlier time. I strongly suspect that if the observers had been in these two classrooms during the first few days of school, they would have seen striking differences in the teachers' behavior.

Once expectations have become established and rules understood, they tend to operate invisibly. Only violations produce reactions on the part of authorities; compliance rarely does. If we want to understand the forces that combine to produce a smoothly running classroom we cannot afford to limit our visits to the periods during which the classroom is running smoothly.

So far I have tried to show that much can be learned about teaching by poking around in the corners of the classroom, as it were, and by sticking around after the dismissal bell has rung. Indeed, if we were to do more than that, if, in addition to staying for longer periods in the classroom, educational researchers were to follow teachers and students out onto the playground, or into the library, or the teachers' lounge, there's no telling how many favorite notions about the teaching process would have to be revised.

Although other educational researchers may not take kindly to the comparison, it seems to me that we have tended to be tourists in the classroom. Of course, no one can expect us to become natives, but we can be asked to extend and supplement our knowledge through more intensive and prolonged studies of classroom culture.

The admonition to stay around and look is not new. In fact, it is old advice, and repeating it makes me feel uneasy, even though I believe in its essential soundness. Therefore, I will now abandon the stance of the proselytizer and speculate about what might happen if we were to alter some of our conventional formulations, including some of our root metaphors, of teaching.

At present, the dominant *geist* is to view teaching as though the teacher's task were principally to produce specific changes within the student; as though there were an intimate and direct relation between teaching and learning. Yet when we try to use evidence of learning as a measure of good teaching, the results are discouraging, to say the least. Here again, we seem to have allowed our logical sense to interfere with our psychological sensitivity.

At least in the elementary school classrooms I have visited (and usually these have been located in so-called advantaged schools), the moments during which the teacher is *directly* involved in the business of bringing about desired changes in the students' behavior are relatively few.

More and more I have come to think of the teacher's work as consisting primarily of maintaining involvement in the classroom; of making an edu-

cated guess about what would be a beneficial activity for a student or a group of students and then doing whatever is necessary to see that the participants remain engrossed in that activity.

The teacher naturally hopes that the involvement will result in certain beneficial changes in the students, but learning is in this sense a by-product or a secondary goal rather than the thing about which he is most directly concerned.

If we allow ourselves to toy with the consequences of such a conception, we must ultimately face the possibility that most of the changes we have come to think of as "classroom learning" typically may not occur in the presence of a teacher. Perhaps it is during seatwork and homework sessions and other forms of solitary study that the major forms of any learning are laid down. The teacher's chief contribution may be that of choosing the solitary activity that he thinks will do the most good and then seeing to it that pupils remain involved.

Of course, the task of keeping pupils involved may entail explanation, demonstration, definition, and other "logical" operations that have come to be thought of as the heart of teaching. But it is also possible that the teacher might perform this vital function by merely wandering around the room while the pupils are engaged in seatwork. To argue that he is not teaching at that moment is to be unnecessarily narrow in our definition.

Once we have loosened the conceptual bonds that have traditionally linked the teacher's work to the details of producing behavioral change, the effects might be felt in many different areas. Take, as an instance, questions of curriculum construction. So long as we think of the teacher as being personally and intimately involved in producing specific changes in students' behavior, it is reasonable to admonish the teacher to define his objectives behaviorally. But do "good" teachers really take this kind of advice seriously? Not in my experience. Rather, they choose an activity, such as a book to read or a topic to discuss, on the basis of its overall relevance to the subject matter under consideration. The success of the activity is measured not so much by concrete evidence of behavioral change as by the more fleeting and subjective evidence of enthusiasm and involvement.

Some curriculum workers may not like this description. And it is bound to upset many test-makers. But in the field of the curriculum, as elsewhere, it is probable that marked adjustments would have to be made if there were a shift of concern from the way teaching ought to be to the way teaching is.

A year or so ago I came across the following statement made by the famous surgeon Sir William Osler: "No bubble is so iridescent or floats longer than that blown by the successful teacher."

Osler's metaphor intrigues me because it calls attention to the fragile quality of the psychological condition that is created and maintained by the teacher. Class sessions, like bubbles, tend to be shortlived, and after a teaching session is finished, its residue, like that of a burst bubble, is almost invisible.

But we already have an abundance of root metaphors with which to consider the teacher's task; teachers have been likened to gardeners, potters, guides, and human engineers. Why add another? The reason is that we need to become more aware than we presently are of the fleeting and ephemeral quality of much of the teacher's work. We need to learn how to sit still and watch carefully as the teacher goes about his work. I hope I am excused, therefore, if I suggest that there might be some value in thinking of the teacher as a blower of bubbles.

Of course, we know that a metaphor is valuable only so long as we treat it as a metaphor. When we begin to believe that the teacher really is a gardener, a potter, a human engineer, or a blower of bubbles, we're in trouble. At that point we leave ourselves wide open for the living, breathing, nonmetaphorical teacher to reply, "That's not the way teaching is. That's not the way it is at all. Come into my classroom tomorrow and see."

2.

Teaching

MICHAEL OAKESHOTT

Professor of Politics, University
of London.

Teaching is a practical activity in which a "learned" person (to use an archaism) "learns" his pupils. No doubt one may properly be said to learn from books, from gazing at the sky or from listening to the waves (so long as one's disposition is that mixture of activity and submission we call curiosity), but to say that the book, the sky or the sea has taught us anything, or that we have taught ourselves, is to speak in the language of unfortunate metaphor. The counterpart of the teacher is not the learner in general, but the pupil. And I am concerned with the learner as pupil, one who learns from teacher, one who learns by being taught. This does not mean that I subscribe to the prejudice which

"Teaching" by Michael Oakeshott is reprinted with permission from the author's chapter, "Learning and Teaching", in The Concept of Education, *ed. R. S. Peters (New York: Humanities Press, 1967), pp. 156–76. The selection here is from pp. 157–59 and 170–76.*

attributes all learning to teaching, it means only that I am concerned here with learning when it is the counterpart of teaching.

The activity of the teacher is, then, specified in the first place by the character of his partner. The ruler is partnered by the citizen, the physician by his patient, the master by his servant, the duenna by her charge, the commander by his subordinates, the lawyer by his client, the prophet by his disciple, the clown by his audience, the hypnotist his subject, and both the tamer and trainer by creatures whose aptitudes are of being tamed or trained. Each of these is engaged in a practical activity, but it is not teaching; each has a partner, but he is not a pupil. Teaching is not taming or ruling or restoring to health, or conditioning, or commanding, because none of these activities is possible in relation to a pupil. Like the ruler, or the hypnotist, the teacher communicates something to his partner; his peculiarity is that what he communicates is appropriate to a partner who is a pupil—it is something which may be received only by being learned. And there can, I think, be no doubt about what this is.

Every human being is born an heir to an inheritance to which he can succeed only in a process of learning. If this inheritance were an estate composed of woods and meadows, a villa in Venice, a portion of Pimlico and a chain of village stores, the heir would expect to succeed to it automatically, on the death of his father or on coming of age. It would be conveyed to him by lawyers, and the most that would be expected of him would be legal acknowledgement.

But the inheritance I speak of is not exactly like this; and, indeed, this is not exactly like what I have made is out to be. What every man is born an heir to is an inheritance of human achievements; an inheritance of feelings, emotions, images, visions, thoughts, beliefs, ideas, understandings, intellectual and practical enterprises, languages, relationships, organizations, canons and maxims of conduct, procedures, rituals, skills, works of art, books, musical compositions, tools, artefacts and utensils—in short, what Dilthey called a *geistige Welt*.

The components of this world are not abstractions ("physical objects") but beliefs. It is a world of facts, not "things"; of "expressions" which have meanings and require to be understood because they are the "expressions" of human minds. The landed estate itself belongs to this world; indeed, this is the only world known to human beings. The starry heavens above us and the moral law within, are alike human achievements. And it is a world, not because it has itself any meaning (it has none), but because it is a whole of interlocking meanings which establish and interpret one another.

Now, this world can be entered, possessed and enjoyed only in a process of learning. A "picture" may be purchased, but one cannot purchase an understanding of it. And I have called this world our common inheritance because to enter it is the only way of becoming a human being, and to inhabit it is to be a human being. It is into this *geistige Welt* that the child, even in its earliest adventures in awareness, initiates itself; and to initiate his pupils into it is the business of the teacher. Not only may it be entered only by learning, but there is nothing else for a pupil to learn. If, from one point of view, the analogies of wax and clay are inappropriate to learning, from another point of view the analogies of sagacious apes and accomplished horses are no less inappropriate. These admirable creatures have no such inheritance; they may only be trained to react to a stimulus and to perform tricks.[1]

There is an ancient oriental image of human life which recognizes this account of our circumstances. In it the child is understood to owe its physical life to its father, a debt to be acknowledged with appropriate respect. But initiation into the *geistige Welt* of human achievement is owed to the

---

[1] The horses I refer to are, of course, those of Elberfield. But it is, perhaps, worth recalling that the ancient Athenians delighted in the horse above all other animals because they recognized in it an affinity to man, and an animal uniquely capable of education. The horse had no *geistige* inheritance of its own, but (while other animals might be set to work) the horse was capable of sharing an inheritance imparted to it by man. And, in partnership with a rider (so Xenophon observed), it could acquire talents, accomplishments and even a grace of movement unknown to it in its "natural" condition.

Sage, the teacher: and this debt is to be acknowledged with the profoundest reverence—for to whom can a man be more deeply indebted than to the one to whom he owes, not his mere existence, but his participation in human life? It is the Sage, the teacher, who is the agent of civilization. And, as Dr. Johnson said, not to name the school and the masters of illustrious men is a kind of historical fraud. . . .

The inheritance of human achievements into which the teacher is to initiate his pupil is knowledge; and (on this reading of it) knowledge is to be recognized as manifolds of abilities, in each of which there is a synthesis of "information" and "judgment." What bearing has this view of things upon the activities of learning and teaching —learning which is succeeding to the inheritance, and teaching which is deliberately initiating a pupil into it? I doubt very much whether there are any practical conclusions to be drawn from it for either learners or teachers; but I think it may have some virtue as part of an attempt to understand what is going on in learning and teaching.

It suggests, first, that what I have called the two components of knowledge ("information" and "judgment") can both be communicated and acquired, but cannot be communicated or acquired separately—at least, not on separate occasions or in separate "lessons." This, I think, is certainly true in respect of all the more important abilities and passages in the inheritance, and it is not seriously qualified by the observations that it is possible to communicate and acquire inert information, and that there are some skills in which the component of information is minimal.

But, secondly, it suggests that these two components of knowledge cannot be communicated in the same manner. Indeed, as I understand it, the distinction between "information" and "judgment" is a distinction between different manners of communication rather than a dichotomy in what is known; and for me it springs from reflecting upon teaching and learning rather than from reflecting upon the nature of knowledge. Thus teaching may be said to be a twofold activity of communicating "information" (which I shall call "instructing") and communicating "judgment" (which I shall call "imparting"); and learning may be said to be a twofold activity of acquiring "information" and coming to posses "judgment."

And the rest of what I have to say concerns this distinction and the understanding it may give of what is going on in learning and teaching.

All teaching has a component of instruction, because all knowledge has a component of information. The teacher as instructor is the deliberate conveyor of information to his pupil.

The facts which compose information are specific, impersonal and mostly to be taken on trust; they are also apt to be hard, isolated, abitrary and inert. They may be stored in encyclopaedias and dictionaries. Their immediate appeal is not to the pupil's desire to understand, but to his curiosity, his desire not to be ignorant—that is, perhaps, to his vanity. And this desire not to be ignorant is, for the most part, satisfied by knowing things in terms of their names and by knowing the signification of words and expressions. From his earliest years the pupil has been used to making such discoveries for himself; he has become accustomed to distinguishing in an elementary way between fact and not-fact—without, of course, knowing the rules he is observing in doing so. And, for the most part, he is used to doing all this as part of the process of coming to be at home in the world he inhabits. Thus, when he falls into the hands of an instructor, he is already familiar with the activity of acquiring information, particularly information of immediate use.

Now the task of the teacher as instructor is to introduce his pupil to facts which have no immediate practical significance. (If there were no such facts, or if they composed an unimportant part of our inheritance, he would be a luxury rather than a necessity.) And, therefore, his first business is to consider and decide what information to convey to his pupil. This may be decided by circumstances: the Sergeant-Instructor does not have to consider whether or not he shall inform his class about the names and uses of the parts of the Bren-gun. But, if it is not decided by such circumstances as these, it is something which falls to the teacher as instructor to consider. What part or parts of our inheritance of information shall be transmitted to his pupil?

His second task is to make the information he has to convey more readily learnable by giving it an organization in which the inertness of its component facts is modified.

The organization provided by an immediate application to the practical life of his pupil is spurious; much of the information he has to convey has no such application and would be corrupted by being turned in this direction. The organization provided by a dictionary or an encyclopaedia is not designed for learning but for the rapid discovery of items of information in reponse to a recognition of specific ignorance. And the organization of information in terms of the modes of

thought, or languages, which are the greatest achievements of civilization, is much too sophisticated for the beginner. In these circumstance, what we have settled for, and what the instructor may be expected to settle for, is the organization of information in terms of the more or less arbitrarily distinguished "subjects" of a school or university curriculum: geography, Latin, chemistry, arithmetic, "current affairs" or what-not. Each of these is an organization of information and not a mode of thought; but each permits facts to begin to reveal their rule-like character (that is, their character as tools to be used in doing, making or understanding) and thus to throw off some of their inertness. Moreover, there is, I think, some positive advantage in devising, for pedagogical purposes, special organizations of information which differ from the significant modes of thought of our civilization. For these modes of thought are not themselves organizations of information; and when one of them appears as a school "subject"—as, for example, "philosophy" in the curriculum of a *lycée*—its character is apt to be misrepresented. No great harm may be thought to come from representing "geography" or even "Latin" as information to be acquired, but there is something odd about "philosophy" when it appears as the ability (for example) to remember and rehearse the second proof for the existence of God or what Descartes said about dreams.

There are, I think, two other tasks which obviously fall to the teacher as instructor. First, he has to consider the order in which the information contained in each of these somewhat arbitrary organizations of facts shall be transmitted to his pupil. It is this sort of consideration which goes into devising a syllabus, writing a textbook, or composing the programme of an instructing machine. And second, he has to exercise his pupil in this information so that what has been aquired may be recognized in forms other than those in which it was first acquired, and may be recollected on all the occasions when it is relevant. That is, the instructor has not only to hear his pupils recite the Catechism, the Highway Code, the Capes and Bays, the eight-times multiplication table and the Kings of England, but he has also to see that they can answer questions in which this information is properly used. For the importance of information is the accuracy with which it is learned and the readiness with which it can be recollected and used.

Nevertheless, our inheritance of information is so great that, whatever devices the instructor may use to modify its inertness, much of it must be acquired with only the dimmest notion of how it might be used. No doubt it would be a good thing (as Lichtenberg said) if we could be educated in such a way that everything unclear to us was totally incomprehensible; but this is not possible. Learning begins not in ignorance, but in error. Besides, in acquiring information we may learn something else, other and more valuable than either the information itself or perceiving that it is something to be used. And to understand what this is we must turn from "information" to "judgment," from the activity of "instructing" to the activity of "imparting."

Now, something of what I mean by "judgment" has begun to appear whenever the pupil perceives that information must be used, and perceives the possibility of irrelevance. And something of this is imparted in the organi-

zation of information itself; although these organizations are apt to give a restrictive impression of relevance. It is clear that this is not itself information; it cannot be taught in the way in which information may be conveyed, and it cannot be learned, recollected or forgotten in the way in which information may be learned, recollected and forgotten. But it is clear, also, that this is only an intimation of "judgment," for there is much more to be noticed which no mere organization of information can impart. To perceive that facts are rules or tools, to perceive that rules are always disjunctive and never categorical, is one thing, to have acquired the ability to use them is another.

"Judgment," then, is that which, when united with information, generates knowledge or "ability" to do, to make, or to understand and explain. It is being able to think—not to think in no manner in particular, but to think with an appreciation of the considerations which belong to different modes of thought. This, of course, is something which must be *learned;* it does not belong to the pupil by the light of nature, and it is as much a part of our civilized inheritance as the information which is its counterpart. But since learning to think is not acquiring additional information it cannot be pursued in the same way as we add to our stock of information.

Further, "judgment" may be *taught;* and it belongs to the deliberate enterprise of the teacher to teach it. But, although a pupil cannot be explicitly instructed in how to think (there being, here, no rules), "judgment" can be taught only in conjunction with the transmission of information. That is to say, it cannot be taught in a separate lesson which is not (for example) a geography, a Latin or an algebra lesson. Thus, from the pupil's point of view, the ability to think is something learned as a by-product of acquiring information; and, from the teacher's point of view, it is something which, if it is taught, must be imparted obliquely in the course of instruction. How this is done is to be understood from considering the character of what has to be imparted.

"Judgment," the ability to think, appears first, not in merely being aware that information is to be used, that it is a capital and not a stock, but in the ability to use it—the ability to invest it in answering questions. The rules may have been mastered, the maxims may be familiar, the facts may be available to recollection; but what do they look like in a concrete situation, and how may a concrete situation (an artefact or an understanding) be generated from this information? How does Latin grammar appear in a page from Cicero (whence, indeed, it was abstracted) and how can it be made to generate a page of genuine Latin prose? What do the copybook maxims look like in moral conduct observed, and how can they be made to generate conduct? These are the facts, but what conclusions do they authorize or forbid? This is the literature—the articulate contents, for example, of current knowledge about magnetic effects—but how does a pupil learn to speak the language in which it is written down: the language of science? How does he acquire the connoisseurship which enables him to determine relevance, which allows him to distinguish between different sorts of questions and the different sorts of answers they call for, which emancipates him from crude absolutes and suffers him to give his assent or dissent in graduate terms?

But learning to think is not merely learning how to judge, to interpret and to use information, it is learning to recognize and enjoy the intellectual virtues. How does a pupil learn disinterested curiosity, patience, intellectual honesty, exactness, industry, concentration and doubt? How does he acquire a sensibility to small differences and the ability to recognize intellectual elegance? How does he come to inherit the disposition to submit to refutation? How does he, not merely learn the love of truth and justice, but learn it in such a way as to escape the reproach of fanaticism?

And beyond all this there is something more difficult to acquire, but more important than any of it; namely, the ability to detect the individual intelligence which is at work in every utterance, even in those which convey impersonal information. For every significant act or utterance has a style of its own, a personal idiom, an individual manner of thinking of which it is a reflection. This, what I have called style, is the choice made, not according to the rules, but within the area of freedom left by the negative operation of rules. We may listen to what a man has to say, but unless we overhear in it a mind at work and can detect the idiom of thought, we have understood nothing. Art and conduct, science, philosophy and history, these are not modes of thought *defined* by rules; they exist only in personal explorations of territories only the boundaries of which are subject to definition. To have command over the languages of our civilization is, not to know the rules of their grammar, but to have the opportunity of a syntax and a vocabulary, rich in fine distinctions, in which to think for oneself. Learning, then, is acquiring the ability to feel and to think, and the pupil will never acquire these abilities unless he has learned to listen for them and to recognize them in the conduct and utterances of others.

Besides information, then, this is what has to be learned; for this (and not the dead weight of its products) is the real substance of our inheritance —and nothing can be inherited without learning. And this is what the teacher has to "impart" to his pupil, together with whatever information he chooses to convey.

It cannot be *learned* separately; it is never explicitly learned and it is known only in practice; but it may be learned in everything that is learned, in the carpentry shop as well as in the Latin or chemistry lesson. If it is learned, it can never be forgotten, and it does not need to be recollected in order to be enjoyed. It is, indeed, often enough, the residue which remains when all else is forgotten; the shadow of lost knowledge.

It cannot be *taught* separately; it can have no place of its own in a timetable of a curriculum. It cannot be taught overtly, by precept, because it comprises what is required to animate precept; but it may be taught in everything that is taught. It is implanted unobstrusively in the manner in which information, in a tone of voice, in the gesture which accompanies instruction, in asides and oblique utterances, and by example. For "teaching by example," which is sometimes dismissed as an inferior sort of teaching, generating inflexible knowledge because the rules of what is known remain concealed, is emancipating the pupil from the half-utterances of rules by making him aware of a concrete situation. And in imitating the example he acquires, not merely a model for the particular occasion, but the disposition to recognize everything as an occasion.

It is a habit of listening for an individual intelligence at work in every utterance that may be acquired by imitating a teacher who has this habit. And the intellectual virtues may be imparted only by a teacher who really cares about them for their own sake and never stoops to the priggishness of mentioning them. Not the cry, but the rising of the wild duck impels the flock to follow him in flight.

When I consider, as in private duty bound, how I first became dimly aware that there was something else in learning than the acquisition of information, that the way a man thought was more important than what he said, it was, I think, on the occasion when we had before us concrete situations. It was when we had, not an array of historical "facts," but (for a moment) the facts suspended in an historian's argument. It was on those occasions when we were made to learn by heart, not the declension of *bonus* (which, of course, had to be learned), but a passage of literature, the reflection of a mind at work in a language. It was on those occasions when one was not being talked to but had the opportunity of overhearing an intelligent conversation.

And if you were to ask me the circumstances in which patience, accuracy, economy, elegance and style first dawned upon me, I would have to say that I did not come to recognize them in literature, in argument or in geometrical proof until I had first recognized them elsewhere; and that I owed this recognition to a Sergeant gymnastics instructor who lived long before the days of "physical education" and for whom gymnastics was an intellectual art—and I owed it to him, not on account of anything he ever said, but because he was a man of patience, accuracy, economy, elegance and style.

3

On the Anatomy
of Teaching

B. OTHANEL SMITH

Professor of Philosophy of
Education, University of Illinois.

The procedures and techniques of teaching, like those of any art, are not to be worked out by reference to ready-made ideas. Rather they are to be devised in terms of the materials and conditions at hand, and by reference to discoveries about these circumstances and what they require for the achievement of intended effects. Knowledge of what teaching is in fact is prerequisite to its systematic improvement.

We shall, therefore, attempt to give an analysis of teaching as it is. We shall begin with the most general conception, namely, that teaching consists of a succession of acts by an individual whose purpose is either to show other persons how to do something or to in-

The article is adapted from the James William Norman Lecture, delivered at the University of Florida, Gainesville, on July 2, 1956.

"On the Anatomy of Teaching" by B. Othanel Smith is reprinted with permission from the Journal of Teacher Education, *7:339–346, December, 1956.*

form them that something is the case. The word "teaching" thus defined is used to refer to what the teacher does rather than to the behavior of the student or to what happens to him as a result of instruction. It makes no sense to say that if the student has not learned, the teacher has not taught. For learning is not stipulated as a characteristic of teaching.

It should therefore be remembered throughout this discussion that we have chosen to separate learning from teaching. We do not even use the hyphenated expression teaching-learning. For if it is intended to signify that learning is supposed to result from teaching, it is superfluous. Were the expression used to indicate that where there is learning, there is teaching, such is obviously not the case. Or if the double-barrelled expression is used to mean that teaching always results in intended learning, again such is not the case. Finally, if it is used to indicate that teaching is not teaching unless it does result in learning, the usage is arbitrary. Connecting learning and teaching verbally in this hyphenated expression serves to increase the complexity of the concept of teaching without compensating gains. So we have decided to treat teaching as teaching and learning as learning.

WHAT TEACHING IS

Before turning to the acts constituting teaching, we shall point out certain things which are not strictly a part of teaching but which are so closely related to it as often to be mistaken for it. These are method, skill, style, and control. By method is generally meant a particular order imposed upon teaching activities. It is a construction of how teaching ought to be done. We speak of the project method, lecture method, question-answer method, and unit method. Of course, to follow any of these methods is to teach. But teaching is more than a method. And the tendency to equate the two of them has led to more than one pedagogical dogma.

When we speak of a teacher's skill we are referring to how well he performs the acts of teaching. It is sometimes said that the proficiency of a teacher is to be decided by the achievement of his students. But this way of thinking about the teacher's skillfulness is a choice among alternatives and is in no sense necessary. It is no less defensible to say that a teacher is proficient if his instruction satisfies criteria derived from pedagogical research and practical experience. In this event, the teacher might be very proficient and still some students learn little or nothing from his instruction. In the same way a physician may be very skilled

and yet some of his patients may not recover. As the doctors say, the operation was a success but the patient died. Or a lawer may display unusual skill in defending a client but still lose the case. No practitioner can rightly be held responsible for the outcome of his practice beyond adherence to the knowledge and techniques of his profession.

By style of teaching we mean the characteristic demeanor in which the teaching acts are performed. For example, a teacher may operate in a sympathetic frame of mind, or he may be aggressive toward both the students and the ideas with which he deals. A teacher may be habitually dramatic, or he may show little or no feeling at all as he teaches. Unlike skill, teaching style is personal and somewhat unique for each individual. The failure to distinguish between style of teaching and teaching itself, is one of the primary sources of the mistaken notion that teachers are born and not made.

The custodial and disciplinary duties of the teacher are frequently confused with teaching. Of course, a measure of order in the classroom is a necessary condition for instruction. But the maintenance of order is not itself instruction. In college and university classrooms the custodial and disciplinary functions of the teacher are negligible, and the distinction between these functions and instruction stands out clearly. In the public schools, however, these duties take so much of the teacher's time and energy that the line between teaching and discipline becomes blurred in his mind. At any rate, the job of housekeeping is one thing and teaching is quite another thing.

However, telling what something is not, does not tell us what it is. So let us turn to a positive description of the teaching process. If we go to the classroom, we shall see what it is that the teacher does. We shall see that what he does follows an order of events which are not of his own making, but which occur because of the very nature of the enterprise going on there. As the teacher faces a classroom group, what do we see him do? First of all he induces the students to give attention to himself. By virtue of his position, he is necessarily the central figure in the classroom, and no amount of ingratiation or sharing in activities on his part can hide the fact. While the day's disasters need not be read upon his morning face, it is still true that the first significant act of the teacher is to focus the attention of his students upon himself. When this has been accomplished, he then directs their attention to what is to be learned. He may do this in a number of ways—by telling the students what to do, by engaging them in planning what to do, or by other means. The teacher then directs the students in those activities which are designed to bring about the desired learning. Such activities may include listening to the teacher, watching him do something, trying to solve problems, practicing exercises, and so on.

These acts of the teacher are, of course, gross performances. And we shall miss the subtle, but significant aspects of his work, if we do not look at the things which the teacher does when he executes them. Throughout his performance the teacher is observing the students, diagnosing their feelings and interests, and following as best he can the progress of their understanding. He also talks, for he is called upon to explain, interpret and give directions, and these duties can be performed in no other way. Then, too, he uses all sorts of pedagogical and social sanctions to approve and disapprove, to reward and to punish, to persuade and to restrain the students at every turn in the day's work.

SIGNS AND SYMBOLS IN TEACHING

An analysis of these elusive aspects of teaching will take us to the heart of the teaching process. Let us see what the teacher does when he is doing these things. We see him use all sorts of signs and symbols as he diagnoses the state of the students' feelings, interests, and understandings, and likewise as he explains, interprets, and persuades. Now, the teacher cannot know the feelings and interests of his students by observation alone; for feelings and interests are not accessible to the senses. The only way he can know them is by inference. Neither a smile nor a frown is a feeling. Nor is anger a sharply spoken reply. These are external manifestations of inner states and processes. Like one who must find out the contents of a sealed box by inference from its external features, the teacher can know the inner facts about his students only by inference from visible signs. From a student's facial expression, he infers that the student does or does not want to do something. The tone of the student's voice and the expression in his eyes tell the teacher whether or not the student is angry, happy, or apprehensive. And the light in his mind shows up in the light on his face.

The fact that the deeper reactions and feeling of the student are hidden and that they are present to the teacher only by implication has been little noticed. Yet it may well be that the success of the teacher depends in large measure upon his accurate perception and understanding of such natural signs as posture, tone of voice, and facial expression. From practical experience it would seem that there is wide variation among teachers with respect to sensitivity to these cues. Some teachers of outstanding intellectual ability appear to be insensitive to what is going on around them, oblivious to the inner life of the student if not to the classroom itself until something happens to jolt them to their senses. Then it is often too late to redeem their status as teachers. Others seem to see all sorts of cues, but, knowing not what they mean, become rattled by them and thus lose control of the teaching process. Still other teachers appear to be keenly aware of every change in these natural signs and to understand their significance. They, therefore, direct their moment-to-moment behavior as teachers in terms of information coming to them by implication from the multiplicity of natural signs around them. If we could but find out how to read these natural signs accurately and how to teach prospective teachers to do so, their proficiency in the art of teaching might be better secured.

The teacher learns about his students not only from natural signs but also from their use of language. What the student says is of significance to the teacher partly because it supplies him with data by which to understand the student. Just as facial expressions and other natural signs convey by implication the feelings and thoughts of the student, so linguistic expressions reveal the inner life to him who is able to interpret them. Suppose a student says, in response to the question of how the streams of New England differ from those of the coastal plains "I ain't sure.

But is it that the rivers run slow in New England and fast in the coastal plains? Well, maybe I'm wrong. I don't know." Now what do these words tell the teacher? It all depends upon how he is tuned in and how versatile he is in changing wave lengths. These data indicate a number of things. They tell the teacher that the student is deficient in linguistic usage, hesitant in answering the question, and deficient in geographic knowledge. Other linguistic expressions of the student may indicate that he is emotionally upset, reasons fallaciously, and does not know how to explicate words.

In general, then, the symbolic expressions of the student tell us: (1) his emotional state, (2) the grammatical and linguistic errors he makes, (3) whether or not he understands something, (4) the values he holds, (5) the logical errors he makes, and (6) his factual errors. Language as a source of information about the student has, of course, been used since teaching first began. But the conceptualization of its functions should enable us to make better use of language as an instrument of instruction. For the teacher can mold his behavior intelligently to the extent that he is aware of the conditions which affect the outcome of his acts. Hence the teacher, at his best, is sensitive to this total spectrum of things which the student's linguistic expressions tell him.

TEACHING AS A LINGUISTIC PROCESS

The teacher not only interprets signs and symbols coming to him from the students, but he also expresses himself to his students by signs and symbols as he instructs. In fact, teaching cannot occur without the use of language. Teaching is, above all, a linguistic activity. The teacher makes assignments, gives directions, explains events and statements, interprets words and other expressions, proves propositions, justifies decisions and actions, makes promises, praises and blames students. He cannot teach without doing these things. And he cannot do any of them without using language. Can an assignment be made without language? Can anything be explained or an action justified without saying something? Can a proposition be proved or an expression interpreted without using language? To raise such question is to indicate the way in which language is inextricably involved in the processes both of learning and of teaching. It is to show that language is at the very heart af teaching.

Let us look at some of the ways in which the teacher uses language. In the first place, he uses language to teach students how to do something. In teaching a student how to typewrite, for example, the teacher may show the student how to do it by performing the activity himself. But this will not be sufficient. The student must himself perform the activity, and he must be directed in the performance of it. So, the teacher will tell him from time to time what to do. But it is not intended that the student remember the sentences spoken by the teacher. The teacher will tell him to try so and so, don't do so and so, or you are making this movement and you should be doing thus and so. The purpose of the discourse is immediate. Its use beyond the moment may be insignificant. For once the student learns to typewrite, what the teacher told him drops out of the picture.

This sort of telling is to be found in nearly all teaching. And it is more com-

plex than we might suppose. It entails a triple relationship in which the elements are the teacher, the student, and a third something, for example, a map, a piece of apparatus, a book, an act of either the student or the teacher. Suppose a teacher is instructing a science class by means of a demonstration. As the demonstration proceeds, the student must observe what is done and what happens. At the same time he must listen to the teacher tell what is being done, why it is being done, and so on. The student is thus in a double role of observer and listener. The teacher, too, is involved in the same way. He must pay attention to what he is doing and at the same time talk about what he is doing. But he must do even more. He must also pay attention to the entire class and choose words and ideas appropriate to the capacities of the students. This three-way intellectual performance is seldom found outside of a teaching situation. It is not an easy one to learn, and many elements of the situation escape the eye of the novice. Even the experienced teacher is seldom well enough aware of his performance to tell the beginner what to do and how to do it.

There is a second and even more significant use of language in teaching. In this instance the teacher tries to increase the student's fund of knowledge. In order to do this he explains, he defines, he justifies, he offers proof, and so on. And, as we have already said, to do these the teacher must use language. But it is a use of language which differs from that employed in the direction of an activity which a student is learning to perform. It is a discourse that expresses ideas which are to be retained, and which can be retained only as they are embodied in linguistic symbols. The teacher who explains Boyle's law by showing its logical relation to the molecular theory of matter does not do so on the assumption that what he says will be forgotten. Nor does a teacher who explains an event in human history by reference to a general proposition about the behavior of human beings intend that the students forget what he says. Of course, the teacher does not intend that the student remember the exact words or the particular sentences. But the teacher does expect the student to be able to express the ideas in his own words and to show in other verbal ways that he graps what the teacher has said.

Since the discourse of the teacher embodies ideas to be learned, it is designed to convey ideas in accurate and succinct statements. In this sense, it is studied discourse. Unlike informal talk, its order is shaped by the nature of the task. Ideas are expressed in a sequence calculated to make them easily understood. Even the teacher's demeanor and tone of voice are affected by the nature of the task. Children recognize this fact, and when they play "school," the one who has the role of teacher adopts the voice and studied manner of the teacher.

Thus the significance of the role of language in teaching is clearly evident when we stop to think about it. Yet the plain fact is that all we know about language in this regard is a kind of unanalyzed common sense distilled from practice. It could be that when we have analyzed the language of teaching and investigated the effects of its various formulations, the art of teaching will show marked advancement.

THE LOGIC OF TEACHING

Teaching involves logic as well as language. This is the case because reasoned discourse leads to conclusions. It begins somewhere and ends somewhere. And logic, in its deductive sense, is a way of clarifying our linguistic expressions and of ordering sentences in such a way that we can decide upon the truth of our conclusions.

Just as we have neglected the role of language in teaching, so have we disregarded logic. This neglect of logic has resulted partly from our erroneous notion that the research which dislodged faculty psychology and its theory of formal discipline also discredited the study of logic, and partly from our erroneous ideas of what logic was supposed to do for us. The overthrow of formal discipline had no bearing upon the uses of logic when properly perceived. Logic does not purport to tell us how we do in fact think. It has nothing to do with the pondering processes, whatever they are, by which ideas occur to us by which we reach conclusions. The principles of logic describe neither thinking nor thought. Nor do they tell us how our thinking ought to proceed. They are not norms to which the thinking process should conform. Rather logic is useful to us when we scan our thinking to tell whether or not the conclusions we have reached follow necessarily from our premises, or, as in inductive thinking, to decide the probable truth of our conclusions.

Seen in this light, logic plays an important role in the process of teaching. For one thing, a statement becomes clear to us either when its key words are adequately defined or when it is fixed in the chain of sentences to which it is logically linked, or when both of these obtain. Now, teaching in its didactic sense embraces both of these performances. For, as we have already said, such teaching includes the activities of defining, explaining, justifying, proving, and the like. And these without exception are logical operations.

The fact that these activities are logical activities is seldom recognized. We have failed to recognize their logical nature because of our tendency in education to psychologize everything. In pedagogical discussion we use two sets of concepts, both of which we believe to be psychological, when in fact only one set is so. One of these sets consists of such concepts as inferring, perceiving, conceiving, generalizing, thinking, and judging. We use these in talking about psychological processes. And we are correct in doing so. Of course, there is a legitimate question as to whether there are internal processes corresponding to these names, but that question is one which we leave to the psychologists. The other set of concepts are identified by such terms as define, interpret, explain, justify, and prove. These are logical rather than psychological. They are operations which we perform with words and sentences and which we cannot perform without words and sentences. And these operations are found in the domain of logic.

For purposes of illustration we shall consider definition and explanation. It hardly need be said that a great deal of school learning consists of definitions. Our books and discussions are filled with definitions. Now in logic we are told that there are different ways of defining words. To define a word is to tell how it is to be used. We can define the word "seed" by saying that "a seed is that part of a flowering plant that holds the embryo and associated structures." What we have done is to tell the class of things to which a seed belongs, by saying that it belongs to the class of things called "parts of a flowering plant." Then we have told how a seed differs from other members of the class of things to which it belongs such as leaves, roots, and stem. Wherever the expression "part of a flowering plant which holds the embryo and associated structures" appears in our discussion we can substitute the word "seed" without changing the meaning. This is what we do when we define a word. Thus a definition represents a decision; for it lays down the rules for the use of a word. Since they are decisions, definitions are neither true nor false.

The amount of time used inefficiently in the classroom because the teacher does not know how to deal with questions involving definitions is greater, I fear, than we like to think. Classroom discussion is often snarled up by disagreements about the meaning of words, as though words somehow had meanings in the same way that dogs have fleas. Many fruitless discussions might be avoided were the teacher capable of handling definitions through a knowledge of logic and its operations.

Similarly, the logic of explanation is appropriate when the teacher is called upon to explain either statements or events, or to evaluate explanations given by students. Suppose the teacher is called upon to explain the fact that in the early morning the wind blows from the land toward the sea. What must he do? The answer is that he must try to find the premises from which the factual conclusion—the wind blows from the land toward the sea in the early morning—can be drawn. Now any number of premises may be chosen, depending upon the teacher's knowledge. But if he is trained in physics, he will reason from the general law that heated bodies expand and thus become lighter per unit of volume. It is not necessary here to follow the logical steps the teacher must take to get from the general law to the particular event to be explained. But he will go on to show that the air over the ocean becomes warmer at night than the air over the land, and that the cold, heavier air over the land then displaces the ocean air which is warmer and lighter. An explanation thus consists in showing that the fact to be explained can be taken as an instance of the general law which has been used as the explanatory principle.

Failure to understand what an explanation is leads to all sorts of entanglements in the classroom. Sometimes the discussion centers in the question of whether or not an explanation is a true one. To answer the question it is necessary that the truth of the premises be tested. But unfortunately the teacher often lacks the knowledge of logic necessary to test the truth of statements used as premises. Then, too, teachers sometimes mistake the mere recounting of events for explanation. A student is asked to tell why the French Revolution happened. So he relates events leading up to the revolution as an explanation of why the revolution occurred. Now, the mere recounting of events is not an explanation in the logical sense, for there is no general principle from which to derive the event to be explained. Sometimes, however, a student, or even a teacher, uses a general principle without making it explicit. Consequently it is subjected neither to critical appraisal nor to the test of fact. Partly for this reason, instruction in history often lacks rigor and thus fails to engage the higher mental processes of students.

CONCLUSION

It has been our purpose in this discussion to describe teaching, teaching as it is in fact. We have not sought to set forth any new theory of how teaching ought to be done. Rather we have analyzed teaching into some of its essential elements because it is our belief that he who would improve an art must first understand it. And the understanding of any art begins not with loose abstractions, but with systematic and painstaking analysis of that art.

It has been common practice to think of teaching almost exclusively in psychological terms. This practice has too long kept us from facing the realities, the hard plain facts of teaching. I have tried to speak in terms of the facts of teaching—of what it is that we actually do when we teach. Our analysis has, perforce, been all too brief. Hence it has presented merely the bold contours and the grosser elements of the general process of instruction. Many details remain to be laid out. And since the present analysis represents an early exploration, it is to be expected that under further study and further elaboration, the present general outline will undergo changes.

Nevertheless, I believe that any candid view of teaching will throw into sharp relief most features of the teaching process that I have described. If we look frankly at teaching, I believe that we shall become aware at least of the truly linguistic and symbolic nature of the teaching process, and that the fundamental role of logical operations in teaching will become abundantly clear. If this be the case, we shall be dealing with problems that we have not recognized heretofore. And yet, it may be that through the solution of these problems the art of teaching will make its most rewarding advancement.

Suggested Concepts of Teaching:
OVERVIEW

What do we mean when we use the word "teaching"? Is there common agreement among us regarding a concept of teaching? At first glance there might appear to be simple questions with simple answers. But a careful look reveals that "teaching," perhaps because it is such a common term, has been defined quite differently by various people. In fact, one group of educators recently chose not to use the term "teaching" at all because it has "almost innumerable meanings."[1] Most people, however, continue and prefer to use this term in spite of the many different usages. Hence, we have the task of answering the two questions raised above. In short, how do we conceive of teaching?

At this point in the development of the literature on teaching it is pointless to launch into a lengthy defense of the analytic approach for examining the concept of teaching. Suffice it to say here that the articles in this section are intended to serve as an invitation to the reader to probe into a fundamental concept in our languages, teaching. Soltis,[2] in justifying this approach of analyzing important concepts says, "Furthermore, I believe that such an attempt to explicate these ideas would invariably result in the unveiling of nuances of meaning which we unconsciously assume in our discourse and in our actions as students or teachers. As a result,

---

[1] Stephen M. Corey, "The Nature of Instruction," in *Programed Instruction,* ed. Phil C. Lange, The Sixty-sixth yearbook of the National Society for the Study of Education, Part II (Chicago: 1967), p. 5.

[2] Jonas F. Soltis, *An Introduction to the Analysis of Educational Concepts* (Reading, Mass.: Addison-Wesley Publishing Company, 1968), p. 2.

we would not only become more sophisticated and careful in their use, but would also gain a deeper insight into education as a human endeavor in which all men take some part sometime in their lives."

In my own article in this section I point out that Marie Hughes, an empirical researcher (not a linguistic analyst) whose work appears in the last section of this book, claims that the definition of teaching we accept does influence the empirical research we do. Since the concepts we hold do influence our practice, it is well to be clear about what we mean when we talk about teaching.

It is in this light that the cluster of articles in this section follows. These articles exemplify the analysis called for by Soltis and Hughes. The point is not to arrive at a single definition, but to alert the reader to some of the various ways people employ the term "teaching" and to the implications of these uses. Some authors, in describing how people use the term, advocate a particular use. Scheffler[3] calls definitions that advocate a practical program (rather than describe prior use) "programmatic definitions." The reader is asked to keep this distinction in mind as he moves through this section.

We may ask, then, in regard to Scheffler's selection, if his statement about teaching is descriptive or programmatic. Scheffler says, "To teach, in the standard sense, is at some points as least to submit oneself to the understanding and independent judgment of the pupil, to his demand for reasons, to his sense of what constitutes an adequate explanation." Is Scheffler describing or advocating?[4] Fowler[5] and Adams,[6] for example, claim that Scheffler is in fact presenting a programmatic definition of teaching. In reply to Fowler, Scheffler[7] has said, "I don't intend it to be (programmatic)." What saith the reader to this issue?

It is precisely his opposition to programmatic definitions that leads Smith to define teaching as he does. Smith seeks to develop "a descriptive rather than a normative concept of teaching" for he opposes the smuggling in of a view on how teaching is to be conducted. The question is, of course, if Smith's definition is indeed descriptive.[8] Does Smith smuggle in his own

3 Israel Scheffler, *The Language of Education* (Springfield, Ill.: Charles C Thomas, Publisher, 1960), p. 19.

4 See also the definition of teaching that Scheffler offers at the beginning of his article in Section E. Is he describing or advocating in that characterization?

5 Elizabeth F. Fowler, "Review of *The Language of Education,*" *Studies in Philosophy and Education,* 4 (Spring 1965), 133.

6 Donald W. Adams, "Some Extraordinary Implications of Scheffler's 'Ordinary' View of Teaching," *Philosophy of Education 1967,* ed. D. B. Gowin (Edwardsville, Ill.: Studies in Philosophy and Education, 1967), pp. 65–76.

7 Israel Scheffler, "Reply to Elizabeth Fowler", *Studies in Philosophy and Education,* 4 (Spring 1965), 135.

8 See also the article by Strasser in Section Five in which he builds on the work of B. O. Smith. Is Smith describing or advocating there?

normative views willy-nilly? What is the "system of actions" that Smith refers to? What happens if the actions Smith refers to do not form a system?

The question about actions brings Green's article to mind. Green states that "teaching is itself an instance of human action aimed at enhancing the human capacity for action." Is Green's definition descriptive or programmatic? What are the implications of Green's definition for teachers? Is "action" for Green the same as "action" for Smith? If not, what is the difference? The reader is also asked to compare Green's definition of behavior with Smith's and others'. Also, does Green need "human action" in both places of his definition? Can the teacher's *behavior* enhance the student's human capacity for *action?* If so, why not call this *behavior* teaching?

Let us return to Scheffler to highlight another point. Scheffler's definition employs an intentional use of the word "teaching." With this Green and Smith have no quarrel, (does the reader?) for they, too, use the words "intend" and "aim" in their definitions. But Scheffler's position on restricting the manner of teaching is a significant point of disagreement between Scheffler and Smith, as I point out in my article in this section. Does the reader accept Scheffler or Smith? Is Scheffler's distinction as to manner similar to Green's claim about enhancing the human capacity for action? Does Scheffler contradict himself regarding the manner of teaching when he says that reason giving is not uniformly appropriate at every phase of the teaching interval? How do we know when reason giving *is* appropriate?

Smith devotes the second half of his article to explicating the system of actions referred to in his earlier definition. His employment of a model by Tolman (please note that it is a psychological model) leads him into theory development. The reader is asked to consider this segment of Smith as belonging to Part Two of this book also. In any case, Smith points out that the teacher performs three types of action with language—logical actions, directive actions, and admonitory or evaluative actions. Are these the only three? Are they equal in importance?

It is critical for the reader to recognize that Green does not define teaching in terms of "change" or "behavioral objectives" as has been most common for many years. What does Green gain by defining teaching as he does and breaking with the past? Why does he not define teaching in terms of changing the pupil's behavior? In a reaction to Green's article Soltis and McClellan[9] claim that Green is wise in his decision. Soltis claims "that the aim of teaching if regarded as the changing of behavior is a short-sighted and dangerous view." Are Soltis and McClellan right? If we do not aim for behavioral change, how can we measure the effects of

[9] Jonas F. Soltis and others, " 'Teaching, Acting, and Behaving': A Discussion," *Harvard Educational Review*, 35 (Spring 1965), 191–209.

teaching? What are the implications of not striving for such change for the evaluation of teaching?

Komisar's article is one attempt to move beyond the issues of intention versus success and distinctions of manner versus no distictions of manner. Within his treatment of recent innovations he introduces the concepts of offerings, gifts, and services. He further claims that teaching is both obtrusive and intrusive. The reader is asked to consider if Komisar's claims apply to teaching in a school or to teaching in general or both. Is all teaching "massive and mandatory"? If a particular teaching situation is not mandatory or massive (for example, Arthur Rubinstein voluntarily teaching a willing and talented young pianist), can it be considered as an offering? As a service? Is Komisar correct that teaching ought to be a simple service like radio repairing?

Komisar begins his article claiming that the new teaching machines represent a new kind of encounter. In what ways will teaching machines and computer-based instruction differ from the encounter we call teaching so as not to be intrusive, obtrusive, and phoney? Will the technological innovations placed in an "institutionalized education" setting also be phoney, obtrusive, and intrusive once this setting is mandatory? Komisar ends by stating that teaching requires mutual confidence and trust between student and teacher. Does it?

In my own article I ask the reader to conceive of teaching as triadic and dynamic. Within this framework I raise questions about programmed instruction. The reader is asked to consider them in light of Komisar's article as well as in the light of a concept of teaching as triadic and dynamic. The reader is urged to pursue the triadic characteristic of teaching in the articles by Henderson and Martin in Sections Five and Six.

4.

Teaching

ISRAEL SCHEFFLER

Victor S. Thomas Professor of
Education and Philosophy, Harvard University.

Doctrines that contradict each other as literal statements may nevertheless, in their practical purport, represent abstractly compatible emphases which may, to be sure, very independently in relevance and moral warrant from context to context. That is, there may be no cause for supposing that we have an irreconcilable conflict of practical proposals of which we must flatly reject at least one. This point may be illustrated by considering a statement that has acquired the typical status of a slogan in education, the statement that there can be no teaching without learning. As there can be no selling without buying, so there can be no teaching without

learning. A recent writer[1] has argued against this statement, asking us to consider as a counterexample the case of a teacher who has tried his best to teach his pupuils a certain lesson but has failed to get them to learn it. Shall we say that such a man has not, in fact, been teaching, has not earned his pay, has not fulfilled his responsibility? Surely this case shows that there can be teaching without learning.

If we take the two statements, "There can be no teaching without

"Teaching" by Israel Scheffler is reprinted from Scheffler, Israel, The Language of Education, 1960. Courtesy of Charles C Thomas. Publisher. Springfield, Illinois. The selection here is from pp. 41–46 and 57–59.

[1] Broudy, H. S. *Building a Philosophy of Education.* Englewood Cliffs, N. J., Prentice-Hall, Inc., 1954, p. 14. Broudy writers, "Many educators rather glibly pronounce the dictum: 'If there is no learning, there is no teaching.'

This is a way of speaking because no educator really believes it to be treu, or if he did he would in all honesty refuse to take most of his salary. There is a difference between successful teaching and unsuccessful teaching, just as there is a difference between successful surgery and unsuccessful surgery.... To teach is deliberately to try to promote certain learnings. When other factors intrude to prevent such learnings, the teaching fails. Sometimes the factors are in the teacher; sometimes in the pupil; sometimes in the very air both breathe, but as long as the effort was there, there was teaching."

learning," and "There can be teaching without learning," simply as literal doctrines, we must agree that they are contradictory. Further, we must agree that the counterexample produced against the first of these statements is effective in showing it to be false. If we have an actual case before us of teaching without learning, then we must reject the doctrine that denies the existence of such cases. The counterexample does, moreover, represent a real case of teaching without learning. Here, in short, does seem to be a flat contradiction between two statements, one of which is wrong.

It is, furthermore, easy to see why the statement, "There can be no teaching without learning," sounds so plausible as a literal doctrine, though it is in fact false. For though in some uses of the verb "to teach" it does not imply success, in others it does. We have already noted the difference between asking, "What have you been teaching him?" ("What have you been trying to get him to learn?") and "What have you taught him?" ("What have you been successful in teaching him?"). The first question, we may say, contains an "intentional" use of the verb, while the second contains a "success" use.[2] It is clear that if the pupil I have been teaching has in fact not learned anything, I may reply to the second question (but not to the first) by saying, "Nothing." For the second question, that is, unless my pupil has learned something, I cannot say I have taught him anything, i.e., there can (here and in all "success" uses) indeed be no teaching without learning.

Some further illustrations may be helpful, especially since the distinction between "success" and "intentional" uses is important and will recur in later discussions. Clearly, if I have been teaching my nephew how to catch a baseball, he may still not have learned, and may in fact never learn, how to catch a baseball. I have, of course, been trying to get him to learn how to catch a baseball, but I need not have succeeded. Generally, then, we may say that the schema "X has been teaching Y how to..." does not imply success. Suppose, however, that I have taught my nephew how to catch a baseball. If I have indeed taught him, then he must, in fact, have learned how. Were I to say, "Today I taught him how to catch a baseball but he hasn't learned and never will," I would normally be thought to be saying something puzzling. We may, then, say that the schema "X taught Y how to..." does imply success. This schema represents a "success" use of "to teach" whereas the earlier schema does not, representing rather an "intentional" use of the verb.

It should be noted, incidentally, that not every use of the simple past tense of the verb implies success, though the above "success" schema contains such a form. It is, for example, true that some teachers taught mathematics last year to some students who learned nothing of mathematics. It should further be noticed that "success" uses of the verb "to teach" do not eliminate distinctions of relative proficiency. To have been successful in teaching implies no more than that students have learned in relevant ways, not that they have become masters. We may ask rhetorically, in traffic, "Who taught *him* to drive?" suggesting that, though he has learned, he is not very good at it. It is minimal

2 I am indebted to the treatment of achievement words in Ryle, G.: *The Concept of Mind*. London, Hutchinson's University Library, 1949. See also Anscombe, G.E.M.: *Intention*. Oxford, Basil Blackwell, 1957.

achievement, sufficient to warrant us in saying that learning has occurred at all, that is normally implied by "success" uses of the verb "to teach."

Finally, we should make note of the fact that "to teach" is not exceptional in having both "success" and "intentional" uses. Indeed, many verbs relating to action have both uses inasmuch as what is done is often described in terms of trying to reach a goal, the attainment of which defines the success of the try. To say a man is building a house does not mean he has succeeded or ever will. He is, of course, doing something with a certain intention and certain hopes and beliefs; he is, in short, trying to bring it about or make it true that there be a house built by himself. It may, further, be normally understood that what he is doing in this attempt is reasonably considered effective. But from the fact that someone is building a house it cannot be inferred that there is (or will be) some house built by him. He may have been building ("intentional" use) until the flood came and wiped away his work, and he then never completed the job. He may thus never have built ("success" use) the house that he had been building ("intentional" use). Or, better, there may never exist any house built ("success" use) by him, though he has, in fact, been house-building ("intentional" use).

If now, with respect to the verb "to teach," we recognise that it has both "intentional" and "success" uses, we see that for the latter uses, there can, indeed, be no teaching without learning. If one's examples are all drawn from such uses, the doctrine that there can be no teaching without learning seems entirely plausible. Nevertheless, the general way in which it is expressed leaves the doctrine open to falsification through a single counter-example, such as has been discussed above. Thus we return, after a long digression, to the conclusion we reached earlier: taken as literal doctrines, the statements, "There can be no teaching without learning," and "There can be teaching without learning" are contradictory, hence irreconcilable, and it is the first statement, moreover, that must be rejected.

If, however, we examine the practical purport of these two statements, it becomes clear that, though their practical emphases are not equally relevant and warranted in every context, neither are they opposed as exclusive alternatives. Rather, they relate to different practical aims that are perfectly compatible. The practical purport of the statement "There can be no teaching without learning" is closely related to that of the slogan "We teach children, not subjects," that is, to turn the attention of the teacher toward the child. But we have here a distinctive emphasis on the child's learning as the intended *result* of teaching, the point being to improve the effectiveness of teaching by referring it to its actual as compared with its intended results. This emphasis hardly strikes anyone today as being either very original or very controversial. It seems rather taken for granted in quite prosaic contexts. Imagine someone saying to a soap manufacturer, "Look here, you'd really do a better job if you systematically studied your product and tried to improve it. You can't really call yourself a soap manufacturer unless you produce good soap, and you can't do that unless you look at what you're turning out and make sure that it is up to par." Such a little speech would seem rather out of place in our consumer-oriented world. Soap makers are looking at their products anyway (not, perhaps, always to make better soap, but at least to make soap more attractive to buyers). No soap maker supposes that, apart from their contribution to his final product, his manufacturing processes have any intrinsic value.

But teachers often have supposed something dangerously like this. They often assume that, apart from their effects on students, their teaching in just the way they habitually do has intrinsic value, and is therefore self-justifying. Instead of achieving attainable improvements through deliberate effort, they thus tend to deny that any improvements are needed or possible so long as they continue to teach as before. When such educational inertia is widespread, as it seemed to many observers to be when our slogan gained currency, the practical purport of the slogan may seem urgent, indeed, revolutionary. To speak, moreover, of teaching as selling and of learning as buying, to suggest that teaching be compared with business methods improvable by reference to effects on the consumer, was to signal strikingly the intent to support reform of teaching.

In part because such reform has become widespread, the practical purport of our slogan appears to many current observers irrelevant or less warranted. Indeed, it has seemed to such observers that the pendulum has in many places swung too far in the direction of orientation to the child's world and preoccupation with the effects of teaching on this world. The schools have, in some respects, been described as too much concerned with their consumers. Teachers, feeling the weight of each student's adjustment and personality conflicts resting on their tired shoulders, have in many instances tried to do too much— to become parents, counselors, and pals as well as teachers. They have (under-

standably, given such aspirations coupled with the emphasis on consequences) felt harried and guilty at not being able to do all that their charges require, accepting meanwhile the responsibility for all failures in learning upon themselves.[3]

If someone should want to help the morale of such teachers, he would hardly keep repeating the old message under the new conditions. Rather, he would want to say, "Stop feeling guilty, give up your attempts at omnipotence, stop paying so much attention to the inner problems and motivations of your students. Do your very best in teaching your subject and testing your students and when you've done that, relax with an easy conscience." This represents just the practical purport of the statement, "There *can* be teaching without learning." It is this emphasis which seems to many current writers relevant and warranted in the present situation.

Both emphases, however,—that of the present statement and that of its opposite—are abstractly compatible in spite of the fact that they may be unequally relevant or warranted in specific educational contexts. It is, possible to hold (and, indeed, to urge) that teaching ought to be appraised and modified in the light of its effects on learners, and at the same time to believe (and to stress) that there are limits to what the teacher can do, with the best will in the world: whatever he does, he may still fail to achieve the desired learning on the part of his pupils.

In given situations, however, it may be considered more important to maintain the teacher's morale by stressing the limits of his responsibility than to

[3] See Freud, A.: The rôle of the teacher, *Harvard Educational Review,* 22:229 (Fall) 1952, and Riesman, D.: Teachers amid changing expectations, *Harvard Educational Review,* 24:106 (Spring) 1954.

try to improve teaching by stressing the need to examine effects. Whether we say "Try to improve!" or "Don't worry, you've done your best!" is indeed, in this way, a function of the context. But these emphases are not, in general, irreconcilable, nor do they require a flat rejection of the one or the other. They may, in fact, occur together and they may alternate in urgency. To sum up, when slogans are taken literally, they deserve literal criticism. We need, independently however, to evaluate their practical purport in reference to their changing contexts, as well as the parent doctrines from which they have sprung. We must, moreover, avoid assuming that when slogans are in literal contradiction to each other, they represent practical proposals that are in irreconcilable conflict....

We may approach the general point we have here been emphasizing by a consideration of the notion of teaching, which is considerably narrower than that of acculturation. Every culture, we may say, normally gets newborn members to behave according to its norms, however these are specified, and many cultures have agencies devoted to this job. But not every way of getting someone to behave according to some norm is teaching. Some such ways are purely informal and indirect, operating largely by association and contact, as languages are normally learned. But not every formal and deliberate way is teaching, either. Behavior may be effectively brought into accord with norms through threats, hypnosis, bribery, drugs, lies, suggestion, and open force. Teaching may, to be sure, proceed by various methods, but some ways of getting people to do things are excluded from the standard range of the term "teaching." To teach, in the standard sense, is at some points at least to submit oneself to the understanding and in-

dependent judgment of the pupil, to his demand for reasons, to his sense of what constitutes an adequate explanation. To teach someone that such and such is the case is not merely to try to get him to believe it: deception, for example, is not a method or a mode of teaching. Teaching involves further that, if we try to get the student to believe that such and such is the case, we try also to get him to believe it for reasons that, within the limits of his capacity to grasp, are *our* reasons. Teaching, in this way, requires us to reveal our reasons to the student and, by so doing, to submit them to his evaluation and criticism.

To teach someone, not that such and such is the case, but rather *how* to do something, normally involves showing him how (by description or example) and not merely setting up conditions under which he will, in fact, be likely to learn how. To throw a child into the river is not, in itself, to teach him how to swim; to send one's daughter to dancing school is not, in itself, to teach her how to dance. Even to teach someone *to* do something (rather than how to do it) is not simply to try to get him to do it; it is also to make accessible to him, at some stage, our reasons and purposes in getting him to do it. To teach is thus, in the standard use of the term, to acknowledge the "reason" of the pupil, i.e., his demand for and judgment of reasons, even though such demands are not uniformly appropriate at every phase of the teaching interval.

The distinctions here discussed between teaching and fostering the acquisition of modes of behavior or belief are, we may say, distinctions of *manner*. They depend on the manner in which such acquisition is fostered. The organic metaphor, as we have seen, focuses on the continuity of the culture's life,—in effect, on the behavioral norms and beliefs forming the *content* of the culture. It makes no distinctions in manner of acquisition of this content, of the sort we have illustrated by referring to the concept of "teaching." It is these distinctions, however, that are central to moral issues concerning social and educational policy. The usefulness of the organic metaphor in certain contexts cannot be taken to show that the distinctions of manner referred to are of no practical or moral moment, that, for example, teachers ought, by any means and above all, to adjust students to the prevailing culture (specified in any way you like) and to ensure its continuity (no matter how specified). Whether teachers ought or ought not to do just that or some alternative is an independent and serious moral question that requires explicit attention. That it receives no emphasis in the organic metaphor indicates not that the question is unimportant, but that this metaphor is inappropriate in practical contexts.

We shall end this discussion by trying to show how fundamental the question of manner is, and we shall refer here again to the concept of "teaching." We have already taken pains to indicate that the notion of teaching is considerably narrower than that of acculturation. The fact that every culture may be said to renew itself by getting newborn members to behave according to its norms emphatically does not mean that such renewal is everywhere a product of teaching in the standard sense we have discussed. To favor the widest diffusion of teaching as a mode and as a model of cultural renewal is, in fact, a significant social option of a fundamental kind, involving the widest possible extension of reasoned criticism to the culture itself.

That this option may, in particular

societies, lead to great changes in fundamental norms, beliefs, and social institutions, with respect to the prevailing culture, is indeed possible, even highly likely. But such a consequence need not always follow. In particular, it is not likely to follow where the culture itself institutionalizes reasoned procedures in its basic spheres, where it welcomes the exercise of criticism and judgment, where, that is to say, it is democratic culture in the strongest sense. To support the widest diffusion of teaching as a model of cultural renewal is, in effect, to support something peculiarly consonant with the democratization of culture and something that poses a threat to cultures whose basic social norms are institutionally protected from criticism. Such support is thus consistent with the vision of a culture where understanding is not limited and where critical judgment of policy is not the institutionalized privilege of one class, where policy change is not perforce arbitrary and violent, but channelled through institutions operating by reasoned persuasion and freely given consent. Many, even most, social thinkers have shrunk before such a vision and argued that culture cannot long survive under democracy in this sense. Others have urged the fullest institutionalization of reasoned criticism, fully aware that such a course indeed threatens societies with rigid power divisions, but denying that all societies are therefore threatened and that *no* culture can survive which rests on free criticism freely interchanged. The issue, in short, is not whether culture shall be renewed, but in what *manner* such renewal is to be institutionalized. It is this fundamental practical issue that must not be obscured in practical contexts by metaphors appropriate elsewhere.

5.

A Concept of Teaching

B. OTHANEL SMITH

Professor of Philosophy of
Education, University of Illinois.

It is well understood that words can be defined to satisfy the purpose of the individual who uses them. For this reason many controversies center in the meaning of terms. The literature of education is filled with claims and counter-claims about the meaning of "education." One authority defines education as growth; another says it is the cultivation of intellectual virtues; and still another claims that education is the means by which civilization is transmitted from one generation to another. These definitions are controversial because each one is packed with a set of preferences about what is to be taught, how it is to be taught, who is to be educated, and so on. And conducting

"*A Concept of Teaching*" *by B. Othanel Smith is reprinted with permission from* Teachers College Record, *61:229–241, February, 1960.*
The analysis reported herein was made pursuant to a contract with the United States Office of Education, Department of Health, Education, and Welfare.

the controversy consists in unpacking the definitions—each side pointing out what the opposing view commits us to, what it denies or fails to include, and at the same time claiming its own conception to be more defensible and desirable.

The word "teaching" is used in various ways also, and definitions of it often lead to or underlie controversial discussions in pedagogical circles. While the unpacking of various definitions of "teaching" would be an interesting undertaking, it is not our purpose to do so in this article. We shall attempt to undercut conventional definitions by developing a descriptive rather than a normative concept of teaching and to distinguish it from other concepts with which it is often confused.

DEFINITIONS OF TEACHING

Three uses of the word "teaching" are found in ordinary discourse. First, it is used to refer to that which is taught, as a doctrine or body of knowledge. In the expression "the teachings of the church" reference is made to a body of ideas or a system of beliefs. Second, "teaching" is used to refer to an occupation or a profession—the profession of one who instructs or educates. And finally, "teaching" is used to refer to ways of making something known to others, usually in the routine of a school.

We are concerned here with the third of these uses and shall disregard the first two altogether. "Teaching" in this third sense has been defined in the following ways:

> Teaching: arrangement and manipulation of a situation in which there are gaps or obstructions which an individual will seek to overcome and from which he will learn in the course of doing so.[1]
>
> Teaching: intimate contact between a more mature personality and a less mature which is designed to further the education of the latter.[2]
>
> Teaching: impartation of knowledge to an individual by another in a school.[3]

From a generic standpoint, each of these definitions suffers from the same defect. It smuggles in its own particular view of how teaching is to be carried on. All are question-begging definitions, for they answer in advance the very question which research on teaching seeks to answer. The first of these definitions commits us to the view that the individual learns by engaging in problem solving, and that he is motivated to learn by involvement in an unsettled

state of affairs for which he has no ready-made response. To teach is to engage and direct the pupil in problem-solving. Once we accept this definition, we commit ourselves to a chain of propositions identified with a particular theory of education.

The second definition just as surely, though perhaps less obviously, incorporates a theory of didactics. Teaching, we are told, consists in contacts between two individuals, one more mature than the other. The contacts are to be intimate and designed to advance the education of the less mature person. Education, in the view of the author of this definition, is the development of the individual through learning, and learning in turn is defined as an adaptive process. Intimate contact supposedly requires the presence of one person in the company of the other. To unpack this definition of teaching would again bring to view a theory of education.

We are no better off when we turn to the last of these three concepts. The definition of teaching as the impartation of knowledge is typically used by persons who think of education as the cultivation of the mind, the mind being thought of as an accumulation of information—factual, theoretical, and practical. Teaching, according to this definition, typically takes on the character of lecturing.

To say that the foregoing definitions are question-begging is to say that teaching is confused with didactics. The way in which teaching is or can be performed is mistaken for teaching itself. In its generic sense, teaching is a system of actions intended to induce learning. So defined, teaching is observed to be everywhere the same, irrespective of the cultural context in which it occurs. But these actions may be performed differently from culture to culture or from

---

[1] Adapted from John Brubacher, *Modern Philosophies of Education* (New York: McGraw-Hill, 1939), p. 108.

[2] Henry C. Morrison, *Basic Principles of Education* (Boston: Houghton Mifflin, 1934), p. 41.

[3] Adapted from common usage.

one individual to another within the same culture, depending upon the state of knowledge about teaching, and the teacher's pedagogical knowledge and skill. Didactics, or the science and art of teaching, are not the same as the actions which they treat. And a definition of teaching as such, which packs a set of biases about how these actions are to be conducted, confuses teaching with its science and its art.

TEACHING AND LEARNING DISTINGUISHED

Furthermore, teaching is frequently assimilated to learning. The belief that teaching necessarily entails learning is widely held, and is expressed in more than one book on pedagogical method. As one of our most distinguished authorities says, unless the child learns the teacher has not taught.[4] Then he goes ahead to say that teaching is to learning as selling is to buying, apparently on the assumption that if there is no buying, there can have been no selling. At first, this binding of teaching and learning together after the fashion of selling and buying seems plausible enough. But the analogy will not bear inspection, although it does highlight the responsibility of the teacher and the importance of active endeavor by the pupil.

To begin examination of the idea that teaching entails learning, let us note first of all that teaching and selling each involve some sort of interaction. We do, perform, or accomplish many acts unaided. We race, hunt, and sing without the assistance of anyone. But

there are actions which can be performed only in association with other persons. We can do business only if there is somebody to do business with. We can negotiate if there is someone to carry on negotiations with, and not otherwise. Likewise we can carry on the activities of selling only if there is someone who will buy our product and we can teach only if there is somebody whom we may instruct. Were there no buyers, there could be no sellers. Unless there were pupils, there could be no teachers. Such verbs as *negotiate, sell,* and *teach* signify proceedings between two or more individuals, involving some sort of deliberation with adjustment of mutual claims and interests in expectation that some result will issue. Lacking a process of interaction there can be neither teacher nor pupil just as there can be neither seller nor buyer.

Beyond this point, the analogy between teaching and selling begins to break down. To see how this is so, let us spell out the analogy. There are four elements in the selling-buying operation: a seller, a buyer, the act of selling, and the act of buying. Similarly, in the teaching-learning combination we find a teacher, a pupil, the action of teaching, and the activities of learning. To say that a teacher is to teaching as a seller is to selling, while not strictly correct, does not do violence to either of these relations. The qualifying expression "not strictly correct" is inserted because there are several different actions which we expect of a teacher: making assignments, grading papers, showing how to do something, telling why something is the case, and so on. But there is little more than one sort of behavior predictable from the statement that one is a seller; namely, that he gives something in return for a consideration, usually money. Looking further we find that

[4] William H. Kilpatrick, *Foundations of Method* (New York: MacMillan, 1926, p. 268). See also John Dewey, *How We Think,* rev. ed. (New York: D. C. Heath, 1934), p. 35f.

learning is not coordinate with buying, because the relation of pupil to learning is not the same sort of thing as buyer to buying. We can say that a buyer is to buying as a pupil is to "pupiling," but the parallel breaks down when we say "as a pupil is to learning." "Pupiling," if there were such a word, would be required by the analogy to mean receiving instruction just as "buying" means receiving something in return for an agreed-upon price. Nor are we any better off if we substitute "learner" for "pupil," since "learner" is defined as one who receives instruction.

Furthermore, the relation between selling and buying is not the same as that between teaching and learning. The statement "I am selling X and someone is buying it from me" is implicitly tautological. It is clear from common usage that in order to be selling something someone must be buying. It would be contradictory to say "I am selling X but no one is buying it,"* or to say "I am buying X from so and so but he is not selling it." If you state "I am selling X" you are stating only part of what you mean, for implicit in this statement is the idea that someone is buying it. On the other hand, "I am teaching X (meaning, say, mathematics) to A and he is learning it" is not tautological. It is not contradictory to say "I am teaching X to A but he is not learning it." Nor is it contradictory to assert "A is learning X but no one is teaching it to him." "I taught X to

A" means that I showed A how to do X, or told him such and such about X. This expression does not include the idea that A learned from me how to do X. It is thus not repeating the idea to add it to the expression. Hence "I taught X to A" says something different from "I taught X to A and he learned X." However, the parallel suggested in the paragraph above is logically similar to that between buying and selling. To assert "I am teaching X (mathematics) and he is 'pupiling' it" (meaning he is receiving my instruction), would be tautological. It would then be contradictory to say "I am teaching X (mathematics) and he is not 'pupiling' it" (meaning he is not receiving my instruction). To give instruction would seem to entail receiving it. It would likewise be contradictory to say "He received instruction, but no one gave him instruction."

The difference between teaching and learning may be further explored by reference to the distinction which Ryle makes between what he calls task words and achievement or success words.[5] Task words are those which express activities such as *racing, treating, traveling,* and *hunting.* The corresponding achievement words are *win, cure, arrive,* and *find. Teaching* is a task word and *learn* is the parallel achievement word. Achievement words signify occurrences or episodes. Thus one wins, arrives, or finds at a particular moment, or a cure is effected at a particular time. Nevertheless, some achievement verbs express a continued process. A boat is launched at a particular instant but it is held at the dock for inspection. On the other hand, task verbs always signify some

---

* There is a sense in which it would not be contradictory to say, "I am selling X but no one is buying it." For example, "I have been selling cars all day but nobody bought one" is not self-contradictory. But in this case it would be more precise to say "I have been *trying* to sell cars," etc., meaning I have been doing things intended to result in the sale of cars.

5 Gilbert Ryle, *The Concept of Mind* (London: Hutchinson House, 1952), pp. 149–52.

sort of activity or extended proceedings. We can say of a task such as play, treat, or teach that it is performed skillfully, carefully, successfully, or ineffectively. We may play the game successfully or unsuccessfully, but we cannot win unsuccessfully. We may treat a patient skillfully or unskillfully, but the restoring of health is neither skillful nor unskillful. It makes sense to say that we teach unsuccessfully. But it is self-contradictory to say we learned French unsuccessfully.

TEACHING AS A SYSTEM OF ACTIONS

That learning does not necessarily issue from teaching, that teaching is one thing and learning is quite another, is significant for pedagogical research. It enables us to analyze the concept of teaching without becoming entangled in the web of arguments about the processes and conditions of learning; in short, to carry on investigations of teaching in its own right. Teaching, like learning, has its own forms, its own constituent elements, its own regularities. It takes place under specifiable conditions —time limits, authority relations, individual abilities, institutional structures, and so on. What is needed for scientific inquiry is a concept which recognizes teaching as a distinctive phenomenon general enough to embrace normative definitions (see page 40) as special cases.

The word "teacher" is a dispositional term in the sense that under specifiable conditions—classroom, pupils, and so forth—the individual referred to as a teacher tends to behave in characteristic ways. He may explain something with the expectation that what he says will be remembered by the pupil; he may

draw a diagram and point out certain features of it, emphasizing that these are to be remembered; he may read from a book and ask a pupil to interpret the passage; and so on. When the teacher behaves in these and many other ways, we say he is teaching. To repeat, teaching thus conceived may be defined as a system of actions directed to pupils. These actions are varied in form and content and they are related to the behavior of pupils, whose actions are in turn related to those of the teacher. From the execution of these actions and interactions of teacher and pupil, learning occurs. But learning, being an acquired disposition to behave in particular ways in particular circumstances, is neither action nor behavior, though it is exhibited in actions. The theoretical conception of teaching we propose to present will include all the actions of teachers necessary to explain and to predict the behavior of pupils and the occurrence of learning, though such explaining and predicting cannot be made from these actions alone.

It is to be kept in mind that the actions which constitute teaching, as defined in this discussion, take place in and are influenced by an environment which typically contains such social factors as mores, organizational structures, and cultural resources, as well as physical objects, persons, and so forth. But this environment is excluded from our conception of teaching, not because it is unimportant or irrelevant to teaching, but because it is not a part of the concept of teaching. Teaching is doubtless related to the mores and to social structures, but it is not the same sort of thing.

To explicate the concept of teaching we shall resort to a model which draws upon the psychological paradigm devel-

A PEDAGOGICAL MODEL

I	III	II
INDEPENDENT VARIABLES	INTERVENING VARIABLES	DEPENDENT VARIABLES
(*Teacher*)	(*Pupils*)	(*Pupils*)
————————→		————————→
(1) Linguistic behavior	These variables consist of postulated explanatory en-	(1) Linguistic behavior
(2) Performative behavior	tities and processes such as memories, beliefs, needs,	(2) Performative behavior
(3) Expressive behavior	inferences, and associative mechanisms.	(3) Expressive behavior

oped by Tolman,[6] although the psychological features of his model are of little interest to us here. All the variables involved in and related to the actions which make up teaching can be classfied into three categories, but the actions themselves belong to only one of these. Although their particular contents continue to be controversial, the categories themselves have been well established in the behavioral sciences. They are (1) independent variables, (2) dependent variables, and (3) intervening variables. By referring to the model it can be easily seen that the actions of teaching belong to the first of these categories, and the actions of pupils to the second. Learning, as achievement, is an intervening variable. The index of its presence is pupil behavior, and this behavior is a dependent variable.

In the course of teaching, these variables are related in various ways. In so far as these relations can be postulated, described, and verified, teaching can be shaped in terms of empirically tested principles. While it is not possible here to deal concretely with these relations, we can discuss them in a very general

[6] Edward C. Tolman, "A Psychological Model," in *Toward a General Theory of Social Action,* edited by Talcott Parsons and Edward A. Shils (Cambridge: Harvard University Press, 1952), pp. 279–302.

way. In the model, the arrows indicate the direction of causal influences. The teacher's actions are followed by postulated states, events, or processes in the pupil and are represented by the intervening variables. Then, as a result of these variables, the pupil behaves in one or more of the ways indicated in the dependent variables column. The teachre can see the pupil's behavior, but he cannot see the postulated events and processes; that is, he cannot observe interests, motives, needs, beliefs, and the like. But these psychological entities and processes are present by implication in the behavior of the pupil. The teacher may therefore infer these psychological factors from the pupil's behavior, and in some instances he actually does infer them, although he may not be aware that he is doing so. Thus the teacher often infers from the reactions of the pupil that he is interested, or that he wants to do so and so, or the contrary.

Our model does not depict the ebb and flow of teaching, nor does it give a complete schema of the cycle of giving and taking instruction, hereafter referred to as the teaching cycle. To complete the picture the model must be extended to the right in duplicate form. Thus extended, the model would show that the pupil's actions bring into operation the teacher's intervening variables.

These variables in turn lead to teacher actions, and at this point the whole cycle begins again. In this way the process of teaching is continued until the teacher believes either that the pupil has achieved what the teacher intended or that it is not profitable to continue teaching at the moment.

The foregoing analysis enables us to describe the teaching cycle, to mark off units of this cycle, and to distinguish the act of teaching from the act of receiving instruction. The teaching cycle is symbolized as follows:

$$\left\| P_t \rightarrow D_t \rightarrow R_t \mid \rightarrow P_p \rightarrow D_p \rightarrow R_p \right\|$$
$$\rightarrow P_t \rightarrow D_t \rightarrow R_t \mid \rightarrow P_p \rightarrow D_p \rightarrow R_p \right\| \rightarrow$$
$$P_t \rightarrow D_t \rightarrow R_t \mid \rightarrow P_p \rightarrow D_p \rightarrow R_p \right\|$$
$$\cdots\cdots\cdots\cdots \rightarrow achievement,$$

where P_t is the teacher's perception of the pupil's behavior; D_t is the teacher's diagnosis of the pupil's state of interest, readiness, knowledge, and the like made by inference from the behavior of the pupil; and R_t is the action taken by the teacher in light of his diagnosis; and where P_p is the pupil's perception of the teacher's behavior; D_p is the pupil's diagnosis of the teacher's state of interest, what he is saying, and so on, as inferred from the teacher's behavior; and R_p is the reaction of the pupil to the actions of the teacher.

Each unit marked off by the double vertical lines is an instance of the teaching cycle. Each one consists of a teacher-pupil interaction. Within this teaching cycle are two subunits divided by the single vertical line. The subunit $\mid P_t \rightarrow D_t \rightarrow R_t \mid$ is what we refer to as an act of teaching; the subunit $\mid P_p \rightarrow D_p \rightarrow R^p \mid$ is what we call the act of taking instruction. These are reciprocating acts, and when performed under proper conditions they issue in achievement.

Teaching, according to our schema, does entail someone to give instruction as well as someone to take it. If a pupil is working on an assignment, he is probably learning. But no teaching is going on. No one is acting toward the pupil as a teacher. However, teaching acts can occur, though in abbreviated form, without the physical presence of pupils. For example, a teacher giving instruction over a television network is not in the physical presence of pupils. He can even be cut off the air by a mechanical difficulty, and being unaware that anything has happened, continue to teach. In a case like this the teacher is shaping his instructional behavior to some generalized pupil group anyway, and the fact that he is off the air consequently makes no difference.

Of course actual classroom teaching is not as simple as our schema. For one thing, more than one pupil is usually involved in classroom teaching. The teacher typically addresses himself to the entire class rather than to a single pupil. Even when he appears to be talking to a single pupil, he usually speaks for the benefit of the whole class. His perception of pupil behavior is likely to be some sort of generalized picture, and his diagnosis a hunch as to the general state of the class as a whole. Finally, his actions are likely to be shaped more by these general considerations and by his habits than by the psychological requirements of any one pupil.

The fact that classroom teaching is more complex than our pedagogical model is no criticism of the model. One of the advantages of models is that they give a simplified picture of the phenomenon they depict. However, the fact that our symbolic schema and verbal performances in the classroom are isomorphic is borne out by our descriptive studies of classroom teaching. By taping classroom discourse and analyzing it into pedagogically neutral units called episodes we have established a context within which to view verbal exchanges comprising the teaching cycle.[7] Acts of teaching as well as acts of taking instruction can be clearly distinguished in the episodic structure.

Our knowledge of the act of teaching as well as that of taking instruction is meager. Neither of these acts has been investigated sufficiently to justify, from a scientific standpoint, fundamental changes in teaching. We have considerable knowledge of how human learning occurs, although much of it comes by extrapolation from studies of animal learning. The amount of adjustment in our current theories of learning which verbal behavior and cognitive processes may require is something about which we can only guess. We do not even know how accurately our learning theory describes what occurs in the act of taking instruction. Be that as it may, the act of teaching has received far less attention than its central role in pedagogy would seem to require.

THE VARIABLES

Intervening variables consist of constructs, or postulated entities and processes, which stand between the independent and dependent variables and are functionally related to them. The independent variables—the teacher's actions—are conceived to be causal factors which evoke or bring into opera-

---

[7] B. Othanel Smith and others, *A Study of the Logic of Teaching.* A report on the first phase of a five-year research project. United States Office of Education. Dittoed 1959. For a more detailed treatment see "The Analysis of Classroom Discourse: A Method and Its Uses," by Mary Jane Aschner (Unpublished Doctor's Dissertation, University of Illinois, 1958).

tion postulated entities and processes, and these in turn are connected by a set of functions to the dependent variables —to the behavior of pupils. An account of these variables would involve us in psychological theory, and consequently, in one of the most controversial areas of the behavioral sciences. In the heyday of radical behaviorism, postulation of entities and processes between stimulus and response was frowned upon. Even Thorndike's postulation of physiological entities and processes was believed to be unnecessary to the explanation of learning. In recent years, however, different schools of psychology have assumed, each in its own way, whatever processes and entities seem to afford the most plausible explanation. To a large extent, differences in schools of psychology hinge upon differences in their conceptual postulations. Fortunately our task is a modest one, requiring us to delineate only the variables of our model. Were we to develop completely a general theory of teaching, we would be required to set forth a set of intervening variables, and to show their postulated causal connections with both independent and dependent variables of our model.

The independent variables consist of linguistic, performative, and expressive behaviors. These behaviors are essential elements of the concept of teaching and are not to be confused with the dependent variables, which are the behaviors identified with the act of taking instruction and are functionally associated with learning.

To continue our discussion of independent variables, teaching acts consist largely in verbal behavior, in what is done with and to pupils through the medium of words. But the fact that language is the primary medium of instruction is not as important as the things we do with language. For if we are to understand teaching, we must know what the actions are that we perform linguistically. Furthermore, it may be supposed that changes in the effectiveness of instruction will follow upon changes in the execution of such verbal actions.

What are the sorts of actions we perform with language in the classroom? First, there is a group of actions which have to do with the performance of what we shall call logically relevant—subject to logical appraisal—tasks. The teacher is called upon to deal with questions whose answers involve logical operations. For example, the teacher defines terms. To define a term is to perform a logical operation. If he gives a classificatory definition such as "A triangle is a plane figure with three sides," the teacher names the class of things (plane figure) to which triangles belong and then gives the attributes (three sides) which distinguish triangles from all other plane figures. We will describe only briefly a few of the logically relevant actions which are found in didactic verbal behavior.[8]

Defining

In general, definitions are rules for using words. There are several ways to

define words, depending upon the rules. Among these ways are classificatory, operational, relational, and nominal definitions.

Classifying

To classify is to put something in a category. The teacher classifies implicitly when he defines, describes, or explains. But the logic of classification is far more involved than the mere verbal act of asserting "X is a Y." Its logic becomes explicit when the teacher attempts to tell why he classifies X as a Y. He is then expected to set forth the criteria (rules) he uses and to show that they apply in the particular case.

Explaining

Explanations are called for when an event or a state of affairs is to be accounted for. To explain is to set forth an antecedent condition of which the particular event to be accounted for is taken as the effect, or else to give the rules or facts which are used to tell why decisions or judgments were made or actions taken. There are at least six different kinds of explanations: mechanical, causal, sequent, procedural, teleological, and normative.

Conditional Inferring

In conditional inferring, a set of conditions is described and the teacher then gives the consequent—the effect, result, or outcome. Sometimes the conditions are fairly simple, so that the path from the conditions to a conclusion is easily followed and the logical connection between the conditions and the outcome is fairly explicit. In other instances the path is complex, involving a number of steps, and is difficult to connect logically with the conditions.

---

[8] For a more extended discussion of these verbal actions see Smith and others, *op. cit.* It should be noted that there are different dimensions of verbal behavior which cannot be discussed here. The teacher not only makes assertions about objects, but also talks about language itself. To ask "What is the author comparing X to?" in a given passage is to direct the pupil's attention to an object, event, and so forth, while to ask "Is this passage a metaphor?" is to ask about language itself. To ask for a definition is one thing, and to ask what a definition *is* is quite another thing.

Comparing and Constrasting

In this sort of verbal action two or more things—actions, factors, objects, processes—are compared; or else something is given and the teacher attempts to interpret it by describing another familiar object or process to which it is compared. Such comparative relations can often be expressed in terms of transitivity and symmetry.

Valuating

To perform the act of valuating, the teacher rates some object, expression, event, or action, let us say, as to its truth and the like. If he gives the complete operation of valuating, the teacher will set forth the reasons for his rating.

Designating

To designate is to identify something by name, word, or symbol. The verbal action here consists in citing instances or examples of a group of things or in giving the name of a particular thing or class of things.

Other Actions

In addition to the foregoing actions, there are verbal actions less closely related perhaps to logical operations. The teacher states theorems, rules, beliefs. He reports what was stated in a book, or verbally by someone. He states something to be the case; for example, that the date and place of a particular event were thus and so.[9]

[9] Our own studies of classroom discourse in English, social studies, science, and mathematics show that episodes involving definitions make up about 4 per cent of the total number of episodes; classifying about 3 per cent; explaining about 13 per cent; conditional inferring about 7 per cent; comparing and contrasting about 3 per cent; valuating about 5 per cent; designating about 15 per cent; and others 50 per cent.

The second group of actions which teachers perform with words is called directive action. In the moment-to-moment tasks of the classroom the teacher is called upon to tell pupils what to do in the performance of some operation or the practice of a motor skill. He may observe a pupil's mistake in the practice of typing and tell him what to do to correct it, just as on the playing field he may tell a player what to do to improve his tackling. He may tell a pupil in the laboratory that a piece of apparatus is to be set up in a particular way, or that he has made an error in reasoning which can be corrected in such and such a way. These verbal actions are all directive in the sense that they instruct the pupil in what he is to do. There are other directive actions which are less specific and only suggest the direction in which the pupil is to move. Verbal actions of this sort always frame a situation in a general way. For example, a teacher may tell a group of pupils that they are to take a trip by automobile and that they need to know how much the gasoline will cost in order to pro-rate the expense among members of the class. He then asks what they need to know in order to find out the cost of the gasoline. In this case, the teacher sets a situation and suggests the line along which the pupils are to work.

In both of these sorts of saying and telling the teacher does not intend that the pupil learn what he says. The pupil is not expected to say back to the teacher, in either the same or different words, what the teacher himself said. In the case of learning motor skills, he does expect the pupil to do what he is told, and thereby to effect changes in his performance. If the pupil forgets entirely what the teacher said, it does not matter so long as the pupil's performance is improved. The same is true with respect to less specific directives, as in the case of the automobile trip. The pupils most certainly will forget all about the situation laid before them by the teacher. This is not what the teacher wishes them to remember. His hope is that the pupils will learn how to analyze a situation and to decide upon the relevant factors in the course of working it out. This use of language is quite different from the expository uses discussed above. There the pupil is expected to remember what the teacher says and to repeat it in his own words in a subsequent situation. If the teacher says that the law of gravity is so and so and that it can be expressed mathematically thus and so, he expects the pupil to remember what he has said and to be able to say the same thing in his own words when he is called upon to do it.

Finally, the teacher performs admonitory acts. He praises and commends; blames and reprimands. He recommends, advises, and enjoins. He says to a pupil, "That is good." He may say to another, "That is not up to your ability. You could have done better." He may say, "You got yourself into this difficulty. You have only yourself to blame." He may suggest some course of action as the way out of the trouble. He may enjoin the pupil to remember so and so when he comes up against a particular sort of situation in the future. These kinds of verbal acts may effect psychological reinforcement or extinctions, depending upon the particular admonitory act and the circumstances in which it occurs. They are conventionally understood to be taken for their social or emotional impact upon the pupil rather than for their cognitive content.

We turn now to consider those independent variables of our model which are nonverbal. The first set of these we call performative actions; that is, actions which are performed for assumed or understood purposes but which are not linguistic. They may be accompanied by verbal behavior but they are themselves mere motor performances. These actions serve to *show* rather than to *tell* something to pupils, and the showing is done by manipulating objects. The teacher shows a pupil how to do something—say, how to regulate a Bunsen burner—by performing the act himself. At the same time, he may say, "Here is the way to do it—you turn this to control the amount of air," and so forth. But the saying is itself directive verbal behavior and not performative in our sense. The act of turning the element of the apparatus, and thus showing the relation between the turning and the color of the flame, is what we refer to as performative behavior. In such cases it is assumed that the pupil is to learn how to perform this action himself, so that the next time he will be able to adjust the burner without the aid of the teacher.

Numerous instances of this type of performative behavior can be found in the day-to-day work of the teacher. In some situations, however, the teacher engages in performative actions which the pupil is not expected to learn, for their purpose is to facilitate the learning of something else. For example, the teacher performs a demonstration in a science class to show the lines of force in a magnetic field. He goes through the usual operations of putting the appropriate piece of paper over a magnet and then sprinkling iron filings on the paper. Of course the pupils may learn from their observation of the teacher how to do the demonstration themselves. But the purpose of the performance is to show the magnetic field rather than how to carry out the demonstration.

The second set of nonverbal variables

is what we call expressive behavior. These behaviors are illustrated in bodily posture, facial expression, tone of voice, expression of the eyes, and other ways. Typically they are neither purposeful nor addressed to anyone. In this respect they differ significantly from both verbal and performative actions, which we always understood as being directed to someone or to a group. Nevertheless, expressive behaviors function in teaching because they are taken by pupils as signs of the psychological state of the teacher. In this sense expressive behaviors are natural signs, like the things we call clouds, lightning, rivers. We take them as signifying something—as a cloud is a sign of rain.

Turning now to the dependent variables of our model—those which make up the instruction-taking part of the teaching cycle—we find a parallel between these variables and the independent ones. The pupil performs linguistic actions. He defines, explains, valuates, and so on, just as the teacher does. He performs these actions at the teacher's suggestion, or often even voluntarily. However, the pupil's purpose is not to instruct anyone, but to bear witness that he is taking instruction—that he understands what is happening or that he is taking part in (accepting or dissenting from) what is going on.

Directive verbal behavior of the pupil occurs infrequently, and usually on occasions when he plays the role of teacher, as chairman of class discussion, for example. The same observation holds for admonitory behavior. Classroom conventions do not permit the pupil to praise, blame, or advise the teacher with respect to his work, but this does happen on occasion. A pupil may complain that the teacher has been unfair, but he is not likely to say either to another pupil or to a teacher, "Your ex-planation was splendid." Such verbal behavior is odd and is likely to be ill received by the pupils as well as by the teacher.

While the pupil exhibits performative behavior (nonverbal behavior carried on for a purpose), he does so typically to practice the actions themselves rather than to instruct anyone. Thus he engages in performative actions when he sets up laboratory equipment, takes part in athletic events, and so on. Actions of this nature under the direct tutelage of the teacher are part of the teaching cycle. If they occur outside of teacher-pupil interaction, they are simply ways of study and practice.

The expressive behavior of the pupil is the same as that of the teacher. The pupil smiles or frowns; he slumps or sits erect in his seat; his voice is firm and convincing or weak and uncertain. Such behavior in the pupil, even more often than in the teacher, is not addressed to anyone. It is not typically intended to communicate. Nevertheless, it functions as signs to the teacher—as the skies, clouds, and winds are signs to the skipper at sea. The posture of the pupil, the light in his eyes, or the frown on his face tell the teacher who can read them about his feelings, intentions, and ideas.

THE LANGUAGE OF DIDACTICS

By "didactics" is meant, of course, the science or art of teaching, and not teaching itself. When we speak of what we know about how teaching is to be conducted we have reference to didactics. The language of didactics traditionally is marked by such terms as "method," "drill," "interest," "learning situation." Discussions of teaching as such are carried on in the terms of the lecture method, problem method, project method, supervised study method. Much of the research on teaching has been framed in terms of these various doctrines. Is the problem method more effective than the lecture method? Is the project method more effective than the recitation method?

Numerous experiments to find answers to these and similar questions have produced only inconclusive results. This fact is often attributed to inadequate control of experimental conditions and to the complexity of the phenomenon itself. No one can doubt the strength of these claims. Nevertheless, the fact that teaching itself has never been analyzed apart from the context of doctrine may contribute to failure to control relevant factors. Has not our theorizing about teaching, even for experimental purposes, become clouded with commitments to the very words we use to discuss teaching?

If what we just said about pedagogical theorizing is only partly correct, it suggests that a new way of talking about didactic questions is in order. Perhaps a new approach to the study of teaching will emerge if we abandon the term "method," which is associated with such heavy-laden terms as "induction," "deduction," and "problem-solving"—terms for which everyone has his own preconceptions and predilections. If we cut through the verbal curtain and look at actual instructional operations in the classroom, we find them to be different from what our linguistic commitments lead us to believe. We see that teachers do many things which cannot be neatly fitted into the traditional theories of pedagogy. For example, at one time a teacher sets up a verbal situation from which he can move in a number of directions, depending upon his assessment of the way his pupils are psychologically deployed. At another time he sets up a nonverbal state of affairs and invites his pupils to explore it, to tell how it can be handled, and so forth. On another occasion a pupil may execute a verbal maneuver to counter the teacher's move. The teacher may then outflank the pupil, leaving one or more members of the class to meet the challenge.

We need studies of the sorts of positions teachers assume, and what maneuvers and detailed actions they take under varying circumstances and with different sorts of materials. If these were made, it would be appropriate to speak of the strategies and tactics of teaching. From such descriptive studies we might then go on to develop experimental as well as more nearly adquate theoretical didactics.

6.

Teaching, Acting, and Behaving

THOMAS F. GREEN

Professor of Philosophy of
Education and Director of The Educational Policy
Research Center, Syracuse University.

Whatever men do may be viewed as conforming to certain generalizations of human behavior; generalizations, which describing and explaining what men have done, afford also some basis for predicting what they shall do. It may be questionable whether a social science is possible which treats of human behavior except in the aggregate and which therefore can explain or predict human behavior except in relation to large numbers and general tendencies. But this question does not concern me. I assume that whatever men may do, in every specific detail, can be *viewed* as conforming to certain generalizations or laws of human behavior even though we may not know what those generalizations or laws may be. When we observe any item of human behavior in this light, we observe it to "fall under" some general law or to be a "special case" of some generalization. The law or generalization may then be cited as an explanation or part of an explanation to account for the occurrence of such behavior and to predict like behavior in the future.

But many times the same behavior viewed as conforming to such a descriptive generalization, may also be viewed as done in *obedience* to certain rules or principles of action. When one views his own behavior in this light, then the principle or rule of action being "followed" or "applied" may be cited as his reason for acting as he did. There is a difference between someone giving an explanation as to why he acted as he did, and giving a good reason for acting as he did. The one involves the citation of a generalization or law of human behavior, and the other involves the citation of a rule of action. That there is a difference here is

Reprinted with permission. Thomas F. Green, "Teaching, Acting, and Behaving," Harvard Educational Review, 34, Fall 1964, 507–524. Copyright © 1964 by President and Fellows of Harvard College. This selection is from pp. 507–511 of the longer original article.

also clear when one considers that my explanation why A acted as he did may differ from A's reason for acting as he did, and indeed, my explanation may not even include *any* good reason for his action. And this can be true even when my explanation is correct or adequate and when A is in no way deceived concerning his "real" reason. That there is no contradiction in such a supposition, shows that there is a difference between an explanation of human behavior and a reason for acting in a certain way; and this difference between explanation and reason is one way of displaying the difference between conformity to rule and obedience to rule. Either an explanation or a reason may be offered in answer to the question "Why did you do such and such?" because that question can be differently interpreted as a request for an explanatory generalization or for a rule of action. It can be a request for a cause or a request for a principle of conduct.

The concepts "explanation" and "reason," "behavior" and "action," "conformity to rule" and "obedience to rule" are ambiguous. It is clear, however, that in some sense each of these is a pair of contrasting concepts, and, moreover, that the contrast drawn in each pair is related to that in each of the other pairs. Thus, the contrast between conformity to a law of behavior and obedience to a rule of action is related to a possible contrast between giving an explanation of one's behavior and giving a reason for acting in a certain way. Similarly, the contrast between conforming to a rule and obeying a rule is the central distinction in a possible contrast between behaving and acting.

This contrast between conformity to rule and obedience to rule lies also at the heart of what we mean by teaching.

For teaching is a rule guided activity, or as I shall say, it is norm-regarding. That is to say, it is important for a teacher not only to understand some explanation of his behavior, but also to have some reasons for acting as he does; and these are different requirements. In a Freudian explanation as to why a gardener behaves as he does, the principles of good gardening may never enter. But presumably his *reasons* for doing as he does *must* include some reference to the principles involved in gardening. Gardening is a rule-directed activity. Similarly, an explanation of a teacher's behavior may have nothing to do with the principles of good teaching or the canons of inquiry. But one's reasons for teaching in a certain way *must* include some reference to such principles. We cannot understand teaching if we study it simply as a species of human behavior. It must be viewed also as a species of human action; that is, not simply as behavior conforming to some laws or generalizations of human behavior, but as conduct obedient to certain principles of action. Teaching, in short, is not simply norm-conforming; it is norm-obeying.

Teaching also has, at least as its partial aim, the development of rule-directed conduct in others. To teach mathematics is to teach obedience to the principles of mathematical inquiry. To teach plumbing is to teach not simply conformity to, but obedience to the principles of plumbing. If we focus our attention upon a possible contrast between acting and behaving and view human action always as norm-regarding and behavior as norm-conforming, then we can say that teaching is itself an instance of human action aimed at enhancinig the human capacity for action. The most direct way to understand such a view of teaching is to grasp the difference between obedience to rule and conformity to rule, and the most immediate way to understand this difference is to observe the ways in which learning a rule or learning to obey a rule of action differs from learning a habit.

I

To acquire a habit is to acquire a disposition to act in a certain way. The same may be said of learning to obey a rule of action. It too, involves a disposition to act in a certain way. How then does acquiring a habit differ from learning to obey a rule? There is such a thing as having good speaking habits, by which we mean having a disposition to speak according to certain rules or principles. But this phrase "according to certain rules or principles" is systematically ambiguous. How can we know whether this "speaking according to certain rules" is the expression of a habit or the result of obedience, whether it is conformity to a rule, or obedience to it? It might be either. Surely it is possible, for example, to obey the rules of English in speaking without being able to state the rules. How then does obeying the grammatical and rhetorical principles of English differ from simply having certain habits of speaking?

A rule of action is intended to discriminate between a right and a wrong, a correct or incorrect way of doing things. To learn to obey a rule is not simply to acquire a disposition to act in a certain way, but a disposition to act in that way *because* it is a correct way. The phrase "because it is a correct way" in no way implies "because it is a good way." We are not concerned with what makes a rule good or valuable or right, but only with what constitutes obeying the rule as contrasted with conforming

to it. What constitutes the value of a rule is a matter not discussed here.

But if learning to obey a rule is a disposition to act in a certain way because it is a correct way, then how can a person learn to follow a rule and yet continue to act in an incorrect way? The answer is clear. When we say "learning to obey a rule is to acquire a disposition to act in a certain way because it is a correct way," the word "because" has the force of "for the reason that" or "on the grounds that." It is perfectly clear that men may act in certain ways for reasons which are quite erroneous or on grounds which are not defensible. In short, there is such a thing as learning to obey a wrong principle; that is, to acquire a disposition to act in a wrong way according to a certain rule on the erroneous grounds that, or for the mistaken reason that, it is a correct rule.

A child, for example, may learn to use an incorrect grammatical construction, say a double negative. He may use it consistently and regard a correct usage as wrong. We would say that he learned to obey a certain principle, but that the principle was wrong. Similarly, a student who, in the solution of certain equations, consistently arrives at wrong answers by a procedure which he regularly follows, and who regards a correct procedure as wrong, would be said to have learned to obey a certain rule, although a wrong rule. Nonetheless, in this case, as in all others, to learn to obey a rule is to acquire a disposition to act in a certain way on the grounds that, or for the reason that, it is a correct way to act. Thus, learning to obey a rule or principle differs from acquiring a mere habit in at least this respect, that it involves not simply acquiring a disposition to act in a certain way, but a disposition to act in that way because it is a correct way. And this is so, even in those cases where people learn to obey *wrong* principles.[1]

It is not a necessary condition for having learned to obey a rule, that one be able to state the rule one is obeying. But it is a necessary condition that one adopt a certain attitude toward violations of the rule. Thus, a "good speaker of English" may obey certain rules even though he is unable to state the rules he obeys. Whether his speech is the expression of habit or of obedience to rule will be most clearly displayed when he is confronted with a case of their violation. If he does not regard the violation of the rules as wrong or incorrect, then that is *prima facie* evidence that what he has learned is not obedience to rule, but only a correct habit. It is evidence, in short, that though his speech may be norm-conforming, it is not norm-obeying.

This is only *prima facie* evidence, however, for the following curious reason. A "good speaker of English" may be indifferent to violations of grammatical rules and rhetorical principles for several different reasons. One who *cannot* state the principles which govern his own case, may be indifferent to violations of the rules simply because he regards all ways of using the language

as differences of taste or habit among which there is no "correct" or "incorrect." We could say that his speech is norm-conforming in the sense that it does in fact conform to the rules of good English usage. We could not, however, say that his speech is norm-obeying. Indeed, we could not say of such a person that he had learned to obey the rules of English grammar because to learn to obey them involves the understanding that good speech is *not* merely a matter of preference, but a matter of being correct or incorrect.

On the other hand, a good speaker of English may be indifferent to violations of the rules of grammar because he regards the choice of grammatical principles as a matter of indifference. He *can* state what rules or principles govern his own speech, but he is also willing to acknowledge that others may adopt other rules. Thus, he can be indifferent to violations of the rules of grammar when discovered in the speech of others and regard them simply as different from his own, but never as incorrect. Such a supposition, however, does not run counter to our thesis concerning the difference between conformity to rule and obedience to rule. For what is our criterion for saying that in *his* speech he is obedient to certain rules or principles? It must include the fact that he regards violations of the rules in his own speech as incorrect and that he seeks to remedy them. In short, a rule of action is intended always to discriminate between right and wrong, correct or incorrect performances. Therefore, in learning to obey a rule, it is not necessary that one be able to state the rule one is obeying, but it is necessary that one adopt the attitude that violations of the rule are incorrect or at least improper. It is this condition which marks the difference between

[1] It is worth observing that just as one can ask what is involved in learning to obey a certain principle, so one can ask what is involved in learning to disobey a certain principle. Similar questions can be asked in both cases. But this much must be observed. Learning to disobey a certain rule or principle clearly presupposes knowledge of the principle. In the absence of such knowledge, such behavior could only be described as incorrect habit. One cannot be said to disobey a principle K unless one regards K as in some sense valid or binding upon him. Thus in learning to obey K, one is not learning to disobey − K.

learning to obey a rule and learning a habit in conformity to the rule.

Thus, if a "good speaker of English" views speech which violates the rules of grammar as wrong or incorrect, then that is evidence that he has learned not simply to conform to the rule, but to obey the rule even though he cannot state the rule he obeys. Good speech is in this sense norm-regarding. It is principled. It is not *merely* habitual, but is rule-guided.

7

Is Teaching Phoney?

B. PAUL KOMISAR

Professor of Philosophy of
Education, Temple University.

To a less than happy degree, a distinct tone of carping has characterized one region of discussion in education. The region I refer to is the debate accompanying the introduction and limited encroachment of machinery and new forms of organization into the classroom, traditionally the precinct of the single, human-type teacher.

It is easy to be displeased by this, but more disheartening yet is the futile way the debate is joined. Controversy seems to have arisen in answer to such a question as "Is programmed instruction better than lecturing?" a question which puts the onus of proof on the innovation. Then demonstrations of greater or, what is more likely, equal effectiveness in the new techniques are countered with claims of further sacrosanct, often indiscernible features in the traditional ways. And so it goes on, jejunely.

"Is Teaching Phoney?" by B. Paul Komisar is reprinted with permission from Teachers College Record, *70:407–411, February, 1969.*

In what follows, I want to do two things: (1) suggest what is wrong with the debate as presently conducted; and (2) even more suggestively do an analysis of teaching which might recast our conception of it. The "it" in the preceding sentence is ambiguous by intent. For it is the hope here that the analysis will contribute something to the rationality of the debate as well as give us a glimpse of the terror that is in teaching, debate or no debate.

The new forms of "teaching" alluded to above include teaching machines, computer-based instruction, and other offsprings of technology, as well as any conception of the teacher as a guide, stage-manager, or resource rather than a director of learning. So the first suggestion is that those in education who advocate these forms are radicals and not merely revisionists. They are radicals because teaching machines *et al.* are *not* new methods of teaching; rather they represent a different kind of social encounter to replace the kind we call *teaching.* The case for claiming radical innovation is as follows:

1. *Offerings.* In all human encounters it can be said a person makes something available to another: our paths intersect, we perceive one another and offer our discourse, demeanor and movements. When the elements are combined in intelligible ways, we get the minimum to be expected in any social encounter, what I will call an offering. An offering, on the view adopted here, is a social object adequately describable on its *own* terms, supplemented perhaps by reference to the offerer. So I may whine, wail, bleat, or blubber in your presence, but that *that* is what I do can be correctly reported *without reference to you.* My act, so to speak, though done in your presence is describable as done by me (of course I may have annoyed *you,* but that is another matter, or act). Indeed I can be said to have done that act in your company without your having noted it or noted it as such, and certainly it is not necessary that you acknowledge it. The point to be made in calling this an *offering* is that the act is made available to you; you *might* be of a mind to notice or even make something of it. But you need not; as an act it remains what it is whether or not it has this effect.

2. *Gifts and Services.* When what we make available to another requires for its completeness participation by the second party (perhaps some *change* in the other), then we have not offerings but gifts and services. Gifts and services, then, are offerings marked by being obtrusive. They have a "built-in" effect and require a recipient in order to achieve their alleged being. Hence an adequate description of either will mention a recipient. We give friendship, sympathy, and advice *to someone;* we

don't just do them of ourselves. So these are gifts or services, not offerings; and we cannot describe what they are without mention of the other to which they are directed.

But what in turn sets off gifts from services is whether solicitation is a precondition for esteem. If I am a therapist and you invite my ministrations, then what I give is (genuine) therapy. But foisted "therapy" is not that at all but rather meddling or impertinence: it gives offense not aid. The same applies to training; to direct it at me without my leave is to be arrogant not helpful, obtuse not obliging. I am not sure, but the same may be true of comedy. If your antics are not invited or, at minimum, welcome, then you are being more vexing than entertaining. Ergo these are all *services,* by which is meant that without solicitation or acceptance they lose the right to be called (simply) by their initial names.

Gifts are the antithesis. My failure to request or accede to your act does not make it lose face or strip it of being; it remains what it is. Like services, gifts essentially intrude on the other, but it is an intrusion lacking power to modify the nature of the act. Thus we *give* friendship, love, joy, loyalty, and, not to side with the angels, subservience, enmity, and hurt. These need not be wanted to be honorably what they allege to be. Whether it sits easily or not with the recipient, friendship given remains friendship. (Indeed to woo or welcome the pain that is given transmutes the gift. It becomes significantly something else.)

On the whole, services are more mundane than gifts, though one can give services to the state, I suppose, or sing for kings. Yet services restrict the other's freedom less than gifts (and offerings seem to restrict it not at all).

There isn't much one can do to choose or control a gift except to avoid the likely circumstances or make oneself an unlikely receiver. To lose a little love may be to gain a little freedom. But if you are given loyalty, then you are one who commands loyalty (that much anyway), and not much is to be done about it *post eventum*. The gift has obliterated the freedom to choose. Not surprisingly this lack of choice tends to characterize the giver, too. Gifts tend to be spontaneous; it detracts from the gift, often, to plot the giving. A *contrived* insult is a mark of respect, and that much easier to bear.

TEACHING AS INTRUSION

To return to our topic. Teaching, I would contend, is obtrusive in two ways. What we call effective teaching is an activity which makes substantial changes in the students' nonsubstantial self, his mind-stuff. (Effective whining can be just whining that makes the whiner less wrought.) More than this, the many expressions we use to label sundry phases of teaching all seem to imply a piercing of the student's perceptual line of defense. Thus we say we reassure the student, give him praise, clear up his muddled ideas, and so on.. All this suggests a necessary intrusion of teacher on student.

So the obvious is true, to teach and to leave the learner unaffected is not to have been teaching at all. To reassure or prove something to a student is *to do something to him*. And one cannot prove the thing so the student can decide whether he wants it proved to him!

But for those who would view reassurance and reports, proofs, and praise as trivial intrusions, not to be taken weightily, another point is waiting. If it is not teaching itself which is essentially intrusive (though I would argue that it is), then no one can dispute that the way we conduct it makes it significantly so. A good part of our institution of education is hedged about with rule and law the upshot of which, it must appear to student and observer alike, is to make the teacher's intrusion on the student massive and mandatory.

The above remarks are all in aid of showing that teaching either by its conception or circumstances is *not* an offering simpliciter. And, consequently, my contention that the advocates of the new methods and machines, in which teachers are supposed not to intrude, are not urging new forms of teaching but urging a substitute for teaching or a radical change in its institutional conditions. But to make teaching an offering by such radical surgery is just one more case of a cure that kills.

It might be objected, however, that the original choice abides; should we or should we not adopt these new forms? To label the innovators radicals would seem to merely reword but not resolve the issue. But I suggest that a smidgin of strictness is just the ticket here. New phraseology inspires new focus. Posed as a radical dichotomy between teaching and some total replacement, we are encouraged to ask: "Is teaching itself obsolete?" And "Is teaching obsolete?" asks not for repeated matching of features in the new with ever more arcane qualities in the old, rather it directs us to seek for some quality in teaching which debilitates it absolutely. I suggest that there is such a quality.

A ROOT PHONINESS

Due to its nature or circumstances, teaching is an inauthentic human encounter. In terms of a distinction made earlier, teaching is service masquerading as gift. Though we present it as a gift, it lacks gift features: teaching has not the immediate and intrinsic worth possessed by joy or splendor (though we try to so ornament it); nor does the activity arise spontaneously, on impulse, without forethought, things which render the meanest gifts as at least honest. No, teaching is a contrivance in two ways: its value is the value of invention and appliance, and its performance arises by craft and emerges in plot. The very model of rational action urged on teachers in conventional educational wisdom is the model of adapting means to ends, the model for planned intervention.

Yet despite these deviations from gift traits, teaching does not wait upon client demand or acquiescence; it is thrust upon minds not fit out to welcome, avoid, or even appraise it. Imagine, as was noted above, trying to make a mind aware so it can choose whether to become so; or imagine a school denied the privilege of instructing unless conducted under the auspices of a contract made with students.

So there is a root phoniness in teaching. It ought to be a simple service like radio repair but we treat it as a gratuity. And this explains much that was heretofore inexplicable. It accounts for our odd fascination with recurrent proposals to conduct teaching by indirection (Education According to Nature; the Project Method), and it explains the dream of teacher as Itinerant Pedagogue. These myths of *Teaching as Offering* are just that, yet the more sensitive among us cleave to them even as the more creative are propounding new instances. Still, worse forms of expiation have been tried.

Atonement for what? Why, for the destruction which comes from viewing teaching as a boon. There is space for but one example. Teaching requires mutual confidence between student and teacher; for the activity to get anywhere, each must have trust in the general credibility and veracity of the other. I suppose each teacher has had moments of terror when this trust dies or even fails to appear. (Some teachers live with this terror.) In any honest service, both parties have an obvious and immediate recourse—termination. We need not brook the tasteless bard or baker. Since teaching cannot prosper without respect, then let it not be tried at all. But in what presently passes for education, we are denied this obliging expedient. The logistics of institutional education seem not to abide the simple graces, and corruption of teaching is seen as a price worth paying.

Furthermore, we have, not unnaturally, fostered a rhetoric that undercuts this essential trust. For the ideology of education holds that teacher authority should not be the main source of student belief; rather the source should be some "objective," impersonal authority. The idea that students can learn only or even mainly from actual experiments, original sources, and hard data is wild doctrine, but one we *need* if we are to pretend that teaching lives after trust in the teacher dies.

Finally, and not the least trivially, it is not now a mystery why there is more strain and fatigue in teaching than any time and motion study would lead one to predict. It is exquisite agony to make condescension a practice, but to make it the practice of a profession is unbearable.

8.

Teaching: Triadic and Dynamic

RONALD T. HYMAN

Associate Professor of Education,
Rutgers University, The State University of New
Jersey.

Teaching is a common phenomenon in our society; so common that everyone age seven and over has been involved in it, so necessary to the maintenance of our society that Congress has recently established the Teacher Corps to provide qualified instruction to those deprived of it.

There are about 53,000,000 pupils and teachers today, and it surely makes sense to know as much about teaching as we can when about one-quarter of our population is involved in it. Yet we do not agree about what teaching is. One need only survey the literature about teaching and also the current programs for preparing prospective teachers to realize this.

The need to know more about teaching stems not only from the common-ness of the phenomenon, but also from the realization that our notion of teaching guides our future endeavors in analysis and research. As Marie Hughes says, "The manner of analysis is controlled to a large degree by the definition accepted for teaching."[1] It is clear then that when we discuss the nature of teaching, we are not engaged in a trivial matter, but rather in one that is central in the field of education. The purpose of this article is to consider some of the relationships involved in teaching and thereby add to the growing list of recent attempts at clarifying the concept of teaching.

Several writers have recently offered definitions of teaching. Two deserve attention here for they have wide coinage and are typical of the others. Scheffler asserts that "teaching may be character-

"Teaching: Triadic and Dynamic" by Ronald T. Hyman is reprinted with permission from The Educational Forum, *32:65–69, November, 1967. Permission granted by Kappa Delta Pi, an Honor Society in Education, owners of the copyright.*

[1] Marie M. Hughes, "Utah Study of the Assessment of Teaching," in Arno A. Bellack (ed.), *Theory and Research in Teaching* (New York: Bureau of Publications, Teachers College, Columbia University, 1963), p. 26.

ized as an activity aimed at the achievement of learning and practiced in such manner as to respect the student's intellectual integrity and capacity for independent judgment."[2] In his definition, Scheffler is careful to use what he calls the intentional use of teaching. This intentional use of a word refers to trying to reach a goal. It does not imply the achievement of a goal. This is opposed to the success use of a word which refers to attaining the goal intended.[3] In this way such words as "teaching" and "building" may be said to have both intentional and success uses. Thus Scheffler calls activities aimed at learning "teaching" whether or not learning subsequently takes place. Also, Scheffler differentiates teaching from indoctrinating and propagandizing by specifying the manner in which teaching takes place.

Smith's definition is "teaching is a system of actions intended to induce learning."[4] This definition is obviously broader than Scheffler's in that it would include indoctrinating and propagandizing within the concept of teaching for they, too, induce learning. Though they disagree about the scope, Smith and Scheffler do agree about employing the intentional use of "teaching." This is in direct contrast to an older though still somewhat prevalent statement about teaching which employs the success use of the word: "Unless the student has learned, the teacher hasn't taught." But the point here is not whether Smith's or Scheffler's definition

regarding the scope of the concept of teaching is acceptable. Nor is it whether or not the intentional use of teaching is the acceptable one, even though both Smith and Scheffler agree on this point. What is significant is that neither definition considers the relationships or the elements involved in the teaching situation. It is to these points that we must now turn since consideration of the aim and scope of teaching alone is inadequate, even though it is necessary, for clarifying the nature of teaching.

To introduce the discussion of the relationships in teaching, let us first turn to an intriguingly entitled article, "Cameras Don't Take Picture."[5] In it Paul Byers studies "the behaviors of the *people* who are involved in photography, the photographer, the subject, and the viewer." Byers denies the validity of the sender-receiver model of photography and argues for a new model which asserts that photography is a social transaction between photographer, subject, and viewer. Within this framework the meaning of the photograph arises out of the interaction between the viewer and the photograph, the latter being an interaction between photographer and subject. This framework emphasizes the relationships in photography and further asserts that the dyadic sender-receiver model is inadequate for understanding still photography. For Byers the relationship in photography must be considered as a triadic one.

This model of photography suggests several important things when we use it as a motivating analogue for studying teaching. We notice that in Smith's and Sheffler's definition there is no mention of "subject," or "subject matter." We have actions to induce learning, presum-

[2] Israel Scheffler, "Philosophical Models of Teaching." *Harvard Educational Review,* 35: 131–143 (Spring 1965).

[3] Israel Scheffler, *The Language of Education* (Springfield, Ill.: Charles C Thomas, 1960), p. 42.

[4] B. Othanel Smith, "A Concept of Teaching," *Teachers College Record,* 61:230 (February 1960).

[5] Paul Byers, "Cameras Don't Take Pictures," *Columbia University Forum,* 9:27–31 (Winter 1966).

ably in a pupil, but no mention of what is to be learned. That is, according to the definitions there is a relationship between teacher and pupil, but there is no mention of the "subject matter." It is as if you could have learning in general but of nothing in particular. But this is clearly impossible. The pupil must deal with a "subject matter" in order to learn.

In addition, these definitions yield dyadic relationships close to the one found in the popular statement, "I teach children." The definitions offered by Scheffler and Smith are apparently so concerned with emphasizing the intentional (task) use of "teaching" that they fail to be explicit about the subject matter element necessary in a teaching relationship. This is strange indeed when we consider the research work of Smith in which he investigated the verbal logical operations performed by teachers and pupils. Smith studied the subject matter element of teaching but later failed to include it in his definition.

It is clear, then, that teaching must be considered as a triadic relationship. That is, we must see that teaching involves at least one teacher, at least one pupil, and subject matter to be taught and learned. We must build this triadic relationship into our definition of teaching, because when one of the three elements is missing, the other two become disconnected and teaching cannot take place. The nature of the teaching triad is such that it is impossible to have a teacher and pupil without subject matter connecting them. Indeed, if the teacher is intending to induce learning, it must be of "something," as stated previously. If he does not intend to induce learning, then the relationship between the teacher and pupil is not a *teaching* relationship. It may be a purely social one where the labels "teacher" and "pupil" are carried over from the classroom situation.

It is also impossible to have a pupil and subject matter without a teacher connecting them. It may be that the teacher is represented by a book, film, a program, or some other instructional device. Or it may be that the pupil himself is playing the role of the teacher as he works with materials he has assembled and directs himself along a particular path. In this latter case a person operates on two levels, as a teacher and as a pupil.

It is also impossible to have a teacher and subject matter without a pupil. A teacher interacts with subject matter only in consideration of his particular pupils. For example, a teacher teaches concepts, facts, and skills in history to a ten-year-old pupil different from those which he teaches to a seventeen-year-old pupil. At times, this adaptation may be minimal, as in the case of the proverbial professor who still uses the same lecture notes after twenty years of experience. Yet, we must recognize that the lecture notes were originally designed for a particular group of pupils. Further, if we claim that a teacher can write a history book without any particular group of pupils in mind, then we must say that he is not teaching history but rather writing history. This is the difference between a historian and a history teacher, or a mathematician and a mathematics teacher, or a biologist and a biology teacher. We cannot equate writing history, for example, with teaching history. If the teacher writes a history textbook, we can indeed say that he is teaching, for we know that a textbook author gears his book to a particular group of pupils and intends for them to learn from it. This is often explicitly acknowledged in the textbook's preface.

Perhaps more important than the idea of multiple connections among the three elements in teaching is the dynamic quality of the triad. This quality is implied in the triadic conception of teaching because as the relationship between teacher and pupil changes, as indeed it must for life is always changing, the teacher must continually change his relationship with the subject matter. This dynamic conception of teaching eliminates, or at least discourages, the professor mentioned above who used the same lecture notes year after year. The world of the 1960's is very different from that of the 1940's. It is apparent that the college freshman of 1967 is quite different from the freshman of 1947 and therefore requires a different course in world history.

This dynamic conception of teaching also means that changes in a body of knowledge will influence the activities teachers perform. In light of Einstein's Theory of Relativity the physics teacher and his pupils perform quite different experiments in the laboratory, and these in turn change the relationship between teacher and pupil. Changes in theories and empirical data require the teacher to adjust his procedures and techniques. These in turn affect the teacher-pupil relationship. Further, if a teacher is especially interested in calculus, for example, as opposed to plane geometry, he will teach pupils older in both age and mathematical knowledge than the teacher of plane geometry.

Finally, as the pupil's relationship with the subject matter changes, the teacher element also needs to change. This is illustrated by the case of the prodigy in music. The teacher must quickly change his method and demands to correspond to the rapid advances of the pupil. If the teacher himself cannot change appropriately, the teacher ele-ment changes when the prodigy moves on to another teacher who can deal with the particular musical ability of the pupil. Similarly, the teacher element changes when we have a retarded pupil. We need a particular type of teacher to suit the pupil's relationship with subject matter.

From the above it is clear that we must view teaching both as triadic and as dynamic. We cannot understand the nature of teaching by looking at only one or two of the elements of the teaching relationship or by thinking of teaching as dyadic. We must consider all three elements together in order to understand the interaction occuring during teaching. We must see that the relationships are always changing. Furthermore, we must note that the interaction between any two elements influences how each of the two will react to the third one and in turn how all the elements will react together.

The concept of teaching suggested here goes beyond the definitions of Smith and Scheffler cited earlier and beyond Smith's model of the teaching cycle wherein the teacher perceives the pupil's behavior, diagnoses it, and acts according to his diagnosis.[6] The teacher must also diagnose his relationship with the subject matter, as suggested here. A teacher needs not only to be aware of his aim in teaching but also of his relationships with his pupil and the subject matter, and the pupil's relationship with the subject matter. This is necessary in order to make the kind of diagnosis Smith and others suggest.

Realization of the nature of teaching relationships also aids us in assessing current innovations in the schools which are being promoted zealously. For example, how will the two-way relation-

---

6 Smith, *op. cit.*, p. 235.

ship between teacher and subject matter be continued in programmed instruction in light of pupil changes that take place after programmed instruction begins? Does the dynamic quality of the relationship between teacher and subject matter cease upon publication of the program? If so, what steps are being taken to restore it? The answers to such questions provide significant data to be used in the assessment of teaching programs.

Realization of the dynamic and triadic relationships in teaching prevents a teacher from trying to teach "the syllabus" as handed out by "headquarters." Doing so constitutes a static and not a dynamic relationship between teacher and subject matter. Teachers guided by the teaching concept offered here are encouraged to put themselves into the teaching act not only in relationship to the pupil but also with the subject matter they teach.

Perhaps most important is the direction this conception of teaching gives to empirical research. This conception requires us to investigate all three elements in teaching and their interrelationships though not necessarily all at the same time. This is precisely what Marie Hughes referred to in her statement cited earlier in this paper, namely, that the definition of teaching guides the manner of analysis in empirical research.

In summary, it is clear that to clarify the concept of teaching we need not only to investigate the aim and scope of teaching but also the relationships involved. I have dealt with these teaching relationships showing that teaching involves a triad of elements (the teacher, the pupil, the subject matter) and that this triad is dynamic in quality. I have not dealt with the aim or scope (are indoctrinating and conditioning, for example, to be considered as teaching?) for others have done that already.[7] And lastly, though a recognition of this dynamic triad will not offer a prescription as to what kind of teacher-pupil relationship ought to be established, it does require us to ask and obtain data about this relationship and the other relationships involved.

[7] Anthony Flew, "What Is Indoctrination?" *Studies in Philosophy and Education,* 4:281–306 (Spring 1966). Thomas F. Green, "A Topology of the Teaching Concept," *Studies in Philosophy and Education,* 3:284–319 (Winter 1964–1965).

Relating Teaching to Other Activities and Concepts:

Overview

The previous two sections have dealt with teaching as it is and with suggested concepts of teaching. This section deals with teaching as it relates to other activities and concepts such as training, instructing, and indoctrinating. Thus, the question is: What is the relation between teaching and its "cousins"? To answer this question it is necessary to compare and contrast as well as to draw connections.

The springboards for preparing an answer are the selections by Green and Macdonald. The reader is asked to consider Green's continuum carefully so as to compare the concept of teaching it presents with that of Macdonald in this section and the five authors in the previous section. Can we place Smith's concept of teaching on this continuum? Scheffler's? Komisar's? Hyman's? Macdonald's? If so, where? If not, why not?

Macdonald presents a systems approach to distinguish teaching from other terms. The reader is asked to compare Macdonald's *action space* with Green's *continuum*. In addition, compare Figures 1 and 2.

Figure 1 is from the committee responsible for developing the 1967 Yearbook of the National Society for the Study of Education, entitled *Programed Instruction*. The committee specifies, "We make clear our position that instruction is a special kind of teaching that has specificity of purpose and an orderliness that does not characterize all teaching."[3] Corey, in speaking for the committee says, "we are defining instruction operationally as the 'process whereby the environment of an individual is

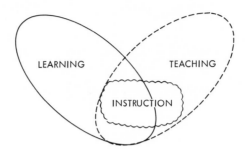

Figure 1. Relation of Instruction to Teaching and Learning[1]

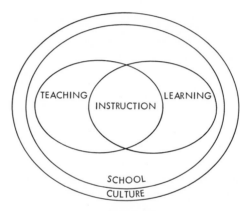

Figure 2. Formal Instruction Within the School[2]

deliberately manipulated to enable him to learn to emit or engage in specified behaviors under specified conditions or as responses to specified situation.' "[4]

Figure 2 is from Maccia,[5] based on her work in the development of a theory of teaching. (See Section Five for an article by her.) Her concern here is with formal work within the school context. For Maccia, "Instruction is teaching-learning viewed as influence toward rule-governed behavior," as she points out in her article in this book. The reader is asked to examine the four figures of Green, Macdonald, the N.S.S.E. Committee, and Maccia

---

[1] "Introduction," in *Programed Instruction,* ed. Phil C. Lange, The Sixty-sixth Yearbook of the National Society for the Study of Education, Part II (Chicago: The National Society for the Study of Education, 1967), p. 4.

[2] Elizabeth Steiner Maccia as reported by John R. Verduin, Jr. in *Conceptual Models in Teacher Education* (Washington, D.C.: The American Association of Colleges for Teacher Education, 1967), p. 132.

[3] See n. 1, p. 3.

[4] Stephen M. Corey, "The Nature of Instruction," in *Programed Instruction,* ed. Phil C. Lange, The Sixty-sixth Yearbook of the National Society for the Study of Education, Part II (Chicago: The National Society for the Study of Education, 1967), p. 6.

[5] See n. 2.

in search of an acceptable distinction between teaching and other activities and concepts.

Green admits that the criteria for distinguishing between specific instances of instructing and indoctrinating, for example, are "neither clearly exemplified nor clearly absent." If this is the case, to what extent is Green's continuum (or anyone else's figure) helpful and illuminating? Is Green's teaching continuum a descriptive topological mapping of the terrain, as he claims, or is it programmatic?

Those readers who wish to compare their reactions to Green's topology with someone else's may wish to see the exchange between Hay and Green.[6] Those readers who wish to pursue the topic of indoctrinating may wish to read a five-article exchange on the topic by Wilson, Flew, and Moore[7] and also the articles by Hare,[8] Butts,[9] Atkinson,[10] White,[11] Crittenden,[12] and Nelson.[13]

Finally, the reader is asked to keep in mind the following quotation from Powell as he reads Green and Macdonald in this section and recalls the articles by Smith, Scheffler, and Green in the previous section.

> Are teaching and indoctrinating really such radically different activities? It is fashionable to suppose that they are; hence the search for unambiguous criteria which will distinguish them. But most of the discussion of this topic is conducted in terms of a model of teaching which is wildly unrealistic: the paradigm classroom situation appears to be one in which the teacher is calmly expounding a Euclidean theorem or the rules of grammar. But this is to ignore a great many other teaching activities which are both characteristic and highly

---

6 William H. Hay, "On Green's Analysis of Teaching", *Studies in Philosophy and Education,* 4 (Fall 1965), 254–63; and Thomas F. Green, "The Concept of Teaching: A Reply," *Studies in Philosophy and Education,* 4 (Spring 1966), 339–45.

7 John B. Wilson, "Education and Indoctrination," in *Aims in Education:* The Philosophic Approach, ed. T. H. B. Hollins (Manchester: Manchester University, 1964), pp. 24–46; Anthony Flew, "What Is Indoctrination?" *Studies in Philosophy and Education,* 4 (Spring 1966), 281–306; John B. Wilson, "Comment on Flew's 'What Is Indoctrination?'" *Studies in Philosophy and Education,* 4 (Summer 1966), 390–95; Willis Moore "Indoctrination as a Normative Conception," *Studies in Philosophy and Education,* 4 (Summer 1966), 396–403; Anthony Flew, " 'What Is Indoctrination?': Comments on Moore and Flew," *Studies in Philosophy and Education,* 5 (Spring 1967), 273–83.

8 R. M. Hare, "Adolescents into Adults, in *Aims in Education: The Philosophic Approach,* ed. T. H. B. Hollins (Manchester: Manchester University Press, 1964), pp. 47–70

9 Robert E. Butts, " 'Indoctrination In,' 'Indoctrination With,' and 'Indoctrination Ints,' " *Bucknell Review,* 10 (May 1962), 347–63.

10 R. F. Atkinson, "Instruction and Indoctrination," in *Philosophical Analysis and Education,* ed. Reginald D. Archambault (New York: Humanities Press, 1965), pp. 171–83.

11 J. P. White "Indoctrination," in *The Concept of Education,* ed. R. S. Peters (New York: The Humanities Press, 1967), pp. 177–91.

12 Brian S. Crittenden, "Teaching, Educating, and Indoctrinating," *Educational Theory,* 18 (Summer 1968), 237–52.

13 Thomas W. Nelson. "Analytical Philosophy of Moral Education," in *Philosophy of Education 1967,* ed. D. B. Gowin (Edwardsville, Illinois: Studies in Philosophy and Education, 1967), pp. 250–58.

valuable activities which involve beliefs, emotions, exhortations and enthusiasms. These less "cerebral" aspects of teaching tend to be undervalued and we feel uneasy about discussing them because they quickly lead to disputes which involve our own attitudes and convictions: it is much less troublesome if we restrict our talk to ."traditions of principled thought." Yet when we look back on our own education, the teachers we remember with gratitude are those who communicated to us their own beliefs, opinions, enthusiasms and convictions with passionate (doctrinaire?) eagerness and a profound concern that one day we should come to share them. Any concept of teaching which excludes this has sadly missed the mark.[14]

[14] John P. Powell, "Philosophical Models of Teaching," *Harvard Educational Review,* 35 (Fall 1965), 496.

9

A Topology of the Teaching Concept

THOMAS F. GREEN

Professor of Philosophy of
Education and Director of The Educational Policy
Research Center, Syracuse University.

I
THE TEACHING CONTINUUM

A concept is a rule. When someone learns a concept, without exception, what he has learned is a rule, a rule of language, or more generally, a rule of behavior. But some of the rules we observe in action and speaking are enormously complicated. Some are "open textured" in the sense that they do not specify with accuracy and precision what is permitted under the rule and what is not. These are the kinds of rules which are vague. They circumscribe the limits of vague concepts.

We can imagine what a vague con-

"A Topology of the Teaching Concept" by Thomas F. Green is reprinted from Studies in Philosophy and Education. *3:284–319, Winter, 1964–65. The journal,* Studies in Philosophy and Education, *is published at Southern Illinois University—Edwardsville. The selection here is from pp. 284–293 of the longer essay.*

cept is like by picturing a modern painting in which the different colors are blurred, one blending into another in degrees more imperceptible and gradual even than those which we discover in the spectrum. Such a painting, when viewed at a distance, clearly possesses a certain order among its several parts. There is a pattern of light and colors which constitutes the structure of the figures in the painting, but which when seen in close proximity, conceals the order of the painting.

How could we draw a clear and precise representation of what is found in such a painting? Here is a certain place where the colors change from red to orange and thence to yellow. Yet we cannot, with any certitude, point to a place and say at that point the color ceases to be red and becomes orange, or ceases to be orange and becomes yellow. Any attempt to specify precisely where the colors change, any attempt to eliminate the delicate blending of one color into another, would misrepresent the order or pattern of the painting. There are many points at which such a line can be drawn. They would all be equally right and all equally wrong.

A vague concept is like such a picture. It is a rule which is enormously complicated, and a part of its complication arises for no other reason than that it is not precise. It allows differences of opinion and differences of judgment at precisely those blurring points where people try to specify where one color begins and another leaves off. Nonetheless, the difficulty of making such differences precise does not mean that there is no order, or that we cannot find it. It means simply that we must not insist on too much precision in the order that we find.

We can, in fact, give a description of such a picture without sacrificing anything in the way of a faithful representation. For if we discover that there are two patches of paint which can be cut out and substituted one for another without in any way changing the picture, then we would be justified in saying that these two patches are related in a certain sense, namely, in the sense that they are exactly similar. And if we discovered that the color in the space intervening between them could be reproduced by imperceptibly and gradually blending the pigment in each of these patches with some second color in ever increasing proportions, then we would be justified in saying that we understand, in a different sense, *how* these two patches of color are related. We would have specified the rule which will suffice to relate the two patches of color. In this fashion we could develop a topology of such a canvas, showiag by what rule each point on the canvas is related to every other point by the gradual blending of the pigments. Thus we could

reveal the structure of the painting without converting it into a line drawing.

The concept of teaching is like such a blurred picture. It is a vague concept. Its boundaries are not clear. However accurately we may describe the activity of teaching there will, and always must, remain certain troublesome border-line cases. In admitting this, the point is not that we have failed to penetrate the darkness and to discover that juncture at which an activity ceases to be teaching and becomes something else. The point is rather that beneath the darkness there is simply no such precise discrimination to be found. There is therefore an initial presumption against the credibility of any analysis which yields precise criteria, which, without a trace of uncertainly assigns to every case a clear identity.

We can, nonetheless, describe the structure of the teaching concept, or if you wish, map its terrain, by standing at a distance and by asking not about teaching itself, but about such patches or parts of teaching as training, indoctrinating, conditioning, showing and instructing. We need not insist that the blur between these patches be removed. We need only show how they are related and how the gradual transition from one to the other may be reproduced. When we have done that, we will have drawn a map of the teaching concept; we will have described a rule or complex set of rules which formulate the structure of the concept.

At the outset, one must recognize then, that the concept of teaching is molecular. That is, as an activity, teaching can best be understood not as a single activity, but as a whole family of activities within which some members appear to be of more central significance than others. For example, there is an intimate relation between teaching and training which can be observed in many ways. There are, for example, contexts in which the word "teaching" may be substituted for "training" without any change of meaning. One reason for this is that teaching is often conceived to involve the formation of habit, and training is a method of shaping habit. Thus, when engaged in training, we may often say with equal propriety that we are engaged in teaching. The two concepts are closely related.

Nonetheless teaching and training are not identical. Training is only a part of teaching. There are contexts in which it would be a rank distortion to substitute the one concept for the other. For example, it is more common, and perhaps more accurate, to speak of training an animal than to speak of teaching him. I do not mean there is no such thing as teaching a dog. I mean only that it is more accurate in this context to speak of training. We can, indeed, teach a dog to fetch, to heel, to point, and to pursue. There is in fact a common saying that you cannot teach an old dog new tricks. The use of the word "teaching" in each of these cases has its explanation. It has to do with the fact that the actions of a trained dog are expressive of intelligence; they involve obedience to orders. Indeed, a well trained dog is one which has passed "obedience trials."

But the intelligence displayed in such cases is limited, and it is this which renders the education of an animal more akin to training than to teaching. What should we think of a trainer of dogs attempting to explain his orders to an animal, giving reasons for them, presenting evidence of a kind that would tend to justify them? The picture is absurd. Dogs do not ask "'Why?"

They do not ask for reasons for a certain rule or order. They do not require explanation or justification. It is this limitation of intelligence which we express by speaking of training rather than teaching in such circumstances. Moreover, those rare occasions in which animals must cleary display intelligence are precisely those in which they appear to ask "Why?" They are the occasions when they do precisely what they have been trained *not* to do, or when they do *not* do what they have been trained to do. The horse, trained to pull the carriage, saves his master's life in the darkness of the night by stopping at the edge of the washed out bridge and refusing to go on. The dog, trained not to go into the street, is killed because he rushed into the path of a truck to push a child to safety. On such occasions, it is as though the animal had obeyed an order which was not given. It is as though he had given himself a reason for acting contrary to his training.

I am not concerned whether this, or something like it, is a correct explanation of such remarkable happenings. I am concerned only to observe that training resembles teaching insofar as it is aimed at actions which display intelligence. In this respect, training has a position of central importance in that congerie of activities we include in teaching. Ordinarily, however, the kind of intelligence aimed at in training is limited. What it excludes is the process of asking questions, weighing evidence and, in short, demanding and receiving a justification of rules, principles, or claims of fact. In proportion as training is aimed at a greater and greater display of intelligence, it more and more clearly resembles teaching, and one of the clues as to how closely training approaches teaching is the degree to which it involves explanations, reasons, argument, and weighing evidence. It is because training sometimes approaches this point, that we can in many cases substitute the word "teaching" for the word "training" without any change in meaning.

This point is strengthened when we consider what happens in proportion as training is aimed less and less at the display of intelligence. In that case, the concept fades off imperceptibly into what we would commonly call conditioning. It is natural to speak of teaching a dog to fetch, to heel, to walk in time to music. It is more of a distortion to speak of teaching a dog to salivate at the sound of a bell. It is in precisely this latter context that we speak of conditioning. Conditioning does not aim at intelligent performance of some act.[1] Insofar as training does not aim at the display of intelligence, it resembles conditioning more and teaching less. Thus, we can see that training is an activity which is conceptually of more central importance to the concept of teaching than is conditioning. We train a dog to fetch; we condition him to salivate. And the difference is a difference in the degree of intelligence displayed.

Instruction also must be numbered among the family of activities related to teaching. Instructing, in fact, is so closely bound to teaching that the phrase "giving instruction" seems only another way of saying "teaching." There seems to be no case of an activity we could describe as "giving instruction" which we could not equally and more simply describe as teaching. Nonetheless, teaching and giving instruction are not

the same thing. For there are almost endless instances of teaching which do not involve instruction. For example, it is acceptable, and even correct, to speak of *teaching* a dog to heel, to sit, or to fetch. It is, however, less acceptable, more imprecise, and perhaps even incorrect to speak of *instructing* a dog in sitting and fetching.

But why, in such contexts, is it more awkward to speak of instructing than to speak of teaching? We need not go far to discover the answer. When we train a dog, we give an order and then push and pull and give reward or punishment. We give the order to sit and then push on the hindquarters precisely because we cannot explain the order. We cannot elaborate its meaning. It is precisely this limitation of intelligence or communication which disposes us to speak of training a dog rather than instructing him. What we seek to express by the phrase "giving instruction" is precisely what we seek to omit by the word "training." Instruction seems, at heart, to involve a kind of conversation, the object of which is to give reasons, weigh evidence, justify, explain, conclude and so forth. It is true that whenever we are involved in giving instruction, it follows that we are engaged in teaching; but it is not true that whenever we are engaged in teaching, we are giving instruction.

This important difference between training and instructing may be viewed in another way. To the extent that instructing necessarily involves a kind of conversation, a giving of reasons, evidence, objections and so on, it is an activity of teaching allied more closely to the acquisition of knowledge and belief than to the promotion of habits and modes of behavior. Training, on the contrary, has to do more with forming modes of habit and behavior

---

[1] There may be circumstances, however, in which it would be intelligent, i.e., wise, to "teach" with the aim of producing a conditioned response.

and less with acquiring knowledge and belief. Instructing, in short, is more closely related to the quest for understanding. We can train people to do certain things without making any effort to bring them to an understanding of what they do. It is, however, logically impossible to instruct someone without at the same time attempting to bring him to some understanding. What this means, stated in its simplest and most ancient terms, is that instructing always involves matters of truth and falsity whereas training does not. This is another reason for observing that instructing has more to do with matters of belief and knowledge, and training more with acquiring habits or modes of behaving. It is not therefore a bit of archaic nonsense that teaching is essentially the pursuit of truth. It is, on the contrary, an enormously important insight. The pursuit of truth is central to the activity of teaching because giving instruction is central to it. That, indeed, is the purpose of the kind of conversation indigenous to the concept of giving instruction. If giving instruction involves giving reasons, evidence, argument, justification, then instruction is essentially related to the search for truth.

The point is not, therefore, that instructing necessarily requires communication. The point is rather that it requires a certain *kind* of communication, and that kind is the kind which includes giving reasons, evidence, argument, etc., in order to approach the truth. The importance of this fact can be seen if we consider what happens when the conversation of instruction is centered less and less upon this kind of communication. It takes no great powers of insight to see that in proportion as the conversation of instruction is less and less characterized by argument, reasons, objections, explanations, and so forth, in proportion as it is less and less directed toward an apprehension of truth, it more and more closely resembles what we call indoctrination. Indoctrination is frequently viewed as a method of instruction. Indeed, we sometimes use the word "instruction" to include what we quite openly confess is, in fact, indoctrination. Nonetheless, indoctrination is a substantially different thing from instruction, and what is central to this difference is precisely that it involves a different kind of conversation and therefore is differently related to matters of truth.

We can summarize the essential characteristics of these differences by saying that indoctrination is to conditioning as beliefs are to habits. That is to say, we may indoctrinate people to *believe* certain things, but we condition them always to *do* certain things. We do not indoctrinate persons to certain modes of behavior any more than we condition them to certain kinds of beliefs. But the important thing is to observe that *insofar as* conditioning does not aim at an expression of intelligent doing, neither does indoctrination aim at an expression of intelligent believing. Conditioning is an activity which can be used to establish certain modes of behavior quite apart from their desirability. It aims simply to establish them. If a response to certain stimuli is trained or conditioned, or has become a fixed habit, it will be displayed in the fact that the same stimuli will produce the same response even when the person admits it would be better if he responded otherwise. This is an unintelligent way of behaving. In an analogous way, indoctrination is aimed at an unintelligent way of holding beliefs. Indoctrination aims simply at establishing certain beliefs so that they will be held quite apart from their truth, their explanation, or their foundation in evidence. As a practical matter, indoctrinating involves certain conversation, but it does not involve the kind of conversation central to the activity of giving instruction. Thus, as the teaching conversation becomes less related to the pursuit of truth, it becomes less an activity of instruction and more a matter of indoctrination. We may represent these remarks schematically:

in different degrees. Thus, we may be uncertain in many concrete cases whether the conversation of a teaching sequence more nearly resembles instructing or indoctrinating. But it does not follow from this that the difference between them is obscure, that we are uncertain about it or that they differ only in degree. It follows only that in such specific instances the criteria that mark the difference though perfectly clear in themselves, are neither clearly exem-

THE TEACHING CONTINUUM

The diagram is not meant to suggest that the distinction between conditioning, training, instructing and indoctrinating are perfectly clear and precise. On the contrary, each of these concepts, like the teaching concept itself, is vague. Each blends imperceptibly into its neighbor. It is as with the well-known case of baldness. We cannot say with precision and accuracy at precisely what point a man becomes bald. There is nonetheless a distinction, clear enough in its extremities, between a bald head and a hairy head. One might say that the difference is a matter of degree. But if the difference between conditioning and training or between instructing and indoctrinating is simply a difference of degree, then one must ask, "What is it that differs in degree?" The fact is that instructing and indoctrinating are different in kind, but the respects in which they differ may be exemplified

plified nor clearly absent.

A parallel example may suffice to make this clearer. To lie is to tell a falsehood with the intent to deceive. But now consider the following circumstances. Two brothers go to bed on the eve of one's birthday. He whose birthday is coming wishes to know what in the way of gifts the next day may hold in store for him; and so he questions, prods, cajoles, and teases his brother to tell him. But he receives only the unsatisfactory but truthful answer from his brother that he does not know. And so the teasing continues and sleep is made impossible. The only recourse for the weary one is to invent a lie. It must, however, be a lie that is believable. It must satisfy and yet must be most assuredly a lie. And so he says what is most improbable, "You will get a bicycle." But now suppose they discover on the morning after that in-

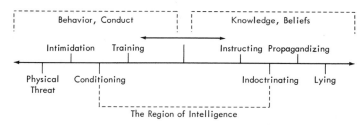

THE TEACHING CONTINUUM EXPANDED

deed the principal gift is a bicycle. The question might arise, did the brother lie or did he not? If the answer is "Yes," the difficulty arises that what he said was in fact the truth. If the answer is "No," the fact will arise that he intended to deceive. A case may be built for both answers, because in this illustration, the criteria for lying and for truth telling are mixed. The case is neither one nor the other. It does not follow, however, that the difference between lying and truth telling is obscure. Such examples show only that the criteria which mark the difference may be in more or less degree fulfilled. It shows there is a degree of vagueness present, a point at which we cannot decide.

And so it is in the present case. The concept of teaching, as we normally use it, includes within its limits a whole family of activities, and we can recognize that some of these are more centrally related to teaching than others. We have no difficulty, for example, in agreeing that instructing and certain kinds of training are activities which belong to teaching. We may have more difficulty, and some persons more than others, in deciding whether conditioning and indoctrinating legitimately belong to teaching. There is, in short, a region on this continuum at which we may legitimately disagree, because there will be many contexts in which the criteria

which tend to distinguish teaching and conditioning or teaching and indoctrination will not be clearly exemplified. Thus, there is an area of uncertainty on this continuum, an area of vagueness neither to be overcome nor ignored, but respected and preserved.

Nonetheless, were we to extend this continuum, we would discover another region of agreement. For we would surely stretch a point too far were we to extend the line on the left and include such activities as intimidation and physical threat, or on the right and include such things as exhorting, propagandizing and just plain lying. The continuum would look like that above.

We would have to strain and struggle to include within the teaching family such things as extortion, lying and deceit. The point is not that such things *cannot* be included among the assemblage of teaching activities. The point is rather that to do so would require an extension and distortion of the concept of teaching. It is clear in any case that such activities are less central to the concept of teaching than conditioning and indoctrination, and that these are, in turn, less central than training and instruction. Thus as we extend the extremities of this continuum we depart from a region of relative uncertainty and enter a segment within which we can agree with relative ease. Lying, propagandizing, slander and threat of physical violence are not teaching activities, although they may be ways of influencing persons' beliefs or shaping their behavior. We know in fact, that these activities are excluded from the concept of teaching with as much certainty as we know that training and instructing are included. This shows approximately where the region of vagueness occurs in the concept of teaching. It occurs in respect to matters of behavior, somewhere between the activities of training and conditioning, and in respect to matters of knowledge and belief, it occurs somewhere between instructing and indoctrinating. The most central properties of the concept of teaching are revealed, in short, within the limits of what we have called the region of intelligence. Or, to put the matter in another way, we can say that teaching has to do primarily with the relation between thought and action.

It is a matter of no consequence that there have been societies which have extended the concept of teaching beyond this limit of vagueness and have thus included even the most remote extremities of this continuum. That propa-ganda, lies, threats, and intimidation have been used as methods of education is not doubted. But the conclusion warranted by this fact is not that teaching includes such activities, but that education may. Propaganda, lies, and threats are more or less effective means of influencing and shaping beliefs and patterns of behavior. It follows that teaching is not the only method of education. It does not follow that the use of propaganda, lies and threats are methods of teaching.

The concept of teaching is thus a molecular concept. It includes a congerie of activities. In order to more clearly understand the concept it may suffice to simply describe in schematic form what are the logical properties most central to this family of activities and to display in what respects other less central activities do or do not bear the marks of teaching. In this way we may gain in clarity without doing violence to the vagueness inherent in the concept. At the same, we may avoid importing some obscure and *a priori* normative definition of teaching.

10.

A Systems Approach for Defining Teaching

JAMES B. MACDONALD

Director of Doctoral Studies,
School of Education, University of
Wisconsin-Milwaukee.

A CONFUSION OF TERMS

A logical assumption would be that, if six educational scholars were asked to present models or theories of instruction, they would have in mind the same phenomenal referent for their thinking. It is apparent from a cursory view of the following section that this is not necessarily true. In fact, there is a confusion of terms about the referent for the word instruction, especially when considered along with such concepts as teaching, curriculum, and learning.

"A Systems Approach for Defining Teaching" by James B. Macdonald is reprinted with permission from James B. Macdonald, "Educational Models for Instruction—Introduction," Theories of Instruction. James B. Macdonald and Robert R. Leeper, editors. Washington, D.C.: Association for Supervision and Curriculum Development, 1965. pp. 1–7. Reprinted with permission of the Association for Supervision and Curriculum Development and James B. Macdonald. Copyright © 1965 by Association for Supervision and Curriculum Development. The selection here is from pp. 2–6.

Just what are we referring to when we talk about instruction? Is this something a teacher does, thus making instruction a sub-aspect of teaching? Or is instruction a process within which teaching is one of many subprocesses, such as learning, which take place? And, is instruction the act of putting a curriculum into operation? Or, is the curriculum the formal set of purposes, etc., which are only a part of the instructional process?

At present it is well to recognize that there is no consistently clear distinction in the use of much educational terminology. One definition of *curriculum* may well turn out to be the same as the next definition of *instruction*, and this definition of *instruction* could quite likely be synonymous with another's definition of *teaching*. It is in fact indicative of the general level of development of the total field that educational definitions are fuzzy and conflicting. Until such time as there can be common agreement upon at least the basic phenomena we are labeling, there will be little chance of making conceptual progress.

A TENTATIVE DISTINCTION

A useful if tentative distinction can be made if one accepts the concept of systems, and the boundaries between systems as suggested by Parsons (1), and Parsons and Shils (2). Accepting this referent, we can examine each of the terms to see if they can be conceptualized as separate systems with distinct (although perhaps open and flexible) boundaries. Such an analysis can be made with reasonable satisfaction.

The idea of systems helps make the distinction clear. The teacher teaches. The teacher is a personality system with needs, predispositions, a set of past experiences, unique values, etc. What the personality system called teacher does when he acts in his professional role is teaching. What he does is influenced by all the factors which make up his personality system, only one facet of which is related to his profession. The professionally oriented behavior of individual personality systems, called teachers by society, makes up the acts of teaching.

Learning is the phenomena or behavior that is noted in the performance of the student. Every student is also a separate personality system with unique patterns of needs, values, past experiences, perceptions, etc. Actions that students perform which teachers perceive to be task related are learning behaviors. Learning is primarily system (student; personality) related and only secondarily related to teaching.

Some researchers prefer to deal only with a teaching-learning system. Thus, it is agreed that neither teaching nor learning is a sensible concept apart from the other. There are cogent arguments for not separating the two; however, accepting the systems analysis already given, neither learning nor teaching is wholly explainable within the limits of a teaching-learning system.

The teaching-learning system, it is argued here, is more aptly called the instructional system. The instructional system is a social system (rather than a personality system). The instructional system usually is bounded by a classroom with a teacher, a group of students, materials, social norms, etc. It is the action context within which formal teaching and learning behaviors take place. The instructional system(s) is (are) made up primarily of classroom action units.

At the next highest (more abstract and removed from teaching-learning) level the Curriculum system becomes operative. The Curriculum system consists of persons who are a part of a social system which eventuates in *a* Curriculum, in the sense of plans for action. The important distinction for purposes here is the boundary between curriculum and instruction. They are essentially two separate action contexts, one (curriculum) producing plans for further action; and, the other (instruction) putting plans into action.

Figure 1 is a graphic representation of the distinction which can be made from a systems viewpoint. Note the four overlapping circles. Each circle shares some space with each other circle, some space with two other circles, and one space with all other circles. The small shadowed spot represents that point of congruence where curriculum goals are operative in the instructional setting through the agency of effective teaching activity as evidenced by the changed behavior or learning of the students. It

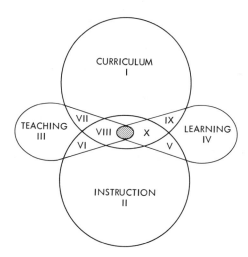

Figure 1

Action Space of Four Systems: Curriculum, Instruction, Teaching, Learning.

is this point of congruence which has created the greatest confusion. In our great desire to arrive at student learning we have failed to distinguish the essential separateness of the vast majority of systems aspects, and have myopically focused upon the area of congruence. Accepting that this space could be either larger or smaller depending upon a variety of possible conditions, we have failed to recognize the separate contexts implied by the four terms.

Since each system is bounded, Figure 1 purposely excludes the possibility of any of the four areas being included in any other space. Traditionally the tendency has been to include instruction within curriculum, and teaching and learning within the instructional setting. This position is impossible to defend from a systems position.

Let us look for one example of what might be considered a part of each space in the diagram and hope that the point is made. One may add other examples with a little reflection. The large separate curriculum space (I) can be illustrated by a course of study or a textbook, perhaps selected by the central staff. Space (II) can be illustrated by the unique quality or flavor of interaction in any given class. Space (III) could refer to unique patterns of experiences, values, attitudes, etc., of a given teacher as these affect teaching behavior. Space (IV) represents unique experiences, values, attitudes, etc., of each individual learner as they affect learning. Space (V) is illustrated dramatically by the phenomena of concomitant learning. Space (VI) would include teacher modification of behavior in response to the immediate feedback of the instructional situation. Space (VII) could be described as in-service experiences. Space (VIII) could include supervision experiences. Although few ready examples come to mind, spaces IX and X might deal with pupil-teacher planning experiences.

The examples given are meant simply to illustrate the existence of separate domains for each concept, and the variety of separable relationships among them. Thus, teaching is defined as the behavior of the teacher, learning as the change in learner behavior, instruction as the pupil-teacher interaction situation and curriculum as those planning endeavors which take place prior to instruction.

Another way of putting this might be: learning is the desired response, teaching is the act of systematically presenting stimuli, and/or cues; instruction is the total stimulus setting within which systematic stimuli and desired responses occur, and curriculum represents the major source of stimuli found in instructional settings to be utilized systematically. When the appropriate sources are utilized in a productively structured setting, and presented in an effective manner, then the desired responses will hopefully occur and the shadowed space, the convergence of all four areas, has been entered.

REFERENCES

1. Talcott Parsons. *The Social System.* Glencoe, Illinois: Free Press, 1950.
2. Talcott Parsons and Edward Shils. *Toward a General Theory of Action.* Cambridge: Harvard University Press, 1952.

The Theory of
Teaching

part two

The Nature of
a Theory of Teaching:
Overview

Although there is not complete agreement as to just what a theory of teaching is or would be, educational writers all agree that there is a need for it. This educational literature calling for a theory of teaching, describing and explaining what such a theory might be like, and clarifying such a theory's functions is all of fairly recent vintage. Indeed, the dates of original appearance of the articles in Sections Four and Five bear witness to this recent surge of interest in theory. Gage[1] claims that the "neglect" of theories of teaching is due to (a) the belief that the development of such theories implies a science of teaching in contrast to an art of teaching, which many writers accept and (b) the presumption that theories of learning are sufficient and adequate for the teacher. Other reasons for neglect of theory may be: a lack of understanding about the nature of theory, lack of awareness as to the benefits of a theory of teaching, lack of professional language needed for theorizing, and a fear of theorizing.[2] But whatever the reasons, the surge of concern for a theory of teaching parallels that in other fields.

The four selections in this section focus on definitions of theory, the likely components of a theory of teaching, the need for and functions of a theory of teaching, and the relation of a theory to practice and research. Many

[1] N. L. Gage, "Theories of Teaching," in *Theories of Learning and Instruction,* ed. Ernest R. Hilgard, The sixty-third Yearbook of the National Society for the Study of Education, Part I (Chicago: The National Society for the Study of Education, 1964), pp. 268–85.

[2] In regard to this issue of neglect for educational administration see Daniel E. Griffiths, *Administrative Theory,* (New York: Appleton-Century-Crofts, 1959).

interesting comparisons can be made regarding these points, especially regarding a definition of theory. The reader is asked to look for common elements in the various definitions offered in the following articles. Is there a common core that most people would accept?

Part of the difficulty in defining "theory" is the fact that people refer to at least three different professional[3] types of theory. Ryans identifies two types as (1) the axiomatic, or hypothetico-deductive type and (2) the empirical, inductive type. Newsome refers to (1) scientific theory and (2) axiological or philosophical theory. Maccia, in introducing her own theory in Section Five, refers to (1) formal theory—theory of pure logic and pure mathematics, (2) descriptive theory—theory of empirical science, and (3) prescriptive theory—theory of philosophy. Ryans' axiomatic theory is a "rapprochement" of logic and deductive empirical science. In consideration of these suggestions by Ryans, Newsome, and Maccia, the reader is asked to use the following list as a guide to his reading of the articles in this section and the next:

1. *Axiomatic: formal,* very often simply called *scientific,* theory.
2. *Inductive: empirical, descriptive* theory.
3. *Philosophical: prescriptive* or *humanistic* or *axiological* theory.

The characteristics of these three types are treated in the various selections. Examples or starting points for developing a theory of a particular type are found mainly in the following section. The reader is therefore asked to direct his attention to comparing these three types.

At this point it is well to point out that Ryans' article also includes some starting points for a theory of teacher behavior. The views presented in this article were updated somewhat in a later book by Ryans. In that book,[4] contrary to the article here, Ryans presents eleven propositions drawn from his basic assumptions. The reader is asked to consider the first five carefully in light of the other articles in Sections Four and Five:

Proposition: General classes of teacher classroom behaviors fall into relatively homogeneous clusters characterized by substantial intercorrelation of behaviors

[3] These do not include the uses of "theory" in common language in such statements as: (a) My theory is that the accident was caused by a blowout in the car's rear tire; and (b) My theory is that we should draft everyone,, male and female, for one year of government service.

[4] David G. Ryans, *Characteristics of Teachers* (Washington, D. C.: American Council on Education, 1960), p. 25. See also Ryans' later very complex formulations in "A Theory of Instruction with Special Reference to the Teacher: An Information System Approach," *Journal of Experimental Education,* 32 (Winter 1963), 191–223; "Teacher Behavior Theory and Research: Implications for Teacher Education", *Journal of Teacher Education,* 14 (September 1963), 274–93; "A Model of Instruction Based on Information System Concepts," in *Theories of Instruction,* ed. James B. Macdonald and Robert R. Leeper (Washington, D. C.: Association for Supervision and Curriculum Development, 1965), pp. 36–61.

within a cluster. Teacher behavior *in toto* may be described in terms of a limited number of such major clusters of behaviors.

Proposition: The major clusters or families formed by teacher behaviors have the characteristics of *dimensions*. Individual teachers, in their manifestations of a particular behavior pattern, vary along a continuum between two behaviorally describable poles.

Proposition: Reliable estimates of teacher behavior constituting a major cluster (positions along a major dimension) may be obtained through assessments derived from the observations of trained observers.

Proposition: The classroom behavior of a teacher with respect to a major dimension, as represented by assessments made by trained observers, is characterized by substantial stability over considerable periods of time.

Proposition: The extent of intercorrelation among major dimensions of teacher behavior varies for different subpopulations of teachers, such as elementary teachers and secondary teachers.

The reader is also asked to compare the criteria offered for assessing a given theory. The ASCD Commission on Instructional Theory lists its criteria with comments. Rose (as cited in Ryans' article), Travers, and Newsome also offer criteria and questions about a theory of teaching. Maccia, in Section Five, also offers criteria before launching into her own theory. Are the criteria of the ASCD Commission, Rose, Travers, Newsome, and Maccia compatible? (Keep in mind that Travers served on the ASCD Commission). What purpose do these criteria serve? Do they supply a guide for theory *builders*?[5] Do they supply a guide for *reviewers* of theory?

Both Travers and the ASCD Commission (in its preface to the criteria)[6] concede that a theory which will meet their criteria is far in the future. How far? Is it indeed possible for a theory of teaching ever to meet these criteria? Does the reader agree with the ASCD Commission's claim that its criteria are realistic? Will the advances gained by having criteria-bound theory outweigh the loss of speculative, non-criteria-bound theory?

In treating the need and utility (that is, function) of a theory of teaching, we quickly come to the relationship between theory and practice. There is little question that theory guides research on teaching, as Rose (in Ryans' article) claims. But we must ask if theory precedes empirical research and shapes it? Does empirical research precede theory building? Also, in what ways—if at all—do axiomatic theories and inductive theories guide the practice of teaching? Do philosophical theories guide practice? These questions form the theme of Newsome's article and they deserve the reader's considered responses.[7] The reader might well keep in mind the popular

[5] *Criteria for Theories of Instruction,* booklet of the ASCD Commission on Instructional Theory, p. 14. This booklet contains Selection No. 14 which appears in this Section. See page 123 for full bibliographical information.

[6] *Ibid.,* p. 6.

[7] See also the three articles by Gowin and Perkinson in *Educational Theory* (January 1963 and April 1964) for further readings related to this issue.

saying that there is nothing so practical as a good theory and also note Travers' references to Newton's work. John Dewey[8], the noted American philosopher and educator, wrote,

> Theory is in the end, as has been said, the most practical of all things, because this widening of the range of attention beyond nearby purpose and desire eventually results in the creation of wider and farther-reaching purposes and enables us to use a much wider and deeper range of conditions and means than were expressed in the observation of primitive practical purposes.

The reader's attention is also directed to the several treatments of the variables to be included in a theory of teaching. Travers treats both dependent and independent variables. How does his treatment of variables compare with Smith's in his article in Section Two? It is noteworthy that Ryans and Travers, psychologists, use a psychological model and Smith, not a psychologist, also uses a psychological model.

In regard to the relationship between teacher variables and pupil variables another point arises. Smith[9] claims that "While the teacher's behavior is influenced by his understanding of the student—by his perception and diagnosis of the student's behavior—still the determining factor in the teacher's behavior is not his understanding of the student but his comprehension of the subject matter and the demands which clear instruction in that subject matter make upon him." Is the teacher independent? Does this claim by Smith conflict with Ryans' formulations? With Travers'?

The reader is asked to consider if Criterion VIII of the ASCD Commission is aimed at Bruner's popular hypothesis,[10] restated in Selection 17 in Section Five as "Any subject can be taught to anybody at any age in some form that is honest." Remember that Travers, a member of the ASCD Commission, specifically mentions that Bruner's[11] speculations "have no place in our kind of activity." Does Travers have Criterion VIII in mind?

Finally, the reader might compare: (1) Criterion ID of the ASCD Commission with the position of Hyman (Section One), Henderson (Section Five), and Martin (Section Six); (2) Ryans' position about good or bad teacher behavior with Newsome's position on the connection between theory and values; and (3) Ryans' definition of teacher behavior with the descriptions by Jackson and Oakeshott in Section One.

8 John Dewey, *The Sources of a Science of Education* (New York: Liveright Publishing Corp., 1929), p. 17.
9 B. O. Smith, "A Conceptual Analysis of Instructional Behavior," *Journal of Teacher Education,* 14 (September 1963), 296.
10 See Jerome S. Bruner, *The Process of Education* (Cambridge, Mass.: Harvard (Cambridge, Mass.: Harvard University Press, 1960), p. 33.
11 Travers refers to Bruner's *Toward a Theory of Instruction,* Chap. 3. This chapter is a direct outgrowth and expansion of Bruner's first article on this topic and this earlier one appears in Section Five. The later piece refers specifically to mathematics whereas the earlier one is general in nature.

11.

In What Sense Is Theory a Guide to Practice in Education?

GEORGE L. NEWSOME, JR.

Professor of
Philosophy of Education, University of Georgia

It is not uncommon to find expressions in the literature of education to the effect that theory is or ought to be a guide to practice. For example, an authority on educational measurement and research has argued that, "The role of basic educational research is to construct and test theories which will serve better to guide educational practice."[1] He implies, however, that guidance from theory is rather indirect, because effective practice also depends on "...ingenious inventions of procedures and materials and skill in their use."[2] One theorist of school administration likens theory to a map and views the theory-practice relationship as symbiotic,[3] while another sees administration as an applied science that uses theory as a guide to action, to collection of facts, to prediction, and to explanation of phenomena.[4]

Many philosophers of education also have stated or suggested that a theory is or ought to be a guide to educational practice. Ernest E. Bayles has maintained that educational theory is concerned not only with what exists but even more so with what ought to exist.[5]

*"In What Sense Is Theory a Guide To
Practice in Education?" by George L. Newsome, Jr. is reprinted with permission from
Educational Theory, 14:31–39, 64, January,
1964.*

[1] Ralph W. Tyler, "Specific Contributions
of Research to Education," *Theory Into Practice* (1: 75–80, April, 1963), p. 77.

[2] *Ibid.*, pp. 78–80.

[3] Jacob W. Getzels, "Theory and Practice
in Education: An Old Question Revisited,"
Administrative Theory as a Guide to Action,
edited by Roald F. Campbell and James M.
Lipham, (Midwest Administrative Center,
The University of Chicago, 1960), p. 58.

[4] Daniel E. Griffith, *Administrative Theory*
(Appleton-Century-Crofts, Inc.: New York,
1959), pp. 24–27.

[5] Ernest E. Bayles, "Research in Educational Theory", *The Philosophy of Education
Society Newsletter* (Northern Illinois University, April, 1962), p. 8.

Broudy has defined "theory" as "a set of ideas so related to each other that they account for or explain a set of facts."[6] Two kinds of theories meet the criteria of this definition; the first, scientific, and the second, axiological or philosophical.[7] Scheffler has stated that "The aim of inquiry is to construct theories adequate to all of the facts, theories that may thus be taken as our best estimates of the truths of nature and as guides to action."[8] Elizabeth Steiner Maccia views theory of education as "interrelations or a system of meanings about ways or methods of carrying on the teaching-learning process."[9] The task of the theorist is, therefore, one of establishing "relationships between knowledge of teaching-learning behavior (means) and knowledge of oughts of teaching-learning behavior (ends)."[10]

The foregoing views of theory and the theory-practice relationship are only a few representative samples from the literature of education. Although these views have been illustrated with very brief quotations out of their larger contexts, they are, nevertheless, suggestive. It appears that there are both points of agreement and disagreement about theory and the theory-practice relationship. It seems likely that some of these differences arise from semantic problems while others reflect different conceptions of theory and practice. Although there seems to be considerable agreement that theory does guide practice, disagreement seems to persist as to just how it does so. Moreover, the points of agreement suggest that an educational theory possesses a moral or prescriptive dimension, though there is disagreement about how such a dimension fits into the theory. Two views are suggested: (1) that a single theory contains both scientific and prescriptive statements or has both an empirical and a normative reference, or (2) that separate scientific and moral theories are related to each other in the guidance of practice. In either case, some questions arise concerning the logical relation of theoretical to prescriptive statements.

The word "theory" has an honorific status. It is said to be a word that is frequently used but seldom defined in educational literature.[11] The same could probably be said for "practice". In the remaining portion of this paper, analysis of the uses of the word "theory" will reveal two different meanings for the term and two different, though similar conceptions of theory.[12] In each case, the logical relationships of theory to practice will be illustrated and evaluated.

I. MEANINGS OF "THEORY" AND "PRACTICE"

According to both etymology and common usage (dictionary definitions),

[6] Harry S. Broudy, *Building a Philosophy of Education,* (Prentice-Hall, Inc.: Englewood Cliffs, New Jersey, 1961), pp. 16–17.

[7] *Ibid.*

[8] Israel Scheffler, *The Language of Education,* (Charles C Thomas Publisher: Springfield, Illinois, 1960), p. 75.

[9] Elizabeth Steiner Maccia, "The Separation of Philosophy from Theory of Education," *Studies in Philosophy and Education* (2: 158–169, Spring, 1962), p. 165.

[10] *Ibid.*

[11] George A. Beauchamp, *Curriculum Theory* (The Kagg Press: Wilmette, Illinois, 1961), p. 18.

[12] Metaethical theories are excluded because they do not conform to either the scientific or the doctrinaire conception of theory. They deserve special consideration on their own merit.

a rather firm distinction is made between theory and practice. Etymologically, the word "theory" means something "seen" in the mind, plan, scheme, guess, or view.[13] The ambiguity of usage is reflected in dictionaries where "theory" is variously defined as contemplation, speculation, a set of facts in their ideal relations to each other, or as a systematic view of a subject. The word "practice" as either a transitive verb or noun, commonly suggests performance, action, or doing based upon habit, art, or strategy. Both etymology and common usage set theory in opposition to practice. A noted philosopher of language has argued that there are logical reasons why "Intelligent practice is not a step-child of theory."[14] Though he does not view theory as necessarily opposed to practice, he maintains that, "We learn how by practice, schooled indeed by criticism and example, but often quite unaided by any lessons in theory."[15]

Examination of selected pieces of literature in several fields, particularly social science, education, and philosophy seems to reveal no standard use of the word "theory." Instead, a variety of uses are found representing ordinary ambiguity. On the other hand, there seems to be little evidence of standard uses of the word "theory" within specific fields. Various uses (meanings) do not appear to be restricted to specific fields, but "spill over" in some measure from field to field. Therefore, terminology which suggests a strictly field dependent use of "theory" reflects linguistic customs and preferences, general tendencies, and convenient illustrations.

II. MEANINGS OF "THEORY" AND CONCEPTIONS OF THEORIES

Among philosophers of science, "scientific theory" has a fairly definite, though not strictly field dependent meaning Feigl has defined "theory as:[16]

... a set of assumptions from which can be derived by purely logico-mathematical procedures a larger set of empirical laws. The theory thereby furnishes an explanation of these empirical laws and unifies the originally relatively heterogeneous areas of subject matter characterized by those empirical laws.

Braithwaite says, "A scientific theory is a deductive system in which observable consequences logically follow from the conjunction of observed facts with the set of fundamental hypotheses of the system."[17] Bergmann states that a theory is "a group of laws deductively connected. ... The laws that serve as premises of these deductions are called *axioms* of the theory; those that appear as conclusions are called theorems."[18] Nagel describes a theory as:[19]

(1) an abstract calculus that is the logical skeleton of the explanatory sys-

[13] Roland Wilbur Brown, *Composition of Scientific Words,* (published by the author: Baltimore, Maryland, 1954), p. 789.

[14] Gilbert Ryle, *The Concept of Mind* (Barnes and Noble, Inc.: New York, 1949), p. 26.

[15] *Ibid.,* p. 41.

[16] Herbert Feigl, "Principles and Problems of Theory Construction" in *Current Trends in Psychological Theory* (The University of Pittsburgh Press: Pittsburgh, 1951), p. 182.

[17] Richard Bevan Braithwaite, *Scientific Explanation* (Cambridge University Press: Cambridge, 1955), p. 22.

[18] Gustav Bergmann, *Philosophy of Science* (Harcourt, Brace and World, Inc.: New York, 1957), pp. 31–32.

[19] Ernest Nagel, *The Structure of Science* (Harcourt, Brace and World, Inc.: New York, 1961), p. 90.

tem, and that "implicitly defines" the basic motions of the system; (2) a set of rules that in effect assign an empirical content to the abstract calculus by relating it to the concrete materials of observation and experiment; and (3) an interpretation or model for the abstract calculus, which supplies some flesh for the skeletal structure in terms of more or less familiar conceptual or visualizable materials.

The most basic conception of theory illustrated by the foregoing definitions and descriptions is that theory, whatever else it may be, is primarily a logical framework. That is, theory consists of classes of statements and rules for their manipulation. Generally speaking, there will be at least two classes of statements deductively related to each other so as to imply another class of statements. In this sense, there can be no theory of particular or single events. Theories are not statements of individual facts, statements of general tendencies, or a statement of some one general law. In a scientific theory, there are, of course, no moral or prescriptive expressions. The major distinction between theories in formal sciences such as mathematics and empirical sciences such as physics is that some of the statements of the latter have or imply an empirical reference. In either case, a theory is usually thought to be adequate, to the degree that it is comprehensive enough to account for relevant facts or cases, internally consistent, and employs as few basic terms as possible.

The foregoing basic conception of scientific theory represents the most fundamental points of agreement among leading philosophers of science, while avoiding many of the terminological differences and controversal issues. For example, the sets of statements which comprise theories are variously called "assumptions," "postulates," "laws," "axioms," "hypotheses," and the like. Numerous interesting issues such as the role and function of primitive or undefined terms, defined terms, types of hypotheses, explanation and prediction, and models or analogies are also avoided. These issues have not been avoided because they are unimportant, but rather because they represent controversal interpretations that go beyond the basic conception of scientific theory.

The basic conception of scientific theory "spills over" into social sciences and non-scientific fields. Among recent and contemporary philosophers, Dewey,[20] Whitehead,[21] and Northrop have suggested that science should have a moral and practical reference to culture. John Dewey and numerous educators appear to believe that science, "properly conceived," and freed from the restraints of dualistic thinking, would possess a moral dimension, and its methods and techniques would be applicable to most any kind of problem. Northrop has sought to describe the moral reference of scientific theory to culture and show the scientific structure and foundation of normative social theories or doctrines.

Northrop states that a deductively formulated theory is:[22]

> ...a body of propositions falling into two groups termed postulates and theorems, where the postulates logically imply the theorems...all of the concepts in these propositions fall also into

[20] John Dewey, *Reconstruction in Philosophy* (The New American Library: New York, 1950), pp. 138–139.

[21] Alfred North Whitehead, *Science and the Modern World* (The New American Library: New York, 1948), p. 157.

[22] F. S. C. Northrop, *The Logic of the Sciences and the Humanities* (The MacMillan Company: New York, 1947). pp. 333–334.

two groups, termed primitive or undefined concepts and defined concepts... the defined concepts are derived from the primitive or undefined concepts by the method of definition. Thus when the primitive concepts and the postulates...of a theory are known, the heart and totality of the theory is possessed. For the remainder follows by the logical method of formal implication and definition.

This statement is much like those made by philosophers of science and suggests the same or similar conception of theory. Northrop claims, however, that political, religious, and economic doctrines in a culture are theories expressing sets of primitive concepts and postulates.[23] These theories, called "philosophies underlying a given culture," have prescriptive references by way of theorems to culture and an empirical reference by way of postulates to "nature and the natural man."[24]

Therefore, the same theory has both a normative and a cognitive dimension.

Northrop is not very clear about the normative reference of a theory. Where is the norm? Is it in the theorems or in the culture? If it is the theorems, then how can a norm logically be derived from postulates which are not themselves normative? If it is in the culture, then the culture, not the theory, is normative. Northrop admits that there is "an apparent paradoxial property of designation" involved here, but he insists that "when the relation between the postulates of the philosophy of culture and the postulates of the philosophy of nature is that of identity, the philosophy of culture is true."[25] For example, he suggests that a doctrine such as Thomistic theology may be checked against Aristotle's

metaphysics, and the metaphysical assertions verified by scientific evidence.[26] Essentially the same view seems to have been held by John Dewey and others who attempt to relate postulates of biological evolution or learning theory to prescriptive postulates of social change or democracy to derive theorems that are alleged to be verifiable by empirical evidence.[27]

Northrop also claims that social and cultural theories are deliberately constructed so as to be incompatible with facts. "This very incompatibility is the argument of the proponents...for its [the theories] acceptance."[28] Yet, strange as it may seem, Northrop claims that, although no social theory ever accords with the de facto state of social affairs, such concordance is "precisely what a normative social theory must achieve if it is to be a theory verified by the methods of natural science."[29]

This view of theory seems to contain some rather questionable metaphysical and logical connotations. The dual is-ought references of the theory is a specific case in point. It suggests a confused and illegitimate combination of two different types of expressions. Northrop, however, is probably correct in assigning a prescriptive dimension to many, though not all, social and culture theories. Such theories probably do attempt to combine into a single theoretical structure or system scientific, metaphysical, and moral expressions. Northrop is also probably correct in calling such theories "doctrines" or "philosophies."

[23] Ibid., p. 334.
[24] Ibid., p. 338.
[25] Ibid.

[26] Ibid., p. 337.
[27] See John Dewey, Democracy and Education (The Macmillan Company: New York, 1961) and Ernest E. Bayles, Democratic Educational Theory, (Harper and Brothers: New York, 1960) pp. 257–259.
[28] Northrop, op. cit., p. 332.
[29] Ibid.

III. CONCEPTIONS OF THEORY AND THE THEORY-PRACTICE RELATIONSHIP

A scientific theory is essentially a logical system of statements. Two questions may be asked in judging it: (1) Is it consistent, comprehensive, and parsimonious (2) Does it generate testable hypotheses? The criteria for answering the first question are facts concerning comprehensiveness and logical standards for parsimony, consistency, and validity of inferences. Criteria for testability of hypotheses are those of meaning and verification. A scientific theory does not contain rules for its own verification. Rules for verification are part of experimentation or testing technique. Neither the theory nor verification techniques provide rules for the application or use of theory.

Practice has been shown to involve actions based upon habit, art, skill, or strategy. Practice, therefore, implies a practitioner. Practitioners may, in varying degrees, utilize knowledge, make decisions, set aims or objectives, and devise ways and means for performing tasks. Practice has outcomes or consequences. One may be said to practice successfully or unsuccessfully, skillfully or unskillfully, but seldom, if ever, truely or falsely. In this sense, practical outcomes are judged against practical contingencies and handicaps, accepted standards of achievement or levels of competency, but not against logical standards of consistency, validity of inferences, or truth of statements.

The link between theory and practice is the practitioner rather than a rule, a term, or a statement. What one practices is not a theory, a set of logically related statements, but an activity. Even theorists do not practice theory, except possibly in memorizing it. They practice theorizing or theory construction. Practice is an art even when scientific knowledge is utilized in carrying on some activity. An activity is carried on in some manner, and the manner is judged as acceptable or unacceptable, approved or unapproved, or even right or wrong. Practice, therefore, has a behavioral dimension. Rules or directives for the guidance of behavior are prescriptive or moral in character.

The manner or morality of practice is not prescribed by a scientific theory because the theory provides no moral rules for practitioners. To logically relate theoretical statements to practice, one of three approaches may be taken: (1) relate theoretical to prescriptive statements so as to derive moral conclusions for practice, (2) relate theoretical statements to conditional statements expressing hypothetical desires, or (3) claim that it is "logically odd" to affirm the truth of a theory and practice in a fashion that suggests that the theory is false or not relevant.

The first alternative, though fairly common, frequently leads either to invalid conclusions, or to valid conclusions that are virtually useless to practitioners. Consider the following argument:

> Children learn faster under conditions x, y, and z than under prevailing conditions.
>
> Schools ought to provide conditions for more rapid learning.
>
> Therefore, schools ought to provide conditions x, y, and z.

This argument, like many moral arguments, is not truly deductive and not valid. One may affirm the premises and reject the conclusion, claiming conditions x, y, or z are not the only conditions or the most effective and desirable conditions for bringing about faster learning.

A valid argument may be formulated as follows:

If children learn fastest, then conditions x, y, and z must be present.

If the purpose of schooling is realized, then children always learn fastest.

If schooling is conducted as it ought, then the purpose of schooling is realized.

If schooling is conducted as it ought, then conditions x, y, and z must be present.

The conclusion necessarily follows from the premises. One can accept the argument, but claim that the conclusion refers to an ideal situation which is not attainable in practice. It is also possible that the conclusion prescribes prevailing practices, in which case, it prescribes that one do what he is doing. Moreover, the conclusion does not specify how the conditions are to be instituted in practice. A wide variety of ways and means could possibly be used to achieve the same end. The conclusion of an argument, even a valid argument, does not imply a particular course of action.

The second alternative says, "If you *wish* to achieve x, then do y." For example, "If you wish to ionize an aqueous solution, add an acid to it." The statement does not suggest that one *should* ionize the solution at all. The theory of ionization is only conditionally (hypothetically) related to action by way of supposed desires of the practitioner. It is not assumed that the practitioner understands the theory, or that he will accept or follow the advice. The argument may be formulated as follows:

1. An ionized solution conducts electricity

2. An aqueous solution can be ionized by adding an acid to it.

3. This solution is aqueous.

Therefore, if you wish it to conduct electricity, then add an acid to it.

The expression, "if you wish," assumes a desire that need not appear in the premises or in the conclusion. The conclusion is that adding an acid to an aqueous solution ionizes it and enables it to conduct electricity. Assumed wishes, assumed rationality on the part of practitioners, or statements about the overt behavior of practitioners are "excessive baggage" or no logical significance.[30] In order to explain one phenomenon, why introduce others more perplexing than the first?

The third alternative may include the second one, but adds something more. In the case just cited, it would be "logically odd" to affirm the truth of the theory of ionization, but refuse to ionize an aqueous solution through which one was attempting to pass an electrical current. The logical oddity seems to be that one's actions are not in keeping with one's beliefs. Such an oddity is not logically self-contradictory because only statements are self-contradictory. It is not false or invalid because only statements and inferences are respectively so labeled. On the other hand, situations

30 For argument to the contrary see C. K. Grant, "Pragmatic Implication," *Philosophy* (33:303–324, October, 1958) and Hobert W. Burns, "The Logic of the 'Educational Implication'," *Educational Theory* (11:53–63, January, 1962). Burns, for example, cautiously proposes that a psychological implication based upon rational action in specific situations may furnish theoretical guides for educational behavior. The concept of rational action can, however, be challenged at numerous points. For example, see Carl G. Hempel, "Rational Action," *Proceedings and Addresses of the American Philosophical Association,* 1961–62 (The Antioch Press, 1962), pp. 5–23.

that first appear logically odd may be reasonable on other grounds. For example, a researcher who was seeking other ways of passing a current through a non-ionized aqueous solution may well affirm the theory of ionization but refuse to ionize the solution. What appears to be logically odd, upon more careful investigation, often proves to be neither logical nor odd.

In summary, a scientific theory may be said to render phenomena more understandable. This end is achieved by simplicity, economy of statements and concepts, and logical systematization. Theory has no direct reference and no formal implications for practice. Reference to practice must be made by way of directions or prescriptions for practitioners. Such references relate to behavior and manner of action, and, hence are moral references. Although valid moral arguments may be formulated by relating theoretical to moral expressions, valid conclusions do not imply feasibility or utility. For this reason, moral arguments can frequently be affirmed and put aside in interest of more practical considerations. An argument based upon assumed desires or rational action adds nothing to the factual content of the argument beyond psychological assumptions of questionable worth. The claims of logical oddity are difficult to maintain because of reasonable and practical deviations from what might be expected on the basis of expressed beliefs or observed behavior.

Unlike scientific theories, doctrines practically never clearly exhibit a logical structure. Sets of related expressions, meanings of key terms, and rather loose rules for manipulating terms can sometimes be explicated by those who are willing to make certain assumptions and offer a scheme for interpretation. The abundance of rival interpretations of religious, political, economic, and educational doctrines do not, however, speak well for this procedure. Doctrines are not as simple, as parsimonious, or as logically rigorous as scientific theories. Emotive, vague, and ambiguous expressions; persuasive definitions, and metaphysical claims are intermingled with descriptions of known events prophecies of future events. Marxism, various forms of Christianity, democracy as a doctrine, and romantic naturalism are cases in point.

In so far as doctrines possess logically related sets of statements that approximate the scientific structure of theory, the same three ways of attempting to relate theory to practice, and the same shortcomings of these relationships also apply *a-fortiori* to doctrines. The shortcomings are more striking, not only because doctrines are less precise than scientific theories, but also because doctrines embody the sentiments and ideals of partisan movements. As a result, doctrines contain many slogans, some of which function ceremoniously, which others summarize and prescribe practices, and still others state or imply aims and values.[31] Slogans, because they are attractive rather than true, are systematically vague and ambiguous, imply no particulars, are open to a variety of interpretations, and ultimately fail when they lose their charm and no longer capture imagination or command the loyalty of disciples.[32] Some individuals have suggested that rationalistic philosophies and theories of education are only slogan systems.[33]

[31] B. Paul Komisar and James E. McClellan, "The Logic of Slogans" in B. Othanel Smith and Robert H. Ennis (eds.), *Language and Concepts in Education* (Rand McNally and Company: Chicago, 1961), pp. 195–200.

[32] *Ibid.*, pp. 200–212.

[33] *Ibid.*, p. 206.

Doctrines are unlike scientific theories in another respect; namely, they do not generate testable hypotheses. For example, Rousseau's doctrine of romantic naturalism has been described as, "based on postulates that are inconsistent with a large body of data concerning both human and animal behavior..." and a theory that generates no testable hypotheses.[34] The Montessori theory, with its postulates of free movement in classrooms and intrinsic value of objects, generates only the hypothesis that children in a free moving situation come in contact with more objects of intrinsic value, and hence learn more than do children in a more restricted situation. The hypothesis, if testable, relates only to the validity of the postulates.[35] Other doctrines on sentiment have similar shortcomings. They specify how teachers *ought* to feel about students—e.g. love them. How love is related to learning is quite mystical.[36] Even Dewey's theory of problem solving, if it can be called a theory, does not seem to have given rise to any scientific studies of consequence.[37]

The rather obvious metaphysical and moralistic aspects of doctrines, and their fabrication and employment in the interest of partisan movements, indicates something about them. How and under what conditions do they arise? Upon what conceptual model are they constructed? Although much study of these questions remains to be done, there is some evidence that doctrines represent the folklore of education,[38] and that they are fabricated on political models

that give "free access" to metaphysical and moralistic dogmas.[39] It is questionable, therefore, that doctrines provide systematic knowledge or understandings. As theories, they appear to be logically inadequate and virtually useless.

Attempts to establish a logical (necessary) relation of scientific theory to practice seem to end in failure. Theory is abstract and logical. It affords economy and system in organization of abstract terms and concepts. In this sense it promotes understanding and provides a basis for rational and scientific explanation. Theory aids and promotes scientific research. Neither theory nor research, however, is the same thing as the practice of teaching. Practices arise in response to custom and demand. Indeed, one may argue with some justification that issues arising from practice stimulate the kind of questions that ultimately lead to scientific research. In any case, between theory and practice is the practitioner facing social and professional demands, customs, technological limitations, and a host of practical problems. What is theoretically possible is not always practical, useful, or desirable. Practitioners must rely heavily, it seems, upon judgment.

Although theoretical knowledge is no guarantee of practical skills, it is very important to science and civilization. Numerous pieces of empirical evidence may be cited in support of having practitioners schooled in theory even if no necessary relationship can be shown to exist between theory and practice. Such evidence, for example, may indicate that theoretical knowledge is likely to provide more reliable,

---

34 Robert M. Travers, *An Introduction to Educational Research* (The Macmillan Company: New York, 1958), pp. 25–26.

35 *Ibid.*, pp. 24–25.

36 *Ibid.*, p. 25.

37 *Ibid.*, p. 24.

38 *Ibid.*, p. 13.

39 George L. Newsome, Jr. and Albert J. Kingston, Jr., "A Critique of Criticisms of Education," *Educational Theory* (12:218–226, October, 1962).

broader, or more systematic understandings of some basic aspects of education. Similarly, evidence may suggest that theoretical knowledge makes phenomena more reasonable, is likely to give one new insights into old problems, or perhaps enables one to better perceive new problems. In this sense, theory possibly provides a useful criterion of reasonableness and hueristic conceptual frame of reference. Finally, one could argue that knowing a theory, say in mathematics or science, is virtually a logically prior condition for teaching it. A necessary condition, however, should not be confused with a necessary relation or with a sufficient condition. Knowing a theory as a necessary condition for teaching it does not mean that theory implies practice, or that knowledge of the theory is a sufficient condition for successful practice.

Doctrines, though they neither logically imply practices nor generate testable hypotheses, nevertheless serve practical purposes. They function chiefly as pseudo-theories which attract followers and give expression for partisan movements. They are misleading and deceptive only to the degree that we are "taken in" by their attractiveness as practical programs of action or theoretical explanations of phenomena.

Theory, primarily scientific theory, is a guide to action or practice only in the sense that relatively reliable, systematic, and perhaps somewhat esoteric knowledge affords a basis for understanding phenomena, serves as a criterion of reasonableness, and affords a hueristic device for conceptualization. Argument in support of these practical claims must rest upon inductive evidence and probabilities. It is only by scientific research, not by philosophical analysis and speculation, that the practical usefulness of theory can be substantiated.

12.

Theory Development and the Study of Teacher Behavior

DAVID G. RYANS

Director of The Educational
Research and Development Center, University of
Hawaii

THE ROLE OF THEORY

Teacher behaviors, their nature, genesis, and cultivation, their identification and their evaluation, constitute the core concern not only of teacher training institutions and school systems, but also of a society at large that depends on teachers to a very great extent for the propagation of accumulated knowledge and cultural values. Considerable opinion is expressed and not a few studies are undertaken in an effort to better understand teacher behavior. (*1, 2, 4, 5, 8, 10, 11, 13, 14.*) [Numbers refer to references.] Relatively little attention, however, appears to have been directed toward the organization or systematization of what is known about teacher behavior or the assumptions on which

"Theory Development and the Study of Teacher Behavior" by David G. Ryans is reprinted with permission from the Journal of Educational Psychology, *47:462–475, December, 1956.*

the study of teacher behavior is based.

In the meantime, strong arguments have been presented by social and behavioral scientitst suggesting that steps toward some sort of a theoretical formulation have considerable utility value; that systematic theories are highly desirable, particularly for guidance, if maximum productivity of research in a field is to be attained. Proponents of this view point out that advanced understanding and usable knowledge frequently have been observed to demonstrate marked increase as the study of problems in an area progressed from exploratory, "catch-as-catch-can," investigations to selective observation guided by hypotheses derived from systematic theory and employing empirical tests to determine the place (if any) of such hypotheses in the basic theory.

Essentially, this approach represents a rapprochement of formal, deductive logic and a modern science that demands the inclusion of pragmatic considerations in judging the admissibility of facts to a body of knowledge. Such axiomatic, or hypothetico-deductive, theory is rather popular at the present time.

Another sort of theorizing attempts to be rigorously inductive and culminates in what may be simply described as an organized body of empirically obtained facts. This kind of theory employs operational definitions extensively and emphasizes reasoning that proceeds from the observed characteristics of sample data to generalizations applicable to larger homogeneous classes. Facts are admissible to such a theory if (1) they are based on fair samples, (2) they satisfy pragmatic criteria, and (3) they fit into a pattern with other known facts in the same area. Hypotheses may be derived from the pattern of accumulated fact (and to this extent the approach is also deductive). Inductively generated theories, or systematizations, are descriptions rather than explanations.

Researchers and practitioners appear to have found little need for either kind of theory development in approaching the problem of teacher behavior. A recent statement attributed the lack of productive research on teacher effectiveness, in part, to such a neglect of theory, declaring:

> ...the present conditions of research of teacher effectiveness holds little promise of yielding results commensurate with the needs of American education. This condition has two significant characteristics: disorganization, and lack of orientation to other behavioral sciences. By disorganization, we mean the condition in which, at present, research too often proceeds without explicit theoretical framework, in intellectual disarray, to the testing of myriads of arbitrary, unrationalized hypotheses. The studies too often interact little

with each other, do not fall into place within any scheme, and hence add little to the understanding of the teaching process. The simple fact of the matter is that, after 40 years of research on teacher effectiveness during which a vast number of studies have been carried out, one can point to few outcomes that a superintendent of schools can safely employ in hiring a teacher or granting him tenure, that an agency can employ in certifying teachers, or that a teacher-education faculty can employ in planning or improving teacher-education program. (*2:* p. 657.)

Something more should be said, perhaps, of the essential characteristics of theories and the values that are claimed for them. Rose, in his volume of essays on theory in the social sciences, states rather well the generally accepted concept of theory viewed from the standpoint of formal logic with appropriate adaptations to make place for a pragmatic criterion of validity. Rose writes that theory is:

> ...an integrated body of definitions, assumptions, and general propositions covering a given subject matter from which a comprehensive and consistent set of specific and testable hypotheses can be deduced logically. The hypotheses must take the form "If *a*, then *b*, holding constant *c, d, e,* ..." or some equivalent of this form, and thus permit of causal explanation and prediction. (*12:* p. 3.)

Rose goes on to say:

> A *good* theory is one which 1) has its definitions, assumptions, and general propositions consistent, insofar as possible, with previous research findings and with careful, although perhaps not systematic, observations; 2) has a minimum number of definitions, assumptions, and general propositions; 3)

has its deduced hypotheses in readily testable form; and, crucially, 4) gets its deduced hypotheses verified by proper scientific methods. (*12:* p. 3.)

Just how does such a theoretical framework, in the view of its proponents, really serve in leading to a more complete understanding of a field? Is all of this merely a scientist's high-sounding words—"gobbledygook" (exposition that is obscured by excessive use of technical terminology and involved phrasing)? Or does it have some real utility? It would seem that such a theory frequently does have utility; that it does provide certain advantages to workers in a field. Thus, it may serve to give proper organization to our thinking about, and study of, a problem. It may help us to specify problems and formulate them in a manner that permits the seeking of direct answers. It may call attention to the probable futility of pursuing certain contradictory hypotheses, hypotheses that might, in the absence of the theoretical setting, seem plausible. It may help us to locate strategic, or crucial, problems. All of these suggestions may be summarized in what many scientists and philosophers feel to be a significant value of theory, the economy of thought and labor that may be affected when investigation is conducted in a theoretical framework.

Rose, to whom reference was made earlier, says of the utility of theory:

...1) It is a guide to the formation of hypotheses and trains investigators to look for facts which may ordinarily not be readily apparent. 2) It permits research to be cumulative; that is, it allows the conclusions of older studies to gain support from new research and allows older studies to provide some of the data for new research. 3) It indicates what studies are crucial; that is,

it provides one guide for the selection of research problems from among the infinitely large number of possible hypotheses. 4) It permits research to proceed systematically and allows conclusions to take shorthand form so they are readily communicable. (*12:* p. 4.)

SOME FURTHER CHARACTERISTICS OF THEORIES

All theories, whether of (1) an axiomatic, hypothetico-deductive type or (2) an empirical, inductive sort, must begin with certain assumptions and perhaps some definitions. In the case of inductive theory, such assumptions are very largely expressions of faith in the inductive method—in the consistency and observability of nature; and the definitions are predominantly of the operational kind. In axiomatic theory the assumptions are likely to be the working premises, or general propositions, from which the theory proceeds to noncontradictory hypotheses (postulates and theorems derived from the assumptions or general propositions), that may be tested to determine their probable validity. Inductive theory plunges at once into observation, stressing classification and cross-classification, on the one hand, and experimental testing of sporadic hypotheses, on the other. The resulting specific descriptions of properties and of functional relationships lead, with confirming replications, to generalizations in the form of inductive principles and laws, which in turn may be systematized and organized into coherent theory. The ultimate goal of theory, either axiomatic or inductive, is prediction.

The assumptions of any theory are simply judgments or propositions that are accepted, or taken for granted.

Thus, depending on the kind of theorizing we are attempting, the assumptions may be based on facts held to be axiomatic; or, they may be propositions deductively derived from either axiomatic or previously confirmed premises; or, they may be based directly on previously obtained and admitted scientific evidence (i.e., evidence accepted as valid, or admissible, because it already has passed satisfactory tests); or, again, the assumptions may even be concepts or propositions that are accepted (even though they are not capable of immediate confirmation in any manner), because they are necessary for the investigation of phenomena in the area with which the theory deals.

In the case of hypothetico-deductive theory, hypotheses are derivable from the assumptions or basic propositions, growing out of questions, problems, or needs suggested by the basic assumptions with which the theory begins. In inductive theory, hypotheses are suggested by experience—previous observations, or empirically obtained evidence. In either case, hypotheses are essentially creations of the imagination of their inventors or originators. In an unrefined and inexact form, they begin to appear as soon as the person develops any definite conception of a thing or an event (e.g., "I think a teacher needs a course in X subject matter to perform his teaching responsibilities adequately." "I think older teachers are more authoritarian than younger ones."). But all such ruminations probably should not be thought of as hypotheses—at least, not in the sense in which the term hypothesis usually is employed in science. There are certain generally agreed-upon restrictions that commonly are applied. Thus, a suitable hypothesis must be in an exact form; must provide a specific answer to a specific question. And it must not be inconsistent with what is known; it must not be contradictory to the basic assumptions and propositions of applicable theory, or with other hypotheses for which there

TABLE I.—THEORETICAL FRAMEWORK

Type I. Axiomatic, Mathematico-Deductive, Hypothetico-Deductive Theory	*Type II. Inductive, Empirical Theory*

A. Assumptions
  Definitions
B. General Propositions
	A. Assumptions
	  Definitions (especially "operational")
	B. Observation
	  Classification and cross-classification
	  Sporadic hypotheses and their experimental testing

C. Hypotheses: postulates and theorems re properties and functional relationships	C. Specified descriptions of properties and functional relationships (generalizable to inductive principles and laws)
D. Observation: testing of postulates and theorems by classification and experimentation	D. Systematization, organization of descriptive principles into coherent pattern (possibly leading to General Propositions)
E. Extension and revision of theory in light of observation and of further deductive analysis F. Prediction	E. Extension and revision of principles, and of theory, as required by further classification and experiment F. Prediction

is extensive supporting evidence. And, again, a suitable hypothesis must be stated in a way that it is capable of being confirmed or refuted at some agreed-upon level of confidence; the consequences that will follow if it is probably true, or probably false, must be describable and such consequences must be capable of observation and recording.

SOME STARTING POINTS FOR A THEORY OF TEACHER BEHAVIOR

Thus far our discussion has been concerned with comments on the nature of theory. Now how can some of these concepts relating to theoretical framework be applied to teacher behavior? What, for example, might be some of the assumptions and definitions that apply to teacher behavior? Those that will be suggested do not constitute a complete set of all assumptions required for a theory of teacher behavior. Nor is any particular claim made at this point for theoretical rigor. But if we do wish to think in terms of theory, a starting point is necessary regardless of how crude and tentative such a beginning may be. Trial and error, criticism, and research may provide the necessary clarification, revision, and extension leading to a generally acceptable theory of teacher behavior.

A DEFINITION

As a point of embarkation, a definition of teacher behavior will be stated. It is suggested that for our purposes teacher behavior may be defined simply as the behavior, or activities, of persons as they go about doing whatever is required of teachers, particularly those activities that are concerned with the guidance or direction of the learning of others.

There are several important implications in this rather straightforward operational definition.

(A) One implication is that teacher behavior is social behavior—that, in addition to the teacher, there must be learners, or pupils, who presumably are affected by the behavior of the teacher. It should also be noted that teacher behavior-pupil behavior relationships may be of a reciprocal nature; that not only do teachers affect pupil behavior, but pupils may affect teacher behavior, as well.

(B) Another implication of the definition of teacher behavior is that there is nothing inherently good or bad in a given teacher behavior, or set of behaviors, but, instead, that teacher behavior is good or bad, right or wrong, effective or ineffective, only to the extent that the behavior conforms or fails to conform to the particular value system, or set of objectives, defining (1) the activities expected of a teacher in a given community or culture, and (2) particularly the kinds of learnings (attainments) and methods of teaching to bring about these learnings, approved by the particular culture (11, 14).

ASSUMPTION I

If we were to state the basic assumption to be made in setting out to describe teacher behavior, we might expect it to bear some resemblance to formulations made for similar purposes in connection with learning theory and personality theory. Indeed, in any and all behavior theory, some expression of faith in the reliability, or consistency of behavior is required. In our case the assumption may be summarized in the proposition that teacher behavior is a resultant of (a) certain situational factors and (b) certain organismic factors, and their interaction; or, simply that teacher behavior is a function of certain environmental influences and characteristics of the individual teacher. Thus:

$$\text{(A)} \quad r_a = f[(S_{1a}M_1{}^oE_1{}^oH_1{}^o)$$
$$+ (S_{2a}M_2{}^oE_2{}^oH_2{}^o)$$
$$+ \cdots (S_{na}M^onE^onH^on)]$$

where:

r_a = teacher behavior r in situation a

S = situational indices

M^o = motivational organismic indices

E^o = experience organismic indices

H^o = genetic organismic indices

$$\text{(B)} \quad R_t = ar_a + br_b \cdots nr_n + e$$

where:

R_t = over-all teacher behavior

a = weight

r_n = z score of teacher behavior n

e = z score of error component

The present treatment is intentionally limited to consideration of teacher behavior per se. Since, however, teacher behavior implies pupil behavior (as previously noted), we might also observe that pupil behavior could be thought of as being similarly influenced by a number of variables, one of which would be teacher behavior R_t. Thus:

$$\text{(C)} \quad r_a + f[(S_{1a}M_1{}^oE_1{}^oH_1{}^o)$$
$$+ \cdots (S_{n_a}M^onE^onH^on)]$$

where:

S represents situational indices such as textbooks, peer behavior, parent behavior, etc.
and

$$\text{(D)} \quad R_p = ar_a + br_b \cdots nr_n + e$$

where: R_p = pupil behavior

What these rather rigid appearing equations say is simply that behavior occurs when an organism is stimulated

and if the variables and mathematical functions are known, the equation may be solved for the unknown (r or R).

Just how these various situational and organismic conditions interact and what takes place in the teacher's nervous system as they interact (how, as some theorists would put it, the energy input-output transfer takes place) certainly is not known and we are completely incapable of describing the process except in terms of inferences based upon observable[1] inputs and observable responses of the teacher. The fact that little is known about how such things take place does not mean that persons interested in behavior theory have not been actively concerned about the problem. Certain groups of theorists have been both active and ingenious. One such group, which incidentally is interested in speculating upon the generality of behavior theory whether the systems involved are atoms, viruses, cells, individual persons, society, solar systems, or what not, view the organism, the teacher in our case, as an open system (i.e., a bounded region in space-time), possessed with negative feedback which provides for the distribution of information to sub-systems to keep them in orderly balance.

Other theorists have been particularly concerned with how individuals in a social environment (e.g., teacher-pupil, teacher-teacher, etc.) interact and condition one-another's behavior, not only in an immediate situation but also in future situations, as a result of the integration of response-produced stimuli into the total stimulus patten. Sears (*15*) has suggested, for example, the necessary expansion of the basic mon-

[1] Observable, as here used, refers to that which may be perceived either by another person or by the experiencing individual, or which may be recorded by some instrument.

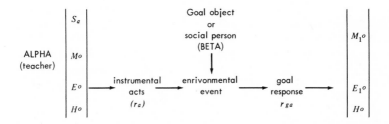

Figure 1. The monadic instigation-action sequence. After Sears (*15*)

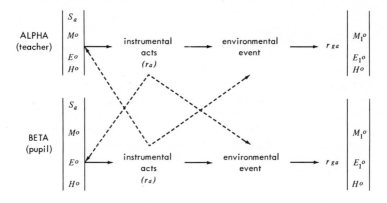

Figure 2. The diadic sequence. After Sears (*15*)

adic unit of behavior, which various learning theories have employed—and in terms of which the foregoing equations (A), (B), (C), and (D) are presented—into a diadic one which describes the combined actions of two or more individuals. That a diadic unit is essential if the relationships between people are to be taken into account in theory should impress the teacher behavior theorist as an entirely reasonable proposition.

The diadic approach strikes at the heart of the teacher-pupil relationship problem. Therefore, it is important to take into account extension of the paradigm represented by our equation (A) to include the significant implications of Sears' model for the diadic behavior sequence. The models which follow

conceptualize teacher behavior first in terms of the monadic and then the diadic behavior sequence. Alpha may be presumed to be the teacher, and Beta the pupil. The symbols S_a, M^o, E^o, H^o, and r_a have the same meaning as in the earlier equations. M_1^o, and E_1^o are employed to represent the modified motivational and experience structures of the teacher resulting from a reinforcement brought about by completion of the behavior sequence.

We are proposing, then, that the basic assumption of teacher behavior theory may be summarized by the equations and the models just presented.

Now growing out of the basic assumption that teacher behavior is a function of the conditions under which it occurs are a number of implications or sub-assumptions, which follow:

(A) An implication of this assumption is, of course, that teacher behavior (and social behavior, with which education deals), is characterized by some uniformity; that, as Mill put it: "... there are such things in nature as parallel cases, that what happens once will, under sufficient degree of similarity of cirumstances, happen again" (*9*: p. 223). We are stating that teacher behavior is, within limits, reliable, consistent, or stable.

(B) Another implication of this basic assumption (perhaps it is so fundamental to any or all scientific theory that it is unnecessary to state it explicitly with respect to teacher behavior), is expressed by Keynes' Postulate of Limited Independent Qualities, which states that: "...objects in a field over which our generalizations extend, do not have an infinite number of independent qualities; ...their characteristics, however numerous, cohere together in groups of invariable connections, which are finite in number" (*7*: p. 256). This is to say that the number of responses the individual teacher is capable of making, and the number of stimulus situations and organismic variables that may affect a teacher's behavior, are limited. The assumption is an important one if the equations noted above are to hold, and, of course, if we hope to predict teacher behavior. It presents the researcher with a "tolerable" problem (as a student recently put it).

(C) In taking cognizance of this basic proposition of teacher behavior, it should be noted that human behavior, characterized as it is by variability (only approximate uniformity, or consistency), always must be considered in light of probability rather than rigid, one-to-one, invariable cause-effect relationships.

The error component (unreliability) resulting from behavior sampling inevitably will be present in any assessment we make of stimulus conditions, of organismic conditions (genetic bases, past experience, motivation), and of the teacher behavior (the dependent variable, or criterion). Teacher behavior can be predicted only with varying degrees of probability; never with certainty. Therefore, r_a and R_t refer to probable behaviors rather than certain behaviors.

Assumption II

When we presume to study teacher behavior we also make the assumption that teacher behavior is observable; that its manifestations are of a tangible nature and may be identified objectively, eithey by direct observation of samples of behavior, or by approaches that provide correlative indices of teacher behaviors (e.g., approaches involving the assessment of pupil behavior, the use of tests of teacher abilities and knowledges, the use of interviews or inventories to elicit expression of teacher preferences, interests, beliefs, and attitudes, etc.).

Several implications (or perhaps subassumptions) may be noted here.

(A) One implication is that different teacher behaviors, or sets of teacher behaviors, are distinguishable from one another; that some behaviors possess characteristics in common, to the exclusion of other characteristics. Teacher behaviors can be distinguished under observation.

(B) A second subassumption is that the distingushing characteristics of a teacher behavior provide the basis for a concept, abstracted from specific instances, which permits common understanding of the behavior and communication of the behavior to others.

(C) These implications lead to a

third aspect of the assumption of the observability of teacher behavior, that teacher behaviors are classifiable, both qualitatively and quantitatively. (1) Teacher behaviors that are similar, that have common elements, may be classified in the same category—apart from other teacher behaviors that are dissimilar. (2) Within any given category teacher behaviors may be further assigned to subclasses that may be treated quantitatively (to which numbers may be attached). These quantitative subclasses may be of a present-absence type permitting enumeration, or counting, only; or, they may be subclasses characterized by continuity and varying as a metric (exemplified by ordinal subclasses at the lowest level of refinement and by equal-interval and equal-ratio subclasses at successively more refined levels).

Various qualitative classifications of teacher behaviors are possible. Thus, for example, we might think of teacher behaviors grouped broadly into such general categories as: (1) those involving instruction and relationships with pupils; (2) those involving relationships with the school, its organization, and its administration; and (3) those involving relationships with the community. Or, we might classify teacher behaviors more specifically, employing such categories as verbal aptitude, emotional stability, favorable attitude toward pupils, friendly behavior toward pupils, and the like, to provide the framework. For any specifically defined category we might conceivably assign quantitative subclasses.

(D) Still a fourth subassumption to the basic assumption of observability of teacher behavior might state that teacher behaviors may be revealed, or may be observed, either (1) by the representative sampling of teacher behaviors or (2) by signs, or indicators, or correlates of the behavior under consideration. In sampling behavior, we assume that the performance of the individual during the behavior sample is proportional to the larger aspects, or universe, of his behavior. In judging behavior from signs or correlates, it is assumed that behavior can be inferred from known correlates of that behavior —from phenomena that have been found to accompany that behavior in the past.

So much for our articles of faith, or general assumptions regarding teacher behavior. With such assumptions stated (and assuming for the present the desirability of inductive theorizing), the teacher behavior theorist might turn to observation—to classification and hypothesis testing.

The number of descriptive classifications and specific hypotheses that might be generated with respect to teacher behavior is almost limitless. Probably no one would be interested in all such hypotheses even if it were possible to assemble them. But some classifications and some hypotheses are more relevant than others. And, moreover, some appear to be quite plausible. In fact, many can even be incorporated in the design of well-controlled study.

At this point it might be well to note that there are various approaches to the testing of hypotheses. Ideally, to test any hypothesis, we would like to design a projected experiment (the basic experimental design) with (1) experimental and control groups equated at the beginning of the investigation, (2) introduction of an experimental variable or treatment (the hypothesized causal factor) with the experimental group while withholding it from the control group, and (3) judgment of the validity of the hypothesis by comparison of the groups with respect to the dependent variable, or criterion behavior. This is the typical application (or, it may involve some more advanced and complex modification to permit analysis of interaction effects and such), of Mill's methods of agreement and difference. But this approach frequently is not possible in the study of teacher behavior. Instead, it usually is necessary to undertake what Chapin (*3*) has called "ex post facto" experiments, or perhaps the comparison of aspects of defined groups, or perhaps intercorrelational studies (classificatory investigation). Much of the research on teacher behavior must be of this nonexperimental (using "experiment" in the strictest sense) type.

No attempt will be made to state specific hypotheses about teacher behavior that might be subjected to testing. Tests of a number of hypotheses have been attempted in connection with various researches (*10*), including the Teacher Characteristics Study (*14*). In the latter research, hypotheses referring to the interrelationships of estimates of teacher behaviors have been extensively tested. Similarly, hypotheses relative to the central tendencies and dispersions of behavior measurements of defined groups of teachers have been given attention, leading to comparisons of teachers with respect to such conditions as age, experience, geographic area of employment, type of college attended, youthful experiences, frequent activities, etc., on a selected set of teacher personal and social characteristics.*

Throughout the country, many similar researches are being directed at the study of comparisons of, and interrelationships among, teacher behaviors. Perhaps we are reaching the point where

patterns among the behavior components may be discerned—where the beginnings of organization of evidence into a theory of teacher behavior may be possible.

Such study and systematization (theory development), in combination with proper attention to specification of problems and careful design, may reasonably be expected to shed increasing light upon our understanding, first, of teacher behavior, and, second (and of ultimate importance), on how teacher behavior influences pupil behavior and how certain kinds of teacher-pupil relationships may be identified, predicted, and cultivated.

REFERENCES[2]

1. A. S. Barr, B. V. Bechdolt, W. W. Coxe, N. L. Gage, J. S. Orleans, H. H. Remmers, and D. G. Ryans, "Report of the Committee on the Criteria of Teacher Effectiveness," *Revue of Educational Research*, 22: 238–253, 1952.

2. A. S. Barr, B. V. Bechdolt, N. L. Gage, J. S. Orelans, C. R. Page, H. H. Remmers, and D. G. Ryans, "Second Report of the Committee on Criteria of Teacher Effectiveness," *Journal of Educational Research*, 46: 641–658, 1953.

3. F. S. Chapin, *Experimental Designs in Sociological Research*. New York, Harper & Bros., 1947.

4. W. W. Charters and D. Waples, *The Commonwealth Teacher Training Study*.

---

* The reader is referred to the Overview to this Section pp. 86–87 in which five of Ryans' propositions are cited from his later work. [Ed.]

[2] References 1, 2, 11, and 14 bear, to some extent, on theory of teacher behavior. References 5 and 10, in particular, provide bibliographies and reviews of studies relating to the evaluation of teacher behavior. It should be noted, also, that the June issues of the *Review of Educational Research* in the years 1934, 1937, 1940, 1943, 1946, 1949, 1952, and 1955 were devoted to "Teacher Personnel."

Chicago, University of Chicago Press, 1929.

5. S. J. Domas and D. V. Tiedeman, "Teacher Competence: An Annotated Bibliography," *Journal of Experimental Education*, 19: 101–218, 1950.

6. E. Greenwood, *Experimental Sociology*. New York, King's Crown Press, 1945.

7. J. M. Keynes, *A Treatise on Probability*. New York, Macmillan Co., 1921.

8. W. A. McCall, *Measurement of Teacher Merit*. Raleigh, N. C., State Department of Public Instruction, 1952.

9. J. S. Mill, *A System of Logic*. New York, Longmans, Green, Co., 1872.

10. J. E. Morsh and E. W. Wilder, *Identifying the Effective Instructor: A Review of the Quantitative Studies 1900–1952*. San Antonio, Texas, Air Force Personnel and Training Research Center, 1954.

11. W. Rabinowitz and R. M. W. Travers, "Problems of Defining and Assessing Teacher Effectiveness," *Educational Theory*, 3:212–219, 1953.

12. A. M. Rose, *Theory and Method in the Social Sciences*. Minneapolis, University of Minnesota Press, 1954.

13. D. G. Ryans, "Appraising Teacher Personnel," *Journal of Experimental Education*, 16: 1–30, 1947.

14. D. G. Ryans, "The Investigation of Teacher Characteristics," *The Educational Record*, 34: 370–396, 1953.

15. R. R. Sears, "A Theoretical Framework for Personality and Social Behavior," *The American Psychologist*, 6: 476–483, 1951.

13.

Towards Taking the Fun Out of Building a Theory of Instruction

ROBERT M. W. TRAVERS

Distinguished University
Professor, Western Michigan University

While the present age is one in which there is considerable interest expressed in the development of a theory or instruction, there is little concern for beginning the task by specifying the formal properties which should characterize such a theory. Yet, at the present time, it is probably much more important for professional educators to acquire some understanding of the nature of theory than it is to develop new theories of instruction. Scientists in the behavioral sciences have had to undertake a similar pause in their building endeavors and, during the last twenty years, have given extensive thought to the problem of why earlier psychological theories were inadequate and what formal properties these earlier

"Towards Taking the Fun Out of Building a Theory of Instruction" by Robert M. W. Travers is reprinted with permission from Teachers College Record, *68:49–60, October, 1966.*

theories lacked. Since there are many psychologists who have had a background in philosophy and many philosophers who study the products of psychologists, an enthusiastic group of well qualified persons has existed for the pursuit of these problems of metatheory. Bergman and Feigl in philosophy, Hull and Spence in experimental psychology, are the names of some of those who have pondered the problems of the inadequacy of early psychological theory and who have paved the way for future generations of theorists. A corresponding movement has not taken place in education with the result that while new theories of teaching are being produced these are not necessarily better theories unless one identifies progress with change. Indeed, the only group exploring the problems of criteria for evaluating theory of instruction at the present time appears to be the ASCD Commission on Theory of Instruction. Theorizing is fun so long as there are no standards involved. I predict that it is going to be much less fun in the future.

THEORIES
OF INSTRUCTION

Theories of instruction found in current literature seem to attempt to provide a set of propositions which are judged to represent an optimum set of learning conditions for achieving what the developer of the theory believes to be the worthy objectives of education. Now scientific theories are not generally focussed on optimum conditions although they occasionally are, but optimum conditions can generally be derived from the propositions which state the theory. The derivations of a set of propositions representing a theory is a compex task, but the production of a set of statements representing optimum conditions is likely to be even more complex.

A scientific theory involves a set of statements concerning the variables that enter into a particular phenomenon. When Count Rumford made the observation that there appeared to be some relationship between heat and work he laid the foundation for the development of a scientific theory of the relationship. Later it was shown that the quantity of heat produced was a function of two variables, *force* and *distance*, the product of which is known as *work*. The establishment of the values of these variables in a given situation permits the prediction of the quantity of heat that will be produced. Once these facts had been established, it became evident that there is no way of obtaining more than a given quantity of heat out of a given amount of work or vice versa. However, optimum con-

ditions for the useful conversion of the one into the other requires that a minimum of heat be needlessly dissipated in nonuseful ways in the process. The latter is the optimum condition for the useful transfer. Optimum conditions of various kinds derive from theories but are not the essence of scientific theories. I could not conceive of a theory of instruction which met acceptable scientific standards just specifying a set of optimum conditions. Indeed, the problem of establishing optimum conditions is likely to represent a much more difficult task than that of stating a theory of instruction.

THEORY
OF INSTRUCTION

I would conceive of a theory of instruction as consisting of a set of propositions stating relationships between, on the one hand, measures of the outcomes of education and, on the other hand, measures of both the conditions to which the learner is exposed and the variables representing characteristics of the learner. Crude types of theory have long been part of the literature of education, but the propositions they have involved have typically been intuitively derived and have not been based on carefully collected data.

In addition, unlike scientific theories current instructional theory involves a language derived from common usage, common forms of irrationally, obscure sources of philosophy, and superstitions which lead man to believe that by naming an obscure phenomenon it then becomes controllable. A major block in the development of a set of propositions or statements representing an instructional theory is that the technical language needed for such a task has not yet evolved. Much more will have to be said about this language problem in connection with the discussion of the independent variables of theories of instruction.

FREEDOM
FROM DATA

A theory of instruction, like a scientific theory, also has to have certain other characteristics. First, it has to be empirically based and the propositions of the theory must have a clear relation to data. While the late Clark Hull's theory of behavior[1] may not offer a convenient model of theory building in the area of instruction, it does provide an excellent example of how the propositions of a behavioral theory must be related to data. Now the data on which the propositions of an instructional theory would have to be based would be vastly different from those used by Hull and would involve an essentially different data language, but the Hull model still reflects a pattern of relating data to theoretical propositions which seems to me admirable. Too much in current educational theorizing involves the statement of propositions are supported by personal experience rather than by the kind of data on which scientists rely.

Much theorizing about instruction which receives widespread acclamation is extraordinarily data free and data uninhibited. Ausubel[2] has already carefully documented the lack of correspondence between the propositions advanced

by Jerome Bruner in various writings as a theory of instruction and the studies cited to support them. Bruner[3] seems to have circumvented this source of criticism in his more recent book by avoiding almost all reference to empirical studies. Indeed, he seems to be moving away from the development of a theory of instruction based on the scientific tradition, and one can predict with some confidence that the type of activity he proposes will long remain more popular than what is proposed here for it is much more fun. There is a place for the undisciplined roving imagination, but it is not in systematic theory construction. While data-free "theorizing" is popular, there is also another trend in the development of theory of instruction which is equally popular and equally misleading. This latter kind of theorizing is evident in the work of educational reformers with backgrounds in experimental research on reinforcement. The theories of instruction they have evolved generally include propositions based on data only very remotely related to the phenomena of the classroom, and the propositions appear to have only a metaphorical relationship to the laboratory derived generalizations from which they are presumably derived. The production of theory by metaphorical extension can be a dangerously misleading activity.

Second, a theory of instruction will have to represent the relationship between a wide range of learning conditions and achievements. Even theories of instruction which deal with very limited areas are likely to be complex in that they will probably involve many variables.

---

[1] Hull, C. L., *Principles of Behavior*. New York, Appleton-Century-Crofts, 1943.

[2] Ausubel, D. P., *The Psychology of Meaningful Verbal Learning*. New York, Grune and Stratton, 1963.

[3] Bruner, J. S., *Toward a Theory of Instruction*. Cambridge, Massachusetts, Harvard University Press, 1966.

Third, the optimum conditions would be those which maximized some function, say a linear function, of the measures of the variables defining the outcomes. The weight given to each variable would reflect a value judgment. In the case of a school program organized into subjects, presumably, the optimum levels for independent variables would be different for each subject-matter field.

Fourth, a theory of instruction of any value will have to be based on quantitative data, but these data will probably be reducible to a set of verbal nonmathematical propositions. This reducibility with little loss simply reflects the limitations of the data. This reduction of quantitative data to qualitative terms can be undertaken without loss because the constant needed for deriving a useful equation from the data cannot be established. This was the problem which Hull[1] encountered in the development of his behavior theory and which has since limited the use of the equations which he introduced in some of the propositions.

DEPENDENT VARIABLES

No theory of instruction, nor the deductions of optimum conditions, can have merit unless the dependent variables of the system are well defined. Since much of what is written on this subject seems to me to be misleading, I would like to comment on why it seems to be on the wrong track.

Merely writing operational definitions of our expected outcomes is not sufficient for the development of an instructional theory. Since Tyler[4] many years ago

[4] Tyler, R. W., *Constructing Achievement Tests.* Columbus, Ohio, Bureau of Educational Research, 1934.

wrote on the importance of defining educational objectives in behavioral terms, vast lists of behavioral outcomes have been prepared. Those who have engaged in this activity seem to agree both on the virtues of undertaking this task and also on the unwieldly and unuseable product which generally emerges from it. What is wrong with this procedure has only slowly become apparent though it has long been evident that something is wrong.

First, let me point out that it is misleading to say that the outcomes should be specified in terms of behavior, as if one were generally interested in the frequency of emission of a particular operant. It is much more precise to say that outcomes should be specified in terms of tasks problem situations and task solutions. The tasks may be anything from that of finding the sum of two numbers to situations which call for decisions reflecting attitudes and values. A task consists of a set of items of information S_1 to be received concerning the existence of a particular state of affairs. The task also provides cues concerning a situation S_2 that is to be produced through the behavior of the student. S_1 might consists of a paragraph of prose and a set of reading comprehension items, while S_2 indicates that the items are to be answered in such a way that the answers provide information consistent with that in the paragraph. Situation S_2 is generated by the behavior of the student. A useful taxonomy of objectives would involve a taxonomy of tasks. What I have said does not mean that educatinal goals do not refer to behavior for clearly they do, but the behavior involved is structured by the tasks and it is behavior in relation to the defining tasks that provide evidence whether a goal is or is not achieved. What I am proposing is a classification of tasks in terms of well-defined task characteristics.

A TAXONOMY OF TASKS

What I believe is needed is a taxonomy of tasks in which tasks are classified as well-defined task characteristics. Now task characteristics can be identified through two kinds of procedures. They may be identified and measured by an inspection of the task itself, as when one counts the number of words in a passage that the pupil is to read, or one can infer task characteristics by observing the responses of pupils to the task, as one would in finding out how long it takes a pupil to read the passage in comparison with other passages. In assessing task characteristics by observing the pupil one is assessing *response-inferred* characteristics. The taxonomy of tasks which appears to be needed for the construction of a theory of instruction would be one in which tasks were classified mainly in terms of the directly observable task characteristics. Response-inferred task characteristics would be avoided as far as possible. The distinction made here has long been recognized by experimental psychologists who prefer to use, wherever possible, direct measure of stimulus properties rather than response-inferred stimulus properties.

The taxonomies prepared by Bloom[5] and Krathwohl[6] are not really taxonomies at all in a scientific sense. They classify tasks in a crude way on the

[5] Bloom, B. S., *Taxonomy of Educational Objectives, Handbook I: The Cognitive Domain.* New York, Longmans Green, 1956.
[6] Krathwohl, D. R., Bloom, B. S., and Masia, B. B., *Taxonomy of Educational Objectives: The Classification of Educational Goals Handbook II: Affective Domain.* New York, David McKay Company, Inc., 1964.

basis of subjective judgment using categories such as knowledge, comprehension, interpretation, analysis, and so forth, derived from common language; but, unlike taxonomies evolved in the sciences, there appears to be no theoretical basis for the classification. These taxonomies are, I suspect, what Alfred North Whitehead had in mind when he said that taxonomies are the death of science, but there is also another reason why the procedures derived from the Bloom and Krathwohl ventures are of little use in the development of theory of instruction. Since the taxonomies classify tasks on a basis which lacks any established scientific utility, the application of the taxonomies results in a bulky and unmanageable collection of tasks which generally cannot be used for scientific purposes. The product which results is reminiscent of those bags of unsorted foreign postage stamps which philatelists like to rummage through in the hope of finding some rare item.

A SYSTEM OF SCALES

The mere fact that outcomes have been operationally defined does not imply that measurable variables exist which can be used to represent the degree to which the outcomes have been achieved. The tasks which define outcomes, before they can be of any particular value, must also have characteristics which permit them to be fitted into a system. The system into which tasks defining outcomes can be most profitably fitted would appear to be a system of scales. For example, if the tasks defining mathematics outcomes in the lower elementary grades can be arranged in order from those involving the addition of single digits to those involving the division of fractions, the extent to which this class of outcomes is achieved can be indicated by specifying the task in the series below which all tasks can be successfully completed and above which tasks cannot be completed. Thus the achievement of a group with respect to this group of outcomes can then be specified in a simple concise form. Most tasks which define outcomes cannot be fitted into such an ideal scale and scaling of tasks will have to be crude with a resulting crudeness of theory. Experience in test construction suggests that the ordering of tasks within subject-matter fields can be more readily undertaken than the ordering of tasks representing objectives that cross subject-matter fields. The scaling of the tasks which define outcomes would appear to be an essential operation for them to have any utility in building a theory of instruction. Such ordered systems of tasks then define the dependent variables of a theory of instruction. Proliferations of lists of tasks which cannot be ordered should be abandoned if only for the fact that they represent a mass of unmanageable rummage, but I also suspect that such tasks would reflect a high degree of specificity of learning and acquisitions which had little transfer value.

Some tasks defining outcomes organize rather well into scaled systems. Those related to mathematics do this extremely well. Almost as easily organized are those related to vocabulary development and spelling and perhaps knowledge related to some scientific areas. At the other extreme are those related to social studies which can hardly be arranged in any meaningful order representing a scale. I take this to mean, on the one hand, that there is no way at present of organizing the outcomes so that a meaningful variable or variables emerge,

and, on the other hand, that the teaching of social studies is not based on a recognition of certain structures within the knowledge itself which suggests how the subject matter has to be arranged. In contrast, mathematics, as a logically organized discipline, requires that at the elementary levels certain concepts be acquired before other concepts. It is this structure which prescribes the organization of the subject matter and which, in turn, makes it possible to arrange into ordered scales the tasks defining outcomes.

Before moving on to a consideration of the independent variables of instructional theory, there is another way of viewing what I have said here about the dependent variables. All outcomes of education can be viewed as the consequences of the production of rule-regulated behavior. Outcomes can be specified in terms of the rules that regulate behavior. These rules can represent narrow rules which specify the orderliness of behavior with respect to single very narrow tasks, in which case the outcomes of any educational program have to be specified in terms of a large number of rules. On the other hand, the rules may be broad in scope and refer to general lawfulnesses covering a wide range of tasks—in which case the objectives can be specified in terms of a set of relatively few rules. While procedures for defining objectives in the past have implied that many rules have to be specified, the proposal here is that these be organized into broader rules covering a wider range of events.

LANGUAGE AND VARIABLES

Language already available seems capable of taking us far in the development of the dependent variables of an educational theory. The long experience which psychologists have had in ordering and scaling tasks provides both the techniques needed for producing the necessary dimensions and also the vocabulary required for discussing the operations to be performed. In contrast, the independent variables of a theory of instruction cannot be discussed except in the most general terms at this time because of a lack of the emergence of a technical vocabulary. The special vocabularies used by some writers on instructional theory bear a much closer resemblance to the language of theology than the technical language of science.

For example, it is my judgment that most of the chapters, although not all, in the 1966 Yearbook of the Association for Supervision and Curriculum Development (Waetjen, W.B., Chairman)[7] are written largely in the language of contemporary theology; but I think it lacks the discipline that most contemporary theologians display. At least a part of the yearbook and many other contemporary documents on instructional theory are sermons on the good life and do not deal with the world as the scientist knows it. One finds some of the chapters loaded with such terms as "self-actualization," "self-identity," "experience," "awareness," "a sense of universality," "self-exploration," "fulfillment education," "insight," "enlightenment," and "eupsychian growth" (Yes, that word is really there in print). One inherent limitation of such a language is that it contains very large numbers of primitive terms which cannot be defined operationally. While a statement of an empirically derived theory of instruction must include some primitive terms, the number of these must be kept to a mini-

mum and the remainder should be tied to publicly observable operations. In keeping with the high concentration of primitive terms is a lack of reference to documented empirical findings, for the ideas flow from one set of primitive terms to another set of primitive terms. One is hardly surprised by the fact that in one of the chapters less than ten percent of the references used to support the theory of instruction presented represent empirical research.

The lack of an appropriate technical language for stating a theory of instruction vastly impedes progress and also reflects why a theory of instruction, with desirable formal properties, has not arisen.

If Isaac Newton had been assigned the task of improving the ways of constructing bridges in his day or of developing a theory of bridge construction, he could not have begun this task with the language and concepts used by bridge builders. The concepts and related language which proved to be of value for this purpose were those of the *Principia* which, today, still form the basis of the study of mechanics by engineering students. Concepts such as force, mass, center of gravity, and equilibrium are necessary for the solution of problems related to bridges. Once these were evolved Newton was able to develop a theory of mechanics and to construct a bridge in terms of the principles. He did actually build a bridge which still bears the weight of those who wish to cross the river Cam. Our problems related to a lack of an appropriate technical language in education are also highly reminiscent of the comments made by Lavoisier 200 years ago on the hopeless inadequacy of the language of chemistry in his day for developing knowledge. He pointed out that chemical nomenclature involved such terms as "flowers of

[7] Waetjen, W. B. (Editor), *Learning and Mental Health in the School.* Washington, D.C., Association for Supervision and Curriculum Development, 1966.

sulphur" and "oil of vitriol" while these substances could not in any way be considered as flowers or oil. Neither was there any imaginary substance called phlogiston. One of Lavoisier's great contributions was the development of a technical language of chemistry which permitted the propositions of the science to be stated in clear and precise terms, and even permitted him to write chemical equations. How can we, in education, evolve a vocabulary of terms suitable for constructing a theory of instruction?

ON BORROWING TERMS

One solution to our problem of lack of vocabulary is to borrow terms and the concepts they represent from related areas which have a higher degree of technical development than the one under consideration. An attempt to perform such a borrowing has been made by Maccia et al.,[8] at Ohio State University. In this connection the latter group have attempted to use, for example, the language of general systems theory as a data language for discussing the independent variables of instructional theory. While explorations of this kind should be undertaken, I do not see them leading to the identification of variables that can at present be regarded as the core of a theory of instruction. The variables turn out to be hypothetical rather than ones which can be operationally defined in terms of useable measuring instruments. The resulting theory appears to have the deficiency of being only remotely related to data. It represents the meta-

[8] Maccia, E. S., Maccia, G. S., and Jewett, R. E., Construction of Educational Theory Models Ohio State University, mimeographed, 1963.

phorical extension of the ideas of one field to another. Such metaphorical extensions must not be confused with legitimate scientific generalizations.

Analytic approaches have obviously evolved languages of a kind, but these have not turned out to be particularly useful for theory construction. While Newton could evolve a technical language for physics as he worked on his manuscript, he was able to do this partly because of the immense amount of empirical data that had already been acquired on the motions of heavenly bodies. The evolution of a language for stating a theory of instruction would appear to require the medium of empirical research. Components of such a language appears to be evolving in such varied work as that of Arno Bellack, Marie Hughes, John Atkinson, B. F. Skinner, Hilda Taba, B. O. Smith and others. One can also point to much armchair activity evolving the contemporary form of educational language which is quite useless for our purpose.

INDEPENDENT VARIABLES

The major independent variables can be conveniently classified into four main classes: pupil variables, pupil task variables, teacher variables, and teacher task variables. There are some other variables such as temperature, lighting, and so forth, which probably have less impact and which I am inclined to ignore at this time. Other classifications are, of course, possible. Pupil variables need not be discussed extensively here because the literature that exists on the subject is already extensive. The only point I want to make is that the pupil variables which are introduced into a theory should be measureable variables and not the hypothetical variables they are in some current theories of teaching.

For example, some current educational literature assumes the existence of a general creativity variable, yet the correlations between different tests of creativity are so small that no variable representing a general creativity factor makes any sense. Again, those who build a theory of instruction around the Guilford[9] model of human abilities are committing the error of introducing large numbers of hypothesized variables which cannot be measured, have no known relationship to human learning, and which may well have little impact on behavior. The wish-it-were type of variable has to be avoided. I think we also have to avoid the current cliché which proposes that the concept of *uniqueness* should replace that of *individual differences*. In my judgment, if uniqueness involves the representation of different individuals in different hyperspaces (that is to say each is described in terms of a different set of variables) then a theory of teaching becomes virtually impossible to develop, as does a science of psychology. This issue was discussed and I think settled over thirty years ago by Allport[10] who first noted the fact that the assumption of individual uniqueness, in the sense under discussion, must lead the psychologist to conclude that psychology as a science cannot be developed. Current educational literature which discusses the issue of uniqueness typically fails to recognize the fact that the problem was explored by outstanding scholars a generation ago and that the implications of this doctrine have been quite clearly stated.

[9] Guilford, J. P., Intelligence. *American Psychologist*. 1966, 21, 20–26.
[10] Allport, G. W., *Personality: A Psychological Interpretation*. New York, Holt, 1937.

There is also another sense in which individuals may be considered to be unique. This is the sense in which all individuals can be represented by different points in a common hyperspace, that is to say, all individuals can be described in terms of the same set of variables but each represents a different combination of values with respect to these variables. In his sense, the problem of uniqueness does not represent insuperable difficulties to the development of a theory of instruction.

PUPIL TASK VARIABLES

Pupil task variables are obviously of immense importance and a focus of central interets in any theory of instructions. These are the variables which describe the tasks which the pupil encounters. They include such variables as reading difficulty level, density of information transmission, sequencing variables, content variables, many of which are time variables (such as how much time is devoted to particular aspects of study, to scientific experimentation, to artistic production,) and many other categories. Here again, one must point out that task variables should be, as far as possible, measured directly, and that one should avoid the use of response-inferred task variables, just as the experimental psychologist attempts to avoid what he calls response-inferred stimulus variables. The crucial importance of these variables stems from the fact that these are the variables that teachers and supervisors can change and manipulate so that they attain optimum values for learning. I think that all the evidence available indicates that teachers are much more likely to be able to control effectively the characteristics of the tasks on which pupils work than they are the characteristics of their own behavior. Modification of pupil tasks is no threat to the teacher's ego but a requirement that the teacher's behavior be modified is obviously a threat.

There are many good candidates for task variables in addition to those I have mentioned, and some have long been proposed by practitioners. For example, Madame Montessori suggested that the child be exposed first to a wide range of simple stimuli and slowly be introduced to the more complex. Again, she suggested that simple discriminations be followed by more complex discriminations. Psychologists who specialize in perception have long proposed a variable of perceptual complexity. Piaget introduces, as have others, the concrete-abstract dimension for describing pupil tasks.

LEARNER CHARACTERISTICS

One may note that, in the actual design of educational materials, the task variables that are taken into account are those which are related to learning and which, hence, are related to learner characteristics. Much of my objection to the concept of a classroom as a computer-based teaching machine stems from a belief that the task characteristics of the computer-based classroom are not compatible with what we know about learner characteristics. For example, I believe that there is considerable evidence that effective learning in the elementary school has to be highly tied to concrete situations which the pupil himself can manipulate. I do not see the computer providing tasks that have that kind of characteristic. In addition the striking control over behavior which can be exercised by the

introduction of new and odd objects which can be handled, manipulated, speculated about, investigated, and so forth, is lost in a computer run classroom. With a few notable exceptions, the characteristic which should probably characterize the tasks of the elementary school child do not appear to lie within the capability of the computer. At higher levels of education there may be greater justification for the computer-based task, although at those levels I would have other questions to raise.

TEACHER BEHAVIOR

As soon as we move to the teacher aspects of the classroom world, we are forced sooner or later to deal with some awkward questions about how to treat the phenomena referred to as teaching methods, styles of teaching, or whatever name one prefers for this class of phenomena. The empirical existence of a pattern of teaching is, I presume, demonstrated by the presence of a common set of rules regulating the behavior of two or more teachers. While hypothetical patterns of behavior which follow certain stated rules can be concocted, the value of writing descriptions of the hypothetical behavior of hypothetical teachers can be looked upon with skepticism. The simulation of such concoctions may not be within human capability. In addition, even the best intentioned attempts to act out the behaviors presented by such concoctions may not be successful. A theory of instruction if it is based on empirical data would probably have to begin by being limited in scope to those forms of rule-regulated behavior that can be observed at this time.

The rules regulating teacher behavior one presumes were partially derived from such diverse influences as the behavior of those teachers to which he, the teacher, had been exposed as a child, events in teacher training, ego defense mechanisms, the immediate pressures of the culture, the controlling effects of syllabi, the controlling effects of pupils and principals. This vast diversity might lead one to conclude that the behavior of each teacher is unique, in the sense that the behavior of no two teachers can be described in terms of the same set of attributes, but empirical evidence such as that collected by Ryans[11] leads to the conclusion that much of teacher behavior can be described in terms of relatively few dimensions and that the unique attributes are, perhaps, of much less significance than are the common attributes which permit us to represent all teachers as separate and distinct points within the same hyperspace. In the Ryans study, three general classes of regularities of teacher behavior emerge. These pertain to scales broadly described as warm vs. aloof, businesslike vs. unplanned, and stimulating vs. dull. While evidence of the relationship of these variables to pupil learning is far from as clear as one would like to have it, some kind of a case could still be developed for including these variables in a theory of instruction. Clearly, other teacher-related variables would have to be included and many of these derive from the tasks which the teacher engages in. Teachers obviously differ in the extent to which they engage in such tasks as informing, demonstrating, controlling pupil movements, listening, questioning, and many others. These I refer to as teacher task variables. Extent

of participation in such tasks has been studied extensively by those engaged in interaction analysis. The work of Bellack, Hughes and others would appear to be leading towards the identification of variables which would have to be included in any theory of instruction.

Teaching methods as they are described in textbooks and as they are observed in schools differ in the amount of time the teacher devotes to different tasks in the classroom. One presumes that, for the achievement of particular objectives, there is an optimum distribution of the teacher's time across the different tasks. The optimum could be derived from the same data that would be used for developing a theory of instruction. While it is obvious that the optimum time distribution must vary from hour to hour, one can reasonably assume that over long periods, such as a semester, the optimum time distribution would show stable characteristics. If a theory of instruction were available to provide the relationship of time distribution to the achievement of particular outcomes, techniques would be available for calculating optimum time distributions. The problem is mathematically complicated, but soluble, and takes the form of what mathematicians have called the transportation problem. The latter problem and its solution arose in a wartime context in which a decision had to be made concerning optimum use of shipping space for guns, rounds of ammunition, personnel, food, general equipment, clothing and so forth. Clearly, some balance of these categories has to be achieved in order to provide, say, maximum military effort at the final port to which it is all shipped; this is very much like distributing the teacher's time in an optimum way over different tasks in order to produce maximum achievement of some kind. Mathematicians

11 Ryans, D. G. *Characteristics of Teachers.* Washington, D.C., American Council on Education, 1960.

undertaking operations research have developed a solution for this kind of problem which should be useful when someone in education becomes interested in it. The solution, of course, could be applied only after the collection of extensive data.

FOR LIMITED EXPLORATIONS

Now it is quite clear that a comprehensive theory of instruction of the kind I have envisaged has to be far in the future. In the meantime, I hope that those interested in this ultimate venture will abandon the present language of instructional theory, despite its popular appeal, and begin to experiment with the development of a technical language. Theories of instruction cannot be developed as a global whole, and, hence, effort should be made to derive from data miniature theories of aspects of the instructional program. I hope that none will consider such limited explorations of theory construction as being beneath their dignity. I suspect that data are sufficient in the area of reading to derive a set of propositions relating some of the independent and dependent variables described here. The latter area is also one where some significant pupil task variables have been developed, and a fairly adequate technical vocabulary has evolved in terms of which the problems can be discussed. In the development of such miniature theories, every proposition should be presented together with a summary of the data on which it is based and proper documentation should be provided concerning the source of the data. The propositions representing such a theory would not have the exotic qualities of Jerome Bruner's speculations which have nice literary color, immense public appeal and widespread influence but they have no place in our kind of activity. There is a place for romantic speculation, but it is not here. The activity proposed is a painstaking and tedious activity and, as I pointed out earlier, much less "fun" than much so-called theory building of the past, but it is the kind of tedious empirically-oriented work that is likely to bring advances in the development of a theory of instruction.

THE PRETHEORETICAL

There are other areas too where some beginnings could be made in developing limited, but clearly stated, formal theories. Examples of such areas include such diverse items as foreign language learning, and the development of logical thinking, and the acquisition of motor skills. I think that at this state of theory development, which some would call pretheoretical development, one will have to make many simplifying assumptions in order to be able to construct a theory at all. In addition, in the application of any limited theory one would also have to introduce additional simplifying assumptions. Suppose, for example, a theory of teaching reading specified that the level of skill acquired was related to the initial level of perceptual development X and a dimension of teacher behavior Y. Now suppose also that a deduction from the theory was that, for optimum learning conditions to occur, teachers should reflect high scores on Y if the level of X, the pupil's perceptual skill, were low. In the application of such a theory, or the deductions from it, one would probably have to assume that the teacher had highly reliable information concerning the status of each pupil with respect to his perceptual skills. The data actually available would probably not be very reliable.

Finally, I would like to make a few points about the application of theories of instruction or deductions from them. First, let me also dispose of a common fallacy which is that the development of a theory of instruction would necessarily result in improved control over the instructional process and hence improve teaching. Many scientific theories do not result in improved control. Kepler's discovery of the lawfulness of the motions of the planets did not result in any control. A theory of instruction might have to postulate that much of the process was controlled by highly stable teacher characteristics which teacher training can do little to change. Even those who today write theories of instruction in the format of a sermon must concede that exposure to sermons does not necessarily make for better ways of living.

Second, from what one can see at this time, theories of instruction which satisfy the kinds of criteria, which the ASCD Commission on Theory of Instruction has developed, are not likely to be particularly enlightening to teachers until teacher training is vastly changed.

One can perhaps reflect on the fact that while Newtonian physics introduced a revolution in bridge design, there was probably not a single bridge builder for 100 years after Newton who had the education necessary to apply Newtonian physics to practical problems of bridge design. The phenomena of instruction are clearly of sufficient complexity that they will not yield concise simple propositions which any teacher can take with her to the classroom. The formulation of a scientific theory is perhaps a long step from any practical application.

Finally, appreciation is expressed for the help provided by my colleague Dr. David Adams who reviewed an early version of the manuscript, and to the Curriculum Professor's Meeting in San Francisco that provided a sounding board for many of the ideas.

14.

Criteria for Assessing
The Formal Properties of
Theories of Instruction

ASCD COMMISSION ON INSTRUCTIONAL THEORY

The criteria presented below include those which apply to the analysis of any scientific theory. They have been made particularly applicable to instruction through the illustrative material. For convenience, they are presented in outline form.

I. A statement of an instructional theory* should include a set of postu-

"Criteria for Assessing the Formal Properties of Theories of Instruction" by the *ASCD Commission on Instructional Theory* is reprinted with permission from Ira J. Gordon, editor, Criteria for Theories of Instruction. *Washington, D.C.: Association for Supervision and Curriculum Development, 1968, Reprinted with permission of the Association for Supervision and Curriculum Development and Ira J. Gordon, Chairman of the Commission. Copyright © 1968 by the Association for Supervision and Curriculum Development. The members of the Commission: Ira J. Gordon, Chairman; Nicholas Fattu; Marie M. Hughes; Grace Lund; E. Brooks Smith; Robert M. W. Travers. The selection here is from pp. 16–24: Chapter 3 of the booklet.*

* On page 3 of the booklet the ASCD Commission writes:

lates and definition of terms involved in these postulates. Pupil, goal, and instructional characteristics should be operationally defined. The theory should include a minimum number of primitive terms which cannot be defined

In this document the term *theory* is used as it is used in the natural sciences to represent a set of interrelated generalizations derived from data, which permit some degree of prediction or control over the phenomena to which they pertain. Thus, a *theory of instruction* would be represented by a set of statements, based on sound replicable research, which would permit one to predict how particular changes in the educational environment (classroom setting) would affect pupil learning.

In this document the word *instruction* refers to the activity which takes place during schooling and within the classroom setting. The term includes both material and human variables. Instruction is differentiated from teaching in that instruction encompasses more of the situational elements. Teaching refers primarily to the human interaction between teacher and pupil. [Ed.]

("experience," "awareness," "real self," "process").

The diagram on this page indicates the network of interrelations between pupil, instructional situation, and goal characteristics. Each of these sets of characteristic needs to be explicated.

A. The pupil characteristics must be specified together with the relationship they have to the goals. The characteristics must be demonstrated as related to learning. If one is developing a theory of reading instruction for sighted pupils, visual form discrimination is a relevent variable; if one is developing a theory of instruction in reading for blind pupils, tactile two-point threshold (at the finger tips) is a relevant variable. The following are some of the dimensions of pupil characteristics which could be specified:

1. Biosocial variables: age, sex, social class, level of physical maturity.
2. Psychological variables: level of intellectual development, academic achievement, cognitive style, self-concept, achievement motivation.

B. The characteristics of the instructional situations must be specified together with the relationship they have to goals. For example, if the goal is the ability to ask questions, then the situation should involve practice in ques-

Pupil Characteristics   Instructional Situation
Characteristics

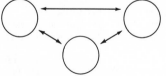

Goal Characteristics

tioning. However, the relationship need not be logical, but must have some rationale. Ability to play scales on the piano rapidly, relates to practice, but practice focusing on accuracy, done

slowly, rather than speed. The following are some of the dimensions which could be specified:

1. Organizational variables: time, space, class size, class composition.
2. Content variables: tasks, media, sequence
3. Teacher behavior variables: acts the teacher is directed to perform, management techniques
4. Teacher personality variables: warmth, openness, control, style.

In addition, the characteristics of the instructional situations must be specified together with the relationship they have to pupil characteristics. In learning an abstract concept in science, for example, the younger the child, the more the abstract terms of the concept have to be derived from concrete situations. A child cannot be expected to master an abstract idea before the concrete groundwork has been laid.

C. Goal characteristics should be dimensionalized. That is, objectives should be described in terms of change with respect to specified dimensions. The outcomes should be specified along a scale. These outcomes are describable as performances on a task. For our purposes, a task specifies the kinds of actions which have to be undertaken to reach a goal. In economics, for example, the task may be to handle the variety of equations utilizing the concepts of C for consumer, I for business investment, G for government, F for foreigners, and the sum of these, GNP, Gross National Product. In Suchman's work using "discrepant event," a task is to ask questions; a goal is to learn how to ask questions.

An objective might be that a child would read each month one book of his own choice from the school library, or the objectives could be multidimensional. For example, at the end of period X of time, a given child should be able to read Y type of material, at a given level of speed with a stated level of comprehension.

Again, it must be stated that these objectives must take into account pupil variables, so that the economics task may be specified for pupils of a given age, level of achievement, etc., rather than necessarily being for all children.

An illustration of the relationship between pupil characteristics and goals may be drawn from The Joint Council on Economic Education Program.[1] The statement of the Council's goals for the elementary level gives an indication concerning the nature of the child. It holds that:

The main purpose of economic education in a free society is to develop the problem-solving ability of our children as it relates to personal and social problems, basically economic in nature. To accomplish this purpose we must:

1. Develop the child's analytic ability
2. Help the child relate his everyday experiences to the big world around him. Even a first-grade child has economic decisions to make.

The child is thus seen as a problem solver, and, more than that, someone who is concerned with utilizing academic concepts to handle his daily needs. "It is important that elementary teachers, supervisors, and school administrators take full advantage of the intellectual curiosity of children. Children are yearning to be identified with the world around them. They should be given that opportunity" (p. 19). A cursory view of the various ideas and concepts to be developed at the elementary, junior, and senior high levels indicates a belief in development of the child from someone who can deal with materials only at a concrete, highly personalized, immediate perception level to a youngster who can relate abstract concepts to other abstract concepts, who can analyze "big ideas," who can engage in the utilization of abstract symbols.

D. A change in pupil characteristics leads to change in instructional situation characteristics. A theory needs to specify how, as pupils progress toward goals, the instructional situation has to change. For example, as the pupil masters vocabulary, the level of the vocabulary used should change. This may be expressed as follows:

$$Pc = f(I)$$

Pupil change is a function of instruction

$$\Delta Pc = \Delta I$$

Increments in pupil change are related to changes in instruction.

The relationships among goal characteristics, instructional situation characteristics, and pupil characteristics may be seen in the work of Montessori.[2]

In defining her goal of educating the senses, Maria Montessori states that the aim is "the refinement of the differential perception of stimuli by means of repeated exercises" (p. 173). One dimension of this goal is to educate the eye to the different perceptions of dimen-

[1] Joint Council on Economic Education. *Teachers Guide to Developmental Economic Education Program.* New York: the Council, 1964. Copyright © 1964 Joint Council on Economic Education and reproduced with their permission.

[2] Maria Montessori. *The Montessori Method.* New York: Schocken Books, Inc., 1964. Reprinted by permission. Schocken Books, Inc.

sions (p. 169). The young child notes different dimensions of solid geometric forms and compares various sizes. He "observes the relationships between the size of the opening in a mould and that of the object which he is to place in the mould" (pp. 100–170). This aspect of the goal of sense education is achieved when the child correctly places the solid geometric forms in the appropriate moulds.

She describes the teacher's role and the didactic materials. The directress makes a pedagogical experiment with a didactic object and awaits the spontaneous reactions of the child (p. 167). The child is caused to exercise the senses (p. 168). With little children, the directress must proceed to the making of trials, and must select the didactic materials in which they show themselves interested (p. 168). The directress presents didactic materials made up of graded stimuli. These provoke auto-education (p. 169).

The didacic object is a block in which solid geometric forms are set.

Into corresponding holes in the block are set ten little wooden cylinders the bases diminishing gradually about three millimetres. The game consists in taking the cylinders out of their places, putting them on the table, mixing them, and then putting each one back in its own place (p. 169).

If he mistakes, placing one of the objects in an opening that is too small for it, he takes it away, and proceeds to make various trials, seeking the proper opening. If he makes a contrary error, letting the cylinder fall into an opening that is a little too large for it, and then collects all the successive cylinders in openings just a little too large for it, he will find himself at the last with the big cylinder in his hand while only the smallest opening is empty. The didactic material *controls every error*. The child proceeds to cor-

rect himself, doing this in various ways. The normal child always repeats the exercise with growing interest (p. 171).

Pupil characteristics which Maria Montessori recognizes, and which might be stated as postulates, are:

1. Little children of two or three years take the greatest pleasure, a spontaneous lively interest, in arranging objects.
2. The young child can perfect himself through his own efforts and without teacher intervention. He is capable of auto-correction and auto-education.
3. Learning proceeds first by perceiving objects and then by understanding motor activities in relation to the objects.
4. Effective use of the senses requires that they be educated.
5. The education of the senses precedes the learning of the names of sensory attributes.

Although these postulates may lack adequate empirical support in contemporary psychology, they illustrate the type of statement which needs to be made in a theory of instruction.

Ausubel's[3] derivatives from Piagetian theory, in which Ausubel postulates that when pupils reach formal operational level of thought they can be instructed more didactically, is another example. Gagne's[4] steps in learning are more formal examples of sequence.

[3] David P. Ausubel. *The Psychology of Meaningful Verbal Learning.* New York: Grune & Stratton, Inc., 1963.

[4] R. M. Gagne. *The Conditions of Learning.* New York: Holt, Rinehart & Winston, Inc., 1965.

II. The statement of an instructional theory or sub-theory should make explicit the boundaries of its concern and limitations under which it is proposed. Theories can be so generally stated that they lose relevance by trying to incorporate the universe. For example, when a theory of conditioning is stretched so far as to include not only psychomotor learning but also literary production, the S-R representation becomes complex to the point of absurdity. It is not a useful theory for predicting such a phenomenon and should be limited to smaller step-like aspects of learning in which conditioning can be plotted within observable boundaries.

An instructional theory which postulates that being taught by a discovery method will produce inquiry in the children should specify:

A. A limited goal, the special type of inquiry to be gained by the children.

B. A particular group type of children, their age and similarity of cultural-social background.

C. A defined instructional situation, materials and the way they are to be used in open ended or directed fashion.

A theory of teaching inquiry could be overly general if it did not, for example, make a limiting statement about the developmental characteristics of the pupils. Discovery strategies that stress formal logical abstraction are not likely to apply at earlier levels where concrete operational thinking is more likely to occur. Teaching inquiry becomes as meaningless as teaching to satisfy children's needs when globally stated.

The way "need theory" is used in many educational circles is a prime example of meaningless generalized explanation that comes from speculating without stating limits or boundaries. In any event, what is proposed must be encompassed by a description of bounds or the theory begins to leak either because too many factors become uncontrollable or because the theory has to be stretched beyond reason to embrace the growing examples of deviant phenomena.

III. A theoretical construction must have internal consistency—a logical set of interrelationships. If a theory has a postulate that the control of learning resides within the learner, it cannot follow it with a second postulate specifying that certain aspects of teacher behavior will influence learning. The inconsistency can be resolved by moving to an interaction theory, which specifies limited control both internal and external to the learner.

IV. An instructional theory should be congruent with empirical data. If the facts from modern investigations of language and linguistics say that vowels change their sounds depending on the consonants before and after them, and upon the dialect of a speech community, then a theory for teaching phonics based on these present discoveries cannot assume that any set number of graphemes can be taught to equal the sounds of the vowels. Yet the Initial Teaching Alphabet instructional system does exactly that.

Propositions of the theory should be properly derived from the data on which they are based. It is of crucial importance to a scientific theory that it be based on data. Each generalization that constitutes a segment of an educational theory must be based on specific protocol statements derived from specific studies. The statement of the theory should be properly documented so that the reader can go back and examine the protocol statements and the data on which the protocol statements are based.

Some contemporary theorizing about

education is completely undocumented and some is even in a worse way in that the references cited to support the postulates of the theory bear little relationship to the generalizations they are claimed to support. Accurate documentation of the sources of evidence on which a theory is based and a credible relationship between the evidence and the theoretical position is a minimum requirement for any scientific theory. Since the development of generalizations from data involves inductive inference, an element of judgment is always involved, and the boundaries of the generalizations thus derived must always be established through further empirical studies.

Personal experience and single case histories are not generally admissable as evidence to support the propositions of a theory. In addition, evidence remote from the generalization should not be introduced, for it can lead to false generalization. For example, much that has been written about the theory of instruction on which teaching machines are based stresses the importance of immediacy of feedback—a position derived from experiments with subhuman subjects. Yet the more recent evidence derived from experiments with human subjects indicates that immediacy of feedback is generally unimportant in concept learning.

V. An instructional theory must be capable of generating hypotheses. If a theory is written in broad terms, poorly defined, it may not be possible to see how aspects of it can be tested. The postulates have to be stated in such a way that hypotheses clearly present themselves. For example, if we look at the model presented at the beginning of the chapter, a whole host of hypotheses are derivable from postulates which state interrelationships among the variables. One such hypothesis might be of the order: Given the goal of developing analytical ability in relation to concept A in social studies, when first graders of average intelligence in a suburban school are presented series X, Y, Z of concrete operations and receive instructions of the type B, C, D from a female teacher located at point E on a circumflex measure of control and warmth, the concept will be attained more efficiently than when taught in other sequences by other teachers.

Of course, for the sake of brevity, the "other" conditions are not specified here, nor are the substantive statements which would take the place of the symbols used above. That would depend upon the theory. The further elaboration of how location of the teacher on the scale, and efficiency, and "receive instructions" are measured would also need to be spelled out in the design. The point is that any instructional theory must lend itself to such statements.

VI. An instructional theory must contain generalizations which go beyond the data. Unless links can be made between the findings of a particular investigation and other investigations, the work does not lend itself to prediction. The power of a concept, or generalization, is that it allows one to deal with unknown events on the basis of known classes. The power of a theory is enhanced only when one can make predictions in like manner. The accumulated bits and pieces of empirical studies only gain utility when they can be interwoven into a set of generalizations at a higher level of abstraction than the conclusions themselves.

VII. An instructional theory must be verifiable. As stated in the first chapter, one of the problems is the language in which postulates or hypotheses are stated. If the terms are ambiguous, then data collection is difficult. There are other problems. It is possible for all the terms to be stated properly, but data to be unobtainable. For example, "When the child is given complex learning tasks, his brain increases its capacity for learning through altered chemistry." It is demonstrable in rats that early complex training leads to higher brain weight and increased secretion of chlorinesterase, but is not demonstrable in humans. Reasoning by analogy does not meet the test of this criterion.

VIII. An instructional theory must be stated in such a way that it is possible to collect data to disprove it. The statement of terms may be tautological, that is, the reasoning may be circular. For example, if reinforcement is defined, in such a way that it is always possible to read its presence in the theory, or if perception is always inferable from behavior, then it is impossible to test some basic postulates from learning theory or perceptual psychology. If one says, "Pupil classroom behavior is a function of teacher personality," he may be expressing a truism, but one that cannot really be tested in the form stated.

IX. An instructional theory must not only explain past events but also must be capable of predicting future events. Many personality theories have been historical in their approach, reading behavior backwards. For example, in psychoanalytic theory, the present behavior of an adult is seen as a function of particular classes of events in his past. The connections are often tenuous, with many missing links. Even if demonstrable, the theory serves to explain how a person became what he is, rather than predicting what he will become in the future.

In instructional theory, if *post hoc* reasoning is used to explain results of investigation, or if one can only go backwards with it, the power of the theory is greatly reduced. Explaining student performance is insufficient; prediction is necessary. It should not be assumed that this means a belief in determinism, or simple antecedent-consequent relations, but rather that predictions must be made concerning the probabilities of a given change in student performance under stated conditions.

X. At the present time, instructional theories may be expected to represent qualitative synthesis. Ultimately, a theory should be expressed in terms of quantitative relationships among variables. Propositions in educational theories may be expected at this time to appear in the general form "Increments in condition X produce increments in achievement Y in pupils characterized by attributes A, B, C, etc." In such a statement, X may be an attribute of teacher behavior, such as how frequently he makes rewarding statements, or it may refer to a property of the physical learning situation such as how frequently the pupil encounters a particular word in context. Y is a measure of achievement derived from a test, an observation procedure, a spontaneous product or whatever else is appropriate.

The statements will indicate virtually nothing about the size of the increment in the one variable that will produce a particular increment in the other variable. In this respect, the statements of any theory of instruction that is likely to be evolved lack precision. However, there are immense difficulties in the way of producing statements for a theory of instruction that have greater precision. The major difficulty is the lack of an appropriate system of units for measuring the variables involved. Insofar as a theory is needed as a general guide to action, qualitative statements could be sufficiently precise. Indeed, little might be gained if the statements of the theory were transformed into more precise mathematical relationships. Although research workers have hopes that the qualitative generalizations that they derive from research may someday be refined to the point where they may assume the form of mathematical equations, many would doubt whether this hope can ever be realized.

section five

Suggested Theories of Teaching:

Overview

It is necessary in introducing this section to remind the reader that parts of several other selections in this book rightfully belong here, i.e., Smith in Section Two and Ryans in Section Four.

The selections in this section deal with the topic of theories of teaching in that they present theories or models of teaching. (These two words, theory and model, often are used interchangeably. Those who do not interchange them at least accept them as closely related.) Obviously, these articles are to be read in light of the articles in the previous section which treated the characteristics of a theory of teaching, the different types of theory, and the criteria for assessing a theory of teaching.

The reader is asked several questions: Do these various suggested theories, separately or together, fulfill the need for a theory of teaching? Do the various suggested theories meet the criteria presented by ASCD Commission or Travers or Newsome or Rose (in Ryans' article) or Maccia? Do they try to meet those criteria? Do they accept those criteria as criteria to be met? It will become obvious that the reader has the task of keeping track of the different ways in which the same words are used (for example, instruction).

These seven selections can be conveniently divided into the three types of theory suggested in the overview to the previous section, though the fit may not be perfect: (1) axiomatic; (2) inductive; and (3) philosophical. The first type includes the articles by Henderson and Maccia. Henderson presents a theory based on logic and uses set relationships. Via algebraic-like notations Henderson presents the triadic aspect of teaching in abstract form. It is well to ask if and how Henderson's components are similar to those presented by Hyman in Section Two and Martin in Section Six. If they are not the same, in which ways do they differ? What does Henderson gain by stating the components as he does? The reader is asked to compare Henderson's variable y with the set of teachable items presented by Pincoffs in Section Six.

Maccia's article is a bridge between axiomatic theory and inductive theory. It is based on a graph theory (which is mathematical) as the author herself acknowledges. Hence, her eight figures manifest the graph theory basis. Maccia then builds upon this mathematical theory to talk about group life, including group dynamics, a part of the social sciences. Maccia's key term is "influence," certainly a fundamental term in the field of political science. Several questions arise. How does Maccia's "instruction" compare with Green's, Macdonald's and that of the NSSE Committee as specified in the overview to Section Three? How does her "rule-governed behavior" compare with Green's concept of rule-governed action as presented in Section Two? Is her "pupil problem solver" similar to the pupil in Dewey's mutual inquiry theory as depicted by Walton in this Section? The reader is asked, naturally, to answer Maccia's own five questions, listed early in her article, so as to be able to draw a conclusion at the end of the article as requested.

The second type of selection includes the articles by Bruner and Strasser. These two approach the construction of a theory of teaching from an empirical social science perspective. Bruner's article is his earliest attempt to deal with a theory of teaching, and it serves as the explicit basis of his later work. Here he does not deal with a specific academic field as he does in his later work.[1] The reader is alerted to several points. First, Bruner's labels of prescriptive theory and descriptive theory differ somewhat from those of the other authors. Second, this article is the attempt at theorizing Travers attacks in his article in Section Four. Is Travers' criticism accepted by the reader? Third, Bruner comes to the topic of a theory of teaching with the perspective of an empirical psychologist long involved in the issues related to learning theory. Perhaps it is for this reason that three of the four elements Bruner includes in a theory stem so clearly from the field of psychology.

This leads to a basic question: Why are there only these four elements in Bruner's theory of teaching? Are these four necessary? Are these four sufficient? If there are other elements, what might they be? Ausubel,[2] another psychologist, in commenting on Bruner's work suggests such ele-

---

[1] Jerome S. Bruner. "Some Theorems on Instruction Illustrated with Reference to Mathematics," in *Theories of Learning and Instruction*, ed. Ernest R. Hilgard, The Sixty-third Yearbook of The National Society for the Study of Education, Part I (Chicago: The National Society for the Study of Education, 1964), pp. 306–35 and *Toward a Theory of Instruction* (Cambridge, Mass.: Harvard University Press, 1966).

[2] David P. Ausubel, "Review of *Toward a Theory of Instruction, Harvard Educational Review*, 36 (Summer 1966), 337–40.

ments as the learner's cognitive maturity and intellectual ability, his subject
matter sophistication, the organizational properties of his existing structure
of knowledge, relevant aspects of his personality and cognitive style, practice,
step size, pacing, peer group and social variables, the teacher's personality
and instructional style, and teaching aids.

Bruner states that he does not have a tested theory of instruction. How
would we test Bruner's proposed theory? The answer is important, for
Bruner repeats his famous but untested hypothesis about teaching any
subject to anybody at any age in some form that is honest.[3]

Strasser, the curriculum worker, presents an interesting contrast to
Bruner, the psychologist, regarding the elements of a theory of teaching.
Yet both Strasser and Bruner are working within the empirical social
sciences. Indeed, Strasser as curriculum worker builds upon the work of
Taba and Smith, two curriculum specialists. Since Strasser builds upon
Smith it is appropriate to ask if the idea of influencing/influenced teacher
behavior calls for equal and mutual influence. If the teacher is influenced
by his observations, interpretations, and diagnosis of the learner's behavior
as suggested by Strasser, then how does he account for Smith's statement
that the determining factor in the teacher's behavior is his comprehension
of subject matter and demands for clear instruction? (See the full citation
from Smith in the Overview to Section Four.) Would Strasser reject Smith
on this matter? Could Strasser's model accommodate Smith's claim? Could
Strasser's four point model subsume the three phases of teaching suggested
by Jackson in Section One? In light of Strasser's summary statement that
teaching is inquiring, the reader is asked to compare this model of teaching
with Dewey's mutual inquiry theory as set forth by Walton in this section.

The third type of theory includes the selections by Walton, Scheffler,
and Scudder. These selections present theories that may appropriately be
labeled philosophical. Walton presents his formulations of four theories,
Scheffler presents his formulations of three theories, and Scudder presents
his formulation of a Buber model of teaching. In this way a broad range
of various philosophical theories is presented within these three selections.
Several comparisons come easily to mind; Walton's maieutic theory with
Scheffler's insight model; Walton's communication theory with Scheffler's
impression model; Walton's comments on self-actualization with Scudder's
Buber model; Scheffler's rule model with Green's (Section Two) concept
of action; and Scudder's interpretation of Scheffler with the reader's own
interpretation of Scheffler.[4]

---

[3] Jerome S. Bruner, *The Process of Education* (Cambridge, Mass.: Harvard University Press, 1960), p. 33.

[4] For two other reactions to Scheffler's article the reader may wish to see the two
letters to the editors by Sterling M. McMurrin and John P. Powell in *Harvard Educational Review*, 35 (Fall 1965), 492–96.

Several specific points deserve mention especially in consideration of other articles. (1) Scheffler refers to conditions for knowing when he treats the insight model and the rule model. Walton, too, deals with ways of knowing when he treats his four theories. Scheffler fully develops the conditions for knowing in his short book *Conditions of knowledge.*[5] The reader may wish to pursue them further for they are important to the various theories. (2) Scudder claims that according to Buber the teacher's primary responsibility is to his student rather than to his subject matter.[6] Is this in conflict with the triadic claim made by Hyman (Section Two), Henderson (this Section), and Martin (Section Six)? Does the reader agree with Buber? (3) The idea that teaching is a moral endeavor is stated by Scudder ("Ethically, he has no right to force the student into a predetermined relationship with a discipline"); by Maccia ("I assume most of our prescriptive theorizing would agree in placing the theiving aspects of human living outside of instructional bounds); and by Scheffler ("Our teaching needs thus to introduce students to those principles we ourselves acknowledge as fundamental, general, and impartial in the various departments of thought and action"). Recall, also, Jackson's opening sentence in his article in Section One. If teaching does include a moral aspect, how can we accomodate it in axiomatic and inductive-type theories? Must we relegate the moral aspect of teaching only to philosophical theories of teaching? (4) Finally, the reader is asked to consider what suggestions or directions for research can be gained from these seven selections, since it is generally accepted that theory does guide research hypotheses. Perhaps a starting point is with Henderson's formulations of M ((X,Y), Z) and C ((X,Y), Z).

[5] Israel Scheffler, *Conditions of Knowledge* (Chicago: Scott, Foresman & Company, 1965).

[6] For a further analysis of Buber as presented by Scudder see the article by Edward David Kiner, "Some Problems in a Buber Model for Teaching," *Educational Theory,* 19 (Fall 1969), pp. 396–403.

15.

A Theoretical Model for Teaching

KENNETH B. HENDERSON

Professor of Secondary and
Continuing Education, University of Illinois.

One does not have to read extensively in the literature of education before he finds that there are various conceptions of teaching. He finds that teaching is arranging conditions which facilitate learning. He also learns that teaching consists in making it possible for students to discover things for themselves. He encounters the slogan, "If the student has not learned, the teacher has not taught," and realizes that the generalization is used as an elliptical biconditional: Teaching occurs if and only if learning occurs.

Reflecting on these different points of view, one realizes that a concept of teaching is not acquired in the way one learns that it is colder in the Northern Hemisphere in January than in July, that frustration often begets aggression, or that learning is enhanced when the

"A Theoretical Model for Teaching" by Kenneth B. Henderson is reprinted with permission from School Review, 73:384–391, Winter, 1965. (University of Chicago Press, publisher).

learner is provided immediate knowledge of the results of his provisional tries. Otherwise, how can we explain the fact that different observers, all careful and objective, arrive at different conceptions? One does not discover by observation what teaching is. Rather, he decides how he wants to conceive of teaching—what he wants to call by the term *teaching* and/or what conditions have to be met before he is willing to say that teaching is taking place. In short, a concept of teaching is a theoretic construct, not an observed phenomenon.

Although a person is free to decide how he wishes to conceive of teaching, if his decision is a thoughtful one it is based on what he considers important. For example, stating that teaching is making it possible for students "to discover for themselves" is an instance of a persuasive definition. It disposes a person (the teacher) to emphasize a certain kind of behavior. A theoretician who advances this proposal may be willing to sacrifice generality for the likelihood of inducing a certain kind of behavior in a person regarded as the teacher.

Regarding teaching as taking place "if and only if learning is taking place" might be advanced by a person who regards the previous conception as too restricted and who values a more extensive concept, one which is based on the reason for teaching. Such a person probably is willing to tolerate the awkward consequence of defining in terms of purpose when the following analogies are presented:

> If the patient does not recover, the surgeon has not operated;
>
> If the jury does not find for the defendant, the defense lawyer has not tried the case;
>
> If no one appreciates the picture, the artist has not painted it.

Nor is he impressed by the difficulty of doing any significant research on methods of teaching when such a concept of teaching is employed.

One who proposes that teaching occurs when someone (the teacher) interprets, explains, defines, justifies, generalizes, relates, demonstrates, and so on, calls our attention to those intellectual and linguistic activities which he considers important and implies that a teacher should be skillful in these activities. He probably is willing to accept the awkward consequence of having to say that teaching in being carried on even though no one is hearing the explanations, interpretations, definitions, or observing the demonstrations.

What I shall propose in this article is a particular conception of teaching which I believe has merit, provided one values structure, generality, fruitfulness for research, and objectivity. It is a concept based on modern logic and utilizes the idea of a relation as a set of ordered *n*-tuples.

Since a relation is a set, it has members. If each member of a relation is an ordered pair of components, the relation is a 2-tuple or *binary relation*. If each member is an ordered triple of components, the relation is a 3-tuple or *ternary relation*. Theoretically, there are relations each of whose members has 4, 5, or more components. Inasmuch as teaching will be explicated in terms of binary and ternary relations, no further mention will be made of the other relations.

Since a binary relation is a set of *ordered* pairs and a ternary relation is a set of *ordered* triples, the order in which the components are listed makes a difference. To indicate the ordering, we speak of the first, second, and third components. Conventional notation for a member of a binary relation is (x, y) and for a ternary relation (x, y, z). Any variables can be used, but once a choice is made, the form (x, y) for a member of a binary relation is effective in indicating that the member is a pair whose first component is x and whose second component is y. Similarly, the form (x, y, z) for a member of a ternary relation is effective in indicating that the member is a triple whose first component is x, second component is y, and third component is z. If we use another variable, say a capital letter, and write $T(x, y, z)$, we can consider the variable T as designating the particular relation being considered.

If teaching is considered as a relation, its form might be expressed by

$$x \text{ teaches } y.$$

One interpretation of this relation would make the domain of x the set of persons who are teachers and the domain of y the set of persons who are taught by x. Hence members of the relation would be just those pairs which make the sentence

x teaches y

true; for example (Miss Taylor, Henry Brown), (Miss Taylor, Alice Lewis), (Mr. Jones, Mike Smith), and (Mr. Latimer, Mike Smith) if, in fact, Miss Taylor teaches Henry Brown and Alice Lewis, Mr. Jones teaches Mike Smith, and Mr. Latimer teaches Mike Smith. But if it is not the case that Mr. Poppins teaches Mary Frazier, then (Mr. Poppins, Mary Frazier) is not a member of the relation. Such a concept of teaching is reflected in the statement, "I don't teach subjects; I teach children" and would be associated with a "child-centered" school.

The relation x teaches y might also be interpreted as the relation from the set of persons called teachers to the set of subjects taught; for example, English, mathematics, auto mechanics, swimming. In this case (Miss Taylor, French), (Mr. Latimer, art), (Mr. Jones, auto mechanics), and (Mr. Jones, machine drawing) are members of the relation if and only if it is a fact that Miss Taylor teaches French, Mr. Latimer teacher art, and Mr. Jones teaches both auto mechanics and machine drawing. Such a concept of teaching might be expected to be associated with a "subject-centered" school.

Teaching can also be regarded as the ternary relation x teaches y to z. A layman's interpretation of this relation would have the domain of x be the set of persons who teach, the domain of y the set of subjects taught, and the domain of z the set of persons taught. The form of the relation would be $T(x, y, z)$. In this case, (Mr. Jones, auto mechanics, Mike Smith) is a mem-

ber of the teaching relation if and only if it is a fact that Mr. Jones teaches auto mechanics to Mike Smith.

Considering teaching as a ternary relation has the advantage of generality. It allows the two binary relations described above to be subsumed under the ternary relation. But it is general enough and is not at all fruitful for purposes of research. In research on teaching, we are interested not in who the teacher is or who the student is, but rather in what the teacher does and in what the student does. In other words, the behavior or actions of a person designated as the teacher and the behavior of the person designated as the student are the significant factors for research. It, therefore, seems desirable to reinterpret the ternary relation $T(x, y, z)$.

Let us say that the domain of x in $T(x, y, z)$ is sequences of "actions" of an object which, in terms of some set of criteria, is identified as a teacher. The term "object" was deliberately chosen as designating a general category and not implying that the members of the category are either human or non-human. This permits a machine, a conventional textbook, or a programed text as well as a human being to be regarded as a teacher. Such a conception is not so bizarre, and, as will be shown shortly, has an advantage of clarifying the nature of one kind of educational research. The quotation marks around "actions" are used to imply that the term is not used in the ordinary sense. Although it makes sense to speak of actions of a human being and of a teaching machine, it is odd to speak of actions of a textbook or other text materials. Yet one step removed from the text is the author of the text who generated the articular sequence of descriptions, explanations, interpretations, or illustrations exhibited in the text. It is in this sense that the term "actions" appears not to be inappropriate.

Let us say that the domain of z in $T(x, y, z)$ is sequences of actions or behaviors of a person who, in terms of some set of criteria, is identified as a learner. The domain of y is the set of whatever is teachable; for example, knowledge, beliefs, attitudes, skills, or values. It is generally agreed, this author believes, that there are some things that are learnable but not teachable. Hence it is proper to stipulate that the domain of y consists of what is teachable rather than what is learnable.

By grouping the components, every ternary relation can be transformed into a binary relation. The teaching relation $T(x, y, z)$ theoretically can be transformed into twelve distinct binary relations by different groupings and permutations of the components. However, only two—perhaps three—appear to have interpretations which are of practical significance, namely $T((x, y), z)$ and its converse $T(z, (x, y))$. In each of these z, standing for sequences of behavior of the learner, is considered by itself. Since the purpose of teaching is to affect the behavior of the learner, considering the behavior of the learner as one component of a binary relation is in keeping with the kind of research that is done in which the behavior of the learner is the dependent variable.

Consider the binary relation $T((x, y), z)$ where y is constant. Research based on this model, where x is considered the independent variable and z the dependent variable seeks conclusions concerning whether x is a sufficient and/or necessary condition for z. In light of the proposed interpretation of x and z, we might call this kind of research *methods research* since what we have in mind when we speak of

teaching methods are patterns of actions. Let us designate research based on this relation as $M((x, y), z)$ with the M reminding us of methods—the invariance of y over a well-defined set of teachable objects.

Theoretically, it is possible to conduct research to discover methods effecting certain behavior in learners—methods which are invariant with respect to what is taught. However, we usually attempt to find the methods which are invariant over a restricted subset of what is taught. For example, we attempt to find methods (a popular synonym these days for *methods* is *strategies*) which are invariant over the set of concepts, skills, or generalizations. In such research the dependent variable z becomes whatever behavior of the learner is defined operationally to indicate the acquisition of the concept, skill, or generalization. Even more restrictive methods research would attempt to find methods which are invariant over generalizations in a particular subject (e.g., mathematics), but not necessarily invariant over the entire set of generalizations; that is, including generalizations in science, economics, sociology, history, or literature. Such restricted research would be justified in case the logic of the subject (e.g., mathematics) is different from the logic of other subjects; for example, an empirically based science.

Consider the binary relation $T((x, y,), z)$ where x is constant. Research based on this model, where y is considered the independent variable and z the dependent variable, seeks conclusions concerning whether y is a sufficient and/or necessary condition for z. In light of the proposed interpretation of y and z, we might call this kind of research *curriculum research*, and denote it by $C((x, y), z)$ with C reminding us of curriculum. Such research attempts to find the knowledge, beliefs, skills, or values which appear to produce certain behavior in students, irrespective of the methods used. If research shows that what is taught is not invariant with respect to the methods used, the relation $C((x, y), z)$ is empty.

Much of the research being carried on in such curricular projects at the Physical Science Study Group, School Mathematics Study Group, University of Illinois Committee on School Mathematics, and the Biological Sciences Curriculum Study is based on $C((x, y), z)$. The projects appear to be attempting to demonstrate y as a sufficient condition for z; that is, they produce evidence that if y is taught z results. An interesting difference is found between the University of Illinois Committee on School Mathematics and the School Mathematics Study Group. The former restricts x (methods of teaching) to inductive methods, hence the independent variable is (x, y). The School Mathematics Study Group speaks as though the subject matter selected will produce mathematical competence whether inductive or expository methods are used by a teacher. It is to be noted that this is a testable hypothesis even if it is ignored.

We use the converse of $C((x, y), z)$ when we select subject matter for some course. Focusing on the behavior we want the student to manifest, we attempt to infer the subject matter which, if taught, will induce this behavior. The assumption is that, irrespective of what subject matter is selected, there exists a method (value of x) for teaching it. If the research based on $C((x, y), z)$ has demonstrated y as a sufficient condition for z (that is, if research shows that if such and such knowledge is

taught, the students behave in such and such ways; e.g., can apply the knowledge in new situations), we have more confidence in selecting subject matter. If research has not demonstrated y as a sufficient condition for z, we still must make a choice, but we have less confidence in the particular choice we make. If the research has demonstrated no necessary conditions, then we have less confidence in choosing one body of knowledge over some other. Much of the debate concerning what ought to be taught can be traced directly to the absence of verified generalizations of the form:

If y is taught, z results;

z results only if y is taught.

Or, more generally,

If (x, y), then z,

z only if (x, y).

A third binary relation which admits a possible interpretation is one in which z (the behavior of the learner) is neither the dependent nor the independent variable. This relation can be symbolized as $P((y, z), x)$, or, more simply $P(y, x)$ if z is ignored. This is interpreted as the relation between what is taught and the methods used. A writer of text materials employs this relation. Since he gets no feedback from the student, having decided what subject matter he wants to teach, he has to select some method of teaching it. Depending on how much he knows about methods of teaching, his choice is wise or unwise. Those of us who have read textbooks are well aware of this.

I stated earlier that I am unaware of useful interpretations of some of the binary relations obtained from $T(x, y, z)$ obtained by permuting and grouping the three components. This is not necessarily a weakness of the model (it may be lack of insight on my part), for it is characteristic of models that at a given time in the development of the theory they may not be completely interpretable.

A model is developed by using some theory; in the case of the model proposed, the theory of relations. One then attempts to state semantic rules for mapping the variables in the abstract model into empirical phenomena. To the extent he can do this, the model becomes an interpreted model and serves to organize knowledge, provide insights, remove semantic confusion, and generate hypotheses. It is toward these ends that I offered the conception of teaching as a ternary relation between methods, teachable objects, and the behavior of students.

16.

Instruction as Influence Toward Rule-governed Behavior

ELIZABETH STEINER MACCIA

Professor of Philosophy of
Education, Indiana University.

The purpose of this paper is to present the results of my inquiry—to present my theory of instruction.

CHARACTERIZATION OF THE THEORY

While it is beyond the scope of one paper presenting a theory to discuss fully the nature and kinds of theory, nevertheless an initial characterization is possible. Theory is taken to be a systematically related set of statements. To be systematically related is obviously to be organized. The paradigm of organization is a deductive system, such

Elizabeth Steiner Maccia, "Instruction as Influence Toward Rule-governed Behavior," in Theories of Instruction. *James B. Macdonald and Robert R. Leeper, editors. Washington, D.C.: Association for Supervision and Curriculum Development, 1965. pp. 88–99. Reprinted with permission of the Association for Supervision and Curriculum Development and Elizabeth Steiner Maccia. Copyright © 1965 by the Association for Supervision and Curriculum Development.*

as Euclidean geometry. As you remember, such a system consists of axioms (statements formed according to rules from undefined terms) and theorems (statements formed according to rules from the axioms). Even though most theory outside of logic and mathematics fails in terms of the paradigm, still no theory is simply a heap of unrelated statements. In fact, formal coherence is a criterion of adequate theory no matter what kind of theory it is.

Theories may be either formal or descriptive or prescriptive. The statements of a formal theory—theories of pure logic and pure mathematics—are given no meaning; they are not interpreted. The statements of a descriptive theory—theories of empirical science—are given meaning through what is; they are interpreted experientially. The statements of a prescriptive theory—theories of philosophy—are given meaning through what ought to be; they are interpreted ideally.

From the preceding discussion, theorizing in which there is a meaning dimension is an attempt to give an organized account of the universe, or a portion thereof, as it is or as it ought to be. To theorize about instruction, therefore, involves a choice as to whether the organized account shall be of instruction as it is or as it ought to be. Shall the theory be a scientific or a philosophic one? I selected the former alternative. The reason for the selection is that without a means of control, ideas as to how the phenomena we are dealing with are related, we have no basis for implementing a philosophic theory of instruction no matter how adequate that philosophic theory might be. A scientific theory of instruction, if adequate, provides such a basis.

CRITERIA FOR JUDGING THE ADEQUACY OF THE THEORY

How are you to judge whether the theory I shall present bears the marks of adequacy or inadequacy? No doubt adequacy criteria are part of the implicit background of the researcher or inquirer, yet there may be merit in making explicit these criteria. The basis for either developing the theory further, and further checking it or for striking out in a different direction, then, will be before the reader as the theory is presented. Perhaps this also will facilitate the intent of the paper.

A scientific theory to be adequate must exhibit formal coherence, observational verification, and observational predictiveness. Formal coherence, the criterion any kind of theory must exhibit to be adequate, has been mentioned already.[1] To repeat, a theory has formal coherence, if its statements

[1] See page 141 of this book.

are systematically related. The parts of the theory must fit together or cohere. There is a fittingness in form. Observational verification and observational predictiveness are the other criteria a theory must exhibit to make it an adequate scientific theory. A theory has observational verification, if its statements correspond to that which can be experienced. It is true in terms of observations. When possible, the observations are made under controlled situations which permit precision and ease of observing. Experimentation, however, is not always possible. A theory has observational predictiveness if statements about what will happen in experience can be derived from it. It permits marking off other observations to be made.

The meaning of this discussion of adequacy criteria can be resolved into questions to ask as the theory is presented. With respect to formal coherence, ask these questions:

1. Do the ideas about instruction fit together?
2. If the ideas about instruction do not fit together, could they be extended or modified or both in order to produce the fit?
   With respect to observational verification, ask these questions:
3. Do the ideas instruction check with experimental or non-experimental observations recorded by others or made by you?
4. If there is no evidence as to whether the ideas about instruction check with observations, could experimental or non-experimental designs for checking them be devised?
   With respect to observational predictiveness, ask this question:
5. From ideas about instruction, could other ideas about instruction be derived (hypotheses be stated), and

could these predictions be observed (experimental or non-experimental designs for checking the hypotheses be devised)?

Through answering these five questions, the reader will face the challenge of this paper.

BROAD OUTLINES OF THE THEORY

"Instruct" comes from two Latin words, *in* and *struere,* expressing direction from a point outside to one within limits and building respectively. But what has this to do with instruction viewed as a process of a person teaching another who thereby learns? Unless this question is answered, I would consider myself not producing results in the realm of inquiry into the problem of education.

The direction is from one person to another person. One person is directed to another person. There is an interpersonal relationship which is an influence relationship. Since influence comes form the Latin word, *influere,* expressing causing to flow in, influence involves the building up in the one influenced. The person influencing the building up is teaching.

Learning, however, is taken to be a change of behavior effected by teaching. What kind of behavioral change is building up? A rare or obsolete meaning of "structure" as action of building coupled with the usual meanings—organized body, and combination of mutually connected and dependent elements—leads one to a behavioral change in which the behavior becomes rule-governed. The content of teaching or the possible building up is knowledge. Knowledge consists of systems of ideas or actions. A system of ideas or actions

is an organized body or a combination of mutually connected and dependent elements. Knowledge, then, consists of structures. In analyzing a structure, it is obvious that there can be no structure unless there are rules for putting the elements together. The following of rules is the heart of organization. Recall what was said earlier about Euclidean geometry, a knowledge structure.[2] The building up of knowledge structures in a person, therefore, becomes affecting his behavior so that it changes to behavior governed by the rules. The person being influenced toward rule-governed behavior is learning.

The broad outlines of the theory to be presented have been sketched. Instruction is teaching-learning viewed as influence toward rule-governed behavior. Some readers may have recognized the centering of this theory in group dynamics and the discipline approach to curriculum. The theory will be developed in terms of these two centerings.

GROUP DYNAMICS: INFLUENCE DIMENSION OF THE THEORY[3]

To some readers, "group dynamics" refers to a political ideology as characterized in the democratic classroom;

---

[2] See page 141 of this book.

[3] See *An Educational Theory Model: Graph Theory,* in *Construction of Educational Theory Models,* Cooperative Research Project No. 1632, The Ohio State University Research Foundation, Columbus, Ohio, 1963, p. 101–38. This paper presents the model from which the influence dimension of this theory was devised, as well as a formal presentation of a tentative educational theory in which the classroom group is viewed as an influence structure. The research reported therein was supported by the Cooperative Research Program of the Office of Education, U.S. Department of Health, Education, and Welfare.

to others, a set of techniques such as role playing; and yet to others, an inquiry to advance knowledge of group life. The group dynamics centering of this theory of instruction relates to the last stated referent. This follows from the decision to present a scientific theory which by its nature rules out the development of instruction as phenomena of an ideal of classroom group life or as techniques of classroom group life. Ideals related to philosophic theorizing, and techniques are the result of scientific theorizing. The primary concern will be with structure variables which are descriptions of the internal behavior of the classroom group and which consist of statements of relations among classroom group members.[4]

The interpersonal relations within a classroom group will be delimited in terms of two clearly identifiable positions: teacher and student. The roles or behavior of the persons occupying these positions will be those of inducer whose behavior brings about a behavioral change in another person or persons and of inducee whose behavior is changed by the inducer's behavior. Unless there is a directed relation between at least two persons, one person is directed to another person to bring about a behavioral change in that person; there can be no teacher (inducer) and student (inducee). This directed relation may be depicted diagrammatically through graph theory, as in Figure 1.

4 See R. B. Cattell, "New Concepts for Measuring Leadership, in Terms of Group Syntality" (*Human Relations* 4: 161–84; 1951), in which three panels of group description are proposed: structure variables as indicated above, population variables which are means (statistical parameters) of the measured characteristics of component individuals, and syntality variables which represent the performances of groups acting as a whole.

Figure 1

This directed relation points to a concept of influence, A influences B, and thus will be called "an influence relation."

Influence relations could be direct or indirect. Figure 1 shows a direct influence relation, while Figure 2 shows a direct influence relation of A over B and of B over C, and an indirect one of A over C.

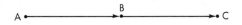

Figure 2

Furthermore, there could be mutual influence, where each person is both teacher and student, as in Figure 3.

It must be obvious from the foregoing statements that there are many possibilities as to the influence structure

Figure 3

of a given classroom. It is not the case that a classroom group necessarily has the influence structure of Figure 4, because A is hired as the teacher and B, C, and D are enrolled as students.

The classroom group might be structured according to Figures 5, 6, 7, or 8.

In Figure 5, A directly teaches B and indirectly C through B directly teaching

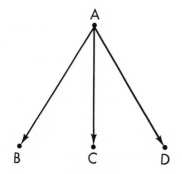

Figure 4

C. D is isolated, and taught by no one. In Figure 6, the hired teacher, A, teaches no one. Student C teaches B and D; and C is actually not a student, since he is taught by no one. In Figure 7, there are two teachers, A and C, who both directly teach B and D, the two students. What if A's and C's teachings are contradictory? In Figure 8, every person is both teacher and student.

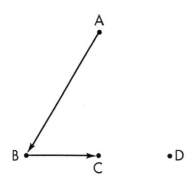

Figure 5

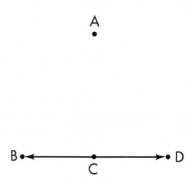

Figure 6

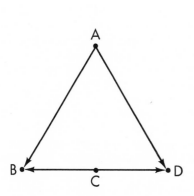

Figure 7

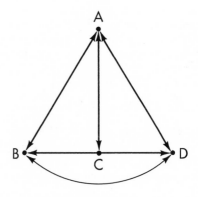

Figure 8

We are faced with the question, of course, as to what kind of influence structure we want in the classroom. This depends upon the individual's philosophic stand. Should the persons who are enrolled as students be influenced only by the person hired to teach? A democratic philosophic stand would lead some to answer in the negative. Others might question the goodness of the behavioral change the teacher is bringing about in the students, i.e., what the teacher is building up. Of what worth is a philosophic stand without scientific knowledge about influence structures? Through science we arrive at means, and so the kind of control dictated by a philosophic stand becomes possible. Scientific inquiry is called for. We can theorize and we have[5] theorized about what structures will do what, and recorded observations suggest adequacy of this theorizing, although more theorizing and experimentation are required. To illustrate, an influence structure as depicted in Figure 8 will produce behavior at the average of the group's initial behavior.[6] Such is the outcome of everyone's taking both the teacher and student roles in the classroom.

We cannot assume that because the teacher is the teacher, because he is hired, that he automatically has influence. As indicated in the use of Flanders' interaction analysis, teacher talk that centers about direction and criticism (Categories 6 and 7) might indicate lack of teacher influence.[7]

[5] See footnote 3.

[6] John R. P. French, Jr. "A Formal Theory of Social Power." *The Psychological Review* 63: 181–94; 1956.

[7] Edmund J. Amidon and Ned A. Flanders. *The Role of the Teacher in the Classroom.* Minneapolis, Minnesota: Paul S. Amidon & Associates, Inc., 1963. p. 32–33.

There might be no basis for teacher influence, because there is an inappropriateness between what is wanted of the student and what he can do and has done. For example, a student who does not understand algebra cannot be influenced to do calculus. In order to have an influence relation, therefore, the content of influence must be appropriate to the one being influenced. Even though appropriateness of content is present, there still might be no basis for teacher influence. A motivational basis, as well as a content basis, must be present.

What, then, are the possible motivational bases of influence? That the teacher is the teacher is one possible motivational basis. It is not the only one. The student also might let the teacher have influence over him because he might be punished, he might be rewarded, the teacher really can teach, or he likes the teacher. These possibilities provide the following kinds of influence with respect to their motivational bases: legitimate, punitive, reward, expert, and affective. Both punitive and reward influences are based upon expectation of behavior by another which is not valued or is valued respectively. A frown, a slap, and an F usually are not valued. A smile, a pat, and an A usually are valued. Legitimate influence is based upon position, while expert influence is based upon idealized role.

Persons are hired as teachers, at least in most contemporary societies. There are positions which they fill. Since they fill positions, they are legitimate. The teachers are the teachers. The strength of the influence based upon position will vary with the degree of recognition of the significance of the position by the group. If a community views its teachers as "persons who can't," there is little basis for legitimate influence. Expert influence, on the other hand, is independent of the valuing of the group. When influence based upon expertise is present, a person is a student to another person, whether that person is hired to occupy the position of teacher or not, because he judges that person to behave as one ought to to be a teacher. The last motivational basis for influence to be mentioned is a positive feeling state toward an individual. When we feel affection for another, then that individual can influence us. It is interesting to note that affect means "to influence."

What ways do we have of observing the bases for influence, both the content bases and the motivational bases? Achievement and aptitude measures offer only limited possibilities with respect to observing the content bases. Achievement measures are attempts to ascertain what the student has learned; and aptitude measures, what the student could learn. There is still the question of the kind and degree of relatedness required to establish appropriateness of content in terms of past learnings and possible learnings. A tentative answer might be given in terms of structural similarity,[8] rather than the usual one in terms of content similarity. Ausubel

and Blake did find that meaningful learning of a passage of Buddhism was not adversely affected by recent prior learning of Christianity. If transfer were not in a context of cognitive structure, proactive inhibition would be expected between the two stimuli.[9]

Sociograms and interaction analysis[10] offer only limited possibilities with respect to observing the motivational bases. The use of sociograms has been largely a matter of graphic representation of the classroom group structure in terms of expressed attraction of students to one another. Strangely, where the teacher fits into the group structure has not been of concern. The use of interaction analysis involves categories that relate to both the content and motivational bases of influence. When the latter categories are sorted out, it is seen that only two bases are considered: punitive—rejection of student as indicated by teacher talk; and reward—acceptance of student as indicated by teacher talk. More complete ways will have to be developed to determine a student's expectations about how the teacher will act and perceptions about the position, role-taking, and attractiveness of the teacher.

When the ways for observing both the content and motivational bases of instruction are delineated, then the influence structure of a given classroom can be revealed. Who is teaching whom

---

[8] See *An Educational Theory Model: Pharmacology and Pharmacogenetics* and *An Educational Theory Model: Information Theory,* in *Construction of Educational Theory Models,* Cooperative Research Project No. 1632, The Ohio State University Research Foundation, Columbus, Ohio, 1963, p. 187–227 and p. 298–334. The tentative educational theorizing found in these two papers has something to say about structural similarity.

[9] David P. Ausubel and Elias Blake, Jr. "Proactive Inhibition in the Forgetting of Meaningful School Material." *Journal of Educational Research* 52: 145–49; 1958.
[10] The interaction analysis being considered is that devised by Ned A. Flanders. See work cited in Footnote 7 and final report of Cooperative Research Project No. 397, *Teacher Influence, Pupil Attitudes, anid Achievement.*

or who is learning from whom will be determinable. We shall know then if instruction is taking place.

DISCIPLINE APPROACH TO CURRICULUM: RULE-GOVERNED BEHAVIOR DIMENSION OF THEORY[11]

Undoubtedly for most readers "discipline" does not have the same meaning. Consequently, the possible meanings must be set forth to render clear the rule-governed behavior dimension of the theory which is centered in a discipline approach to curriculum.

"Discipline" comes from the Latin, *discipulus,* meaning disciple. Because a disciple is one who learns (*discipulus* comes from *discere,* to learn) by following another person, in its most general sense "discipline" means

1. instruction or teaching.
   Sense 1 could be stated too as instructions or teachings, if the emphasis is shifted from process to content. Sense 1, obviously, adds nothing to the explication of instruction. Another meaning of "discipline," however, does. This second sense of "discipline" is
2. regulation or control.
   Again, due to the shift of emphasis from process to content, there is an alternate way of statement, i.e., rules.

[11] See Occasional Paper 63–143, *The Scientific Perspective: Only One Curricular Model,* published by The Center for the Construction of Theory in Education, The Ohio State University, Columbus. This paper deals with curricular problems within a discipline perspective.

Sense 2 of "discipline" clearly points to the rule-governed behavior dimension of the instructional theory. Instruction involves learning or behavioral change as regulated or controlled behavior—behavior governed by rules. Consider what a rule is. A rule is a reason or criterion which leads to one behavior rather than another behavior. It is a way of behaving rather than another way. It is judgmental or selective in nature. The selective characteristic of a rule also makes it a way of solving problems, since problems are sets of alternatives. In an individual a rule is a cognitive structure.[12] Through teaching, cognitive structures are built up in a student, or to state the matter in another way, the student becomes a problem-solver.

There are yet other meanings of "discipline" which are more specific in regard to control. We must take these into account, since some will hinder our theorizing and others help our theorizing. Some meanings of "discipline" carry with them an interpretive context which runs counter to controlled behavior as rule-governed behavior. The other meanings are not in such a context, and hence could be used for further description of instruction as influence toward rule-governed behavior.

The meanings which through context hinder our theorizing are:

3. control through punishment, and
4. submission to authority.

Both of these meanings involve only what we have called "motivational

[12] The presence of cognitive structures in an individual is not meant in any spatial sense.

bases." In 3, there is the punitive basis. In 4, the most general sense of "authority" implicates any of the five motivational bases—reward, legitimate, expert, punitive and affective as well; a less general sense, only legitimate and expert bases; and the least general sense, the expert basis alone. There is a neglect of the content basis in relation to behavioral control. This neglect seems to indicate an interpretive context in which human behavior is taken as reactive. Behavior is controlled by someone acting upon another. Action by someone produces a concomitant reacting by another, provided the someone has influence over the other through punishment or authority. Behavior is not controlled by the one who behaves, because of his cognitive structures. Behavior is not rule-governed.

The content basis of influence must be considered also, and so the above interpretive context with its meanings of "discipline" (3 and 4) is set aside. Even though a person can punish another or is an authority to another, if the another does not understand in the sense that the person's demands are not appropriate to him, he will not act. The human being cannot be divested of his cognitive structures. Cognition is present. There are rules which an individual has and which govern his behavior. A human being is a problem-solver. Human behavior is active and not reactive. Human behavior must be so described. The inadequacy of the view of human behavior as reactive is not a philosophic inadequacy. It is a scientific one.

We are not prescribing that human beings behave humanly. What sense would this make, since a human being must of necessity so behave? In the instructional process, therefore, the student is not passive but active. He is a problem-solver. Provided there is a motivational basis, the student will want to relate to the content presented by the teacher; but no building up of cognitive structures will occur, unless the content has structural fit to the cognitive structures of the student. If the cognitive structures are built up, learning occurs. New or modified foci of behavior—rules—control the student. The student has new or modified ways of solving problems.

The remaining two meanings of "discipline" which will be utilized to explicate further the rule-governed behavior dimension of the theory are:

5. organized branches of knowledge, and

6. rules of practical conduct.

Senses 5 and 6, I suspect, would be taken as meanings which distinguish the theoretical from the practical disciplines and which restrict cognitive or knowledge structures to the former. The disciplines of instructional concern, hence, would be the organized branches of knowledge which exclude rules of practical conduct. Depending upon whether you embrace a nineteenth century or twentieth century viewpoint, the organized branches of knowledge would be either the traditionally recognized subject-matter fields including more than the sciences, e.g., literature, or the sciences alone. In either case much of the business of human living or rule-governed behavior would be outside of instructional bounds.

Need we take these two meanings of discipline as mutually exclusive? Cannot the remainder of the business of human living be brought within instructional bounds? There are rules that govern all aspects of human living, even the rather more important aspects. Businessmen, doctors, lawyers, artists, carpenters, drivers, swimmers, mothers, etc., do have their ways of solving problems as well as academicians. Rules or ways of solving problems are not restricted to the doings of science, literature, etc.

In order to stretch instructional bounds, we must analyze structure. We have done little in this realm. To be sure, the philosophers of science have been hard at work.[13] The structure of science or scientific ways of solving problems are no longer a mystery. Scientific ways of solving problems are not the only ways. The scientific community is a small segment of the total human community. What of other philosophy? The structure in the humanities is quite mysterious. Even more so is the structure of the so-called practical endeavors, as lawyering, mothering, etc. Basic curricular inquiry which is not scientific but analytic or logical in nature is required.

At this point, I imagine some readers are thinking that I am making the matter too difficult. What is required is simply the introduction into the content of instruction (the curriculum) problems covering all aspects of human living. But the introduction of problems demands knowledge of structure. To introduce a problem of a given aspect of human living is to introduce at the

same time the way of solving the problem. A problem to be a problem must have some structure or organization.[14] A problem is present, only if there is doubt or uncertainty. Doubt or uncertainty is present if alternatives are present and so require selection. To select is to solve a problem. If content is completely unstructured or disorganized, alternatives cannot be discerned and no selection is possible. If content is completely structured or organized, there are no alternatives and no selection is required. Total uncertainty or certainty is nonproblematic. A problem, therefore, to be a problem of a given aspect of human living must have some structuring or organizing along the lines of the organization of that aspect of human living. The problem must incorporate rules or cognitive structures or ways of solving problems distinctive to that kind of human living.

The discipline approach to the curriculum has led to learning as rule-governed behavior or problem solving. The possible learnings, and so the possible instructional content (curriculum), have not been restricted within narrow bounds. All possibilities of human living could be matters of learning. The "could" looms large, since actualization of possibilities awaits analysis of the structure of realms of rule-governed behavior other than science. Such analysis would provide the teacher the necessary knowledge to be the kind of problem-maker who could offer instructional content which, if also appropriate, could lead to rule-governed behavior for all aspects of human living. Whether the teacher ought to offer all or only some

[13] See: R. B. Braithwaite. *Scientific Explanation.* Cambridge, England: The University Press, 1955; E. Nagel. *The Structure of Science.* New York: Harcourt, Brace and World, Inc., 1961; and other similar works.

[14] See work on Information Theory cited in Footnote 8, p. 147.

instructional content would be a matter of prescriptive theorizing. I assume most of our prescriptive theorizing would agree in placing the thieving aspects of human living outside of instructional bounds.

CONCLUSION

The results of my descriptive theorizing about instruction are now before the readers of this paper. The conclusion is theirs to make.

17

Needed :
A Theory of Instruction

JEROME S. BRUNER

Professor of Psychology and
Director of The Center for Cognitive Studies,
Harvard University.

Over the past several years it has become increasingly clear to me, as to any thinking person today, that both psychology and the field of curriculum design itself suffer jointly from the lack of a theory of instruction. Such a theory of instruction would indeed be interesting just for its own sake, for purely theoretical reasons. There cannot be, for example, a theory of development which leaves somehow to chance the question of the way in which societies pace and structure the experiences with which children come in contact; and to talk about the nature of development without talking about the way in which

This article is adapted from Dr. Bruner's address at the Second General Session during ASCD's Eighteenth Annual Conference March 10, 1963 in St. Louis, Missouri.

Jerome S. Bruner, "Needed: A Theory of Instruction." Educational Leadership 20 (8): 523–532; May 1963. Reprinted with permission of the Association for Supervision and Curriculum Development and Jerome S. Bruner. Copyright © 1963 by the Association for Supervision and Curriculum Development.

society does and can structure the sequence, is to be as intellectually foolish as it is to be morally irresponsible. So even as if one were seeking only a better theory about the nature of man, one would indeed want a theory of instruction as one of the instruments by which one understood man and how he was shaped by his fellow man.

Yet we also realize that a theory of instruction is about as practical a thing as one could possibly have to guide one in the process of passing on the knowledge, the skills, the point of view and the heart of a culture. Let us, then, see whether we can set forth some possible theorems that might go into a theory of instruction.

ELEMENTS OF A THEORY

What do we mean by a theory of instruction? I found myself beginning this exercise by putting down theorems that tried to separate what we might mean by a theory of instruction from other kinds of theories that have been current. The first thought that occurred to me is that in its very nature a theory of instruction is *prescriptive* and not *descriptive*. Such a theory has the aim of producing particular ends and producing them in ways that we speak of as optimal. It is not a description of what has happened when learning has taken place—it is something which is normative, which gives you something to shoot at and which, in the end, must state something about what you do when you put instruction together in the form of courses. Now, this is not a very surprising thing, yet I am struck by the fact that many persons in the field of education have assumed that we could depend on other kinds of theories than the theory of instruction to guide us in this kind of enterprise. For example, I find that the dependence upon learning theory among educators is as touching as it is shocking. The fact of the matter is that the learning theory is not a theory of instruction; it is a theory that describes what takes place while learning is going on and after learning has taken place.

There is no clear-cut way in which one can derive wisdom, or indeed implication, from learning theory that will guide him in the constructing of a curriculum. When I say a theory of instruction is prescriptive, I mean it is *before the fact*. It is before learning has taken place and not while and after learning has taken place. Let me give you an example of the kind of difficulty you get into when you assume that you can use the slender reed of learning theory to lean on. Take, for example, the case of programed instruction.

There is in the current doctrine (I will call it) of programed instruction the idea that somehow you should take small steps, that each increment should be a small step. Now, this idea is derived willy-nilly from a theory of learning which states that learning is incremental and goes in small steps. Nowhere in the evidence upon which such a theory is based—and it is only partial evidence—nowhere is there anything that says that simply because learning takes place in small steps the *environment* should be arranged in small steps. And so we set up a curriculum that also has small steps. In doing so we fail to take sight of the fact that, indeed, organisms from vertebrate on up through the highest primate, man, operate by taking large packets of information and breaking these down into their own bite size and that unless they have the opportunity to do that, learning may become stereotyped. At least it is a worthy hypothesis about instruction.

A theory of instruction must concern itself with the relationship between how things are presented and how they are learned. Though I myself have worked hard and long in the vineyard of learning theory, I can do no better than to start by warning the reader away from it. Learning theory is not a theory of instruction. It describes what happened. A theory of instruction is a guide to what to do in order to achieve certain objectives. Unfortunately, we shall have to start pretty nearly at the beginning, for there is very little literature to guide us in this subtle enterprise.

What shall a theory of instruction be about? I would propose that there are four aspects of such a theory. First, a theory of instruction should concern itself with the factors that predispose a child to learn effectively; and there are many such factors that predispose. These are factors which, on the whole, precede the child's entry into our scholastic care. These factors relate to his earliest childhood and indeed one might say that we should provide some theorems for a theory of toys, and for a theory of family, and for a theory of stimulation, because the thing that comes to mind here is the question of what kind of stimulation ought a child to have before he is faced with this formidable thing we call a schoolroom and a teacher. What sorts of identification might he best form? How shall we bring his linguistic level up to a point where he is able to handle things symbolically ?I shall not treat further these predispositions because what I want to do after this introduction of the different aspects of the theory is to go back and have a look at each one of these in detail, so let me pass on now to a second aspect of a theory of instruction.

It should concern itself with the optimal structuring of knowledge. By this, I mean that for any body of konwledge there is a minimal set of propositions, or statements, or images from which one can best generate the rest of what exists within that field. For example, from the conservation theorems plus a little more, a great deal of physics can be reconstructed. This is the "guts" of physics.

Now, I think when we speak of the optimal structuring of knowledge, we probably have three things in mind about this set of underlying propositions. They should have the power of simplifying the diversity of information within the field, somehow rendering the particular redundant, making it clear that this case is just a sub-case of something else, that one fact is not the same as every other fact. I speak of this power of simplification as the economy of a structure. Secondly, such a structure would enable you to generate new proposition, to go beyond the informa-

tion given. This I would speak of as the productiveness of a structure. And finally, there is another aspect to the structure of knowledge which has to do with the extent to which it increases the manipulability of knowledge. It is classically the case, for example, that when you put something into words it now becomes possible for you to take that thing which before you only intuited in some rough way and to subject it to the combinings and re-combinings that are made possible by the transformative powers of language. And this I want to speak of as the power of a structure. In thinking of structure, then, we shall want to consider economy, productiveness, and power. All of these things are relative to a learner. It does not do to say simply that because physics has great economy, great productiveness, and great power as practiced by a Feinman or a Purcell, that therefore you have children ape those distinguished scientists. You take the child where you find him and give him the structure that is economical, productive and powerful for him and that allows him to grow.

A third aspect of a theory of instruction deals with the optimal sequence that is required for learning. In what order do we present things? If you are presenting the Napoleonic period, where do you start? If you would give a sense of the sixteenth century, do you begin with the fact that mercantile prices and prosperity were going up at a booming rate, whereas the rents that were got by the landlords were not going up because there were long-term leases? You might. If you want to produce drama, you would. But, we will return to that because there is a question of how to give the learner a place from which to take off, something upon which to build. What order to do it? What exercises do you give him to strengthen the sinews of his own thinking? What type of representation do you use? How much particular? How much generality?

Finally, a fourth aspect of a theory of instruction should concern itself with the nature and pacing of rewards and punishments and successes and failures.

To sum up then, a theory of instruction should be constructed around four problems: predispositions, structures, sequences, and consequences.

PREDISPOSITION

What can we say about the factors that predispose a student to be a learner? Let us begin with the following simple proposition: that in order to learn or to solve problems, it is necessary that alternatives be explored and that you cannot have effective learning or problem solving without the learner's having the courage and the skill to explore alternative ways of dealing with a problem.

It seems that if you take this as the first proposition concerning predisposition, there are three things that immediately can be said. First, that if this is the case, learning in the presence of a teacher, or a tutor, or an instructor should somehow minimize the risks and the severity of the consequence that follows upon exploration of alternatives. It should be less risky for a child to explore alternatives in the presence of a teacher, than without one present. It is obvious that, at the level of coping with nature in the raw, the child searching for food on his own would stand more risk of eating toadstools and poisoning himself, and thereby bringing exploration to a close.

Yet there are other less obvious things that have to do with the closing down

of the exploration of alternatives. A teacher or parent can instill the fear of being a fool. That can surely paralyze the will to explore alternatives, for the moment an unreasonable alternative is made to seem like a foolish one, the inner freedom to explore is limited by the requirements of face saving. The encouragement of exploration of alternatives requires some practical minimization of the severity of consequences following exploration.

It seems to me, further, that one of the ways in which a sense of alternatives to be explored can be opened, is to increase the informativeness of error. To increase the informativeness of error essentially involves making clear to the child what produced a failure. One of the major functions of a teacher is to lead the child to a sense of why he failed. I do not mean why he failed in terms of a characterological analysis; I mean in terms of the nature of what it is that he is doing. If you can somehow make the child aware that his attempted answer is not so much a wrong answer, as an answer to another problem, and then get him back on the track, it becomes possible for the child to reduce the confusion that is produced by picking a wrong alternative. One of the things that, I believe, keeps us from exploring alternatives is precisely the confusion of making the wrong choice.

Still another goad to the exploration of alternatives is through the encouragement of "subversiveness." I mean that you must subvert all of the earlier established constraints against the exploratoin of alternatives. This kind of subversiveness has to do with a healthy skepticism toward holy cows, prefabricated doctrines, and stuffed shirtliness. Let there be no question or doubt that is "not nice to express." The moment you as teachers lose your role as subversives in this respect, you are doing the child an injustice and yourself an injustice as a teacher. I want to rescue the word "subversion" from the wrong senses to which it has been put in recent years.

When we think about predispositions to learn, we have to bear in mind that the very relationship that we have with our pupils is a privileged relationship involving authority and direction; that is to say, the exchange is uneven. We know; they do not. Since that is the case, it becomes very necessary for us not to use this implicit authoritative relationship as a means of using our own office as a way of establishing truth and falsity. It is so easy in the mind of the impressionable child to equate truth with Miss Smith!

The nature of learning in a school situation requires as least a dyadic relation; at least two people are involved, and usually many more than two. This obvious point requires that there be some set of minimal social skills that a child brings with him to a learning situation. We do not know much about the nature of these social skills that are required for an exchange of information. The act of exchanging information mutually, or even of accepting information and working on it until you make it your own, is not well understood. In addition to minimum social skills, there are elementary intellectual skills that are necessary for a first encounter with school learning. We "know" this, but we do little either to investigate these elementary skills or to devise ways of strengthening them. I am thinking principally of linguistic skills. Where a child has been socially underprivileged in his early years, it may be necessary for example to look squarely at the situation and say: This child, before he

can go on in these subjects, simply needs more linguistic training or all of our words will be just mere wind going by his ears. I do not mean vocabulary, but, rather, the development of the full transformative power of language which our linguists are only now beginning to understand.

It is necessary for the beginning child to have certain kinds of manipulative and almost intuitive geometric skills. We have started studies of children on the borders of the Sahara in the interior of Senegal. We are struck at the difference in the behavior of American children and children in the African bush who do not have toys with mechanical or geometrical constraint to play with. We take it for granted that our children can deal with geometrical forms, put them together and take them apart, yet the fact of the matter is that it should not be taken for granted. The experience of manipulating materials gives our children a stock of images and geometric transformations that permit him to work geometrically and mechanically in a way that our African subjects cannot. These elementary forms of intellectual skills are essential. Is there more that we can do that we are not doing?

My last point before passing on to the topic of structure in learning has to do with attitudes toward the use of mind. These are predisposing factors of an enormously important kind. For example, we know that these vary to some extent, speaking sociologically, by class, by ethnic group, by culture. There is no question, for example, that in terms of social class, very frequently you will find in the lowest social class an attitude toward life that is governed by the concept of luck. This means that there is really nothing you can do by your own efforts, that things happen to a considerable extent by luck. The business of applying the mind, the idea that man has a chance if he will use his mind, is an attitude which is not frequently present and which has to be created. This is an extremely difficult thing to do and I hope no one asks me how do you do it, because I do not know. Yet it is quite clear that we must use the most intelligent opportunism we can muster, to do anything we can to get the idea started that by the use of mind one can increase effectiveness or any other desired state. We also know that different ethnic groups have different attitudes toward the use of mind, and again, I do not think we take full advantage of this. The Muslim-African culture, for example, has an attitude toward the use of mind that it should be used principally for grasping the word that has been passed on. This is not the kind of use of mind that makes for what might be called a very active, vigorous mind.

STRUCTURE OF KNOWLEDGE

Now let us turn to the question of the structure of knowledge, its economy, productiveness, and power as related to the capacities of a learner. The first point relates to theorem in the theory of computation proposed by Turing. Turing proposed that any problem that can be solved can be solved by simpler means. That is the theorem. Out of this theorem has come the technology of computing machines. What it says—and it says this only for so-called well-defined problems with unique solutions —is that however complicated the problem, we can break it down into a set of simpler elementary operations and finally end up with operations as simple as: make a mark, move a mark, take the

mark out, put the mark back, etc. These elementary operations are then combined into sub-routines that are more complex and then these are combined, etc. The machine succeeds in being practically interesting because it can run off so many of these operations in so short a time. Turing's theorem has a certain relevance to the structure of knowledge; it, in a sense, is another way of stating what by now I am afraid has become an old saw: that any subject can be taught to anybody at any age in some form that is honest. There is always some way in which complicated problems can be reduced to simpler form, simple and step-by-step enough for a child to grasp.

Now, to move ahead one step, I believe it can be said that knowledge about anything can, generally speaking, be represented in three ways, three parallel systems of processing information. One of these is what I call the enactive representation of knowledge. How do you tie a running bowline? You will reply that you can't quite say it or draw it, but that you will show me by tying one. Try to tell somebody how to ride a bicycle, or ski. It is knowing by doing. It is the way in which the young child on a seesaw "knows" Newton's Law of Moments. He knows that in order to balance two children on the other side he has to get farther out on his side, and this is the Law of Moments, but known enactively. Only with time do children free themselves from this tendency to equate things with the actions directed toward them. We never free ourselves from it completely. Let me now speak of ikonic representation. if somebody says to me, for example, "What's a square?" I might say, "Well, a square is a set of sets such that the number of elements in each set is equal to the number of sets." This is a good definition of a square, formalistically. Yet the fact of the matter is that there is another way of representing a square, by an image. It isn't a square it's an image of a square, and it's a useful image—we can start with it. Many of the things we use in representing knowledge have this ikonic property. I use the word "ikonic" because I do not really mean a kind of imitation of nature. Let us not run down the importance of these useful images. They have limits, these representing pictures.

Finally, a third way in which knowledge can get represented is symbolically. By this I mean in words or in those more powerful versions of words, powerful in one way in any case, mathematical symbols. I think you can turn around the Chinese proverb to the effect that one picture is worth a thousand words. For certain purposes one word is worth a thousand pictures. For example, draw a picture of "implosion"; and yet the idea of implosion as such was one of the basic notions that led to the idea of thermonuclear fusion. Implosion is the concept that results from the application of a contrast transformation on the more familiar concept of explosion. The word was so important that it was classified as top secret during the war. It is this capacity to put things into a symbol system with rules for manipulating, for decomposing and recomposing and transforming and turning symbols on their heads that makes it possible to explore things not present, not picturable, and indeed not in existence.

Now the three modes of representation do not disappear as we grow older; quite to the contrary, they remain with us forever. When we speak of the application of Turing's theorem to the question of structuring of knowledge, it is in reference to the representation forms we have been discussing. Early in life and also early in our mastery of a subject we may have to represent things in terms of what we do with them—in much the same way as a child "knows about" balance beams by knowing what to do on a seesaw. We may then emerge with an image of it, however nonrigorous the image may be. Then and only then can language and symbol systems be applied with some degree of likelihood that their reference will be understood. I do not think I can say anything more important than that. You create a structure, not by starting off with the highest brow symbolic version, but by giving it in the muscles, then in imagery and then giving it in language, with its tools for manipulation. The basic task is to orchestrate the three kinds of representations so that we can lead the child from doing, to imaging what he has done, and finally to symbolization.

Usually in a college catalog when a course is listed it will say something about a "prerequisite." Let me urge that any topic also has internal prerequisites in addition to the things that you are supposed to have mastered beforehand. The internal prerequisites may indeed be just precisely the easier modes of representation that get one to a less rigorous, more imageful or enactive grasp of a subject before it gets converted either into ordinary or mathematical language. The way you get ahead with learning is to translate an idea into those non-rigorous forms that can be understood. Then one can, with their aid, become more precise and powerful. In mathematics such techniques are called "heuristics." Their use often constitutes a prerequisite to grasping a subject in its full depth. This is most of what is meant when we speak of "spiral curriculum."

OPTIMAL SEQUENCE

With respect to the sequence in which material is presented, different sequences are obviously needed to achieve different objectives. The idea of one right sequence is a myth. You have to be quite clear about what kind of learning you are trying to produce before you can specify what is a good sequence for presenting it. There are sequences that can be described for the production of parrots. We use them all the time. But there is also a sequence that is particularly interesting in that it seems to increase the likelihood that knowledge will be converted into a structure that is economical, productive and powerful—and therefore transferable. It is worth pausing over.

I would like to suggest that if you wanted to do this, the first thing that you might do is to try leading the child to grasp a structure by induction from particular instances. You would give him lots of particular instances and let him recognize their underlying regularity. If you want the child to transfer his learning to new situations you had better give him some practice in transfer while he is learning.

The second thing you might try is the use of contrast in your sequence. The fish will be the last to discover water. Economy of representation often makes it necessary for the child to see the contrasting case. Often concepts are structured in terms of contrast and can only be fully understood in terms of them. To grasp the meaning of commutativity in arithmetic—that $3 \cdot 4 = 4 \cdot 3$ —often may require that we recognize the non-commutative case of ordinary language—that for quantifiers, for example, "very much" is not equal to "much very" or as a little girl once put it "black shoe" isn't "shoe black."

Third, if one wants a sequence that is going to produce powerful learning, avoid premature symbolization. Do not give them that word to parrot before they know what it is about either by manipulation or in images. Ask yourselves how much you understand about simultaneous equations.

Forth, you might try to give the child practice at both leaping and plodding. Let him go by small steps. Then let him take great leaps, huge guesses. Without guessing he is deprived of his rights as a mind. We cannot get all of the evidence. It is often by guessing that we become aware of what we know.

Another question related to sequence has to do with what I would call "revisiting." Rarely is everything learned about anything in one encounter. Yet we seem to be so impelled to cover, to get through the Elizabethan Period, and on through such-and-such period that we forget the obvious point—that the pot is rarely licked clean at one swipe. Perhaps we would do well to take music listening as a model. It is not simply a matter of mastering this subject, or even of converting it into more powerful form. Rather, revisit means an opportunity of connecting what we have learned now with what else we know. Why is such an obvious point so often ignored?

REWARD AND PUNISHMENT

Now the question of pacing reward and punishment for success and failure. First distinguish two states. One is success and failure; the other one is reward and punishment. By success and failure, I mean the end state that is inherent in a task. The problem is solved or not solved or close to solved. By reward and punishment, I mean something quite different. It relates to the consequences that follow upon success and failure—prizes, scoldings, gold stars, etc.

It is often the case that emphasis upon reward and punishment, under the control of an outside agent such as a teacher or parent, diverts attention away from success and failure. In effect, this may take the learning initiative away from the child and give it to the person dispensing the rewards and punishments. This will be the more likely if the learner is not able to determine the basis of success and failure. One of the great problems in teaching, which usually starts with the teacher being very supportive, is to give the rewarding function back to the learner and the task. Perhaps we can do this by rewarding good errors so that the child becomes aware of the process of problem solving as worthy as well as the fruits of successful outcome. In any case, I wish to mention these matters to suggest that old dogmas about the role of "reinforcement" can be looked at afresh. The independent problem solver is one who rewards and punishes himself by judging the adequacy of his efforts. Equip him with the tools for thinking and let him be his own man.

SOME CONCLUSIONS

I should warn you, in conclusion, to beware of the likes of us. We do not have a tested theory of instruction to offer you. What is quite plain is that one is needed and I would propose that we work together in its forging.

I warn you for a good reason. Educators are a curiously doctrinal or ideological kind of people. You are given to slogans and fight and bleed in their behalf. You have looked to psychology for help and have often been misled into accepting mere hypotheses as the proven word. It is partly because it is so hard to test the adequacy of ideas in an educational setting.

Now we are living through a great revolution in education. Our survival may depend on its successful outcome —our survival as the human race. I know no group in our society more devoted to the common weal than our educators. In this era of new curricula, new teaching arrangements, new automated devices, your best rudder is a healthy sense of experimentation backed by a skepticism toward educational slogans.

If we are to move toward a serviceable and sturdy theory of instruction— and I think we are—then your greatest contribution will be a willingness to give new ideas a try and full candor in expressing your reactions to how things worked. The prospect is strenuous, but gains to be won are enormous. I wish you well.

18.

A Conceptual Model
of Instruction[1]

ben b. strasser

Consultant in Curriculum and
Instruction, Office of Los Angeles County
Superintendent of Schools.

The motivation which led to the evolution of the Conceptual Model of Instruction is common to all who are in education: a desire to understand more of what teaching is all about.

A point of departure for this work was the notion of teaching strategies and tactics as evolved by Taba.[2, 3] To

"A Conceptual Model of Instruction" by ben strasser is reprinted with permission from the Journal of Teacher Education, 18:63–74, Spring, 1967.
[1] Printed in the February and March 1966 issues of the Curriculum Exchange, a department periodical published by the Division of Elementary and Secondary Education, Office of the Los Angeles County Superintendent of Schools. The author would like to acknowledge the reactions, suggestions, and encouragement of the many individuals and groups to whom the ideas for this model were presented at different stages of development, among whom were Art Costa, Eugenia Bernthal, Marie Dickinson, Helen James, and particularly J. Richard Suchman, whose formulations have helped the writer increase his understanding of the nature of instruction.
[2] Taba, Hilda, and Elzey, Freeman S. "Teaching Strategies and Thought Processes."

what aspect of instruction does the term teaching strategy refer? What activities of the teacher can be described as tactics? What do the learners do while a teacher is engaged in such activities? And finally, how does this notion of strategies, tactics, and learners' responses interrelate in a picture of instruction?

To begin with, a series of lessons ranging in grade level from first grade through college was studied in an attempt to identify various tactics and strategies of teachers in order to evolve an operational definition of each of the terms. As a frame of reference for his observations and reflections, the author accepted a definition of teaching by

Teachers College Record 65: 524–34; March 1964.
[3] Taba, Hilda, "Teaching Strategy and Learning." The California Journal for Instructional Improvement; December 1963. p. 3.

B. Othanel Smith,[4] which he outlined as follows:

Teaching is a system of action involving an agent, an end in view, and a situation including two sets of factors—those over which the agent has no control (class size, size of classroom, physical characteristics of pupils, etc.) and those which he can modify (ways of asking questions about instruction and ways of structuring information or ideas gleaned).

Smith points out that it is by means of the set of factors the agent can control that the particular end in view is reached. It might be concluded, then, that the dimension of the instructional situation which includes those factors the agent can modify is, in sum, the *strategies* and *tactics* of the teacher. This definition of teaching is also of aid in identifying those elements of teaching over which teachers have little or no control, thus helping one to be consciously aware of the limitation of the model, that it focuses only on factors over which the teacher has control.

SOME ASSUMPTIONS ABOUT INSTRUCTION USED AS A BASIS FOR OBSERVATIONS

1. *What the teacher does is a critical factor in determining what the pupil learns.*
   Implied in this assumption is the notion that teachers have to display some behavior so that the learners will know what is expected of them: what goals they are to work toward, what they are expected to do, and how they are to do it.

[4] B. Othanel Smith, "Toward a Theory of Teaching," in *Theory and Research in Teaching,* Arno A. Bellack, ed. (New York: Bureau of Publications, Teachers College, Columbia University, 1963), p. 4.

James Gallagher,[5] in reporting his study of productive thinking, stated, "The teacher is the key in the *initiation* and *stimulation* of productive thinking in the classroom."

2. *Children can set goals in the instructional situation; teacher behavior determines if they will.*

3. *Children can do productive thinking in the instructional situation; teacher behavior determines if they will.*

4. *Some aspects of learner behavior in an instructional situation may be directly related to specific units of teacher behavior; that is, learner behavior is influenced by the behavior of the teacher.*
   In a meeting at the Manhattan Beach Unified School District in 1965, Marie Hughes stated, "There is a syndrome of teaching acts that will (1) lead to good order and management in the classroom, and (2) lead to the development by the learners of higher mental processes; and there is also a syndrome of acts that will lead to involvement and self-commitment on the part of the learners."

5. *Some aspects of teacher behavior in an instructional situation may be directly related to learner behavior; that is, teacher behavior is influenced by the behavior of the learners.*

6. *Other factors being equal, certain units of teacher behavior (tactics) generally elicit learner behavior within a given range.*
   This is not to imply that all teachers need do is to behave in a certain way and the learners will respond accordingly. Certainly teaching is not so simple. But with students of our culture, our range of socioeconomic backgrounds and kinds of past ex-

[5] Gallagher, James. "Problems in Stimulating Productive Thinking of the Gifted." A presentation made at the California Teachers Association in Los Angeles, December 1963.

periences, the responses of the learners in a given learning situation are generally predictable. The work of J. Richard Suchman in the Illinois Studies in Inquiry Training is interpreted as evidence in support of this assumption. When a teacher creates a certain kind of structure (conditions for inquiry among the structural factors), learners usually do inquire—and in a more or less predictable fashion.[6]

STRATEGIES AND TACTICS

From the observation and analysis of 49 tape-recorded lessons, the following operational definitions of strategy and tactic, as these terms apply to instruction were developed:

Strategy: A generalized plan for a lesson(s) which includes structure, desired learner behavior in terms of the goals of instruction, and an outline of planned tactics necessary to implement the strategy. The lesson strategy is part of a larger development scheme—the curriculum.

Strategies are, in a sense, the "why" of specific teacher behavior. Some are a function of more explicit "now" goals, or "one-lesson-accessible" stragies; others which take more than one lesson to develop and usually continue over a period of several lessons are referred to as "overtime" strategies.

Either one-lesson-accessible or overtime strategies may be changed, modified, or discontinued (with another substituted perhaps) as a lesson proceeds and the teacher interprets feedback from the students. One factor which may give rise to such change in

a lesson strategy is the nature of that strategy in relation to the hypothesized and real readiness and rate of progress of the unique group of students.

Strategy planning is done at a time other than that at which the teacher is teaching, however, this is not to deny that the teacher may get some ideas for future strategies while in the process of teaching.

Tactic: Goal-linked influenced/influencing behavior of the teacher—the way a teacher behaves in the instructional situation in working toward the development of the strategy; units of teacher behavior through which the teacher fulfills his various instructional roles with the students of his class from moment to moment; the components of teacher behavior through which the teacher, the students, and the subject matter interact.

A tactic may range from no overt teacher behavior (e.g., using silence for a specific purpose) to one question or statement to a complex of verbal or purposeful nonverbal teacher behavior interlaced with student behaviors.

In the lessons observed, it was found that one lesson may vary from one tactic for the whole lesson to a highly complex interweaving of several different tactics In some cases, while using one tactic with an entire class, a teacher may employ several different tactics at different times or at the same time with different individuals within the total group. Some tactics may be directed toward one child and some toward a group of children; some may be in the form of one teacher behavior directed toward one learner response, while others are more complex and dependent upon a sequence of teacher-student interactions; still others may be directed to learner responses at some time in the future.

---

[6] This assumption is drawn from the author's experience in Inquiry Training during the last five years and from many discussions with Dr. Suchman.

It also became evident that a given lesson may illustrate two different kinds of teacher tactics, *planned tactics* and *responsive tactics*. The difference between the two is that planned tactics are those a teacher decides to use to implement his strategy; they are planned before the lesson takes place. Then, as the teacher uses these tactics with the class, certain responses by the children may clue him to apply a different tactic with a particular child in terms of the goals established or in order to enhance the child's self-concept. In this case, the teacher draws from his tactic repertory, or he may consciously or subconsciously invent a new (new to the teacher) tactic to meet the specific situation.

INSTRUCTION

After an operational definition of tactics and strategies had been built, attention was turned to searching for the ways in which tactics and strategies fit into the total picture of instruction; that is, an attempt was made to seek relationships among tactics, strategies, teacher behavior, goals of education, and the learners.

Smith provided the idea which led to the development of the Conceptual Model of Instruction:

> Everyone knows that the teacher not only influences student behavior, but that he is also influenced by student behavior. The teacher is constantly observing the student and modifying his own behavior in terms of his observations. ... We may therefore say that instructional behavior consists of a chain of three links—observing, diagnosing, acting.[7]

[7] B. Othanel Smith, "A Conceptual Analysis of Instructional Behavior," *Journal of Teacher Education,* 14: 296, September, 1963.

The idea of influencing/influenced teacher behavior seemed most intriguing, as was the picture of the teacher as behaver, observer, and diagnoser. By applying these two ideas, the following four aspects of instruction were identified:

1. *Teacher planning*—in terms of what the teacher knows of the learner, the curriculum, the situation.
2. *Teacher behavior, initiatory*—to create a focus for thinking and working, what the teacher does to get things started.
3. *Teacher observation, interpretation, and diagnosis of learner behavior*—in terms of the situation, knowledge of prior experiences of the learner, prior observations of learners' behaviors, enhancement of child's self-concept, the curriculum (affective, cognitive, and action dimensions).
4. *Teacher behavior, influenced/influencing*—influenced by the observations, interpretations, and diagnosis of learner behavior, and influencing to the degree that teacher behavior stimulates further learner behavior.

Consideration of the flow of those aspects during the process of instruction led to the development of the Conceptual Model of Instruction (Figure 1), from which it can be seen that the potential lesson takes shape as the teacher, making decisions about goals, structure, and planned tactics, begins the development of the strategy. *Teacher planning* (1) is completed.

Teacher behavior, initiatory (2) is a tactic(s) which creates the focus for the lesson and sets the appropriate structure. As a result of the teacher behavior, initiatory, the children becomes aware of some of the goals that will direct their activity as well as their evolving responsibilities in the specific instruc-

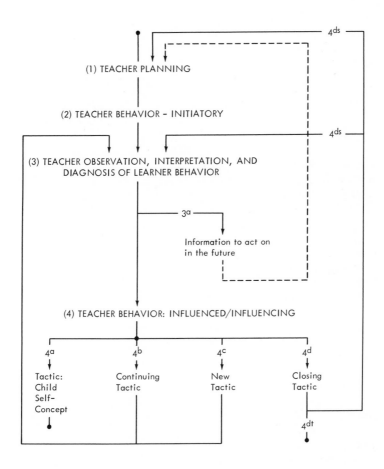

Figure 1

A Conceptual Model of Instruction

tional situation. The lesson begins to unfold.

At the same moment the initiatory tactic takes place, *teacher observation, interpretation, and diagnosis of learner behavior* (3) take place. The teacher observes the consequences of his influencing behavior. Some observations may be singular in nature, leading directly to influenced teacher behavior; some may take place for a longer period of time over a more complex series of learner-teacher behaviors as related to the purpose of the tactic; some may yield information about the learners that is not directly related to following the teacher behavior. For example, while a group of third-grade children were working to make a compass, one said, "The north part of one magnet will attract the north part of another magnet." Rather than stop the lesson to attempt to correct this misconception, the teacher made a mental note of the response, which became *information to act on in the future* (3a) and possibly the basis of planning for a future lesson. In this case, the observation, interpretation, and diagnosis of the learner behavior did not lead to influenced teacher behavior—at that particular moment.

As the lesson continues, the teacher's observation and interpretation may lead to the diagnosis that the initiatory tactic is developing according to plan, and the tactic is therefore continued (4b—*continuing tactic*). It may be, however, that the initiatory tactic is not achieving the intended purpose, and the planned teacher behavior is consequently modified or discontinued and another initiatory tactic started (4c—*new tactic*); or the lesson may be aborted (4d—*closing tactic*). Thus, *teacher behavior, influenced/influencing* (4) is initiated. The teacher behaves according to a previous observation, interpretation, and diagnosis of learner behavior (*influenced teacher behavior*). And in that the teacher behavior is intended to feed forward to new learner behavior (back to (3)), the teacher behavior is *influencing*.

Once having achieved the focus and structure for the lesson, the strategy implementation tactic(s) evolves. A 4, 3, 4, 3 . . . behaving-observing cycle develops; this 4, 3 cycle is the interactive heart of instruction. During this sequence, one kind of tactic a teacher might use which is an exception to the development of the lesson strategy is teacher behavior designed to enhance immediately a child's self-concept (4a—*tactic: child self-concept*).

If the strategy is won or time has run out, a closing tactic (4d) is employed. In one case, the topic may be closed off,

not to be reconsidered ($4d_1$); in another case, the closing tactic may set the stage directly for work next time ($4d_2$). The teacher may say, "We will not be able to complete this work today. Tomorrow, let's begin just where we left off. When you come into the room after recess you may get the materials with which you were working and continue." The use of $4d_3$ implies that the day's closing tactic provides information which the teacher will consider in planning the next lesson.

The ways in which the strategies and tactics relate to the four aspects of instruction visualized in the model are:

1. The first step, *teacher planning*, is devoted to developing a strategy for a lesson or for a series of lessons in terms of selected goals. Planned tactics are decided upon.

2. *Teacher behavior* in the class situation initiates the tactics in action.

3. *Teacher observation, interpretation, and diagnosis* are made in terms of the purpose for which the tactic was initiated.

4. Teacher behavior proceeds with tactic as planned or the tactic is modified as a result of prior observation, interpretation, and diagnosis. In reaction to students' interactions, teacher may draw on responsive tactics to pull certain students into class interaction, to take advantage of problems, questions, etc., which arise.

It may be concluded, therefore, that the central directive element of instruction is the lesson strategy, and the essence of classroom interactions, the lesson tactic(s).

TACTICAL ELEMENTS

As attention is turned to classroom interaction, all tactics, whether they are directed toward a convergent behavior such as interpreting a contour map or a more divergent behavior such as setting the stage so that the students can generate theories about a given event, consist of the four elements introduced in the model as *teacher behavior, influenced/influencing* (4) and *teacher observation, interpretation and diagnosis* (3). A behavior-observing cycle develops.

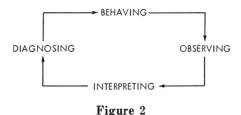

Figure 2

Tactical Element Loop

In the light of some previous diagnoses and in terms of explicit goals, a teacher behaves. Simultaneously, he observes the students. Such observations are interpreted in terms of the purposes of the tactic. With this information, diagnoses about continuing or new teacher behaviors are made which lead to continuing behaving. Thus, a tactical element loop takes shape which involves *diagnosing, behaving, observing,* and *interpreting* by the teacher.

TEACHING AS EXPERIMENTING

In making a diagnosis, the teacher generates a hypothesis about a relationship between his potential behavior and its effect upon the students. In effect, he is saying, "If I..., then the learners will...."

Following the formulation of such a hypothesis, the teacher experiments: he behaves and observes the responses of the students, viewing such responses largely as a consequence of his behavior. These observations are then interpreted in terms of the purposes which motivated his behavior in the first place. Thus, if a tactic does not seem to be successful in helping the learners move toward the purposes for which it was hypothetically designed, the teacher, either by drawing on his repertory of tactics, by creating a new tactic (spontaneous teacher behavior), or by modifying the purpose for which the tactic was designed, may change his behavior sequence.

Viewed in this way, instruction is experimental in nature. Knowing the goals appropriate for a child or group of children, a teacher hypothesizes about his own behaviors which may stimulate certain kinds of productive behavior of the learners. In his behaving and observing, the teacher experiments. He interprets his observations in terms of their relevancy to the goals of instruction. Hypotheses may then be discontinued, modified, or discarded in favor of new ones. Thus, instruction is regarded as a dynamic and, over a period of time, self-correcting, continually redirected, influenced/influencing, interactive process.

Smith points out that teaching includes two sets of factors. One of these sets is those (factors) over which the agent (teacher) has no control. Other extrasituational factors which add the dimension of the past and future to the tactical element loop affect that loop to an unknown degree. The following diagram identifies some of these factors as well as the points at which they affect the elements of the loop (Figure 3).

As attention is directed to some of the "knows" in instruction, the question of relative uncertainty about instruction

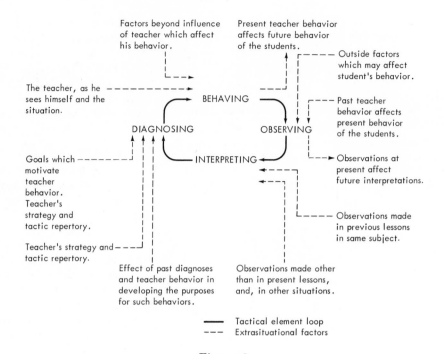

Figure 3

Some Extrasituational Factors That Affect the Nature of Instruction

arises. One group of such knowns is those factors which Smith defines as being modifiable by the teacher; another is the body of educational goals which motivate teacher behavior. As the teacher interacts with the students, a third group of knowns—the teacher's past experience (strategy and tactic repertory) and present awareness—is marshalled in directed effort. To what degree, however, are all of these knowns in instruction *operationally* known?

When these groups of factors are combined (the one set over which the agent has no control, extrasituational factors, and the limit of the degree to which the "knowns" are known) with the idea that in instruction attention is directed toward new or future experiences in which the instructional knowns are largely of value only in a predictive

sense and in which every instructional excursion is in reality an unknown, it is readily apparent that the number of "unknowns," "barely knowns," and "I-think-I-know's" in any instructional situation necessitates an experimental approach: continually redirected, influenced/influencing teacher behavior founded on a continuing stream of data from and about the learners.

LIMITATIONS OF THE MODEL

Most of this paper has been centered on communicating the various dimensions and development of the model. But models are simplifications or generalizations of that which they are designed to represent; hence, it is useful to direct some attention to looking at and thinking about what they don't do, to look at their limitations.

In this case, the limitations discussed serve to identify some holes in the tactical element loop. Although they have been alluded to in prior discussion, the following list has been included in order to make them more explicit.

1. *Instruction is not a closed loop as implied.*

   In considering the tactical element loop of instruction at any one moment of instruction, two kinds of extrasituational factors that affect the nature of instruction may be identified. These include one group which is more or less bound to the specific situation, such as class size, district policies, size of the classroom, availability of instructional materials, etc. A second group of factors adds the dimension of outside experiences of the learner, which may affect his behavior and his ouside observations, which may affect the teacher's interpretation and diagnoses.

2. *Instruction is not purely linear in nature.*

   The model suggests that, first there is a teacher behavior, then learner behavior, then teacher behavior, then learner... This, however, is not necessarily the case. A kind of feed forward and feedback exists. That is, teacher behavior in previous situations and on previous days may affect the present behavior of the learners, and present teacher behavior may affect the future behavior of the learners in like manner. In addition, a present observation of a learner may provide the key through which prior observations may be more clearly understood.

3. *Observing, interpreting, diagnosing, and behaving are cumulative.*

   The longer a teacher works with a given group of children the more data he brings to each observation, interpretation, and diagnosis; thus,

hopefully, the more rational is his behavior.

4. *The behavior of a learner at any one moment is the result of a complex of affective factors, rather than of teacher behavior alone as implied.*

5. *The behavior of one student in a class may affect the behavior of another students(s).*

   The effect of the behavior of one child on another is not discussed as a factor of the instructional situation. It is recognized, however, that such influence may be significant in some classes in some instructional situations.

6. *Tactical elements may occur simultaneously.*

   Human behavior is such that a teacher may be behaving and at the same time observing the effects of that behavior, interpreting it, and forming diagnoses. Thus, teacher behavior may appear to be continuous even though the discrete tactical elements are aspects of that continuous teacher behavior.

IMPLICATIONS FOR INSTRUCTION

After a look at the Conceptual Model of Instruction and consideration of some of its more apparent limitations, attention is turned to what this model implies about instruction, how it ties together past experiences and opens up some new hypotheses for further consideration.

1. *Instruction is viewed as a two-way situation.*

   In one case, students are growing toward the stated curricular goals; in the other, teachers are learning about the children or their classes, the effect of their behavior upon a specific group of students, ways to behave in terms of certain goals, and the limitations of present instructional goals: students grow toward curricular goals and teachers' tactic and strategy repertoire is empirically extended.

2. *One relationship between learner behavior and ongoing instruction is indicated.*

The tactical element loop illustrates the role of the learner behaviors in instruction and identifies some specific points at which learner behaviors affect the nature of instruction.

3. *The necessity for continuous feedback (completing the tactical element cycle) in shaping instruction is highlighted.*

According to the model, it may be predicted that if part of the tactical element loop were eliminated the effectiveness of instruction would become limited. When the loop of tactical elements is destroyed, effectiveness is diminished and the cumulative learning effect of instruction for *both* teacher and student is impeded.

4. *Use of the model provides one basis from which some aspects of instruction may be observed, discussed, and experimented with.*

The notion of tactics and strategies provides one useful organizer for observing, classifying, and experimenting with teacher-learner behavior.

5. *Implicit in the model is the goal-directed behavior of the teacher; the control points at which goals affect the behavior of those involved in instruction are suggested.*

The model indicates the specific points at which goals affect the instructional process—as the bases for strategy decisions, as planned tactics are decided upon, as responsive tactics come into the situation, and as the tactical element loop proceeds from moment to moment during instruction.

6. *Evaluation in instruction is not something unique to the instructional situation; rather, it is a part of the tactical element loop.*

Viewed from the perspective of the tactical element loop, instructional evaluation proceeds *while* the students learn, during instruction rather than apart from it (although it is recognized that for some purposes some evaluation takes place apart from instruction).

7. *One route to increasing teacher effectiveness is through a purposeful experimental approach to instruction.*

Implied is a relationship between a teacher's tactic repertory (both planned and responsive) and the variety of instructional goals accessible through his behavior. Thus, one route to extending one's tactic repertory may be through reflecting on his spontaneous behavior as well as purposeful experimenting to discover the real effect of a certain hypothesized tactic upon the students.

8. *The model provides a unifying element through which some of the studies about various aspects of instruction may be related.*

The model may serve to place goals, curriculum, pedagogy, teacher, students, materials, etc., in perspective so that increased understanding of what such factors are and how or where they relate to the total picture of instruction may be further hypothesized.

In summary, perhaps the essential implication of the model about teaching is that teaching is inquiring and invites a teacher's thinking and behaving in terms of certain goals or enduring purposes. In another sense, teaching is viewed as learning—learning about the learners; learning about the effect of one's behavior on the learners, based on a continuing stream of feedback from and about the learners; and learning as the teacher extends the goals which direct his activity.

A MODEL, FOR WHAT PURPOSE?

The model is an attempt to make sense out of experience. It may serve to facilitate educational dialogue about the topic, that is, a way to talk and think about instruction. Models also suggest what is to be observed and imply the meanings ascribed to such observations. They also outline ways certain facts may be organized, classfied, and interrelated. Furthermore, models usually stimulate the derivation of hypotheses and/or new questions which may serve to substantiate the relationship postulated or suggest a new model.

In *Theories of Instruction*, Ryans[8] indicates that the chief function of theory (a model) is to serve as a framework for observation and analysis rather than a once-and-for-all description of how certain kinds of phenomena operate.

The criterion by which a model is judged is its usefulness in tying together past experience and ideas and in opening new doors for continuing research. At this time, the Conceptual Model of Instruction provides some basis for looking at and thinking about instruction: the limitations pointed out illuminate several paths for reflection and the ideas generated suggest inviting explorations. As it now stands, the model is incomplete; it represents only a point on the time line of our growing understanding of the nature and essence of instruction. Hopefully, many new questions about instruction may arise which will demand our attention and lead to the extension of our awareness. If so, this model will have served us well.

[8] Ryans, David G. "A Model of Instruction Based on Information System Concepts." *Theories of Instruction.* Papers from the ASCD Ninth Curriculum Research Institute, San Francisco, December 1963, and Washington, D.C., February 1964.

BIBLIOGRAPHY

1. Amidon Edmund, and Simon, Anita. "Teacher-Pupil Interaction." *Review of Educational Research* 35: 130–39; April 1965.

2. Amidon, Edmund, and Giammatteo, Michael. "The Verbal Behavior of Superior Teachers," *Elementary School Journal* 65: 283–85; February 1965.

3. Bellack, Arno A., editor. *Theory and Research in Teaching.* New York: Bureau of Publications, Teachers College, Columbia University, 1963. See articles by Aschner, Flanders, Hughes, Medley and Mitzel, and Smith.

4. Cyphert, Frederick R., and Openshaw, Karl. "Research in Teacher Education: Practices and Promises." *Theory into Practice,* Vol. 3, No. 1. Columbus, Ohio: The Ohio State University, 1964.

5. Eisner, Elliot W. "Instruction, Teaching, and Learning: An Attempt at Differentiation." *Elementary School Journal* 65: 115–19; December 1964.

6. Flanders, Ned A. "Intent, Action and Feedback: A Preparation for Teaching." *The Journal of Teacher Education* 14: 251–60; September 1963.

7. Gage, N. L. "Toward a Cognitive Theory of Teaching." *Teachers College Record* 65: 408–12; February 1964.

8. Hughes, Marie M. "What Is Teaching? One Viewpoint." *Educational Leadership* 19: 251–59; January 1962.

9. Macdonald, James B., and Leeper, Robert R., editors. *Theories of Instruction.* Washington, D.C.: Association for Supervision and Curriculum Development, National Education Association, 1965. See articles by Beatty, Bellack, Macdonald, and Ryans.

10. Scheffler, Israel. "Philosophical Models of Teaching." *Harvard Educational Review* 35: 131–43; Spring 1965.

11. Smith, B. Othanel. "A Conceptual Analysis of Instructional Behavior." *The Journal of Teacher Education* 14: 294–98; September 1963.

12. Taba, Hilda. 'Teaching Strategy and Learning." *California Journal for Instructional Improvement;* December 1963. pp. 3–12.

13. ——————. "Strategy for Learning." *Science and Children* 3: 21–24; September 1965.

14. Taba, Hilda, and Elzey, Freeman F. "Teaching Strategies and Thought Processes." *Teachers College Record* 65: 524.34; March 1964.

15. Taba, Hilda; Levine, Samuel; and Elzey, Freeman F. *Thinking in Elementary School Children.* U.S. Department of Health Education, and Welfare, Office of Education, Cooperative Research Project No. 1574. San Francisco, Calif.: San Francisco State College, 1964.

16. Withall, John. "Mental Health-Teacher Education Research Project." *The Journal of Teacher Education* 14:. 318–25; September 1963.

19.

Philosophical Models of Teaching

ISRAEL SCHEFFLER

Victor S. Thomas Professor of
Education and Philosophy, Harvard University.

I. INTRODUCTION

Teaching may be characterized as an activity aimed at the achievement of learning, and practiced in such manner as to respect the student's intellectual integrity and capacity for independent judgment. Such a characterization is important for at least two reasons: First, it brings out the intentional nature of teaching, the fact that teaching is a distinctive goal-oriented activity, rather than a distinctively patterned sequence of behavioral steps executed by the teacher. Secondly it differentiates the activity of teaching from such other

activities as propaganda, conditioning, suggestion, and indoctrination, which are aimed at modifying the person but strive at all costs to avoid a genuine engagement of his judgment on underlying issues.

This characterization of teaching, which I believe to be correct, fails, nevertheless, to answer certain critical questions of the teacher: What sort of learning shall I aim to achieve? In what does such learning consist? How shall I strive to achieve it? Such questions are, respectively, normative, epistemological, and empirical in import, and the answers that are provided for them give point and substance to the educational enterprise. Rather than trying to separate these questions, however, and deal with each abstractly and explicitly, I should like, on the present occasion, to approach them indirectly and as a group, through a consideration of three influential models of teaching, which provide, or at any rate suggest, certain relevant answers. These models do not

This paper was presented at Brown University as the Marshall Woods lecture on Education for 1964. Variant versions were delivered to the Harvard-Lexington Summer Program for 1964, and to the Boston University Philosophy Club.

so much aim to *describe* teaching as to *orient* it, by weaving a coherent picture out of epistemological, psychological, and normative elements. Like all models, they simplify, but such simplification is a legitimate way of highlighting what are thought to be important features of the subject. The primary issue, in each case, is whether these feature are indeed critically important, whether we should allow our educational thinking to be guided by a model which fastens upon them, or whether we should rather reject or revise the model in question. Although I shall mention some historical affiliations of each model, I make no pretense to historical accuracy. My main purpose is, rather, systematic or dialectical, that is, to outline and examine the three models and to see what, if anything, each has to offer us in our own quest for a satisfactory conception of teaching. I turn, then, first to what may be called the "impression model."

II. THE IMPRESSION MODEL

The impression model is perhaps the simplest and most widespread of the three, picturing the mind essentially as sifting and storing the external impression to which it is receptive. The desired end result of teaching is an accumulation in the learner of basic elements fed in from without, organized and processed in standard ways, but, in any event, not generated by the learner himself. In the empiricist variant of this model generally associated with John Locke, learning involves the input by experience of simple ideas of sensation and reflection, which are clustered, related, generalized, and retained by the mind. Blank at birth, the mind is thus formed by its particular experiences,

which it keeps available for its future use. In Locke's words, (Bk. II, Ch. I, Sec. 2 of the *Essay Concerning Human Understanding*):

> Let us then suppose the mind to be, as we say, white paper, void of all characters, without any ideas; how comes it to be furnished? Whence comes it by that vast store, which the busy and boundless fancy of man has painted on it with an almost endless variety? Whence has it all the materials of reason and knowledge? To this I answer, in one word, From experience; in that all our knowledge is founded, and from that it ultimately derives itself. Our observation, employed either about external sensible objects, or about the internal operations of our minds, perceived and reflected on by ourselves, is that which supplies our understandings with all the materials of thinking. These two are the fountains of knowledge, from whence all the ideas we have, or can naturally have, do spring.

Teaching, by implication, should concern itself with exercising the mental powers engaged in receiving and processing incoming ideas, more particularly powers of perception, discrimination, retention, combination, abstraction, and representation. But, more important, teaching needs to strive for the optimum selection and organization of this experiential input. For potentially, the teacher has enormous power; by controlling the input of sensory units, he can, to a large degree, shape the mind. As Dewey remarked,

> Locke's statements...seemed to do justice to both mind and matter.... One of the two supplied the matter of knowledge and the object upon which the mind should work. The other supplied definite mental powers, which

were few in number and which might be trained by specific exercises.[1]

The process of learning in the child was taken as paralleling the growth of knowledge generally, for all knowledge is constructed out of elementary units of experience, which are grouped, related, and generalized. The teacher's object should thus be to provide data not only useful in themselves, but collectively rich enough to support the progressive growth of adult knowledge in the learner's mind.

The impression model, as I have sketched it, has certain obvious strong points. It sets forth the appeal to experience as a general tool of criticism to be employed in the examination of all claims and doctrines, and it demands that they square with it. Surely such a demand is legitimate, for knowledge does rest upon experience in some way or other. Further, the mind is, in a clear sense, as the impression model suggests, a function of its particular experiences, and it is capable of increased growth with experience. The richness and variety of the child's experiences are thus important considerations in the process of educational planning.

The impression model nevertheless suffers from fatal difficulties. The notions of absolutely simple ideas and of abstract mental powers improvable through exercise have been often and rightly criticized as mythological:[2] Simplicity is a relative, not an absolute,

[1] John Dewey, *Democracy and Education.* New York: The Macmillan Company, 1916, p. 62.

[2] Dewey, *Ibid.,* "the supposed original faculties of observation, recollection, willing, thinking, etc., are purely mythological. There are no such ready-made powers waiting to be exercised and thereby trained."

concept and reflects a particular way of analyzing experience; it is, in short, not given but made. And mental powers or faculties invariant with subject matter have, as everyone knows, been expunged from psychology on empirical as well as theoretical grounds. A more fundamental criticism, perhaps, is that the implicit conception of the growth of knowledge is false. Knowledge is not achieved through any standard set of operations for the processing of sensory particulars, however conceived. Knowledge is, first and foremost, embodied in language, and involves a conceptual apparatus not derivable from the sensory data but imposed upon them. Nor is such apparatus built into the human mind; it is, at least in good part a product of guesswork and invention, borne along by culture and by custom. Knowledge further involves *theory,* and theory is surely not simply a matter of generalizing the data, even assuming such data organized by a given conceptual apparatus. Theory is a creative and individualistic enterprise that goes beyond the data in distinctive ways, involving not only generalization, but postulation of entities, deployment of analogies, evaluation of relative simplicity, and, indeed, invention of new languages. Experience is relevant to knowledge through providing tests of our theories; it does not automatically generate these theories, even when processed by the human mind. That we have the theories we do is, therefore a fact, not simply about the human mind, but about our history and our intellectual heritage.

In the process of learning, the child gets not only sense experiences but the language and theory of his heritage in complicated linkages with discriminable contexts He is heir to the complex culture of belief built up out of innumerable creative acts of intellect of the past, and comprising a patterned view of the world. To give the child even the richest selection of sense data or particular facts alone would in no way guarantee his building up anything resembling what we think of as knowledge, much less his developing the ability to retrieve and apply such knowledge in new circumstances.

A *verbal* variant of the impression model of teaching naturally suggests itself, then, as having certain advantages over the *sensory* version we have just considered: What is to be impressed on the mind is not only sense experience but language and, moreover, accepted theory. We need to feed in not only sense data but the correlated verbal patterning of such data, that is, the *statements* about such data which we ourselves accept. The student's knowledge consists in his stored accumulation of these statements, which have application to new cases in the future. He is no longer, as before, assumed capable of generating our conceptual heritage by operating in certain standard ways on his sense data, for part of what *we* are required to feed into his mind is this very heritage itself.

This verbal variant, which has close affinities to contemporary behaviorism, does have certain advantage over its predecessor, but retains grave inadequacies still, as a model of teaching. To *store* all accepted theories is not the same as being able to *use* them properly in context. Nor, even if some practical correlation with sense data is achieved, does it imply an understanding of what is thus stored, nor an appreciation of the theoretical motivation and experimental evidence upon which it rests.

All versions of the impression model, finally, have this defect: They fail to make adequate room for radical *innovation* by the learner. We do not, after all, feed into the learner's mind all that we hope he will have as an end result of our teaching. Nor can we construe the critical surplus as generated in standard ways out of materials we do supply. We do not, indeed cannot, so construe insight, understanding, new applications of our theories, new theories, new achievements in scholarship, history, poetry, philosophy. There is a fundamental gap which teaching cannot bridge simply by expansion or reorganization of the curriculum input. This gap sets *theoretical* limits to the power and control of the teacher; moreover, it is where his control ends that his fondest hopes for education begin.

III. THE INSIGHT MODEL

The next model I shall consider, the "insight model," represents a radically different approach. Where the impression model supposes the teacher to be conveying ideas or bits of knowledge into the student's mental treasury, the insight model denies the very possibility of such conveyance. Knowledge, it insists, is a matter of vision, and vision cannot be dissected into elementary sensory or verbal units that can be conveyed from one person to another. It can, at most, be stimulated or prompted by what the teacher does, and if it indeed occurs, it goes beyond what is thus done. Vision defines and organizes particular experiences, and points up their significance. It is vision, or insight into meaning, which makes the crucial difference between simply storing and reproducing learned sentences, on the one hand, and understanding their basis and application, on the other.

The insight model is due to Plato, but I shall here consider the version of

St. Augustine, in his dialogue, "The Teacher,"[3] for it bears precisely on the points we have dealt with. Augustine argues roughly as follows: The teacher is commonly thought to convey knowledge by his use of language. But knowledge, or rather *new* knowledge, is not conveyed simply by words sounding in the ear. Words are mere noises unless they signify realities present in some way to the mind. Hence a paradox: If the student already knows the realities to which the teacher's words refer, the teacher teaches him nothing new. Whereas, if the student does not know these realities, the teacher's words can have no meaning for him, and must be mere noises. Augustine concludes that language must have a function wholly distinct from that of the signification of realities; it is used to *prompt* people in certain ways. The teacher's words, in particular, prompt the student to search for realities not already known by him. Finding these realities, which are illuminated for him by internal vision, he acquires new knowledge for himself, though indirectly as a result of the teacher's prompting activity. To *believe* something simply on the basis of authority or hearsay is indeed possible, on Augustine's view; to *know* it is not. Mere beliefs may, in his oponion, of course, be useful; they are not therefore knowledge. For knowledge, in short, requires the individual himself to have a grasp of the realities lying behind the words.

The insight model is strong where the

3 *Ancient Christian Writers,* No. 9, St. Augustine, "The Teacher," edited by J. Quasten and J. C. Plumpe, translated and annotated by J. M. Colleran, Newman Press, Westminster, Md: 1950; relevant passages may also be found in Kingsley Price, *Education and Philosophical Thought,* Boston: Allyn and Bacon, Inc., 1962, pp. 145–159.

impression model is weakest. While the latter, in its concern with the conservation of knowledge, fails to do justice to innovation, the former addresses itself from the start to the problem of *new* knowledge resulting from teaching. Where the latter stresses atomic manipulable bits at the expense of understanding, the former stresses primarily the acquisition of insight. Where the latter gives inordinate place to the feeding in of materials from the outside, the former stresses the importance of firsthand inspection of realities by the student, the necessity for the students to earn his knowledge by his own efforts.

I should argue, nevertheless, that the case offered by Augustine for the prompting theory is not, as it stands, satisfactory. If the student does not know the realities behind the teacher's words, these words are, presumably, mere noises and can serve only to prompt the student to inquire for himself. Yet if they *are* mere noises, how can they even serve to prompt? If they are not understood in any way by the student, how can they lead him to search for the appropriate realities which underline them? Augustine, furthermore, allows that a person may believe, though not know, what he accepts on mere authority, without having confronted the relevant realities. Such a person might, presumably, pass from the state of belief to that of knowledge, as a result of prompting, under certain conditions. But what, we may ask, could have been the content of his initial belief if the formulation of it had been literally unintelligible to him? The prompting theory, it seems, will not do as a way of escaping Augustine's original paradox.

There is, however, an easier escape. For the paradox itself rests on a confusion of the meaning of *words* with that of *sentences.* Let me explain. Augustine holds that words acquire intelligibility only through acquaintance with reality. Now it may perhaps be initially objected that understanding a word does not always require acquaintance with its signified reality, for words may also acquire intelligibility through definition, lacking such direct acquaintance. But let us waive this objection and grant, for the sake of argument, that understanding a word *always* does require such acquaintance; it still does not follow that understanding a true sentence similarly requires acquaintance with the state of affairs which it represents. We understand new sentences all the time, on the basis of an understanding of their constituent words and of the grammer by which they are concatenated. Thus, given a sentence signifying some fact, it is simply not true that, unless the student already knows this fact, the sentence must be mere noise to him. For he can understand its meaning indirectly, by a synthesis of its parts, and be led thereafter to inquire whether it is, in reality, true or false.

If my argument is correct, then Augustine's paradox of teaching can be simply rejected, on the ground that we *can* understand statements before becoming acquainted with their signified realities. It follows that the teacher can indeed *inform* the student of new facts by means of language. And it further seems to follow that the basis for Augustine's prompting theory of teaching wholly collapses. We are back to the impression model, with the teacher using language not to prompt the student to inner vision, but simply to inform him of new facts.

The latter conclusion seems to me, however, mistaken. For it does *not* follow that the student will *know* these new facts simply because he has been

informed; on this point Augustine seems to me perfectly right. It is knowing, after all, that Augustine is interested in, and knowing requires something more than the receipt and acceptance of true information. It requires that the student earn the right to his assurance of the truth of the information in question. New *information,* in short, can be intelligibly conveyed by statements; new *knowledge* cannot. Augustine, I suggest, confuses the two cases, arguing in effect for the impossibility of conveying new knowledge by words, on the basis of an alleged similar impossibility for information. I have been urging the falsity of the latter premise. But if Augustine's premise is indeed false, his conclusion as regards knowledge seems to me perfectly true: To *know* the proposition expressed by a sentence is more than just to have been told it, to have grasped its meaning, and to have accepted it. It is to have earned the right, through one's own effort or position, to an assurance of its truth.

Augustine puts the matter in terms of an insightful searching of reality, an inquiry carried out by oneself, and resting in no way on authority. Indeed, he is perhaps too austerely individualistic in this regard, rejecting even legitimate arguments from authority as a basis for knowledge. But his main thesis seems to me correct: One cannot convey new knowledge by words alone. For knowledge is not simply a storage of information by the learner.

The teacher does, of course, employ *language,* according to the insight model, but its primary function is not to impress his statements on the student's mind for later reproduction. The teacher's statements are, rather, instrumental to the student's own search of reality and vision therefore; teaching is consummated in the student's own insight. The reference to such insight seems to explain, at least partially, how the student can be expected to apply his learning to new situations in the future. For, having acquired this learning not merely by external suggestion but through a personal engagement with reality, the student can appreciate the particular fit which his theories have with real circumstances, and, hence, the proper occasions for them to be brought into play.

There is, furthermore, no reason to construe adoption of the insight model as eliminating the impression model, altogether. For the impression model, it may be admitted, does reflect something genuine and important, but mislocates it. It reflects the increase of the culture's written lore, the growth of knowledge as a public and recorded possession. Furthermore, it reflects the primary importance of conserving such knowledge, as a collective heritage. But knowledge in this public sense has nothing to do with the process of learning and the activity of teaching, that is, with the growth of knowledge in the individual learner. The public treasury of knowledge constitutes a basic source of materials for the teacher, but he cannot hope to transfer it bit by bit in growing accumulation within the student's mind. In conducting his teaching, he must rather give up the hope of such simple transfer, and strive instead to encourage individual insight into the meaning and use of public knowledge.

Despite the important emphases of the insight model which we have been considering, there are, however, two respects in which it falls short. One concerns the simplicity of its constituent notion of insight, or vision, as a condition of knowing; the other relates to its specifically cognitive bias, which it

shares with the impression model earlier considered. First, the notion that what is crucial in knowledge is a vision of underlying realities, a consulting of what is found within the mind, is far too simple. Certainly, as we have seen, the knower must satisfy *some* condition beyond simply being informed, in order to have the right to his assurance on the matter in question. But to construe this condition in terms of an intellectual inspection of reality is not at all satisfactory. It is plausible only if we restrict ourselves to very simple cases of truths accessible to observation or introspection. As soon as we attempt to characterize the knowing of propositions normally encountered in practical affairs, in the sciences, in politics, history, or the law, we realize that the concept of a *vision of reality* is impossibly simple. Vision is just the wrong metaphor. What seems indubitably more appropriate in all these cases of knowing is an emphasis on the processes of deliberation, argument, judgment, appraisal of reasons *pro* and *con,* weighing of evidence, appeal to principles, and decision-making, none of which fits at all well with the insight model. This model, in short, does not make adequate room for principled deliberation in the characterization of knowing. It is in terms of such principled deliberation, or the potentiality for it, rather than in terms of simple vision, that the distinctiveness of knowing is primarily to be understood.

Secondly, the insight model is specifically cognitive in emphasis, and cannot readily be stretched so as to cover important aspects of teaching. We noted above, for example, that the application of truths to new situations is somewhat better off in the insight than in the impression model, since the appropriateness of a truth for new situations is better judged with awareness of underlying realities than without. But a judgment of appropriateness is not all there is to application; habits of proper execution are also required, and insight itself does not necessitate such habits. Insight also fails to cover the concept of character and the related notions of attitude and disposition. Character, it is clear, goes beyond insight as well as beyond the impression of information. For it involves general principles of conduct logically independent of both insight and the accumulation of information. Moreover, what has been said of character can be applied also to the various institutions of civilization, including those which channel cognition itself. Science, for example, is not just a collection of true insights; it is embodied in a living tradition composed of demanding principles of judgment and conduct. Beyond the cognitive insight, lies the fundamental commitment to principles by which insights are to be criticized and assessed, in the light of publicly available evidence or reasons. In sum, then, the shortcoming of the insight model may be said to lie in the fact that it provides no role for the concept of *principles,* and the associated concept of *reasons.* This omission is very serious indeed, for concept of principles and the concept of reasons together underlie not only the notions of rational deliberation and critical judgment, but also the notions of rational and moral conduct.

IV. THE RULE MODEL

The shortcoming of the insight model just discussed is remedied in the "rule model," which I associate with Kant. For Kant, the primary philosophical emphasis is on reason, and

reason is always a matter of abiding by general rules or principles. Reason stands always in contrast with inconsistency and with expediency, in the judgment of particular issues. In the cognitive realm, reason is a kind of justice to the evidence, a fair treatment of the merits of the case, in the interests of truth. In the moral realm, reason is action on principle, action which therefore does not bend with the wind, nor lean to the side of advantage or power out of weakness or self-interest. Whether in the cognitive or the moral realm, reason is always a matter of treating equal reasons equally, and of judging the issues in the light of general principles to which one has bound oneself.

In thus binding myself to a set of principles, I act freely; this is my dignity as a being with the power of choice. But my own free commitment obligates me to obey the principles I have adopted, when they rule against me. This is what fairness or consistency in conduct means: if I could judge reasons differently when they bear on my interests, or disregard my principles when they conflict with my own advantage, I should have no principles at all. The concepts of *principles, reasons,* and *consistency* thus go together and they apply both in the cognitive judgment of beliefs and the moral assessment of conduct. In fact, they define a general concept of rationality. A rational man is one who is consistent in thought and in action, abiding by impartial and generalizable principles freely chosen as binding upon himself. Rationality is an essential aspect of human dignity and the rational goal of humanity is to construct a society in which such dignity shall flower, a society so ordered as to adjudicate rationally the affairs of free rational agents, an international and democratic republic. The job of education is to develop character in the broadest sense, that is, principled thought and action, in which the dignity of man is manifest.

In contrast to the insight model, the rule model clearly emphasizes the role of principles in the exercise of cognitive judgment. The strong point of the insight model can thus be preserved: The knower must indeed satisfy a further condition beyond the mere receiving and storing of a bit of information. But this condition need, as in the insight model, be taken to involve simply the vision of an underlying reality; rather, it generally involves the capacity for a principled assessment of reasons bearing on justification of the belief in question. The knower, in short, must typically earn the right to confidence in his belief by acquiring the capacity to make a reasonable case for the belief in question. Nor is it sufficient for this case to have been explicitly taught. What is generally expected of the knower is that his autonomy be evidenced in the ability to construct and evaluate fresh and alternative arguments, the power to innovate, rather than just the capacity to reproduce stale arguments earlier stored. The emphasis on innovation, which we found to be an advantage of the insight model, is thus capable of being preserved by the rule model as well.

Nor does the rule model in any way deny the psychological phenomenon of insight. It merely stresses that insight itself, wherever it is relevant to decision or judgment, is filtered through a network of background principles. It brings out thereby that insight is not an isolated, momentary, or personal matter, that the growth of knowledge is not to be construed as a personal interaction between teacher and student, but rather as mediated by general principles definitive of rationality.

Furthermore, while the previous models, as we have seen, are peculiarly and narrowly *cognitive* in relevance, the rule model embraces *conduct* as well as cognition, itself broadly conceived as including processes of judgment and deliberation. Teaching, it suggests, should be geared not simply to the transfer of information nor even to the development of insight, but to the inculcation of principled judgment and conduct, the building of autonomous and rational character which underlies the enterprises of science, morality and culture. Such inculcation should not, of course, be construed mechanically. Rational character and critical judgment grow only through increased participation in adult experience and criticism, through treatment which respects the dignity of learner as well as teacher. We have here, again, a radical gap which cannot be closed by the teacher's efforts alone. He must rely on the spirit of rational dialogue and critical reflection for the development of character, acknowledging that this implies the freedom to reject as well as to accept what is taught. Kant himself holds, however, that rational principles are somehow embedded in the structure of the human mind, so that education builds on a solid foundation. In any event, the stakes are high, for on such building by education depends the prospect of humanity as an ideal quality of life.

There is much of value in the model, as I have sketched it. Certainly, rationality is a fundamental cognitive and moral virtue and as such should, I believe, form a basic objective of teaching. Nor should the many historical connotations of the term "rationality" here mislead us. There is no intent to suggest a faculty of reason, nor to oppose reason to experience or to the emotions. Nor is rationality being construed as the process of making logical deductions. What is in point here is simply the autonomy of the student's judgment, his right to seek reasons in support of claims upon his credibilities and loyalties, and his correlative obligation to deal with such reasons in a principled manner.

Moreover, adoption of the rule model does not necessarily exclude what is important in the other two models; in fact, it can be construed quite plausibly as supplementing their legitimate emphasis. For, intermediate between the public treasury of accumulated lore mirrored by the impression model, and the personal and intuitive grasp of the student mirrored by the insight model, it places general principles of rational judgment capable of linking them.

Yet, there is something too formal and abstract in the rule model, as I have thus far presented it. For the operative principles of rational judgment at any given time are, after all, much more detailed and specific than a mere requirement of formal consistency. Such consistency is certainly fundamental, but the way its demands are concretely interpreted, elaborated, and supplemented in any field of inquiry or practice, varies with the field, the state of knowledge, and the advance of relevant methodological sophistication. The concrete rules governing inference and procedure in the special sciences, for example, are surely not all embedded in the human mind, even if the demands of formal consistency, as such, *are* universally compelling. These concrete rules and standards, techniques and methodological criteria evolve and grow with the advance of knowledge itself;

they form a live tradition of rationality in the realm of science.

Indeed, the notion of tradition is a better guide here, it seems to me, than appeal to the innate structure of the human mind. Rationality in natural inquiry is embodied in the relatively young tradition of science, which defines and redefines those principles by means of which evidence is to be interpreted and meshed with theory. Rational judgment in the realm of science is, consequently, judgment which accords with such principles, as crystallized at the time in question. To teach rationality in science is to interiorize these principles in the student, but furthermore, to introduce him to the live and evolving *tradition* of natural science, which forms their significant context of development and purpose.

Scholarship in history is subject to an analogous interpretation, for beyond the formal remands of reason, in the sense of consistency, there is a concrete tradition of technique and methodology defining the historian's procedure and his assessment of reasons for or against particular historical accounts. To teach rationality in history is, in effect, here also to introduce the student to a live tradition of historical scholarship. Similar remarks might be made also with respect to other areas, e.g. law, philosophy and the politics of democratic society. The fundamental point is that rationality cannot be taken simply as an abstract and general ideal. It is embodied in *multiple evolving traditions,* in which the basic condition holds that issues are resolved by reference to *reasons,* themselves defined by *principles* purporting to be impartial and universal. These traditions should, I believe, provide an important focus for teaching.

V. CONCLUSION

I have intimated that I find something important in each of the models we have considered. The impression model reflects, as I have said, the cumulative growth of knowledge in its *public* sense. Our aim in teaching should surely be to preserve and extend this growth. But we cannot do this by storing it piecemeal within the learner. We preserve it, as the insight model stresses, only if we succeed in transmitting the live spark that keeps it growing, the insight which is a product of each learner's efforts to make sense of public knowledge in his own terms, and to confront it with reality. Finally, as the rule model suggests, such confrontation involves deliberation and judgment, and hence presupposes general and impartial principles governing the assessment of reasons bearing on the issues. Without such guiding principles, the very conception of rational deliberation collapses, and the concepts of rational and moral conduct, moreover, lose their meaning. Our teaching needs thus to introduce students to those principles we ourselves acknowledge as fundamental, general, and impartial, in the various departments of thought and action.

We need not pretend that these principles of ours are immutable or innate. It is enough that they are what we ourselves acknowledge, that they are the best we know, and that we are prepared to improve them should the need and occasion arise. Such improvement is possible, however, only if we succeed in passing on, too, the multiple live traditions in which they are embodied, and in which a sense of their history,

spirit, and direction may be discerned. Teaching, from this point of view, is clearly not, as the behaviorists would have it, a matter of the teacher's shaping the student's behavior or of controlling his mind. It is a matter of passing on those traditions of principled thought and action which define the rational life for teacher as well as student.

As Professor Richard Peters has recently written,

> The critical procedures by means of which established content is assessed, revised, and adapted to new discoveries have public criteria written into them that stand as impersonal standards to which both teacher and learner must give their allegiance.... To liken education to therapy, to conceive of it as imposing a pattern on another person or as fixing the environment so that he "grows," fails to do justice to the shared impersonality both of the content that is handed on and of the criteria by reference to which it is criticized and revised. The teacher is not a detached operator who is bringing about some kind of result in another person which is external to him. His task is to try to get others on the inside of a public form of life that he shares and considers to be worthwhile.[4]

In teaching, we do not impose our wills on the student, but introduce him to the many mansions of the heritage in which we ourselves strive to live, and to the improvement of which we are ourselves dedicated.

[4] *Education as Initiation,* an inaugural lecture delivered at the University of London Institute of Education, 9 December 1963; published for The University of London Institute of Education by Evans Brothers, Ltd., London.

20

Four Theories of Teaching

JOHN WALTON

Professor of Education, Johns Hopkins
University.

THE MAIEUTIC THEORY

The maieutic, or "midwifery," theory
of teaching is Socratic in origin and
comes to us by way of Plato. Based
on the anamnesis theory of knowledge,
which holds that learning is recollection
or recovery of knowledge which the
immortal soul possesses but forgets at
birth, it conceives of teaching as a
process that aids recall, articulation,
and recognition. In a beautiful passage
in the *Meno,* Socrates "teaches" an
uneducated slave to "recall" a proof of
a special case of the theorem of
Pythagoras.[1] Although rather optimistic
in his earlier writings about the number
of people who could arrive at ideal
divine knowledge, Plato later despaired

of this possibility except for the few;
but about them he remained wildly
optimistic.

In the *Theaetetus,* Socrates describes
teaching:

Socrates: All this, then, lies within the
midwife's province; but her performance falls short of time. It is not the
way of women sometimes to bring forth
real children, sometimes mere phan-
toms, such that is hard to tell the one
from the other. If it were so, the highest and noblest task of the midwife
would be to discern the real from the
unreal, would it not?
Theaetetus: I agree.
Socrates: My art of midwifery is in
general like theirs; the only difference
is that my patients are men, not
women, and my concern is not with the
body but with the soul that is in travail
of birth. And the highest point of my
art is the power to prove by every test
whether the offspring of a young man's
thought is a false phantom or instinct
with life and truth. I am so far like
the midwife, that...I cannot myself

*"Four Theories of Teaching" is from John
Walton,* Toward Better Teaching in the
Secondary Schools, *pp. 73–90.* © *Copyright
1966 by Allyn and Bacon, Inc., Boston. Reprinted by permission.*
[1] B. Jowett, *The Dialogues of Plato,* II
(London: Oxford University Press, 1892), pp.
42–47, or 82 B ff.

give birth to wisdom; and the common reproach is true, that, though I question others, I can myself bring nothing to light because there is no wisdom in me. The reason is this: heaven constrains me to serve as a midwife, but has debarred me from giving birth.

. . . . .

Those who frequent my company at first appear, some of them, quite unintelligent; but as we go further with our discussions, all who are favored by heaven make progress at a rate that seems surprising to others as well as to themselves, although it is clear that they have never learnt anything from me; the many admirable truths they bring to birth have been discovered by themselves from within. But the delivery is heaven's work and mine.

The proof of this is that many who have not been conscious of my assistance but have made light of me, thinking it was all their own doing, have left me sooner than they should, whether under others' influence or of their own motion, and henceforth suffered miscarriage of their thoughts through falling into bad company.

. . . . .

And now for the upshot for this long discourse of mine. I suspect that, as you yourself believe, your mind is in labour with some thought it has conceived.

Accept, then, the ministration of a midwife's son who himself practices his mother's art, and do the best you can to answer the questions I ask. Perhaps when I examine your statements I may judge one or another of them to be an unreal phantom. If I then take the abortion from you and cast it away, do not be savage with me like a woman robbed of her first child. People have often felt like that towards me and been positively ready to bite me for taking away some foolish notion they have conceived. They do not see that I am doing them a kindness. They have

not learnt that no divinity is ever ill-disposed towards man, nor is such action on my part due to unkindness; it is only that I am not permitted to acquiesce in faleshood and suppress the truth.[2]

The doctrine that teaching is an activity that helps the learner recall the knowledge that lies somewhere within his memory is based on certain metaphysical and epistemological assumptions that become more explicit in Plato's later writing. However, it is never quite clear in Plato to what extent knowledge is a priori, despite the fact that in the *Meno* he says that what is true of mathematical knowledge is true of all other branches of learning. But we need not go into the difficult problem in Platonic exegesis of the relation between sense perception and the recognition of a priori knowledge; the recollection theory is clearly stated, as is the teaching method. The latter is systematic questioning. The steps in this method are three: (1) the process of disillusionment, which succeeds in getting the learner to recognize that what he believes to be true is false; (2) leading the learner to recognize that certain propositions are true; and (3) helping him to recall the reason why these propositions are true. The final result is knowledge.

From St. Augustine, who said

Oh, but I think there is a certain kind of teaching by means of reminding, indeed a very important kind. . .[3]

[2] From Francis MacDonald Cornford, *Plato's Theory of Knowledge* (London: Routledge and Kegan Paul, Ltd., 1959), pp. 25–27. See also Norman Gulley, *Plato's Theory of Knowledge* (London: Methuen & Co., Ltd., 1962), pp. 1–47.
[3] St. Aurelius Augustine, *Concerning the Teacher and on the Immortality of the Soul* (New York: Appleton-Century-Crofts, Inc., 1938), p. 3.

to Kahlil Gibran, who spoke thus of teaching:

> No man can reveal aught but that already lies half asleep in the dawning of your knowledge.[4]

the Platonic theory of teaching has often appeared in poetry and philosophy. In the modern litrature on education it is difficult to identify, although it probably does persist, particularly among those who view learning as kind of growth or development of the self and teaching as an activity that deliberately encourages the development of something that already exists within the person. In describing the Idealist view of the teacher, Lodge says that he, the teacher, can help his pupils to self-education and self-development in three distinct ways: (1) by associating himself with them; (2) by never "telling" them, but asking questions which suggest where and how an answer can be obtained; and (3) by inducting them into the methods of analysis and synthesis. He says, furthermore, that

> ...it is his business to help his pupils to become themselves, to develop what they have it in them to be.[5]

This development may be referred to as "self-realization" or, as some prefer, "self-actualization." Questions may arise about how the teacher decides which traits, tendencies, and potentialities to encourage. Certainly it would be incorrect to identify self-realization

[4] Kahlil Gibran, *The Prophet* (New York: Alfred A. Knopf, 1942), p. 64.
[5] Rupert C. Lodge, *Philosophy of Education* (New York: Harper and Bros., 1937), pp. 49–50. See also John Dewey, *Democracy and Education* (New York: The Macmillan Company, 1928), pp. 65–70.

with self-expression, since it is conceivable that the former may be attained only by submitting to restraint. All the paradoxes about finding freedom in obedience and service are based on the idea that our higher selves can be developed only by a considerable degree of subordination of the self. But whatever the metaphysical, axiological, and methodological assumptions, the maieutic theory holds that teaching is an activity which aids, encourages, or compels students to discover the truth which lies within them.

In summary we shall now list the essential and distinguishing characteristics of the maieutic theory of teaching in order to distinguish it from the theories that follow.

1. The subject matter to be learned is assumed to lie within the learner. It is a kind of a priori knowledge. This is both an essential and a distinguishing characteristic; it is essential to the doctrine of pedagogical midwifery, and it is an assumption found in none of our other theories of teaching.

2. This theory relies on the anamnesis or recall theory of learning. This, too, is both an essential and a distinguishing characteristic. This is clearly true of the Platonic version, but it is less so of the modern ideas of self-realization. The recall of forgotten knowledge may be a different thing from the introspective discovery of the self's true nature. In any case, the fundamental difference is whether or not the learner once knew what he now recalls or rediscovers. The difference, therefore, is largely metaphysical, although it may have epistemological implications. If, therefore, we are to include in this theory the modern ideas of self-realization as the end of teaching, it would probably be more

accurate to say that it rests on recall and self-discovery as principles of learning.

The Socratic method is, in its broadest sense, essential to this theory but it does not distinguish it from some of the other theories.

The maieutic theory of teaching is, therefore, distinguished from the others which follow by unique conceptions of the locus of subject matter and of the nature of learning. It is superfluous to say here that it is distinguishable by virtue of the combination of three characteristics that are not found in the other theories; but, in view of the subsequent summaries, it is appropriate to point out that a theory may be distinctive by containing either unique components or a unique cluster of components, all of which may appear in other theories but never in the same combination.

THE COMMUNICATION THEORY

Teaching is often, perhaps most often, thought of as telling, demonstrating, or dispensing information, attitudes, or skills. This idea of teaching is based on the assumptions that the teacher possesses, or has access to, preferred information which the student does not possess; and that the best way for the student to learn this information is for the teacher to present, explain, or perform what the student should know. The teacher may do this in the presence of the student or through some form of extended communication. This we have chosen to designate as the *communication theory* of teaching. It will be well to recall here that our definition of teaching includes both successful and unsuccessful teaching, and that

an attempted communication that is not completed can nevertheless be referred to as teaching.

Those who hold to the communication theory are, by definition, maintaining certain stated or implied beliefs about the nature of knowledge and of learning. For example, they must surely believe that those things which a student should learn—attitudes as well as facts—lie outside him and not within. They usually believe that there are special conditions for optimum communication. Also, "[whether], then, knowledge be presented by reading or by learning, it is assimilated only when it is actively thought, and not passively received by the sense and the understanding."[6]

It is, of course, possible to argue that communicating knowledge or information to a student causes him to recall what he already knows, that is, the communication of knowledge serves as a mnemonic device. But this interpretation of communication is rarely, if ever, invoked. Adherents to the communication theory are usually concerned about the means of telling and demonstrating, and about the selection, organization, and presentation of whatever subject matter the students are expected to learn. The office of the teacher is viewed as somewhat mediatorial, and its responsibilities extend simultaneously in the directions of both subject matter and students.

As an illustration of the communication theory in practice we shall use a general, and somewhat complicated, teaching method known as the "famous five steps." Teachers have long been familiar with the five steps in teaching.

[6] J. Welton, *The Psychology of Education* (London: Macmillan Company, Ltd., 1911), p. 357.

McMurry,[7] DeGarmo,[8] and Morrison,[9] whose names are usually associated with the unit plan of teaching, popularized these five steps in the United states. Herbart was the source,[10] for it was he who described the general outline of teaching as *analysis, synthesis, association, system,* and *method.* Central to the theory underlying this method is Herbart's notion of *apperception,* which may be defined

> as that interaction of two analogous presentations or groups of presentations, whereby the one is more or less reformed by the other, and ultimately fused with it. Every presentation [perception] is formed more or less under the cooperating and determining influence of apperception; that is to say, under the influence of the elements acquired by the mind's previous activity.[11]

The first step in teaching, then, is the preparation of the student for the learning of new facts, skills, and ideas. According to Rein,

> [preparation] proceeds at once from some conception contained in the aim. It analyzes the mental content of the

child for the purpose of getting at the possible ideas upon the subject in hand that are already present in the child's mind. The purpose of preparation, therefore, is subservient to that of apperception; it aims to prepare the way for the acquisition of the new by calling up and ordering the related old.[12]

Herbart's cycle was phrased in a variety of ways in Europe, and in the United States, where Morrison's version is the most familiar today. The key phase *preparation* he called *exploration* and said that in this phase the teacher should try to discover what there was in the experiential background of the students that could be related to the new unit of subject matter. This could be done through a written test, class discussion, or an oral examination; the purpose is to establish "the apperceptive sequence between the present experience of the pupils and the new unit."

The second step, according to Morrison, is *presentation,* and it consists in the direct teaching, i.e., communication, of a bold sketch or outline of the essential parts of a unit of subject matter and their relations. The third step he called *assimilation,* during which the teacher's function is largely that of assembling the materials for study and placing the students in effective contact with these materials. The fourth step is *organization,* which includes flushing out what has been learned with essential supporting facts and figures, and forming significant new patterns of relations and meanings. *Recitation* is the fifth and final step; it involves the application of what has been learned and, at the same time, provides a further opportunity for its ordering and classification.

This cycle is repeated with each unit

---

[7] Charles A. McMurry, *The Elements of General Method* (New York: The Macmillan Company, 1903).

[8] Charles DeGarmo, *The Essentials of Method* (Boston: D. C. Heath and Company, 1905).

[9] Henry C. Morrison, *The Practice of Teaching in the Secondary School* (Chicago: The University of Chicago Press, 1926).

[10] Johann Friedrich Herbart, *Outlines of Educational Doctrine,* trans. by Alexis F. Lange (New York: The Macmillan Company, 1909), pp. 54–59; and *The Science of Education,* trans. by Henry and Emma Felkin (Boston: D. C. Heath and Company, 1892).

[11] Henry M. and Emmie Felkin, *An Introduction to Herbart's Science* (Boston: D. C. Heath and Company, 1900).

[12] W. Rein, *Outlines of Pedagogics* (New York: E. L. Kellogg and Co., 1893), p. 107.

of subject matter. Obviously, the teacher must have his material organized and under control. At times he communicates directly to students, as in the *presentation;* at other times his direct communication is limited to telling students where to look for information, which is then communicated through books, maps, and other reading materials. Finally, the student communicates what he has learned to the teacher and to other students, and this communication helps to organize and clarify what he has learned.[13]

This widely-used method, commonly known as the unit plan of teaching, is an elaborate form of teaching through communication. The Herbartian concept of apperception, which underlies the method, lacks firm empirical verification, but it does persist in the still rather popular idea that to a degree we learn new information in terms of what we already know or believe. It is not an idea to be discarded. However, at this point in our discussion, it is merely an illustration of the way the communication theory of teaching may proceed. When a person, directly or indirectly, presents, shows, or explains any kind of subject matter to another, with the belief that the latter can consciously and actively perceive, teaching by communication has occurred. The teacher may present the subject matter in any number of ways: he may simply tell it to students or learners with the expectation that they will understand, or he may devise complicated and subtle devices to help them grasp the information. He may, as a matter of fact, use any of the means employed by those who hold other theories of teaching, with the possible exception of the mutual inquiry theory.

[13] *Ibid.,* pp. 225–231.

One of the newer methods of teaching, which developed out of a theory of learning that relies not at all on the notion of conscious communication, is based on use of the teaching machine and other devices for programmed learning. Sometimes referred to as "controlled communication"—justification, certainly, for using it as an illustration here—it has been described as follows:

> Instruction is the process in which a teacher presents subject matter to a learner so that he responds to it in a way that enables the teacher to determine the next item of information to be presented.[14]

Here the teacher is the indirect medium of communication. He does, however, control what is taught in a predetermined teaching-learning situation, which may be described in psychological terms as a "stimulus-response-reinforcement-stimulus" succession. He begins with precise knowledge of what he wants the learners to know and with clear and well-defined criteria for acceptable responses from the learners. Various stimuli are employed both *to convey* this information and *to test* how well the learners know it. The teacher, via the book or machine, may state the information directly, refer to written materials, present analogies, or develop a sequence, all of which are intended to communicate indirectly the preferred information. After the learners indicate how well they know what the teacher is teaching, the latter provides them with knowledge of their success. The next step is determined by the learners' responses. This is referred to as "controlled communication" because the degree,

[14] Lawrence M. Stolurow, *Teaching by Machine* (Washington: U. S. Department of Health, Education, and Welfare, 1961), p. 4.

extent, and continuity of control are greater in programmed learning than in a situation where the teacher as an individual attempts not only to present information, but also to determine each student's mastery as the instruction proceeds.

As an illustration let us assume that a teacher wants his students to learn that any unmber, when multiplied by itself a particular number of times, can be written as that number with the exponent representing the number of times it is multiplied by itself. He begins with a clear example of this principle by writing on the blackboard $5 \times 5 = 5^2$; then, after a brief pause, he writes $5 \times 5 \times 5 = ?$ If the student responds $5 \times 5 \times 5 = 5^3$, he indicates approval and gives other examples, say $13 \times 13 \times 13 \times 13 \times 13 = ?$, or $4 \times 4 = ?$ He may then generalize by using letters instead of numbers, $N \times N \times N = N^3$, pointing out that N stands for any number; and he may generalize further by pointing out that any number N, when multiplied by itself any number of times, can be written N^n.

That programmed learning should be used as a method to illustrate in a practical way the communication theory of teaching may seem a bit farfetched, particularly since it is based on a theory of learning that does not necessarily take conscious communication into account. The fact is, however, that programmed learning does present new information after the manner of lectures and text books. And when inductive approach—which is frequent in this method—fails, the programmed text or machine gives answers forthrightly. This point in machine learning already has a name; it is called "the doctrinnaire loop.". . .

A summary similar to that we did for the maieutic theory is now in order.

An essential, but not necessarily distinguishing, component of the communication theory is that the subject matter to be taught lies outside the learner.

In addition, teaching as communication requires a cognitive theory of learning—gestalt, purposive, or any of the theories that assume a conscious perception on the part of the learner. This again, is essential but not necessarily distinguishing.

The principal method is didactic. It consists of telling, showing, presenting in their various forms, a general method which is not unique to the communication theory.

No one of the above aspects of this theory can be classified as peculiar to it. The distinguishing feature, therefore, is this combination of essential elements, a combination which occurs in none of our other theories.

THE MOLDING THEORY

A third general notion of the nature of teaching we have chosen to call the molding theory. John Dewey said: "When we have the outcome of the process in mind, we speak of education as shaping, forming, molding activity";[15] but there are those who think this way when they have the process itself in mind. According to this theory, teaching may be defined briefly as that activity which seeks to form associations, habits, and automatic responses in oneself or others that will produce patterns of desirable behavior. Although it resembles in striking ways the communication theory, it does not necessarily involve a conscious "give and

[15] John Dewey, *Democracy and Education* (New York: The Macmillan Company, 1928), p. 12.

receive" relationship between teacher and learner.

The basic assumption about human nature which this theory takes into account is that human personalities are formed by their environment, and that formation occurs, in part at least, through personal as well as social experience. The capacity of each individual to be modified and formed by his environment is due allegedly to the biological "plasticity" of the nervous system, particularly during the period of childhood and youth.

> The fact remains that there is a plastic period during which education does its best work, and after which its effective power rapidly diminishes.[16]

Many psychologists and educators have relied on this general assumption in their recommendations for teaching. Among them was William James, who compared the study of habit formation to the study of physics. Habits are formed, he believed, by the infinitely attenuated currents that pour in through the sensory nerve routes and modify the operations of the brain.[17]

> ...The whole plasticity of the brain sums itself up in two words when we call it an organ in which currents pouring in from the sense organs make with extreme facility paths which do not easily disappear.[18]

Teaching, therefore, through the manipulation of appropriate stimuli, seeks to establish preferred habits. The

neurological correlates, which once were given considerable emphasis, are not stressed so much today; the attention rests rather on the manifest correlation of stimuli and responses, which forms an external model.

A cluster of learning theories, all ignoring, or at least minimizing, any mentalistic conceptions of how learning occurs, form the learning counterpart to the molding theory of teaching. Variations in these theories produce modifications in teaching methods, but over them hovers the general idea that teaching is the shaping and forming of pliable material. Conditioning, connectionism, associationism, and behaviorism (if the last is not a generic term that includes the others) all regard teaching as the forming of models of behavior through the deliberate manipulation of stimuli which impinge on the learner and shape him. Let us look at what Thorndike, the connectionist, has said:

> The laws whereby these connections are made are significant for education and all other branches of human engineering. Learning is connecting; and teaching is the arrangement of situations which lead to desirable bonds and make them satisfying. A volume could well be written showing in detail just what bonds certain exercises in arithmetic, spelling, German, philosophy, and the like, certain customs and laws, certain moral and religious teachings, and certain occupations and amusements, tend to form in men of given original natures, ...[19]

Thorndike did assume that the "original nature" of an individual places some limitations on what could be done in the way of forming connec-

[16] John Adams, *The Evolution of Educational Theory* (London: Macmillan and Company, 1922), pp. 65–66.
[17] William James, *Principles of Psychology* (New York: Henry Holt and Company, 1890), p. 105
[18] *Ibid.*, p. 107.
[19] Edward L. Thorndike, *The Psychology of Learning,* II (New York: Teachers College, Columbia University, 1913), p. 55.

tions, which are behaviors, and that the establishment of connections was facilitated by a "satisfying state of affairs." However, the latter was not defined as a conscious reflection on the value of the connection.

Another learning theorist of the conditioning school, E. L. Guthrie,[20] believes that in any one response to a stimulus, learning occurs on an all-or-none basis; but, since all aspects of any recognizably stimulating situation which affect the learner may not be present at any one response, several responses may have to be made to what appears to be the same stimulus in order to guarantee that the response will recur. It is important, nevertheless, that the first response be correct, because this response is learned at the moment it is made. The following illustration may be repellent to some people because of the analogy with animals (who probably do not mind.) Earlier in life the author had some experience in training foxhounds. The simple model of training was for the young hound to follow a fox trail, and only a fox *trail,* baying as he ran. If he ran after rabbits or racoons or any animals other than the fox, he was not properly educated, and, as a matter of fact, he disgraced both himself and his trainer. To establish the preferred behavior, the trainer made sure that the hound would be following a fox trail the first time he ran and bayed; running and baying would thereby become associated only with the scent of the genus Vulpes.

There are other equally familiar examples that could be drawn from the literature of behaviorism, but these will serve to illustrate the learning theory that underlies the molding theory of teaching. In its simplest and most direct application it advocates the establishment of a response to a stimulus. The teacher, for example, may arrange to have a student respond "phenomena" when she asks "what is the plural of phenomenon?" and so relate stimulus and response that they become more or less permanently associated. Or the teacher may see to it that the name "El Greco" is established as the response to a certain rather attenuated human figure on a canvas, and he may seek to extend this same behavior to other similar situations; for example, the studednt who responds "El Greco" to a portrait of St. Paul in the St. Louis City Museum should respond the same way when, on a Cherry Blossom excursion to Washington, D.C., he sees the face of the Repentant St. Peter in the Phillips Gallery. And so on, until his behavior in the presence of pictures is a model of correct responses.

This theory of teaching implies that the teacher has a model in mind, but it does not imply that under all conditions he selects the model in whose image he fashions the behavior of the student; someone other than the teacher may dictate the model, or the student himself may select the model. Pygmalion, a legendary king and sculptor of Cyprus, made a statue of a beautiful girl and married her after Aphrodite gave life to the image.[21] Bernard Shaw, in his dramatic version of this story, has the student select the model she wishes; the Flower girl says of Mr. Higgins:

I want to be a lady in a flower shop

---

[20] E. L. Guthrie, *The Psychology of Learning,* 2nd ed. (New York: Harper and Bros., 1952); see also, W. K. Estes, "The Statistical Approach to Learning Theory" in Sigmund Koch, ed., *Psychology:A Study of a Science* (New York: McGraw-Hill Book Co., Inc., 1959), II, pp. 399–403.

[21] Ovid, *Metamorphoses,* X, 243.

stead of selling at the corner of Totten-ham Court Road. But they won't take me unless I can talk more genteel. He said he could teach me. Well, here I am ready to pay him—not asking any favor—and he treats me as if I was dirt.[22]

It is true that the modeling theory of teaching has been an integral part of Utopias, in which some personal, social, or political power has decided what the models should be. One modern Utopia builder who has been intensely inter-ested in teaching and teaching machines is B. F. Skinner. He wrote a novel, *Walden Two,* in which teaching is re-garded as a kind of behavioral engineer-ing.[23] In his society people are fashioned into models of predictable and desirable behavior.

Again, a summary of the character-istics of the theory may be helpful.

The concept of subject matter is a model of behavior which must be rec-ognized by the teacher. This is an essential, but not a distinguishing, feature of this theory of teaching.

The learning theory upon which this notion of teaching relies is unique as well as essential. All our other theories of teaching are based on recognition, understanding, and appropriation of subject matter by the learner. This one is not based on assumptions about con-sciousness; but rather, it assumes that correlations between stimuli and behav-ior can be established, with or without the postulation of intervening variables.

The essential method, which is the contiguous arrangement of stimulus, response, and, frequently, reward or reinforcement so familiar in condition-

[22] Bernard Shaw, "Pygmalion," in *Andro-cles and the Lion* (New York: Brentano's, 1916), p. 131.

[23] B. F. Skinner, *Walden Two* (New York: The Macmillan Company, 1948).

ing, is not unique; it may accompany other teaching theories.

THE MUTUAL INQUIRY THEORY

In a graduate seminar, and advanced science laboratory, or an art class in an elementary school, one is likely to ob-serve that the teacher acts as a kind of a guide, who, because of his greater experience in method and recognition of appropriate learning, is able to help the student discover or produce knowl-edge that is new to both of them. This concept of teaching may be referred to as mutual inquiry. To extend it to all teaching would require that all knowl-edge acquired through the aid of teach-ing be "socially" new, or at least new to teacher and student; otherwise there could be no genuine mutual inquiry.

This theory of teaching is clearly applicable to research and art, although there are those who would question whether the teacher in these situations is indeed actively teaching. However, in our definition of teaching as seeking, either successfully or unsuccessfully, to make known, there is no explicit or im-plicit notion that the teacher must know what he will make known. He must, however, know some of the methods of inquiry and be able to rec-ognize the nature and worth of the knowledge that is discovered. It might be argued that he is merely teaching methods of inquiry which he knows; yet it is from the use of these methods that discoveries derive.

Out of the catholicity of John Dewey's ideas about education we may select a great many which appear to be consonant with the theory that teaching is a kind of mutual inquiry; the follow-ing will suffice:

When the parent or teacher has provided the conditions which stimulate thinking and has taken a sympathetic attitude toward the activities of the learner by entering into a common or conjoint experience, all has been done which a second party can do to instigate learning. The rest lies with the one directly concerned. If he cannot devise his own solution (not of course in isolation but in correspondence with the teacher and other pupils) and find his own way out he will not learn, not even if he can recite some correct answer with one hundred per cent accuracy.

This does not mean that the teacher is to stand off and look on; the alternatives to furnishing ready-made subject matter and listening to the accuracy with which it is reproduced is not quiescence, but participation, sharing, in an activity. In such shared activity, the teacher is a learner, and the learner is, without knowing it a teacher—and upon the whole, the less consciousness there is, on either side, of either giving or receiving instruction, the better.[24]

Implicit in this conception of teaching are some assumptions about the nature of knowledge and the ways of knowing. Dewey refers to the whole body of recorded facts as "information" knowledge, which, in schools and out, is often substituted for inquiry:

> The mind of man is taken captive by the spoils of its prior victories; the spoils, not the weapons and the acts of waging the battle against the unknown, are used to fix the meaning of knowledge, of fact, and truth.[25]

Apparently, then, true knowledge is inquiry used to apply efficient methods and relevant information to the solution of problems. In this undertaking the

[24] Dewey, *op. cit.*, p. 188.
[25] *Ibid.*, p. 220.

teacher is usually, but not always, more sophisticated than the learner, and the knowledge acquired is new spoils, new for both teacher and learner. At least, this conclusion seems to follow.

Let us look more closely at this idea of teaching. As has been indicated above, it clearly applies to any kind of original investigation, and, by taking some liberties with the word inquiry, to the creative arts. In neither kind of activity can the teacher or the learner foresee the precise outcome of their efforts, and they share in the anticipation of the results. But if we take the generic and well-worn phrase "problem-solving," we find, perhaps more often than not, that teaching directs the learning activities of the students to preconceived and familiar answers; the outcomes of inquiry, as well as the methods, are well-known by the teacher before the student comes upon them. This can hardly be called mutual inquiry. The teacher in fact is not engaged to the extent that he looks forward to learning what the answer is, although he may, through empathy, identify himself with the student's employment of the tools of inquiry. It is possible of course that the students will discover knowledge that is new to their teacher as well; but in most teaching the results of the students will be new only to them. For example, a teacher may set the stage, year after year, so that the students genuinely want to know why Lancaster, Pennsylvania, which was the largest inland city in the colonies, did not continue its growth; and he may reasonably expect, or even require, the students to come up with a familiar and accepted answer. In some of the newer mathematics, this kind of teaching is also advocated. Certainly the problems set for, or adopted by, the students are artificial ones for the teacher, but it appears that some teaching is bound to proceed in this manner.

Far too much, perhaps. It might be argued that if answers are recorded to many problems which students, as newcomers to the world of knowledge, do not know, the teacher should set students on problems that are real for both and allow the student to learn the recorded "informational" knowledge not for its own sake but as it applies to the solution of these latter sort of problems. For example, instead of going through the routine of rediscovering the well-known reasons why the Lancaster's growth was arrested, the student may ask what the *prospects* are for Fairbanks, taking into account during the course of the inquiry the recorded information on Lancaster; or he may come up with an original hypothesis about what happened to Lancaster, in which case mutual inquiry can begin.

At this point it is advisable to digress for a moment and to point out that in making so clear a distinction between the kind of inquiry that leads to knowledge already possessed by the teacher but not by the learner, we have drawn a line that is too hard and fast. For most teaching situations the teacher is bound to discover facts of which he was hitherto unaware. These is, therefore, likely to be true mutual inquiry that proceeds as problem solving, if the teacher is willing to admit that he, too, is seeking answers.

A more detailed description of teaching as mutual inquiry would show it to be very much like learning expect for two important features: (1) the teacher is responsible for the learning of others; and (2) he generally is better prepared in the methods of inquiry and in his knowledge of relevant recorded information than is the learner. His first concern is the identification of those various problems or tasks which make up the subject matter. Kilpatrick's classification of types of projects (although project may be a more inclusive term than problem solving) may be helpful here:

1. where the purpose is to embody some idea or plan in external form, as building a boat, writing a letter, or presenting a play;
2. where the purpose is to enjoy some (aesthetic) experience, as listening to a story, hearing a symphony, appreciating a picture;
3. where the purpose is to straighten out some intellectual difficulty, to solve some problem, as to find out whether or not dew falls, or to ascertain how New York outgrew Philadelphia;
4. where the purpose is to obtain some item or degree of skill or knowledge, as learning to write at a level of grade 4, or learning the irregular verbs in French.[26]

After a problem or a project has been adopted by an individual learner, a group of learners, or the whole class, then, except under the most extraordinary circumstances, they should go through with trying to solve it. This, in Dewey's mind, is discipline.[27] He believes that it can be induced by the end in view; that is, the solution to the problem or the outcome of the project should be of such concern to the learner that he will be eager to go on to the conclusion. The teacher's role lies largely in assisting with the identification of real problems; with the spacing of the "ends in view" so that they will serve as lodestones to the learner as he struggles

26 William Heard Kilpatrick, *The Project Method* (New York: Teachers College, Columbia University, 1926), p. 16.
27 Dewey, *op. cit.*, pp. 146–162.

through arduous inquiry; and with aiding in the selection of methods and means. All the while he is a sharer in the inquiry being carried on by many learners, who are referred to as his students.

The activities of the classroom may be expected to reflect the rhythm of inquiry and discovery, of effort and accomplishment. While learners are engaged in the solution of intellectual problems, the attainment of skills, and the production of art, music, or literature, the classroom is likely to present the appearance of tension and disorder, of search and experiment, of trial and error and more trial. True inquiry is a difficult and probing business. But upon the completion of a project or the solution of a problem, there comes a tidying up, a release from the tension of inquiry, and the contemplation and enjoyment of what one has done. It is in the very nature of things, however, that one cannot enjoy for long his intellectual accomplishments—they begin soon to cloy—and he naturally will become engaged again in the active phase of learning. Thus, the endless cycle of activity, achievement, consum-

mation, and renewal charts the course of the teacher-learning experience. This picture of the classroom is usually the one portrayed by the adherents to the mutual inquiry theory of teaching.

We shall review briefly, then, the basic assumptions of the mutual inquiry theory with respect to subject matter, learning theory, and method.

The subject matter to be learned may have its locus inside or outside the learner. With some adherents it may lie in experience, and experience may be conceived of as both the learner and the things to be learned. This rather indeterminate placing of subject matter is both an essential and a distinguishing characteristic.

The learning theory is difficult to identify. Perhaps learning by experiencing in a cognitive way is as precise a definition as can be given. If so, it is not clearly distinguishing.

As for method this theory demands exclusively inquiry and problem-solving in which both teacher and learner participate. These methods are not unique here—although their exclusiveness may be—but they are unmistakably essential.

21

Freedom With Authority : A Buber Model for Teaching

JOHN R. SCUDDER, JR.

Professor of Philosophy and
Education, Lynchburg College, Lynchburg, Virginia.

How can one teach with authority, as an expert in a discipline, without violating the integrity of students? Achieving a satisfactory relationship between freedom and authority is a perennial problem of education in a democratic society. It is a crucial one today when many educators are attempting to restore to the teacher the authority which was lost by the "democratic" educators, led by John Dewey and William H. Kilpatrick. They attempted to rid education of the authoritarian model of teaching prevalent in the nineteenth century by limiting the role of the teacher to assisting students in solving their own problems. This undermined the traditional authority of the teacher as the mediator of the academic disciplines to students. Restoring this authority will be difficult in a time when intellectuals are challenging the root as-

"Freedom with Authority: A Buber Model for Teaching" by John R. Scudder, Jr. is reprinted with permission from Educational Theory, *18:133–142, Spring, 1968.*

sumptions and values common to all the contesting ideologies of the last century. Can teachers regain authority when even students are exceeding their traditional right to challenge the authority of the older generation by questioning the validity of all authority?

Martin Buber spoke for and to a generation skeptical of traditional beliefs and values and in search of a meaningful and responsible life. Instead of the ideological approach of the preceding century and the impersonal, scientific perspective of the early twentieth century, he advocated the sharing of deep convictions between persons in a manner which respected and encouraged individuality. His interpretation of dialogue, lays the foundation for a model of teaching which combines freedom with authority within the context of the intellectual and moral confusion of our time.

A Buber model for teaching contrasts sharply with attempts to restore authority to teaching on traditional grounds.

This difference can be clearly defined by contrasting a Buber model with the able attempt of Israel Scheffler to restore authority to teaching through the use of three traditional philosophical models. He well states the nature and function of philosophical models of teaching.

> These models do not so much aim to describe teaching as to orient it, by weaving a coherent picture out of epistemological, psychological, and normative elements. Like all models, they simplify, but such simplification is a legitimate way of highlighting what are thought to be important features of the subject. The primary issue, in each case, is whether we should allow our educational thinking to be guided by a model which fastens upon them, or whether we should rather reject or revise the model in question. Although I shall mention some historical affiliations of each model, I make no pretense to historical accuracy. My main purpose is, rather, systematic or dialectical, that is, to outline and examine the three models and to see what, if anything, each has to offer us in our own quest for a satisfactory conception of teaching.[1]

First, Scheffler presents an "impression model" based on Locke's belief that the mind is a *tabula rasa* on which experience records simple ideas perceived by the senses and ordered by reflection. Second, he develops an "insight model" founded on the view of Plato and of Augustine that significant understanding comes through intuition "by an insightful searching of reality, and inquiry carried out by oneself and resting in no way on authority." Finally,

he constructs a "rule model" drawn from Kant's stress on reason as consistent application of principles in thought and morals.[2] Using these three philosophical models, Scheffler gives his interpretation of teaching.

> I have intimated that I find something important in each of the models we have considered. The impression model reflects, as I have said, the cumulative growth of knowledge in its public sense. Our aim in teaching should surely be to preserve and extend this growth. But we cannot do this by storing it piecemeal within the learner. We preserve it, as the insight model stresses, only if we succeed in transmitting the live spark that keeps it growing, the insight which is a product of each learner's efforts to make sense of public knowledge in his own terms, and to confront it with reality. Finally, as the rule model suggests, such confrontation involves deliberation and judgment, and hence presupposes general and impartial principles governing the assessment of reasons bearing on the issues. Without such guiding principles, the very conception of rational deliberation collapses, and the concepts of rational and moral conduct, moreover, lose their meaning. Our teachings needs thus to introduce students to those principles we ourselves acknowledge as fundamental, general, and impartial, in the various departments of thought and action.[3]

For Scheffler, the rule model encompasses the impression and the insight model. He concludes that teaching is "passing on those traditions of principled thought and action which define the rational life for teacher as well as student."[4]

[1] Israel Scheffler, "Philosophical Models of Teaching," *Philosophy and Education* (Israel Scheffler, editor) (Boston: Allyn and Bacon, Inc., 1966). [Reprinted on pp. 173–183 of this text.]

[2] *Ibid.,* pp. 100–113.
[3] *Ibid.,* p. 113.
[4] *Ibid.,* p. 114.

Scheffler's position begs the question: are there traditional principles of thought and action on which the intellectual community agrees? The fallacy of attempting a rule model without such agreement is evident in Mark M. Krug's criticism of Jerome Bruner for applying to sociology and history the structures-of-knowledge approach to curriculum drawn from the natural sciences.[5] Before one attempts to find common principles for interdisciplinary endeavor, however, he should confront the lack of agreement on principles within the separate disciplines. Certainly, there are few in the two disciplines with which educational philosophers are most directly concerned. In philosophy, having failed to resolve the difference between the idealist, realist, and pragmatist, we now face the deep cleavage between the existentialist and linguistic analyst. Even within these schools, there is much controversy. Education appears more confused. We cannot even agree on whether or not our pursuit can properly be called academic or a discipline. In our day this lack of agreement is characteristic of many disciplines. Are sociology and psychology sciences? Is there a scientific method? Is history a social science or humanity? Can one speak meaningfully of God? Indeed, is He dead? Granted the desirability of a rule model, how can one be developed given the intellectual confusion of our time?

Buber believed that a rule model was neither possible nor desirable. He contended that we live in "the hour of the crumbling of bonds in which the young no longer respond to appeals to prin-

ciple."[6] He felt that this was regrettable because no "responsible person remains a stranger to norms."[7] In fact, one of the major concerns of his life was how to develop responsible persons without the absolute ideas which guided past generations. But, he had no desire to return to the rule model.

The great character can be conceived neither as a system of maxims nor as a system of habits. It is peculiar to him to act from the whole of his substance. That is, it is peculiar to him to react in accordance with the uniqueness of every situation which challenges him as an active person. Of course there are all sorts of similarities in different situations; one can construct types of situations, one can always find to what section the particular situation belongs, and draw what is appropriate from the hoard of established maxims and habits, apply the appropriate maxim, bring into operation the appropriate habit. But what is untypical in the particular situation remains unnoticed and unanswered. . . . In spite of all similarities every living situation has, like a new-born child, a new face, that has never been before and will never come again. It demands of you a reaction which cannot be prepared beforehand. It demands nothing of what is past. It demands presence, responsibility; it demands you.[8]

A rule model tends to make teaching the impartial application of predetermined principles to knowledge and events. Thus, it squeezes the uniqueness out of each situation and idea encountered in the classroom.

The rule model also opposes Buber's conception of teaching by allowing the

[5] Mark M. Krug, "Bruner's New Social Studies: A Critique," *Social Education,* Vol. XXX (October 1966), pp. 400–401.

[6] Martin Buber, *Between Man and Man* (New York: The Macmillan Company, 1965), p. 93.

[7] *Ibid.,* p. 114.

[8] *Ibid.,* pp. 113–114.

teacher to impose on the student his relationship to the truth under the guise of "shared impersonality." Scheffler argues that the teacher has the right to require his students to adhere to certain principles provided that they are used by the teacher himself, agreed on by many experts, and sanctioned by tradition. If this is the case, according to Scheffler, "we do not impose our wills on the students."[9] Actually, the teacher imposes on the student his relationship to the truth by requiring him to follow the same rational and ethical principles which the teacher uses as a basis for decision-making. But who determines what these principles are? The authorities in the field? Tradition? Those in power? Even an intellectual coward must decide who will make his decisions for him. For Buber the "education of men by men means the selection of the effective world by a person and in him."[10] Thus, the teacher must decide which principles will guide, but not determine, his pursuit of knowledge and his behavior.

Rather than shared impersonality, Buber contended that the teacher-student relationship should be a personal I-Thou relationship. He believed that there are two basic modes of existence.

For man the existent is either face-to-face being or passive object. The essence of man arises from this two-fold relation to the existence. These are not two external phenomena but the two basic modes of existing with being. The child that calls to his mother and the child that watches his mother...show the twofoldness in which man stands and remains standing.... What is here apparent is the double structure of human

existence.... Because these are the two basic modes of our existence with Being, they are the two basic modes of our existence in general—I-Thou and I-It.[11]

Scheffler fashions his teaching model from the I-It relationship. The function of the teacher is to bring the student into the correct relationship with an academic discipline by putting him under the control of its principles. Scheffler tries to lessen the impersonality of the teacher as a middle man between the structures of knowledge and the student by relating the teacher personally to knowledge. For him, teachers "introduce" the student "to the many mansions of the heritage in which we ourselves strive to live, and the improvement of which we are ourselves dedicated."[12] Certainly, this model is more desirable than a program-learning model in which one imparts textbook knowledge which is external to himself. But, a personal relationship to knowledge, however desirable, does not create a personal relationship between teacher and student. The teacher is still an "It" who functions to relate the student to knowledge and the student is the "It" to be initiated into this relationship. Thus, a rule model fails to relate either the student or teacher to the other as Thou.

Scheffler does force us, however, to face seriously the relationship of the teacher to his discipline. Certainly a teacher, as an authority in comparison to his students, should select the principles to be introduced to them. Surely, students should be required to under-

---

9 "Philosophical Models of Teaching," p. 114.
10 *Between Man and Man*, p. 101.

11 Martin Buber, *Eclipse of God* (New York: Harper and Brothers Publishers, 1952), p. 44.
12 "Philosophical Models of Teaching," p. 114.

stand and master these principles. After all, the teacher has been given his position as teacher because he is responsibly related to the world of scholarship and especially to the subject which he is to teach. Although this is an I-It relationship, Scheffler does insist that it should not be an impersonal one. Indeed, the most important aspect of this relationship which a teacher has to communicate is the relevance of his discipline for him and the meaning that has come from his relationship to it. But, in a dialogue, a teacher must share, explicitly as his views, the convictions which have grown out of his decisions in the world of scholarship.

In a dialogue model, the teacher shares with his student what he has learned as a man living responsibly in the world of letters. From this experience, rather than impersonally imposing principles on his students, he gives of himself because his relationship with knowledge has in part made him what he is and has led to his becoming a teacher. Unfortunately, he cannot share this relationship directly with his students because, as Buber saw clearly, there is a one-sidedness in teaching. The teacher can imaginatively enter into the life of the student, but the student lacks the background and capacity to enter into the teacher's life in the same way.[13] Therefore, the teacher should not attempt to share what he knows directly, as beginning teachers are prone to do. Instead, at the same time he participates in conversation with his students, he should engage in dialogue with the academic world. From this dialogue he brings understandings, principles, and convictions to bear on the problem being considered, always weighing and deciding what is appro-

[13] *Between Man and Man*, p. 100.

priate, significant, and relevant to the conversation.

His primary concern should be the issue under consideration and not the promotion of his point of view. Therefore, he ought to give the views of those with whom he disagrees when their thought makes a significant contribution to the dialogue. To do this he must have a deep appreciation for views other than his own. For example, one of my professors so vividly presented the contribution of the Renaissance humanists to western culture that the members of his class were completely dismayed when they discovered that his approach to knowledge was not primarily a humanistic one. By drawing on a wide appreciative acquaintance with divergent thought, a good teacher will encourage and enrich meaningful conversation.

The purpose of the discussion, however, is not to share divergent points of view so that the student can choose the one that best suits him. Students often respond to courses treating idealism, and pragmatism as if the purpose for taking the course was to select the best fitting suit of intellectual clothing. In one class, students following this fallacious way of thinking mistakenly typed me as a pragmatist. They so labeled because I had used Dewey's insights frequently in dealing with the problems we discussed. To be mistaken for a disciple of Dewey would be a compliment according to the canons of objective democratic education. According to this view, the proper way to teach the philisophy of education would be to treat each theorist so impartially as to be completely nondirective. Then, the student could choose for himself. Thus, education would be objective and democratic.

Buber rejects both the claims that

education should be non-directive and that freedom is the end of education. In a fascinating dialogue with Carl Rogers, Buber gently but firmly rejects the claim that Rogers engages in dialogue. According to Buber, one cannot adhere to the theory of non-directive counseling and engage in dialogue because dialogue requires mutual sharing of experience from both sides.[14] For example, in following Buber's model of counseling with a young man who was having difficulty relating himself to the institutional side of education, I commented that we shared the same problem. After his initial reaction of utter disbelief, we discussed levels of institutional alienation. I *hope* that he understood my contention that, although one can improve his relations with an instituiton, he can never solve this problem. I *know* that a new dimension entered our relationship when he understood that I was neither an intellectual sounding board reflecting back his ideas, nor an expert who had the answer to his problem, but rather a fellow pilgrim who shared his situation.

Few persons exceed Buber's zeal for freedom. Yet, he rejected it as the goal of individual or social life.

Freedom—I love its flashing face: it flashes forth from the darkness and dies away, but it has made the heart invulnerable. I am devoted to it, I am always ready to join in the fight for it.... I give my left hand to the rebel and my right to the heretic: forward! But I do not trust them. They know how to die, but that is not enough.... But they must not make freedom into a theorem or a programme. To become

free of a bond is destiny; one carries that like a cross, not like a cockade. Let us realize the true meaning of being free of a bond: it means that a quite personal responsibility takes the place of one shared with many generations. Life lived in freedom is personal responsibility or it is a pathetic farce.[15]

Thus, freedom for the teacher is not to be prized as an end, but because it increases the opportunity for responsible action.

Buber deplored indecisive neutrality. He would have applauded the three history professors—a Marxian, a Jeffersonian agrarian, a sophisticated rationalist—who made my graduate study exciting by sharing not only the events of history but its meaning for them. Dialogue meant for Buber that the teacher should share the significant results of a scholarly decisive life in a manner which would evoke the kind of decisive response from the student which would cause him to grow.

In practice, the crucial issue in this type of teaching is often testing and evaluation. If I explicitly present my views in dialogue, expecting my students to respond to them but not accept them, how do I test? Do I have the right to ask students to give the effect of the American frontier on American character and expect them to respond with the Turner thesis? If I ask them to evaluate the Turner thesis, do I expect my evaluation or theirs? How do I compare the interpretations of juniors in high school with my own critical work as given back by students who honestly or dishonestly claim to hold my views? What do I say to a student who gives an inadequate evaluation, but defends it on the grounds that he

14 "Dialogue Between Martin Buber and Carl R. Rogers," contained in the appendix of Martin Buber, *The Knowledge of Man* (New York: Harper and Row, Publishers, 1965), pp. 166–184.

15 *Between Man and Man,* pp. 91–92.

has a right to his opinion? I am indebted to Professor William Cartwright for his treatment of this problem in lectures in his classes at Duke University. He contended that, as an authority in comparison to his students, the teacher has the right to require his students to understand his position but not to make them plagiarize themselves in order to pass his examination. A student should be required to give the position of the teacher, the textbook, some authority, or his classmates, individually or collectively. Then, he should be required to respond to this position. His grade would be determined by his mastery of the material in the dialogue and his skill in responding to it. The teacher's evaluation of the student as a person should have nothing to do with the grade. The teacher has neither the ability nor the right to make this type of judgment of the student. He has the duty to test and grade the I-It relationship but not the right to test or grade the I-Thou relationship.

The teacher's primary responsibility is not to the scholarship, but to his students. This involves an I-Thou relationship. To this relationship the teacher contributes from his personal relations with a discipline and his personal views growing out of this relationship. His responsibility is to evoke a response from the students which will promote the growth of the student. It is not to offer them a cafeteria of ideas and ideals from which to select, nor to subtly guide their personality growth, nor impersonally to initiate them into the prescribed principles of a discipline or ethical system. He openly, honestly, and personally shares his relationship to this discipline and the meaning he has found from this relationship in such a way as to cause the student to respond. But, he must not violate the integrity of the student by attempting to control his response.

The correct response to the contention of a teacher would be for the student to test it against his experience. For instance, suppose a responsible teacher states to white students in black-belt Alabama that there is no scientific evidence of significant individual differences in intelligence based on race. A student should respond by asking why, if this is so, do all the Negro tenant farmers he knows seem to be less intelligent than white persons. If he raises this issue in dialogue, the knowledge becomes relevant. It is irrelevant if the student dismisses it because he values only his experience, accepts it merely because the teacher says it is true, or memorizes it in order to make a higher grade in the course. When there is dialogue between knowledge and experience, knowledge becomes relevant to the student. This develops appreciation for knowledge which, according to Alfred North Whitehead, is the goal of education. For Buber, however, the goal of education goes beyond Whitehead's "appreciation by use."[16] The purpose of education is to help the student fulfill his potential through decisive response to what the teacher decides to include in the dialogue.

The role of the teacher becomes one of selecting from the cultural heritage what to include in the dialogue and injecting it in a way which will evoke response and decision. He can set the atmosphere for evoking response but he cannot cause it. Pedagogically, he cannot make knowledge relevant for the student. Ethically, he has no right to force the student into a predetermined

[16] Alfred North Whitehead, *The Aims of Education* (New York: The New American Library, 1929), p. 15.

relationship with a discipline. He is dealing with a person, a Thou, a child of God, whom he has no right to manipulate. The teacher, therefore, is in a position of great power fraught with danger.

> If education means to let a selection of the world affect a person through the medium of another person, then the one through whom this takes places, rather, who makes it take place through himself, is caught in a strange paradox. What is otherwise found only as grace, inlaid in the folds of life—the influencing of the lives of others with one's own life—becomes here a function and a law. But since the educator has to such an extent replaced the master, the danger has arisen that the new phenomenon, the will to educate, may degenerate into arbitrariness, and that the educator may carry out his selection and his influence from himself and his idea of the pupil, not from the pupil's own reality.[17]

Buber believed that the teacher could avoid arbitrariness by creating an atmosphere of mutuality. This atmosphere is one of trust, which grows out of the concerned presence of the teacher.

> He need possess none of the perfections which the child may dream he possesses; but he must be really there. In order to be and remain truly present to the child he must have gathered the child's presence into his own store as one of the bearers of his communion with the world. Of course, he cannot be continually concerned with the child, either in thought or in deed, nor ought he to be. But if he has really gathered the child into his life then that subterranean dialogic, that steady potential presence of the one to the other is established and endures. Then there is

reality between them, there is mutuality.[18]

The source of mutuality is not mutual inclusion, as in friendship, for a student cannot truly experience the teacher's side in a dialogue. Mutuality is present when one becomes "aware of the other's full legitimacy, wearing the insignia of necessity and of meaning."[19] Thus, mutuality results from our recognition that the student shares our necessary relationship to the cultural heritage, to others, and to God and from our actual *acknowledgement* of each student as "Thou."

For this acknowledgement "to be real and effective" it must spring from "an experience of inclusion, of the other side."[20] This inclusion requires learning "what this human being needs and does not need at the moment" and thereby being led "to an ever deeper recognition of what he, the educator, is able and what he is unable to give of what is needed—and what he can give now, and what not yet."[21] This, of course, implies adjusting instruction to fit the limits and potentials of students. In adapting education to the needs and capacities of the student, Buber seems to be in line with much of the pedagogical thought of our century. This is certainly not the case. Nothing would be more inimical to his views than to gear education to "the needs" and "the capacities" of "the child" derived from the latest "scientific" studies in child development. He argues that one learns about children from being personally related to individual children as a teacher. In this way, the teacher comes to know chil-

---

[17] *Between Man and Man*, pp. 99–100.

[18] *Ibid.*, p. 98.
[19] *Ibid.*, p. 99.
[20] *Ibid.*, p. 97.
[21] *Ibid.*, p. 101.

dren in a manner analogous to an artist's learning to know color and form through painting. Teaching, thus, is more akin to art than to technology. In addition, the purpose of knowledge about the needs and capacities of children is not to fit them into the mold of THE CHILD by leading them through a series of development tasks. Knowledge of children makes it possible for a teacher to enter into the life of the "individual and unique" person who is "confronting him, and who stands with him in the common situation of 'educating' and 'being educated.' "[22] Through this act of inclusion, the teacher avoids the arbitrariness which denies the individuality of the student and creates the mutuality necessary for dialogue.

Buber would never sanction using one's knowledge of children to subtly guide their personality growth. Attempting to mould the personality of another person runs counter to Buber's view of the nature of man.

Buber's philosophical anthropology, his study of the problem of "What is man?," sets before us man as the one creature who builds up his existence through attaining a distance from the things and other persons with whom he lives and then overcoming that distance in relation. Men are able to enter into relationship with each other because they set each other at a distance and make each other independent. . . . But to exist as an individual—to realize one's created uniqueness, one must be confirmed by others in his personal qualities and capacities, in his right and responsibility to become what only he can become. . . . True confirmation accepts the independent otherness of one's partner and does not wish to

impose upon him one's own relation to truth.[23]

The degree to which Buber rejected squeezing one personality into a mould of another, however ideal, is perhaps best expressed in "The Query of Queries" in one of Buber's *Tales of the Hasidim.*

Before his death, Rabbi Zusya said, "In the coming world, they will not ask me: 'Why were you not Moses?' They will ask me: 'Why were you not Zusya?' "[24]

In fact, by refusing to attempt to direct the development of the student, the teacher affirms the true purpose of education.

Man, the Creature, who forms and transforms the creation, cannot create. But he, each man, can expose himself and others to the creative Spirit. And he can call upon the Creator to save and perfect His image.[25]

A Buber model for teaching has much to contribute to education in our confused time. In a day when traditional principles and values are in question, it makes it possible for a teacher, as an expert in comparison to his students, to present his relationship with the truth and alternative possibilities with real authority, but without the authoritarian claim that students must accept his relationship to the truth. He shares this relationship, not in a detached objective manner, but with the conviction of one whose life of pursuing basic

[22] *Ibid.,* p. 100.

[23] Maurice Friedman, "Martin Buber's 'Theology' and Religious Education," *Religious Education,* Vol. LIX (January–February 1959), p. 9.
[24] Martin Buber, *Tales of the Hasidim,* Vol. I (New York: Schocken Books, 1947), p. 251.
[25] *Between Man and Man,* p. 103.

issues has produced answers. Furthermore, these answers are to be expressed in the kind of person he is and in his relationship with his students. But, his students are not to accept his principles and values. Instead, they are to respond to them by saying "yes" to some and "no" to others. Thus, they are to develop their own individuality by responding to one who is in dialogue with the world of scholarship and who has become in part what he is from saying "yes" and "no" in this world. But, being related to the academic world is not sufficient. He must enter into an I-Thou relationship with his students. Achieving this requires engaging in dialogue from their side by understanding their needs, limitations, and potentials. This act of inclusion creates the mutuality and trust which makes true dialogue possible. It also helps avoid arbitrariness. But, the real bulwark against violating the integrity of the student is recognition by the teacher that he shares the student's necessary relationship with nature, the cultural heritage, other persons, and God, and actual acknowledgement by the teacher that the student is a "Thou" who is ultimately responsible to God. Thus, in dialogue the teacher has the authority which valid education requires. At the same time, each student has the opportunity to develop his individuality and the respect for his integrity as a person which true democracy demands.

The Evaluation
of Teaching

part three

section six

Problems in Evaluating Teaching:
Overview

This cluster of selections focuses on the significant problems involved in evaluating teaching: what is good teaching in general and what is good teaching in a particular instance or series of instances. In evaluating teaching we face definitional questions (for example, what do we mean by "good" teaching?), philosophical questions (for example, is it valid to treat good teaching in general or must we treat only specific situations?), and empirical questions (for example, how long after the teaching situation is completed shall we wait before measuring pupil growth in learning so as to get the most reliable data?).

Pincoffs, in a complex technical analysis, asks the philosophical question which needs answering before any evaluation begins, "What can be taught?" (Note that he uses the success rather than the intentional sense of teaching as presented in the articles in Section Two.) If something cannot be taught (successfully) by its very nature, then obviously there is no point at all in launching a costly evaluating project to measure success. The evaluator must seriously ask himself, "What am I evaluating?"

Rabinowitz and Travers dwell on the critical issue that to call a teacher's activity "good"—or "effective," "desirable," or "worthwhile"—requires the evaluator to have criteria—openly acknowledged value judgments. That is, the evaluating of teaching is not simply an empirical task with empirical, technical problems. Jane Roland Martin concedes that this matter of establishing criteria is a valuative one and concentrates on whether the criteria established can be universally applied. Do we need specific criteria for each specific teaching situation? Thus, the evaluator must ask himself,

"What are the criteria that I am using?" and "Do these criteria apply to the case at hand?"[1]

The evaluator also faces issues regarding the collection of data. He collects data about teaching, compares them with the agreed-upon criteria, and renders a decision. If the data (what is) meet the criteria (what ought to be), then he declares the teaching to be good teaching. If the data do not meet the criteria, then the teaching situation does not deserve the label "good." But the collecting of usable acceptable data is not a simple matter, as Rabinowitz and Travers and Taylor point out so clearly. Nevertheless, these authors are optimistic as they refer to the trends for the future. The evaluator must ask, in addition to the questions suggested before, "Are the data acceptable?," "Are the data adequate?," "Relevant?," "Reliable?," "Trivial?"

Evaluating teaching involves several steps[2] that can be stated in terms of the questions to be asked. The difficulty of evaluating teaching and the possible strange results are portrayed in the tongue-in-cheek, but pointed, evaluation of Socrates reported in Figure 1 by Gauss.[3]

The reader is asked to consider other items and relationships. The article by Martin continues the teaching as triadic theme raised by Hyman in Section Two and Henderson in Section Five. Would they accept Martin's thesis? Would Taylor accept Martin? Does the reader accept Martin's thesis? What are these criteria discussed by Martin? Are these criteria product criteria, or process criteria, or presage criteria, using the terms suggested by Mitzel (in Taylor's article)?

Taylor treats the historic development of the research on teacher effectiveness and points to the rise of scientism in educational thinking. Is this what Combs and Herbst in Section Seven oppose? If we do not accept scientism as an approach to the evaluating of teaching, what shall we accept? Taylor, Rabinowitz, and Travers, all measurement specialists, call for experimental studies in laboratory conditions to further research. What experimental studies shall we begin with? What factors shall we control?

---

[1] For the classic article on evaluative criteria in general see J. O. Urmson, "On Grading," *Mind,* 59 (April 1950), 145–69. For a comment on Urmson and Scheffler (Section Two) see Joan Cooper, "Criteria for Successful Teaching: Or an Apple for the Teacher," in *Procedings of the Annual Conference 1966* (London: Philosophy of Education Society of Great Britain, 1966), pp. 5–18. For a comment on Scheffler and Cooper see J. P. Powell, "Teaching Successfully and Just Teaching," *Educational Theory,* 18 (Spring 1968), 112–17.

[2] See the short, excellent article on evaluation steps by Wilbur Harris, "The Nature and Function of Educational Evaluations," *Peabody Journal of Education,* 46 (September, 1968), 95–99. For a lengthy, technically complex article on evaluation of educational programs see Robert E. Stake, "The Countenance of Educational Evaluation," *Teachers College Record,* 68 (April, 1967), 523–40.

[3] John Gauss, "Teacher Evaluation—Socrates," *Phi Delta Kappan,* 43 (January 1962), back cover.

TEACHER EVALUATION

TEACHER: *Socrates*

A. PERSONAL QUALIFICATIONS

	Rating (high to low) 1 2 3 4 5	Comments
1. Personal appearance	□□□□[X]	Dresses in an old sheet draped about his body
2. Self-confidence	□□□□[X]	Not sure of himself--always asking questions
3. Use of English	□□□[X]□	Speaks with a heavy Greek accent
4. Adaptability	□□□□[X]	Prone to suicide by poison when under duress

B. CLASS MANAGEMENT

1. Organization	□□□□[X]	Does not keep a seating chart
2. Room appearance	□□□[X]□	Does not have eye-catching bulletin boards
3. Utilization of supplies	[X]□□□□	Does not use supplies

C. TEACHER-PUPIL RELATIONSHIPS

1. Tact and consideration	□□□□[X]	Places student in embarrassing situation by asking questions
2. Attitude of class	□[X]□□□	Class is friendly

D. TECHNIQUES OF TEACHING

1. Daily preparation	□□□□[X]	Does not keep daily lesson plans
2. Attention to course of study	□□[X]□□	Quite flexible--allows students to wander to different topics
3. Knowledge of subject matter	□□□□[X]	Does not know material--has to question pupils to gain knowledge

E. PROFESSIONAL ATTITUDE

1. Professional ethics	□□□□[X]	Does not belong to professional association or PTA
2. In-service training	□□□□[X]	Complete failure here--has not even bothered to attend college
3. Parent relationships	□□□□[X]	Needs to improve in this area --parents are trying to get rid of him

RECOMMENDATION: DOES NOT HAVE A PLACE IN EDUCATION-- SHOULD NOT BE REHIRED.

Figure 1.

Does Henderson in Section Five offer any clues that these three psychometricians would accept? Is there hope, as they suggest?[4]

Finally, the article by Pincoffs because it is technically complex may be made easier for the reader if he keeps in mind the matrix in Figure 2. The

[4] See also the pair of articles by Arthur W. Combs and Harold E. Mitzel, "Can We Measure Good Teaching Objectively?" *NEA Journal,* 53 (January 1964), 34–36, 73.

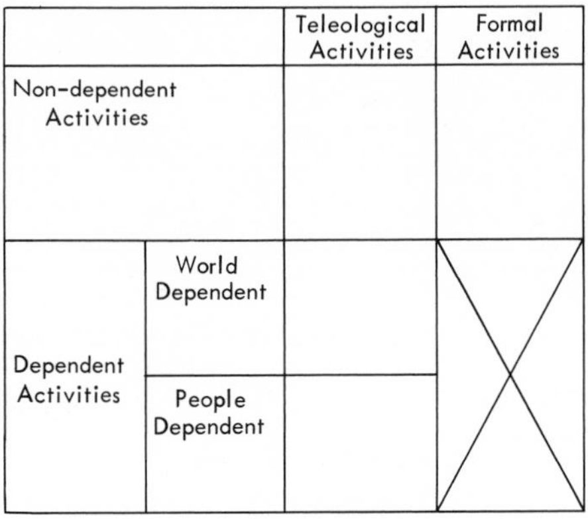

		Teleological Activities	Formal Activities
Non-dependent Activities			
Dependent Activities	World Dependent		✕
	People Dependent		✕

Figure 2.

matrix is offered simply as a facilitating schema within which to consider Pincoff's points, to note definitions of the terms used, and to note examples of the various types of activities. For example, is it acceptable to claim that the *purpose* of golfing or playing chess (teleological activities) is to win? Can we rightly claim that just as dancing and painting (formal activities) have no intrinsic purposes, neither do golfiing and playing chess? Can a man golf on his physician's orders just as he may paint on his physician's orders, to use Pincoffs' example? Is Pincoffs' treatment of purpose and success the same for formal activities and teleological activities?

22

Problems of Defining and Assessing Teacher Effectiveness

WILLIAM RABINOWITZ / ROBERT M. W. TRAVERS

William Rabinowitz is Professor of Educational
Psychology, Pennsylvania State University; Robert
M. W. Travers is Distinguished University Professor,
Western Michigan University.

A recent annotated bibliography dealing with teacher competence[1] lists over 1,000 articles in which some attempt has been made to discuss or investigate one or more aspects of teacher effectiveness. Throughout this material certain persistent problems recur which made the conduct of research in this area particularly difficult. It is the purpose of this paper to state and examine these problems. For purposes of discussion they may be divided into two main categories. In the first category are those related to the definition of teacher effectiveness and in the other are those related to its measurement. By identifying and summarizing these problems it is hoped that some service will be

rendered to research workers who plan studies in this area in the future.

THE ULTIMATE CRITERIA OF TEACHING EFFECTIVENESS

Any study of ability depends upon a conception of what constitutes successful functioning. Before definitive research on the factors associated with effectiveness can be pursued, it must be possible to specify some criterion through which effectiveness may be identified. Research based upon a clearly unacceptable criterion cannot produce results of any great significance. Why then do we not develop more adequate criteria of teacher effectiveness?

In the study of teaching ability great use has been made of strictly empirical and statistical procedures. The use of observations, questionnaires, inventories, schedules, ratings, and tests have been standard practice. Despite this fact, it must be recognized that the ultimate

"Problems of Defining and Assessing Teacher Effectiveness" by William Rabinowitz and Robert M. W. Travers is reprinted from Educational Theory, 3:212–219, July, 1953.
[1] Domas, S. J. and Tiedman, D. V. "Teacher Competence: An Annotated Bibliography." Journal of Experimental Education, 1950, 19, 101–218.

conception of the effective teacher is neither an empirical nor a statistical matter. There is no way to discover the characteristics which distingush effective and ineffective teachers unless one has made or is prepared to make a value judgment. The effective teacher does not exist pure and serene, available for scientific scrutiny, but is instead a fiction in the minds of men. No teacher is more effective than another except as someone so decides and designates. Teachers are real enough, and methods are available or can improvised to study these real teachers. But the effective teacher is only an abstraction. The process of designating any particular teaching practice as effective or ineffective inevitably stems from a reasoned judgment. The ultimate definition of the effective teacher does not involve discovery but decree.

The most fundamental view one can adopt toward teacher effectiveness is to consider it a scientific concept. In searching for the criteria of teacher effectiveness we are in effect attempting to define the term. Flanagan[2] has clearly expressed this equivalence of a criterion and a definition of an activity: "It is impossible to study the requirements for success in an activity without defining the activity. A complete definition of what is meant by success in the activity is practically identical with a statement of the procedure for obtaining a criterion." It would appear that the criterion problem is largely definitional in nature. It we can satisfactorily define "teaching effectiveness," "teaching efficiency," or "teaching competence," we will at the same time produce the criteria

we seek. A definition as Feigl[3] has pointed out is really the statement of a rule describing the conditions under which the term being defined will be used. It states that when certain specified conditions obtain, the term is applicable. Dictionary definitions customarily indicate the meaning of a term by equating it with other terms presumably more familiar to the user of the dictionary. Thus the *Dictionary of Education*[4] defines teacher efficiency as "the degree of success of a teacher in performing instructional and other duties specified in his contract and demanded by the nature of his position." Definitions of this sort are common enough to occasion no concern. Yet it is obvious that this definition, and any other like it, is not a statement of the criterion of teacher effectiveness. Such defining terms as "success," "instructional and other duties," and "nature of his position" require further definition. In this situation, securing an adequate definition involves a regressive process in which more concrete and specific terms are substituted for those on an abstract level. What we mean by the original term, in this case "teaching efficiency," becomes progressively more clear. We obtain maximum clarity and semantic precision when we specify reproducible operations as the defining properities of the term.

By considering teacher effectiveness as a term to be defined, a serious source of confusion is avoided. Selection is so throughly dependent upon statistical checks that one is prone to regard evidence of this sort as universally appropriate. In a certain limited sense

[2] Flanagan, J. C. "Personnel Psychology" In *Current Trends in Psychology,* University of Pittsburgh Press, 1947.

[3] Feigl, H. "Operationism and Scientific Method." *Psychological Review,* 1945, 52, 243–246.

[4] *Dictionary of Education.* ed., C. V. Good, New York, N. Y.: McGraw-Hill, 1945.

this is true for it is quite legitimate to speak of the reliability and validity of a criterion. Statistical and empirical findings are frequently introduced in the evaluation of criterion measures. They have no proper place however, in the development of ultimate criterion measures. In the final analysis a criterion is based not upon evidence but judgment. But let the experts speak:

"In the development of an original criterion...validity is a logical rather than a statistical concept." (Bechtoldt, p. 359)[5]
"The criterion...can be subjected to no wholly satisfactory empirical test of its adequacy. The criterion, must, consequently, be logically justifiable as valid in its own right." (Brogden and Taylor, p. 160)[6]
"...there is no way in which criteria of success can be established on an empirical basis. The definition of success in any activity must always be based on rational considerations." (Flanagan, p. 162)[7]
"The ultimate criterion of success in any duty must always be determined on rational grounds. There is no other basis on which this choice can be made." (Thorndike, p. 123)[8]
"The particular statements of what constitutes a good teacher in any particular locality are in the nature of *policy statements*—emphasizing those qualities which are deemed to be acceptable to the person or group whose

thinking has dominant force..." (p. 141)[9]

A criterion then is first and foremost a matter of decision. Effectiveness as an attribute does not inhere in teaching but is imposed upon it from without. Imposition, in this context, is neither necessarily offensive nor arbitrary. It merely signifies that in the final analysis a criterion rests upon consensus. There is no higher authority to which one can appeal, nor is there any way to escape the judgmental origin of the criterion.

This is a point of rather widespread significance, and one which has too seldom been made explicit. There are those who naively believe that knowledge of teacher effectiveness is facilitated in the simple accretion of facts. These persons invariably insist that their facts exist independent of any judgments whose truth cannot be demonstrated empirically. From this viewpoint, we can by observing many teachers, and by extending our observations over long periods of time, eventually discover those characteristics which distinguish effective and ineffective teachers.

We must register our emphatic disagreement with this brand of empiricism. In studying teacher effectiveness, our efforts always involve a value judgment concerning what are the worthwhile consequences of effective teaching. This decision may be explicit, or it may be implicit in our procedures, but it is always there.

If we are to establish an ultimate criterion of teacher effectiveness, it is apparent that we must do so on the basis of the goals of education. Obviously, a teacher is effective only insofar as he facilitates the achievement of

[5] Bechtoldt, H P. "Problems in Establishing Criterion Measures. In *Personnel Research and Test Development in the Bureau of Naval Personnel*, ed., D. B. Stuit. Princeton, N. J.: Princeton University Press, 1947.
[6] Brogden, H. E. and Taylor, E. K. "The Theory and Classification of Criterion Bias." *Educational and Psychological Measurement*, 1950, 10, 159–186.
[7] *Op. cit.*
[8] Thorndike, R. L. *Personnel Selection: Test and Measurement Techniques,* New York: John Wiley & Sons, Inc., 1949.
[9] Scates, D. E. "The Good Teacher: Establishing Criteria for Identification." *Journal of Teacher Education*, 1950, 1, 137–141.

these goals. The entire problem of teacher effectiveness must begin then, with an examination of the goals of education.

THE GOALS OF EDUCATION

For centuries men have argued over the desirable goals of education. The dispute is probably an eternal one. Certainly there are no signs that it is subsiding at present. We will not subject our reader to another of these seemingly endless expositions and critiques, for that would be alien to our purpose. Our concern is for the manner in which *any* expressed goals of education may become the seminal point for the evolution of criteria of teacher effectiveness.

In general, it may be stated that American educators have, in defining desirable goals toward which education might aspire, contributed little to the clarification of the teacher effectiveness problem. Assessment and prediction require a rigorous specification of what is to be assessed and predicted, but methods of defining measurable objectives of education are still in their infancy. This statement is not intended to belittle the efforts of those who have contributed to the development of more adequate techinques than ones immediately available. Their contribution has been immense, but the proplem of developing an adequate taxonomy of human behavior is of such magnitude that even the greatest can expect to make only small advances. Except in the case of the simplest skills, the objective of education, even when they are defined by currently approved methods, tend to be vague, ephemeral things, which we do not quite know how to measure because we do not know quite what they are.

This was not always so. Not many years ago, education in America consisted largely of indoctrinating a heterogeneous group of youngsters with a limited subject matter. In those days the entire concept of education was narrowly defined. Teachers were expected to be hard-headed and practical, "drill-sergeants in skirts." They knew little about "the emotional needs of the child," and they cared even less. It was considered important for pupils to respect and fear their teachers, and teaching effectiveness was directly reflected in the capacity for reading, writing, and arithmetic which a class possessed. Obviously the goals of education were comparatively simple matters then.

Today educators emphasize the infinite complexity of the educational process. A teacher is considered to be far more than an instrument through which information is imparted. One can discern an unmistakable trend toward defining the teacher's role in broad and inclusive terms, and is expected that an effective teacher will function with skill in a wide variety of situations. According to Barr[10] a teacher is thought of "(a) as a director of learning, (b) as a friend and counselor of pupils, (c) as a member of a group of professional persons, and (d) as a citizen participating in various community activities —local, state, national, and international." This list could, no doubt, be extended without undue distortion of the contemporary concept of the teacher. Extension is unnecessary, however. The reader has only to appreciate the magnitude of the measurement task involved in the evaluation of so inclusive an activity.

[10] Barr, A. S. "Teaching Competencies." In *Encyclopedia of Educational Research.* ed., W. S. Monroe. New York, N.Y.: Macmillan Co., 1950.

Notwithstanding the inclusiveness of current conceptions of teaching, there is one assertion upon which virtually everyone is in accord. It is universally agreed that effective teachers are primarily those who contribute to the growth of the pupil. Education is designed to develop in the pupil certain knowledges, skills, attitudes, and appreciations most of which he could not be expected to acquire to any great extent without the benefit of formal education. But there is no universal agreement as to what aspects of growth are considered desirable.

In recent years a number of attempts have been made to study the characteristics of effective and ineffective teachers using pupil growth as the validating criterion. It seems likely that this trend will continue. Though pupil growth is unquestionably the most defensible criterion possible, undeniable difficulties are involved in its widespread use.

PUPIL GROWTH AND TEACHER EFFECTIVENESS

The effort to determine the characteristics of effective and ineffective teachers defined in terms of pupil growth proceeds within a framework. This framework may be expressed in the form of the equation:

$$\underset{\text{Pupils}}{\text{Behavior}} = f(\underset{\text{Teacher}}{\text{Behavior}})$$

The relationship stated here is a basic one. The equation indicates that the behavior of the pupil is a function of the behavior of the teacher. As an equation it is merely an educational adaptation of the familiar psychological formula:

$$\text{Response} = f(\text{Stimulus})$$

It is within this framework of $R = f(S)$ that many of the principles of psychology are sought. In adapting this formula to the educational context it is necessary to consider the teacher as a complex stimulus to which the pupils are responding. Our task involves the specification of a number of desirable pupil behaviors inherent in acceptable educational goals. After specifying these behaviors an effort must be made to discover relationships between these behaviors of the pupil and behaviors of the teacher. This approach is designed to reveal teacher behaviors and characteristics which under specifiable circumstances can be expected to produce desirable types and amounts of pupil growth. Although the definition of "desirable pupil growth" is a matter of judgment, the relationships between this growth and teacher behavior must be determined empirically. Knowledge of these teacher behaviors will, it is assumed, provide a basis for the selection, training, and evaluation of teachers. The task seems simple enough when described so superficially. In actual practice the problems associated with this apparently uncomplicated procedure are so great as to make universal application at this time impossible.

The great difficulties encountered in the use of pupil growth as the criterion of teacher effectiveness arise from the diversity of outcomes to be achieved, the impossibility of adequately defining each of these outcomes, and the lack of measures for most of these outcomes. These are indeed formidable obstacles, and it is unlikely that they will be over come in the very near future. But for a moment let us assume that these difficulties do not exist. Let us assume that the pupil outcomes, though numerous and diverse, are adequately defined and easily measured. Unfortunately, even under these ideal conditions a number of still unresolved difficulties would be present. These may be outlined as follows:

1. In the first place there is the problem of context. As the Gestalt psychologists have so often reminded us, behavior can be understood only insofar as it is seen in some setting. The "same" behaviors in different contexts have different meanings. A teacher employing "identical" techniques in quite different classes is not likely to obtain "identical" results (pupil responses). The "same" classroom practices employed by different teachers will probably produce different pupil behavior. The entire matter of context presents a thorny research problem. For the most part we have few methods with which to describe and assess the setting in which events occur. Research has always been oriented toward the study of the figure and not the ground.

2. A second problem is apparent when one considers that in a class, though there is a single teacher, there are many pupils. Obviously the teacher does not have the same effect on all of the children. Some will show what might be called progress, others will not. Even if the same effect is found in all pupils, it is highly unlikely that it will be found in all to the same extent. An acceptable use of pupil growth as a criterion requires attention to the individual child. Though time-consuming and sometimes expensive, this seems necessary. It must be recognized that variability in growth from pupil to pupil presents a serious difficulty. An arithmetic average of growth scores is only a partial solution since such averages may on occasion obscure more than they reveal.

3. One of the most troublesome factors in using the criterion of pupil growth is *time*. Ordinarily tests are given immediately before and after a period of instruction. This may be a matter of one hour or one year depending upon various considerations. It seems obvious that the practice of assessing the pupils *immediately* after a period of time with a teacher is defensible only on practical grounds. There is ample reason to assume that there may be effects not immediately measurable. The probability of long range consequences in teaching seem real enough and cannot easily be ignored. On the other hand, some growth which is immediately measurable will rapidly disappear. Here too, it would seem wise to delay measurement until some time has elapsed.

4. Though we describe the behaviors of the pupils as some function of the behaviors of the teacher, we are not prepared to speculate upon the exact nature of these functions. It seems likely that few of them are simple linear relationships. A particular type of teacher behavior may have as a consequence a type of pupil growth. Nevertheless, it would be unreasonable to assume that an increase (or decrease) in this teacher behavior would result in a corresponding increase (or decrease) in pupil growth.

5. Ordinarily we think of the pupil behavior as influenced by the teacher. We seldom consider the behavior of the teacher as a function of the behavior of the pupils. Yet such relationships seem likely. In actual classroom practice a kind of reciprocity is encountered which makes it unprofitable to search for simple functional equations. The facts of school life suggest that the interaction of teacher and pupil is complex and reciprocal, not simple and unilateral.

6. Probably the most serious difficulty encountered in research employing the pupil growth criterion is exercis-

ing the necessary experimental controls. If we are to show relationships between teacher behavior and pupil behaviors, our experimental procedures must be free from sources of contamination. But pupil behavior is obviously determined by a large number of variables, and it is virtually impossible to control them all. To isolate and assess the influence of the teacher independent of other influences (parents, relations, past teachers, friends, self, books, etc.) requires specialized techniques which cannot easily be applied to the classroom situation.

These difficulties are apparent in spite of the fact that we have assumed the existence of instruments to measure all facets of pupil growth. Actually, of course, these instruments do not exist. Growth in skills such as reading or arithmetic are measurable but few are willing to limit assessment so narrowly. Though available tests are almost all in the field of subject matter achievement, a broad concept of effectiveness includes the teacher's influence on emotional adjustment in pupils, social attitudes, creative expression, and the like. These are eminently commendable goals toward which a teacher might aspire, but we have, sad to say, few acceptable methods of measuring progress toward these goals.

A CONCLUSION

It is a simple matter to offer criticism. Suggesting the means to obviate these criticisms is much more difficult, however. It would be pleasant indeed if, following these somewhat gloomy words, the authors could now proceed to surmount the obstacles to which they have alluded. But the reader must not antici-

pate this happy circumstance. If a pessimistic note has been sounded, it will not be resolved in a serene and secure chord of triumph.

Obviously some action is necessary. Nothing contained in this article should be taken as advocacy of a doctrine of despair. An attack upon the problem is urgently needed, but the nature of this attack must be carefully considered. Research which attempts to study teacher effectiveness in the complex world of the classroom inevitably faces the difficulties just described. These difficulties are, in part, a function of our limited understanding and also, in part, a function of the inherent complexity of the problem. Both sources of difficulty suggest the need for some form of simplifying control. Accordingly, it would seem that research is best conducted in situations in which deliberate simplifications have been introduced. Research limited in this way generates findings which may not be fully and immediately applicable to the complicated "real-life" classroom, but, at least, the findings can be free from contamination and equivocal interpretation.

The reasoning behind this suggestion and its implications should be clearly kept in mind. Education is so practical and vital an activity that answers to its problems have been typically sought in the most realistic setting available, the classroom. Using the classroom as the locus of research activity helps insure applicability for one's results, but the obvious merit of this viewpoint does not mean that it is universally appropriate. The crucial factors are the number and nature of the variables which determine the phenomenon under consideration. The advisability of using the classroom as a laboratory is indicated when the number of variables is small, when complicating interactions are minor, and when it is possible to secure independent and accurate measures of them. Whenever these conditions are not fulfilled, it seems likely that some form of artificial simplification will prove necessary. The problem can be stated in purely statistical terms: Whenever there are more variables (including interactions) than there are observations an indeterminacy is introduced which can only be resolved by making a number of assumptions. Thus it may be assumed that differences in teaching method do not contribute to pupil growth, or pupils of different socio-economic background are influenced in the same way by any particular teacher, or all pupils have the same capacity for growth, or some such assumption. These assumptions are almost always implicit and unexpressed, but they are rarely absent. The knowledge which we now possess clearly indicates that these assumptions are largely unjustified and thus other means of simplification must be introduced.

A sound research procedure in this area seems to require the use of artificially simplified teaching situations which are carefully set up according to some experimental plan. Of course, by deliberately introducing control it inevitably happens that situations are studied which are somewhat remote from the "real-life" classroom in which educators are interested. This is unfortunate though necessary. However, the procedure gains more than it loses. It permits the drawing of valid conclusions from data since the experimental situation can be arranged so that there are more observations than determining variables. Only in this type of situation can generalizations be made which are firmly rooted in the experimental data and which are relatively unencumbered by dubious assumptions.

23.

Educational Goals and
Teacher Effectiveness

MARVIN TAYLOR

Associate Dean of Teacher
Education, Queens College, City University of
New York.

Educators have long sought to assess and evaluate teacher performance. In this paper we shall trace the development of research on teacher effectiveness from 1900 to 1964, to suggest some of the pitfalls in research on effectiveness and to indicate, in very general terms, what the future may hold.

Scientific thinking as a process of the human mind is a relatively recent development. By the beginning of the twentieth century the physical sciences had led to an advanced technology which began to produce radical changes in our styles of life. Such was the aura of the sciences that the large industries, public schools, political movements and teacher training institutions began to

This article is adapated and updated from an address at the Administrators' Institute on the Processes of Instruction sponsored by the New York State Department of Education through Queens College of the City University of New York at Smithtown, New York, February 10, 1966. "Educational Goals and Teacher Effectiveness" by Marvin Taylor is printed with the permission of the author.

adopt the methods of science as a means for improving their operations. Thus we have vast volumes written concerning scientific management in industry and schools.

Concurrent with the advance of "scientism" in educational thinking was the development of the Educational Measurement movement. Here was the technology which would help the schools arrive at efficient, precise, effective management and teaching procedures. Such was the attractivess of the scientific model of thought that attempts were made during the first two decades of the twentieth century to establish the aims of education by scientific means. Such was the apparent power of science that man was certain he was on the way to Utopia.

According to Joncich (1962):

The scientific movement is a collective title for a variety of activities which operated on a broad front and which touched virtually every aspect of education. By the turn of the century these various impulses had crystallized into a distinct belief that the next great chapter in the story of the American school would be the wholesale turning of education into a rational systematic and respectable enterprise.... (pp. 3–4)

Interest in evaluating teacher performance began as a branch of the more grandiose school survey movement begun prior to 1900. The survey movement was the parallel of the management in the large industries. No doubt a great impetus to the school movement was the beginning of the educational measurement movement. During the latter part of the 1890's and the first decade of the 1900's Rice devised standardized spelling tests, Thorndike developed standardized procedures for measuring arithmetic, handwriting and quality of English composition, Binet and Simon developed an individualized intelligence test. Joncich (1962) points out that "Many came to believe that any sincere efforts to make education a science must translate human behavior, school subject matter, administrative organization, teacher efficiency, and the products of learning into measureable units, for the results of scientific effort in education must be expressed in the univeral terms of science, numbers. 'All that exists, exists in some amount, and can be measured' became the catch phrase...." (p. 5)

Hazel Davis (1964) points out that during the period 1900–1912:

> School surveys placed great emphasis on testing the efficiency of teaching, most often utilizing the newly developed standard tests in school subjects, such as arithmetic, handwriting and others. There was little interest in indi-vidual tests of individual teaching efficiency. The survey movement did succeed in keeping the idea of efficiency in the forefront of educational concern. However, the growing use of individual efficiency ratings for teachers seems to have been stimulated by the efficiency movement, by interest in educational measurements, and possibly by fear of the surveys rather than by direct use of teacher ratings by the survey teams. (p. 45)

As the study of school systems increased in magnitude and intensity, reaching its zenith during the 1920's, many investigators began devising methods for evaluating teacher efficiency or effectiveness or competency. Undoubtedly there were many motives underlying this trend. Among these was the apparently logical argument that pupil growth was a function of "good" teaching and the more practical question of the need of the school's administrative staff to decide which teachers should be retained and which should not be retained. At the same time most departments of teacher education began to be concerned about the selection of potentially effective teachers. Probably one of the most important motives, and one which persists even today, was the belief that the use of scientific thinking would permit us to isolate those factors which are related to effectiveness. With this knowledge in hand the schools would be in an excellent position to select and educate young people who would be superior teachers, thus ensuring an excellence of educational experience for All American Youth. One may summarize the years 1900–1930 as a period of great enthusiasm and almost naïve belief in the merits of scientific procedures.

The period form 1900–1935 was

replete with efforts to develop scales of various kinds for the measurement of teaching efficiency. According to Barr (1950):

> Elliot (1915), Boyce (1915) and Buediger and Strager (1910) were among the first to use rating scales as means of evaluating teacher efficiency. Many different types of scales have been developed: point scales, graphic scales, diagnostic scales, quality scales, man to man comparison scales, and conduct scales. (p. 1447)

Elliot, a professor at the University of Wisconsin, developed a numerical rating scale with which to collect data about teachers. It was a score card which included seven main headings: physical efficiency, projected efficiency, achieved efficiency, moral-native efficiency, administrative efficiency, dynamic efficiency, and social efficiency. There were sub-items within each category with maximal values totaling to 100. Elliot proposed that the score card be used by teachers for their own guidance. (Davis, 1964)

In 1915 Boyce (Davis, 1964) sent inquiries to 350 cities of over 10,000 population requesting a statement of their methods of determining and recording the efficiency of teachers. Of the 242 replies received, 60 per cent of the schools were using some types of rating or formal evaluation of their teachers. These were used primarily for administrative purposes and should not be confused with the later attempts of the researchers to evaluate teacher competence.

According to Davis (1964) "Boyce reported that the number of items on which teaching efficiency was judged ranged from as few as two items to as many as eighty....Many evaluation forms used in 1962 are similar to the 'efficiency records' puplished by Boyce in 1915." (p. 49)[1]

Not everyone was completely satisfied with the attempts to measure teacher efficiency. In 1924 Monroe and Clark (Davis, 1964) summarized the research of the preceding twenty years. They cited studies that had shown the lack of reliability of existing rating devices. They suggested that the rater's general estimate of the teacher produced a generalized feeling tone (halo) which influenced ratings on particular traits.

Knudsen and Stephens (1931) examined fifty-seven teacher rating scales. They found a total of 199 different traits to be rated with frequencies ranging from inclusion on 43 scales to traits appearing on only one scale. Some of the variability was due to the use of different terms to express essentially the same traits, but examination of the partial list of items given in the report makes clear that there was considerable disagreement about which items should appear in a teacher-rating scale.

With the advent of the 1930's teacher effectiveness became a subject of considerable interest to a new group of educational researchers. These men, primarily college professors, well versed in research techniques and in educational measurement, attacked the problem with enthusiam and slightly dif-

[1] Commensurate with the attempts to measure teacher efficiency was the attention paid to improving our technical skills in assessing intelligence, achievement, personality and aptitude. After the First World War group tests of intelligence, achievement, personality and aptitude were developed. All of this activity impressed many educators, and much of the public, and the tests were hailed without questioning the inherent limitations of all tests. It appeared certain that the tests would provide the necessary technology with which to assess teacher effectiveness.

ferent motives. They did not seek answers to practical questions, but rather sought to understand and explain the relationship between teaching behavior and the goals of education. Obviously if their endeavors were successful the practical questions of school administrators would be answered.

The efforts of the "researchers" considerably widened the avenues of search for important variables. The chief modus operandi of these investigators was the correlational study in a field setting. Typically, data relevant to two or more variables was collected and correlated. According to Biddle and Ellena (1964),

> Investigators have looked at teacher training traits, behaviors, attitudes, values, abilities, sex, weight, voice quality, and many other characteristics. Teacher effects have been judged by investigators themselves, by pupils, by administrators and parents, by master teachers, by practice teachers, and by teachers themselves. The apparent results of teaching have been studied, including pupil learning, adjustment, classroom performance, sociometric status, attitudes, liking for school, and later achievement.... (p. vi)

During the fifties and sixties we note a more sophisticated attempt to assess teacher behavior. One should note here, however, that a different reference term has been used; instead of effectiveness (which is a judgment) we now speak of behavior (which is descriptive). The shift of emphasis is as important to consider as is the strategy underlying the shift.

After all the activity of the thirties and forties Barr (1950) concluded that no adequate definition of teacher efficiency had as yet been devised. Several years earlier Barr (1948) reviewed a large number of studies and reported that forty years of research on teacher effectiveness had resulted in little practical information of use to school administrators for making tenure decisions and to teacher educators for making training decisions. Mitzel in the 1960 issues of the *Encyclopedia of Educational Research* indicated that "More than a half century of research effort has not yielded meaningful, measureable criteria around which the majority of the nation's educators can rally. No standards exist which are commonly agreed upon as the criteria of teacher effectiveness." (p. 1481)

Biddle and Ellena (1964) comment that "With all this research activity, results have been modest and often contradictory. Few, if any, facts are now deemed established about teacher effectiveness and many former 'findings' have been repudiated." (p. vi)

In short, the quest for criteria with which to define teacher effectiveness was not fruitful. Many people believe that research on teacher effectiveness is premature and doomed to failure until we have developed better technology for assessing teacher-behavior, classroom interactions, and for assessing critical student behaviors related to teacher behavior. It may seem surprising to most that the great effort over five decades devoted to assessing teacher effectiveness has resulted in so many negligible results. Biddle (1964) suggests that there are two major reasons for these results, "confusion" and "complexity." He indicates that "confusion" involves several aspects among which the following seem to be most important:

1. Some teachers see classroom behavior as an idiosyncratic function and not accessible to measurement, and "some school administrators, in

contrast, convinced of their ability to judge teacher competence, see no reason for research on the subject." (p. 3)

2. The lack of agreement concerning the effects a teacher's behavior should produce. Indeed, the views held by the public, by the administration of a school, by the teachers, and by teacher-educators are often contradictory and mutually exclusive.

3. The use of the same concepts for disparate purposes. In other words, we have not clearly defined, in operational terms, those variables which we wish to isolate and study.

Biddle (1964) is undoubtedly accurate in his account of the aspects which lead to confusion. However, it seems more likely that "complexity" accounts for the majority of non-significant findings. The nature of classroom interactions, the nature of isolating teacher effects on student behavior from other influences on student behavior are so difficult of definition that a higher level of conceptual and technological sophistication is necessary to solve the problem that existed during the last four decades. Combined with the need for greater sophistication is the need to discipline our energies into the crucial task of defining, in behavioral terms, the desired outcomes of the vast variety of classroom experiences. It is this author's contention that the lack of clearly defined outcomes prevents us from gaining access to the variable we seek, teacher effectiveness. This is not to say that we cannot reliably assess teacher behavior, but without knowledge of objectives, we cannot know if the teacher's behavior is effective or ineffective; that is, have the desired outcomes been achieved or not?

As suggested above, one of the chief problems associated with this area of research is the nature of the criteria of teacher effectiveness. Mitzel (1960) suggests that "The term criterion is commonly attached to any set of observations that may be used as standards for evaluative purposes. In this sense a criterion measure cannot be merely any dependent variable which happens to be at hand. . . . Criteria cannot be trivial, otherwise evaluations are made against trivial standards. . . . (pp. 1481–1482)

In considering the development of a criterion one should take into account "a) relevance, b) reliability, c) freedom from bias, and d) practicality." (Mitzel, 1960, p. 1482). Of these four characteristics the two most important are relevance and freedom from bias. According to Mitzel (1960) "Relevance is the product of a rational analysis of the job functions and the job objectives. Insofar as a criterion measure reflects the behaviors required in the achievement of job objectives, it is relevant. . . ." (p. 1482)

The difficulty in defining relevant criteria stems from the complexity of the teaching-process, the unknown relationship between particular teacher behaviors and their consequences (for example, pupil learning), and from a lack of agreement among educators on a hierarchy of desired goals and objectives.

The question of the goals of schooling is a hotly debated philosophical issue. Many educators would place the goals of the schools on a continuum which extends from the immediately attainable to the ultimate; for example, from learning to spell a list of words in the spelling book to the goal that all youth should be educated to become good citizens. The obvious difficulties with the ultimate goals of education are that they manifest themselves after the school experience is ended and are undoubtedly influenced by many factors. How does one isolate the effects of any single teacher? One should not assume that the goals of education have ever remained static or unquestioned. The problem, rather, is that the goals have continuously changed and the number of aims have grown in astronomical proportions. Many of these statements are broad and ambiguous. Hence, it has been suggested by both Cureton (1951) and Ebel (1955) that schools must be practical and turn their efforts to the measurement of goals which are immediate and measurable.

Yet the question remains, "What goals?" How are they to be defined in operational terms so that we may obtain relevant data? Mitzel (1960) suggests that we utilize the terms product criteria, process criteria, and presage or predictive criteria. If one applies these terms to the body of accumulated literature he finds that presage criteria have been the primary concern of researchers. Presage criteria refer to teacher personality attributes, characteristics of teacher training, teacher knowledge and achievement, and in-service teacher status characteristics. Typically in a study of this type the investigator collects data by means of a questionnaire or paper-pencil test. This is administered to the prospective teacher, or to college personnel, or to master teachers. Frequently the college files are searched to obtain information. Frequently pupils and other school personnel are requested to rate the teacher on some check list or rating scale. Ultimately the ubiquitous correlation coefficient is calculated.

Although the above procedure fits one model of scientific procedure, it leaves a great deal to be desired in terms of relevance of criterion, stability of opinion obtained, ambiguity of the terms "good" and "bad". Furthermore it assumes that there is agreement amongst each group as to what the desired goals of education are and it assumes that effectiveness is a generalizable characteristic over all grades and all activities engaged in by the teacher. Perhaps the most crucial point to be made, however, is that there is little logical relationship between the goals of education and the personal characteristics of the teacher. An assumption that there is such a relationship is far too simple and neglects many variables which probably intervene between teacher personality and pupil change in behavior. The achievement of any goal of education results not only from the effect of the teacher's personality but also from a whole host of complicated interactions between teacher, pupils, and a wide variety of environmental factors. To expect to obtain valuable insight into the "most effective way" of obtaining a desired goal by examining any one variable in isolation from other sources of variation is to act in the most naïve fashion.

In regard to these presage criteria one could also spend considerable time, frustratingly so, examining the huge literature accumulated by asking the opinions of pupils, supervisors, principals, parents, and other people what made teachers "effective." In 1938 Barr, Burton, and Brueckner puplished their monumental book *Supervision* in which they reviewed a large number of studies concerned with the reasons why teachers "fail." They concluded there were seventeen causes of failure. Among these were: 1) lack of control over the technique of teaching, 2) lack of ability to maintain order and discipline, 3) lack of mastery of subject matter, 4) lack of intelligence, and 5) lack of effort. One must wonder by what means the data were collected and what the categories meant in any specific instance.

Paul Witty (1948) collected evidence by analyzing the letters of 37,000 pupils who were asked to describe the teacher who had helped them the most. The most frequently mentioned positive traits were: 1) cooperative, democratic attitude, 2) kindliness and consideration for the pupil, 3) patience, 4) wide interests, 5) personal appearance and pleasing manner, 6) fairness and impartiality, 7) sense of humor, and many others. The most frequently mentioned bad traits were: 1) bad tempered and intolerant, 2) unfair and inclined to have favorites, 3) disinclined to help pupils, 4) unreasonable in demands, 5) tendency to be gloomy and unfriendly, 6) sarcastic and inclined to use ridicule, 7) unattractive appearance, and many others.

Even though the above studies involved large samples, the results do not provide us with much insight. How can we determine which teacher has been most helpful and under what specific situations? It is likely that pupil experiences with their teachers are tempered a great deal by expectations, needs and prestige of the teacher. Indeed, what is a sense of humor? Can we all agree on the merits of a particular comedian, book, opera, or other common experience? What is fairness? What is sympathetic understanding? Let it suffice to say that it is questionable whether teacher characteristics, i.e., presage criteria, represent relevant criteria of teacher "effectiveness."

Similarly, studies using product criteria and process criteria, the other two types suggested by Mitzel (1960) have not yielded very fruitful results. It would appear that product criteria, i.e., pupil growth, should be most relevant. There are, however, a great many technical problems in using pupil growth criteria. For example, what pupil growth are we to assess? How are we to isolate the contribution of any single teacher? Are the effects of the teacher at one grade the same as that teacher's effect at another grade? Are the effects of teacher A in school 1 the same as the effects of teacher A in schools 2, 3, etc.? It is the question of generalizability that is among the most important for the educational scientist. The answer directly affects practice, and because we have so often generalized without sufficient care we have instituted practices which later create new and more complex difficulties.

Mitzel and Gross (1956) summarized twenty studies which utilized pupil growth criteria. They suggest that "teacher effectiveness" is multidimensional rather than unidimensional. They indicate that, "The practical importance of the probably multidimensional nature of teaching effectiveness arises when it is necessary to decide whether or not to combine different pupil growth measure into a single composite labeled 'effectiveness'...perhaps a rule of thumb would be that two or more pupil growth measures should not be combined unless their inter-correlations are of the same magnitude as their separate reliabilities." (p. 11) Ackerman (1954) concurs in this and adds, "Research can attempt to discover the various kinds of effectiveness. It cannot tell us which is the best or most desirable. This is a judgment which each individual must make according to his own educational goals and values." (p. 285)

Other technical factors regarding pupil growth which are rarely taken into account are the prior knowledge of pupils, the private value system of the teacher, the types of questions the teacher asks, and the "ceiling" and "floor" effects of the examinations utilized. For example, if we compare two classes in terms of change in achievement test scores from the beginning of the term to the end we must be certain that the classes are at the same level of prior knowledge at the beginning of the term. If one class is more advanced, we must adjust the final scores berore the differences are interpretable. It we select a measuring device which is too "easy" many pupils will score near the top of the pre-test and thus appear to make less growth than a student who scored near the bottom of the pre-test. At the high school level "effectiveness" measures are even more difficult to isolate because the students are involved with a variety of teachers. Of course, differences in learning materials, organization of materials, differences in topics and emphasis and differences in schools, all influence research results. These latter may be called biasing factors and must be accounted for in planning research.

One may correctly ask, "Is there any hope?" Our hope probably lies in research efforts which will require a change in approach and the development of more qualified educational research personnel who can work cooperatively with puplic school personnel. Research in the last ten years has begun to focus on teacher and pupil behavior and their interactions rather than on "teacher effectiveness." This is one very important step. We have increased considerably our technical proficiency in obtaining relevant and reliable data from observations of classroom behavior. The approach is non-evaluative and seeks to establish descriptions of behav-

ior. Ryan (1963) in his review of the literature indicates that:

A second trend, which is undoubtedly related to the development of the improvement in the quality of research, has been an increase in attention given to methodological problems. The criterion problem is no longer neglected as it was a few years ago, methods for observation and data collection have been refined and improved; and relatively sophisticated design and analysis techniques increasingly have been employed. (p. 415)

In the next few years the literature will surely begin to reflect these new techniques and strategies of research.[2]

In addition to a powerful technology, one capable of producing objective, relevant, and bias free data, we must concern ourselves in the future with a second aspect of the problem which has not been approached, as yet, with a great deal of sophistication. This is the problem of the objectives of schooling. It is clear that the goals of education, if we are to assess teacher "effectiveness", must be defined behaviorally, in terms of a particular grade, in a particular school, in a particular community, and in regard to particular topics and materials. Lest this be interpreted as calling for complete standardization, it is necessary to add that there is no necessity for all communities and schools to agree on goals. Indeed, one might expect that the goals should be determined on the basis of the observed needs of a particular community, or potential job market, or other more ultimate goals. What is needed is a rational analysis of the

---

[2] See the excellent anthology of research on classroom behavior of teachers edited by Hyman, *Teaching: Vantage Points for Study,* 1968.

desired outcomes in terms of community, nation, and world. Bloom (1954) in his taxonomy of educational objectives dealt with the cognitive objectives of educational experience. Krathwohl, Bloom and Masia (1964) dealt with the educational objectives in the affective domain.[3] Kearney (1953) explicates the objectives for elementary schools. We do not need greater proliferation of aims; we need to agree on a hierarchy of aims and define these in terms of observable behaviors.

The future efforts to assess teacher "effectiveness" look promising but not immediately attainable. The present attempts to better define criteria and to develop better technologies for obtaining prime data are encouraging; for example, new observation schedules and various electronic devices for immediate recording, both visual and aural. As we become more proficient we shall no doubt begin to obtain insights concerning the relationship of such variables as teacher-pupil interaction, teacher internal processes, pupil internal processes, other environmental factors as they impinge on pupils and teachers and such ends as pupil change in the cognitive, affective, and skill domains of behavior.

The promise of the future suggests, however, several other necessary steps. We shall need more time and money for the research effort. The latter hardly seems a problem any longer with the

stimulus provided by the U.S. Office of Education.[4] We shall, in addition, need to change our attitudes concerning the model to be applied in our research efforts. In adapting the model of science to research in Education, and the Social Sciences in general, we have tended to adopt the notion or the descriptive, correlational, field study rather than the experimental approach. Although the former approach appears to be more attractive, that is, it does less violence to the concept of on-going processes and their study, it is in effect less powerful as a generator of knowledge about cause and effect. One of the primary kinds of errors that many educational researchers have committed is the interpretation of a high relationship between two variables as indicating cause and effect. Thus, we may observe that in the classes of highly dominating teachers (defined operationally) the pupils are highly submissive. It would be an error to conclude, however, that highly dominating teachers cause pupils to become highly submissive. We can test this cause and effect hypothesis under experimental conditions only. This, for example, was what Lewin, Lippitt, and White (1939) did in their famous study of authoritarian, democratic, and laissez faire leadership. We have begun to turn to experimental studies more and more in recent years as may be seen by the rapid rise of the experimental child psychology and the social psychology movements. The experimental approach does not necessarily

[3] In 1969 the National Science Supervisors Association published a pamphlet called "Behavioral Objectives in the Affective Domain," by Eiss and Harbeck. This pamphlet is an attempt to define affective outcomes in science instruction in behavioral terms and will be most useful to those seeking to assess teacher efficiency in the classroom. This, of course, is based on the presumption that the objectives defined are those that the school and the science teacher hold to be important to them.

[4] There is nothing as humbling as reading a manuscript prepared several years ago. In 1966 the future of educational research seemed assured with the advent of large sums of money becoming available for a wide variety of research efforts. Today, other national events seem to have taken precedence over educational research and funds are not readily available.

mean a laboratory outside of the school with white coated technicians running back and forth with test tubes in hand. The laboratory does mean devising controls such as two teachers creating lessons around the same topics and materials. They would both be observed closely a number of times by trained observers utilizing an observation schedule. The experimental approach does mean assigning children to experimental and control classes on a random basis. (This is perhaps the most violated of all principles in educational research when conducted in field settings.) The experimental approach does not mean that the control class received "bad" teaching or that it shall receive "no" teaching; it means that the two classes are treated differently on a planned basis. Science depends upon replication of experience in order to produce generalizable results and we may expect that the newer approaches will require programatic research efforts, i.e., a systematic and long range program of research. We cannot expect much progress until we develop theories and models to guide our research efforts. These are beginning to develop and the reader is advised to consult Gage's (1963) chapter in the *Handbook of Research on Teaching*.[5]

Finally, one cannot conclude a paper on teacher "effectiveness" without pointing to two further necessary conditions. We must prepare more and better qualified research workers who understand the problems encountered when teaching in the schools and who possess adequate training in the highly complex and sophisticated research techniques of today. The second necessary condition is a bit more difficult to obtain. We

must prepare teachers who are sympathetic to the necessity for research and who are not suspicious and afraid of being observed in their everyday behaviours in the classroom. Administrators and college professors must learn to respect each other and to cooperate together. In the near future schools and universities will need to develop a relationship much like in baseball—the colleges would be the farm teams and the schools the major leagues. We would have professional administrators and researchers who would move with equal facility and freedom among the various levels and the teachers also would have a continuing experience, that is moving freely between levels. Their behavior would be studied at each level and the goals of education would be understood by all involved in the enterprise. Although the search for knowledge and insight is never concluded we are on the verge of a major step forward in the next few decades.

REFERENCES

Ackerman, W. I., "Teacher Competence and Pupil Change." *Harvard Educational Review* 24:273–289, Fall, 1954.

Barr, A. S., Burton, W. H., and Brueckner, L. J., *Supervision.* New York: Appleton-Century 1938.

Barr, A. S., "The Measurement and Prediction of Teacher Efficiency: A Summary of Investigations." *Journal of Experimental Education* 16:203–83, 1948.

Barr, A. S., "Teaching Competencies." In W. S. Monroe (Editor), *Encyclopedia of Educational Research.* Revised edition. New York: Macmillan, 1446–1454, 1950.

Biddle, B. J., "The Integration of Teacher Effectiveness Research." In B. J. Biddle and W. J. Ellena (Editors), *Contem-*

[5] One should also consult the excellent *Conceptual Models in Teacher Education* by Verduin in 1967.

porary Research in Teacher Effectiveness. New York: Holt, Rinehart and Winston, 1–40, 1964.

Biddle, B. J. and Ellena, W. J. (Editors), *Contemporary Research on Teacher Effectiveness,* Preface. New York: Holt, Rinehart and Winston, v–vii, 1964.

Bloom, B. S. (Editor), *Taxonomy of Educational Objectives.* New York: Longmans, 1954.

Cureton, E. F., "Validity." In E. F. Lindquist (Editor), *Educational Measurement.* Washington, D. C.: American Council on Education, 695–763, 1951.

Davis, Hazel, "Evolution of Current Practices in Evaluating Teacher Competence." In B. J. Biddle and W. J. Ellena (Editors), *Contemporary Research on Teacher Effectiveness.* New York: Holt, Rinehart and Winston: 41–66, 1964.

Ebel, R. J., "Using Tests for Evaluation." *National Elementary Principal.* 35: 29–31, 1955.

Eiss, A. F. and Harbeck, Mary B., *Behavioral Objectives in the Affective Domain.* National Science Teachers Association, Washington D. C., 1969.

Gage, N. L., "Paradigms for Research on Teaching." In N. L. Gage (Editor), *Handbook of Research on Teaching.* Chicago: Rand-McNally, 94–141, 1963.

Hyman, R. T. (Editor), *Teaching: Vantafe Points for Study.* Philadelphia: J. B. Lippincott, 1968.

Joncich, Geraldine, "Whither Thou, Educational Scientist?" *Teachers College Record.* 64: 1–12, October 1962.

Kearney, N. C., *Elementary School Objectives.* New York: Russell Sage, 1953.

Knudsen, C. W. and Stephens, Stella, "An Analysis of Fifty-Seven Devices for Rating Teaching." *Peabody Journal of Education* 9:15–24, July, 1931.

Krathwohl, D., Bloom, B. S. and Masia, B. B., *Taxonomy of Educational Objectives* Handbook II: Affective Domain. New York, David McKay, 1964.

Lewin, K., Lippitt, R., and White, R., "Patterns of Aggressive Behavior in Experimentally Created Social Climates." *Journal of Social Psychology* 10: 271–299, 1939.

Mitzel, H. E. and Gross, Cecily F., *A Critical Review of the Development of Pupil Growth Criteria in Studies of Teacher Effectiveness.* Mimeo paper of Office of Research and Evaluation. Division of Teacher Education Board of Higher Education of the City of New York, April, 1956.

Mitzel, H. E., "Teaching Effectiveness." In C. W. Harris (Editor), *Encyclopedia of Educational Research,* 3rd Edition. New York: Macmillan, 1960.

Ryan, D. G., "Assessment of Teacher Behavior and Instruction." *Review of Educational Research* 33: #4, 415–441, October, 1963.

Verduin, John R., *Conceptual Models in Teacher Education: An Approach to Teaching and Learning.* American Association of Colleges for Teacher Education, Washington, D.C.: 1967.

Witty, P. A., "Evaluation of Studies of the Characteristics of the Effective Teacher," in *Improving Educational Research.* Official Report of American Educational Research Association, Washington, D. C.: 198–204, 1948.

24.

Can There Be Universally Applicable Criteria of Good Teaching?

JANE R. MARTIN

Lecturer, Harvard Graduate School
of Education, Harvard University; Visiting Associate
Professor in the Departments of Philosophy and
Educational Foundations, University of Alberta,
1969–1970.

In an article entitled "Educational Research: A Criticism," G. H. Bantock claims that there are, and can be, no universally applicable criteria of what constitutes a good teacher (1961, p. 276). He bases his argument on the fact that teaching is a triadic relation, i.e., it is describable by the form "A teaches B to C." Bantock points out that when we speak of teaching we imply both a direct and an indirect object, in other words we teach something to someone (p. 275). Subjects differ, moreover, in the demands they make on the teacher's capacity (p. 276). For example, having a good voice may be a requisite for the teacher of poetry but not for the teacher of woodwork (p. 276). Since a teacher always acts in concrete situations "which will

vary the demands made upon his skill" (p. 277), no general answer to the question "What makes a good teacher?" can be given. At the least, we consider separately "the French teacher," "the history teacher," "the nursery school teacher" (p. 277).

It is imporatant to examine Bantock's claim and the argument on which it rests for two reasons. In the first place the claim can be generalized so that it extends not only to criteria of the good teacher or good teaching[1] but also to principles of teaching, methods of teaching, and so on. For the argument Bantock gives to support the claim of the impossibility of universally applica-

[1] It should be noted that Bantock believes the notion of teaching unsuccessfully involves a contradiction in terms (p. 275); that he does not differentiate the good teacher from the successful teacher (pp. 275–76); and that he views the criteria in question as criteria of what constitutes a good (successful) teacher or good (successful) teaching. For the present purpose there is no need to question these assumptions.

ble criteria would seem equally able to support analogous claims respecting principles and methods. Now such claims cannot be taken lightly for they deny the possibility of finding general answers to questions about teachers and teaching and, in effect, advise those engaged in educational research to limit their inquiry to the teacher or teaching of particular school subjects. Insofar, then, as Bantock's claim serves as a guide or directive to educational research, it has practical implications of prime importance.

There is a second reason for examining Bantock's claim and argument carefully. In his article Bantock analyzes the concept of "teaching" and from this analysis purports to draw his conclusion about the impossibility of universally applicable criteria. This procedure is presumably an application of his general thesis that conceptual clarification is necessary if educational research is to be successful (pp. 274ff). But any procedure which results in the attempt to limit inquiry requires analysis. It is one thing to advocate conceptual analysis for the purpose of clearing up ambiguities in the terms employed in research, as Bantock does (p. 272), but it is another thing to conclude from any particular conceptual analysis that certain types of inquiry are illegitimate. One cannot help wondering, when such a conclusion is reached, if conceptual analysis has not overstepped its bounds.

THE ARGUMENT FROM TEACHING AS A TRIADIC RELATION

Briefly, the argument on which Bantock's claim rests runs as follows: When we teach, we teach someone some subject; hence, when we speak about teach-

ers or teaching, we must speak about them in relation to some subject. Moreover, since every subject is different from every other subject, it follows that whatever we have to say about teachers or teaching will vary from subject to subject. To state the case metaphorically, subject matter dictates method.

Now this argument may have initial plausibility insofar as the claim that there can be no universally applicable criteria of good teaching is concerned, for it is true that when we teach we always teach some subject, and it might seem to follow from this that there can be no criteria which are independent of particular subjects. But it is difficult to see how the argument can be thought to function as support for the companion claim that "at the very least one needs to create 'homunculi' called 'the French teacher,' 'the history teacher,' or 'the nursery teacher'" (p. 277). For if the fact that teaching is a triadic relation supports the view that criteria of good teaching must be specific with respect to subject, it would seem also to support the view that they must be specific with respect to student. Why should the B of the form "A teaches B to C" be singled out for special attention and the C ignored? But then, letting $P_1, P_2, \ldots, P_n$ stand for particular pupils and $S_1, S_2, \ldots, S_n$ stand for particular subjects, we would not be able to talk simply about criteria of teaching S_1, criteria of teaching S_2, etc.; we would have to talk about criteria of teaching S_1 to P_1, criteria of teaching S_1 to P_2, criteria of teaching S_2 to P_1 etc.

Indeed, to be consistent, if the fact that teaching is triadic made it necessary to speak of it relative to subject and student, it would be necessary also to speak of it relative to teacher—the A of the form "A teaches B to C."

Letting T_1, T_2, ..., T_n stand for particular teachers, then if there were criteria of good teaching, they would on this view be criteria of teaching S_1 to P_1 by T_1, criteria of teaching S_1 to P_1 by T_2, etc. But the end of making the criteria of good teaching relative is not yet in sight. For it can be argued that "A teaches B to C" is elliptical and that teaching is really a tetradic relation describable by the form "A teaches B to C at D" where D stands for some time period. According to the logic of the original argument, any criteria of good teaching there might be would be criteria of teaching S_1 to P_1 by T_1 at time t_1, criteria of teaching S_1 to P_1 by T_1 at time t_2, etc. In other words, we would have to distinguish not merely "the French teacher" from "the history teacher," as Bantock suggests, but "Jones teaching French to Smith in 1962" from "Jones teaching French to Smith in 1963." Moreover, if teaching implies some subject and some student and some time, it also implies some place. It would seem, therefore, that principles of teaching would have to be made relative to place too.

Even if we assume that we can exhaust the respects in which criteria of good teaching must be made relative, there is the problem of deciding what constitutes proper substitutions for the various letters of the form "A teaches B to C..." It might seem that this question ought to be answered by empirical research and ought not to be decided in advance. But Bantock asserts that "the search for criteria all too often rests purely on empirical grounds" (p. 275). The whole thrust of his argument seems to be that conceptual analysis is necessary in order to determine the proper range of application of criteria of good teaching. If empirical research is not needed in order to determine that criteria of good teaching must be relative to particular subjects, then it would seem not to be needed in order to determine just what constitutes a particular subject (or time, place, etc.) either.

Now it may be fairly easy to determine what constitutes a teacher and a pupil—although one may wonder if a group of persons can be substituted for C or if only an individual person can be—but it is not at all clear what can be substituted for the variables of time, place, and subject in our form. Is it legitimate, for example, merely to distingush "Jones teaching French to Smith in 1962 in the United States" from "Jones teaching French to Smith in 1963 in the United States" or must we distinguish between "Jones teaching French to Smith in May 1962 in the United States" and "Jones teaching French to Smith in June 1962 in the United States" and between "Jones teaching French to Smith...in Massachusetts" and "Jones teaching French to Smith...in Colorado'? Are French and history to be treated as subjects or are they to be broken down, e.g., French into grammar and reading, and history into ancient, medieval, and American?

Surely it will be granted that if we follow the argument from teaching as a triadic relation to what seems to be its logical conclusion, it provides no warrant at all for the view that there can at best be criteria of teaching particular subjects. For according to this line of argument, if there are any criteria of teaching, they will not merely be specific to some subject but will be specific also to some teacher, student, time, place, and, indeed, to anything else, e.g. purpose, in respect to which teaching may be relative. This conclusion presents a gloomy prospect for anyone interested in the systematic study of teaching. Indeed, for all practical purposes it rules out such study. Fortunately, however, there is no reason to accept it. The argument from teaching as a triadic relation to the impossibility of universally applicable criteria of good teaching and the possibility, at best, of criteria applicable to the teaching of particular subjects is simply fallacious.

In recent years writers on education have stressed the fact that "teaching" is a triadic term (e.g. Scheffler, 1958, 1960; Gowin, 1961). In doing so they have been concerned, among other things, to remind their readers that phrases such as "I teach children" or "I teach history" are elliptical. It would be unfortunate if more were to be read into their analyses of teaching as a triadic relation than was originally intended. To argue as Scheffler does (1960, pp. 38–9), for instance, from an analysis of the term "teaching" to the conclusion that "I teach children, not subjects" is not to be taken literally, is one thing; to argue from an analysis of the term to the impossibility of certain kinds of criteria of good teaching, is another.

The argument from teaching as a triadic relation to the possibility or impossibility of certain sorts of criteria of teaching will be seen to be invalid once it is recognized that a term capable of behaving as a relative term can also be used as an absolute term (Quine, 1950, p. 119; 1960, p. 106). "Teaches," for example, is capable of behaving triadically but also monadically or, for that matter, dyadically, tetradically, etc. We analyze a term to fit our purpose by making explicit in the analysis as much or as little information as is needed. It begs the question, therefore, to say that *because* teaching is a triadic relation, criteria of good teaching must be made relative, at least to subject matter. For the question at issue is how, given the purpose of constructing criteria of good teaching, we are to construe "teaching," i.e. whether for this purpose it should be analyzed as triadic, tetradic, dyadic, etc.

Suppose we wanted to establish criteria for the teaching of children of a particular ethnic group. Such criteria would be relative not to particular school subjects but to a particular type of pupil. "Teaching," for this purpose, would be analyzed as a dyadic term, "A teaches C." On the other hand, suppose we were interested in formulating criteria for the teaching of science and mathematics in high school. Such criteria would be relative to pupil *and* to school subject. "Teaching," for this purpose, would be construed as a triadic term, "A teaches B to C." Now suppose a historian were trying to formulate criteria of teaching which applied to different areas, e.g. criteria of teaching in the 18th century, the 19th century, the 20th century. Such criteria would be relative to time. To determine if they would also be relative to pupil or school subject we would have to examine the historian's purpose more closely in order to see if he were interested in the differences, say, between secondary and primary education or between the teaching of history and the teaching of languages. In any case, time, which does not even enter into Bantock's analysis of "teaching" as a triadic term, would in this context be a crucial element of the analysis of "teaching."

But if "teaching" can be construed as dyadic given one purpose, triadic given another, and tetradic given another, why can't it be construed as monadic given yet a different purpose? Given purpose of formulating universally applicable criteria of teaching, for example, pupil, school, subject, time, etc., need not be "unpacked" in the analysis of "teaching." There is no reason why for this purpose "teaching" cannot be analyzed as a monadic term.

THERE CAN BE UNIVERSALLY APPLICABLE CRITERIA

The argument from teaching as a triadic relation fails to support Bantock's claim that there can be no universally applicable criteria of teaching; indeed, the argument is incapable of supporting *any* thesis about the range of application of criteria of teaching. It remains possible, of course, that the thesis under consideration is valid on independent grounds, and it is to that question that we must now address ourselves. The reader may have noticed a similarity between Bantock's claim and a view of scientific method widely held today. Such eminent writers as James Conant (1951) and Gerald Holton (1958) have maintained that there is no one scientific method, but at the very best only scientific methods. These writers hold that the search for "the" or "a" scientific method is misguided, for there is no single set of rules or procedures which holds across all sciences; each science is unique and has its own methods. To speak of scientific method as if it were something general, then, is to ignore the actual variations among the sciences.

Now the fact that there are many sciences and that great variation among them exists is undeniable. But this in itself does not require one to abandon the belief that there is "one" scientific method. As Ernest Nagel has pointed out, any two inquiries

will exhibit identifiable and important differences; and it is possible to argue from these differences to the conclusion that in pursuing their objectives the sciences employ a variety of methods. But it is equally clear that any two inquiries will possess some common features, so that by insisting on these to the exclusion of the manifest differences one can without difficulty maintain the unitary character of scientific method (1958, p. 147).

It is the differences which are uppermost in the minds of Conant and Holton, e.g. the differences in instruments employed, in skills exercised, in points of view, in modes of descovery. Yet the various sciences *can* be examined with an eye to their similarities rather than their differences.

Nagel suggests that common features of the various sciences will become apparent if we focus our attention on the way in which statements in the sciences are evaluated. Indeed, he believes that there is a body of principles which applies to all the sciences with respect to the validation of their claims to authentic knowledge. There is no need to assess Nagel's belief here, for regardless of the validity of his substantive claim concerning scientific method, his theoretical point holds good. Moreover, it is not merely the case that any *two* inquiries will exhibit common features; in principle, *any* number of inquiries will. It is fallacious, then, to conclude that because the sciences differ among themselves there are and can be no general principles of scientific method. Of course, we might find that the common features exhibited by a variety of inquiries were quite uninteresting to one attempting to formulate principles of scientific method. However, this is not a conclusion that can be reached *a priori*. Whether the common features among inquiries yield interesting or uninteresting, important or trivial, principles of scientific method can only be decided *after* these features have been investigated.

To return to our original topic, it should be clear, in view of the very obvious variation among school subjects, that those concerned with teaching might wish to focus attention exclusively on the diffences in teaching one subject rather than another. There is no doubt that skill in using a saw is a requisite for the teacher of woodwork but not for the teacher of poetry, that the ability to determine a student's understanding of Keats is essential for the teacher of poetry but not for the teacher of mathematics, that knowledge of the best order for introducing algebraic concepts is necessary for the teacher of mathematics but not for the teacher of French. However, just as the various sciences exhibit common features, so does good teaching of the various subjects; and, if one wishes to focus attention on them, one can.

If the features common to good teaching of the various subjects are emphasized, then criteria can be formulated which apply not merely to the teaching of a particular subject, but to the teaching of all subjects. It seems clear, therefore, that the claim under consideration is untenable. In denying the possibility of universally applicable criteria of good teaching and asserting the possibility of, at most, criteria of teaching particular subjects, Bantock overlooks the simple theoretical point that any group of things will exhibit common, as well as differentiating, features. That the features common to teaching the various subjects will lead to the formulation of uninteresting, unimportant, and unhelpful criteria of teaching is, of course, a possibility. But on the one hand, it should be recalled that the claim in question denies the possibility of any sort of universally applicable criteria of teaching, not merely the possibility of interesting or helpful criteria. On the other hand, even if the claim were limited to the denial of interesting or helpful universally applicable criteria, it would be invalid, for the question of the importance or helpfulness of the criteria cannot be decided in advance.

CONCLUSION

We must conclude that the argument from "teaching" as a triadic term does not support the claim that there are and can be no universally applicable criteria of the good teacher. Moreover, on independent grounds the claim can be seen to be unwarranted. Educational research can continue to seek an answer to the question "What makes a good teacher?" if it wishes; inquiry into teaching in general need not stop. This is not to say that such inquiry will necessarily be successful or that universally applicable criteria of good teaching which are fruitful will be discovered. But it is to say that Bantock has produced no grounds *a priori* for supposing such research to be doomed to disappointment.

Bantock is surely right that conceptual analysis is needed if educational research is to be effective. Moreover, there is every reason to believe that its relevance for research does not consist merely in the clearing up of ambiguities in the terms used by scientists. But it is very doubtful that conceptual analysis has the power that Bantock would attribute to it, namely that of providing a rationale for placing a straitjacket on the scientist. In using conceptual analysis to this end, Bantock does it a disservice. For who is going to take seriously the valid, but modest, claims for conceptual analysis in the light of the rash, invalid use of it to restrict inquiry?

REFERENCES

Bantock, G. H. Educational research: a criticism. *Harvard Educational Review,* 1961, *31,* 264–280.

Conant, J. B. *Science and common sense.* New Haven: Yale Univ. Press, 1951.

Gowin, D. B. Teaching, learning and thirdness. *Studies in Philosophy and Education,* 1961, *1,* 87–113.

Holton, G. & Roller, D. H. D. *Foundations of modern science.* Reading, Mass.: Addison-Wesley, 1958.

Nagel, E. The methods of science: what are they? can they be taught In I. Scheffler (Ed.), *Philosophy and education.* Boston: Allyn & Bacon, 1958. Pp. 146–153.

Quine, W. V. O. *Methods of logic.* New York: Henry Holt, 1950.

Quine, W. V. O. *Word and object.* New York: The Technology Press & John Wiley, 1960.

Scheffler, I. Justifying curriculum decisions. *The School Review,* 1958, *66,* 461– 472.

Scheffler, I. *The language of education.* Springfield, Ill.: Charles C Thomas, 1960.

25.

What Can Be Taught?

EDMUND L. PINCOFFS

Professor of Philosophy,
University of Texas.

If we are interested in the question whether virtue or anything else can be taught, we would do well to begin by asking what sorts of things *can* be taught. What, in general, are the distinguishing characteristics of those things that can and cannot be taught? On what ground can the distinction between the teachable and the nonteachable be made?

Before we can even begin to approach these difficult questions we must dispose of two objections: that the question concerning the limits of teachability is an empirical and therefore not a philoso-

"What Can Be Taught?" by Edmund L. Pincoffs is reprinted with permission of the Philosophy of Education Society and the author from Philosophy of Education, 1967 *edited by D. B. Gowin. (Edwardsville, Ill.: Studies in Philosophy and Education, 1967), pp. 44–54; reprinted with permission from THE MONIST, Vol. 52, No. 1 (January, 1968), pp. 120–32. With permission of The Open Court Publishing Company, La Salle, Illinois.*

phical one, and that the answer to the question is so clear that it need not be taken seriously.

The objection that there is only an empirical question about the limits of teachability might go as follows. If you want to know what can be taught, then there are two, and only two, places where you can expect to find an answer: the experience of the human race, and trial and error. To rely on the first alone would obviously be mistaken; the experience of the human race has been that things previously not taught have come to be taught. But to suppose that the philosopher can from his study dictate what can and cannot succeed is repugnant to common sense. How can philosophers know what cannot be taught until they have tried? This is, of course, not so much an argument as insistence that the burden of proof lies on the other side. It can be shouldered if the philosopher can produce one statement about what can or cannot be taught, which can be shown to be true on nonempirical grounds. Here is one. You cannot teach a person how to do something which is beyond his control. Much of this paper will be devoted to an expansion of this remark. The objection might be raised that we cannot know what is beyond the control of a person until he has tried, so that the supposed answer fails to meet the challenge. But I shall argue that there are types of activities which we can know *a priori* to be beyond the control of the individual.

It might be supposed that the boundary between the teachable and the non-teachable is obvious: whatever can be learned can be taught. Not everything that is learned is taught, it might be held, but whatever is learned could be taught, if only some qualified and interested teacher were present at the appropriate time and in the appropriate circumstances. The difficulties with this supposedly obvious truth are that, first, it is debatable; and, second, even if it were true it would be unilluminating. It is debatable because there at least seem to be numerous things. I can learn but which no one could teach me. I can learn to control my temper, for example. To learn this, I did not merely learn to count to ten, which someone could have taught me, but to calm my temper as I counted ten. How could someone teach me that? It surely is not obvious that anyone can. But suppose for the sake of argument that whatever can be learned can be taught. Then we must ask what can be learned. We have simply substituted one difficult question for another. We are no closer than we were before to an analysis of the boundaries of teachability; even though it might turn ont that we would do better to begin with learning rather than teaching.

SUCCESS AND NON-SUCCESS SENSES OF "TEACH"

As a preliminary move, it is necessary to insist upon a familiar distinction between two uses of the verb, "to teach." If I say that I taught Jamie to read, to play the cornet, or to do sums, it is not clear whether I mean merely that I gave him lessons over a period of time, or that I succeeded in teaching him to read, play, or do sums. It may well be true that I gave him lessons, but false that he learned anything. The two senses of the verb can appear in one sentence, as when I confess that although I have been teaching Jamie cornet (giving him lessons) for a year, I fear that (judging by the sounds he makes) I have taught him nothing.

In this paper, I shall be concerned with "teach" in the success sense: not with whether lessons can be given in X, but whether X can successfully be taught. And I shall confine my remarks to teaching to, or how to; not discussing teaching that, teaching to be, teaching the difference between, etc. I wish to discuss the question which kinds of activity are amenable to teaching to (success sense) and which are not.

This requires that I distinguish between teleological and formal activities, and work out some of the ramifications of that distinction.

TELEOLOGICAL AND FORMAL ACTIVITIES

I use the term, "activities," as a general term for all of the kinds of things that people do: broad enough to include everything from twiddling thumbs to conquering continents, from criticizing poetry to day-dreaming, from issuing a warrant to building a boat. There are some things people do which cannot even *prima facie* be learned or taught. With these I am not concerned here. Of the things people do which cannot *prima facie* be taught, I will mention two classes: instinctive activities, and (though it is strange to call them activities) accidental, inadvertent, or mistaken activities.

The list of instinctive activities includes breathing, scratching, moving one's limbs, and blinking one's eyes. How far it extends, is a question for comparative anthropology. We *can* learn, and be taught, to do better, or at any rate in a special way, some of the instinctive things we were not taught in the first place. For example, a part of learning to sing is learning to breathe "properly"; but this is not learning to breathe as breathing is normally done. Tripping and stumbling are things we do, but are not taught to do normally: (Ryle's clown's stumbling is a special case). Besides the things that we do inadvertently, there are things we do by mistake, as, for example, pitching onto the wrong green, or accusing Jones of Smith's misdeed; or by accident, as when we break a window with our golf ball, or level a town while welding a pipeline. None of these things can be taught.

I want, rather, to linger over a distinction between two kinds of activity which can, at least *prima facie*, be taught.[1] Both of the kinds of activity I shall distinguish have the characteristic that they are purposive: that is, they

---

[1] I use the expression "kinds of activity" merely for ease of presentation. I do not mean to imply that there are "kinds of activity" that one could find as clearly exemplified in the world, and as easy to distinguish, as the hyena from the hippopotamus. Rather, I have a distinction which I think it useful to push a certain distance.

are not accidental, inadvertent, etc. on the one hand; and they are not merely instinctive on the other. Persons who engage in them do so thinking what they are doing, exercising care or being careless (we do not breathe carefully or carelessly), striving for improvement or heedless of improvement, aware or unaware of their failures and successes.

One of these kinds of activity I dub "formal," the other, with many philosophers, but with special qualifications, I call teleological. In making this distinction I wish to call attention to two points: that all purposive activity is not teleological and that teleological activities differ essentially with respect to their teachability and non-teachability.

By "formal activity," I mean an activity which (1) is purposive; (2) does not, as such, have a purpose; and (3) may nevertheless be done well or ill, poorly or brilliantly, satisfactorily or unsatisfactorily. As examples of formal activities, I will mention dancing, painting, riding (as for the show ring), singing, figure skating, arranging flowers, writing (poetry, philosophy), and acting. I have explained what I mean by saying that formal activities are purposive; that they do not, as such, have a purpose must now be explained. By this I mean that to say of a person that he is engaged in the activity is not, normally, to attribute some purpose to him. A man may dance to win a contest, or a heart, or for his health, or to appease the gods. But merely from the statement that he is dancing, nothing follows about what purposes he may or may not have.

The point may be put in a different way. There is no answer to the question what the purpose of a formal activity is. If we are asked what is the purpose of dancing, we are bewildered. It can have a purpose on particular occasions, but what is, in general, its purpose, has no answer; unless it is some such answer as, "We dance because we want to," or "It gives us pleasure." But this is not necessarily (contra the utilitarians) to state a purpose. It may be a way of saying that the request for the purpose of dancing has no answer. It might be objected that there is one purpose which all dancers have, and that is to dance well. But this is not true. A man may dance from a sense of duty (arrange flowers as a chore, paint on his psychiatrist's orders) and have no ambition to do well at his activity.

By "teleological activity," I mean an activity which, while (1) purposive; (2) does have, as such, a purpose; and (3) may be appraised as done well or ill by reference to its purpose. As examples of teleological activity, I mention adding and subtracting, predicting the weather, selling insurance, shooting rapids, prospecting, debating, playing chess or golf, running for office, gambling, proving theorems, fishing, and farming. If we are told that a man is adding a column of figures, we are entitled (normally) to infer that he wants to get the correct answer. If we are told that he is engaged in a debate, or playing chess, we may assume that he wants to win, and that this is at least one of his purposes. These purposes may be said to be intrinsic to the activities in question. This is not to say that a man may not play golf with the president of his company, and want not to win; but that normally when we learn that a man is playing golf, we have a right to assume that he wants to win.

It follows that normally we may appraise a man's performance of an activity by reference to the purpose which is intrinsic to that activity. That is, whatever else may be said about a man's golf game, it is not good if his score is above average; he is not a good chess-player if he never wins against amateurs; and he is an unsuccessful politician if he is repeatedly defeated. It is, thus, a necessary and sufficient condition of a man's doing well at a teleological activity that he regularly attains the goal which is intrinsic to that activity. Exceptions are allowed, but they must be shown to be exceptions: a good golfer can shoot a high score to butter up his boss; but his claim to be a good golfer rests on his shooting low scores consistently.

Concerning formal activities, we may say that an individual is a good dancer but is not likely to win the contest; or that he is a fine painter, even though he has not yet exhibited. But we cannot say that an individual is a good weather predictor even though he has not yet been successful in predicting the weather; or that he is a good accountant even though he has so far failed to balance the books of any of his clients; or a good salesman who can make no sales. We cannot normally say these things: if we do say them, the burden of proof is upon us to make sense of our claim; for given no special explanation, they are self-stultifying assertions.

Because there are purposes intrinsic to teleological activities but not to formal ones, the notion of a successful performer of an activity applies differently in the two cases. If we say of a man that he is a successful prospector, then, normally, we mean that he has found gold or other minerals. But if we say that he is a successful dancer, we mean that he has been acclaimed for his dancing, or has earned a large sum of money by it. His success as a dancer is extrinsic to the quality of his dancing in that it is logically possible that he should be a successful, even though not a good, dancer. But a man cannot be a successful, though not a good, prospector; or anyway not beyond a certain limit. If throughout his active life, and through his own efforts, he repeatedly finds new deposits of gold, then, no matter how he has done it, he is good as well as successful. But even though a ballerina always dances like an angel, she may nevertheless not be successful. Since a good prospector is normally a prospector who consistently finds gold, and since the intrinsic purpose of prospecting is finding, then every good prospector is a successful one; but since there is no purpose intrinsic to dancing, it does not (normally) follow that a good dancer is successful.

Finally, it may be useful to point out that, to use Professor Scheffler's distinction,[2] exhaustive rules cannot be given for teleological activities without adding some such unhelpful rule as "win the game," or "find gold." But the notion of an exhaustive set of rules does not apply in the same way to formal activities. The unhelpful added rule would have to be something like, "move your body in such a way that you satisfy me and all competent critics that you are dancing."

SOME VARIETIES OF TELEOLOGICAL AND FORMAL ACTIVITIES

Since the claim to have taught Jamie (success sense) to do this or that may refer to formal or to teleological activities (I have not, by the way, claimed that this is an exhaustive classification), it is obviously important to distinguish different kinds of claim that can be

[2] Israel Scheffler, *The Language of Education,* (Springfield, Ill.: Charles C Thomas, 1960), p. 70.

made. Before explicitly considering these, I must draw attention to the wide difference in types of activity which can fall under these headings.

Teleological activities may be classified according to the degree of what I shall call people-dependence and world-dependence they exhibit. People-dependent activities are successful only if one bests the people with whom one must compete in carrying them on. Thus, one may participate in contests like debates, games, law suits, fights, races, and battles. Whether one will win these contests depends not only on one's talents and training, but also upon the talents and training of the opposition. Or one may enter into competitive activities like trading in commodities, or selling insurance, publishing books, applying for a position, taking an examination for a scholarship, etc. Here whether or not one attains one's goal depends not only on oneself but on the caliber of the competition. There is not a contest in the sense that the whole object is to best the other men; and that success consists in besting one's opponent. But a number of people are attempting the same thing, in circumstances which are such that only some of them can succeed. Success consists in winning the scholarship, not in beating out Jones; but it can not be won without beating him out.

Mountain-climbing, shooting rapids, riding broncos, gliding, weather-predicting, shooting par, raising crops, building dams, fishing, and mining are world-dependent activities. That is, the world must cooperate if they are to be successfully carried on. The mountain must not be too treacherous, the rapids not too turbulent, or the attempt to climb one or shoot the other fails. Many activities are, of course, both people- and world-dependent. One cannot succeed in a turkey-shooting contest unless the turkey is cooperative, and the competition not too fierce. Earning a living, driving without accident, making reservations, are both people- and world-dependent. Shoeing a horse, estimating distance, building a bridge, weaving cloth are (ordinarily) world- but not people-dependent. But one could imagine special circumstances in which there would be shoeing, estimating, bridge-building, or weaving contests or competitions. It is contests and competitions which differentiate people- from merely world-dependent activities. Success in people-dependent activities depends on the competition; success in world-dependent activities does not. It is trivially true that all people-dependent activities are world-dependent. If my car skids in an oil slick, I lose the race as surely as if Jones is a better driver.

Quelling a riot is not, on this distinction, a people-dependent activity. What makes an activity people-dependent is not the fact that the activity can only be carried on in the presence of, or with the cooperation of other people; it is that success in carrying on the activity depends on the kind of competition one meets, and not merely on one's own efforts. Quelling a riot is, on this distinction, a world-dependent activity. That is, the world, including the people in it (not the competition in it) must "cooperate" for the activity to come off successfully. If the mob is too wild and wooly, then it will not stop rioting.

All activities are to some extent world-dependent. If the earth quakes I cannot walk in a straight line. But the earth can be depended upon pretty regularly not to quake, so we do not regard walking in a straight line (in non-drunkenness-test situations) as a feat. In climbing mountains, shooting rapids,

quelling riots, and other world-dependent activities proper, the cooperation of the world is in doubt.

TEACHING SKILLS

In person- and world-dependent teleological activities, success is beyond our control. Learn what we will, train as we will, take lessons as we will, it is always a live possibility that we will fail at the activity in question. So different sorts of claim to have taught Jamie (success sense) to engage in these activities must be distinguished.

Suppose the activity's successful pursuit is very much beyond our control, like shooting Niagara in a barrel. Then the claim to have taught Jamie to shoot Niagara (and survive) is clearly specious. No one can teach a teleological activity the success of which is in the lap of the gods. Indeed, techniques of barrel-construction and fall-navigation could improve, so that shooting Niagara successfully could be done by everyone's mother on a weekend holiday. But I assume that the chances of survival are not great, no matter what we do, under present circumstances. To make the claim plausible at all, and not simply absurd or even unintelligible, there must be something that can be taught, that might help: the techniques of tight barrel-construction, and the monthly record of flow, for example. But learning these things clearly does not add up to learning to shoot the falls.

Clearly we could construct a spectrum of teleological activities ranging from very much beyond control, like shooting Niagara, to very much in control, or potentially in control once the pupil has learned the appropriate techniques, like shooting fish in a barrel. Sometimes failure at a teleological activity because people or the world do not coooperate is only a remote possibility, and not what might normally be a possibility. Then we would say that the activity in question is not (normally) either people- or world-dependent. Examples might be balancing a bank account, proving a theorem, telling time, baking a cake, making a reservation, writing a check, or cutting the grass. I dub such teleological activities non-dependent. A skeptical philosopher might raise the question whether even such activities as these can be taught; for it is always logically possible that, no matter what drills, hints, nudges, encouragement, examples are given the pupil, he will still fail to carry out the activity in question. He might go through all the right motions and fail to write a check because he is out of ink, or because he ignites the paper with his cigarette before completing it, or because a tornado whisks it away as he is about to sign it. And these activities do differ from formal activities in this respect; for if a man goes through the right motions then, tornado or fire be damned; he has danced. He has not failed to achieve the intrinsic purpose of dancing, and thus failed to dance, because there is no purpose intrinsic to dancing.

If the skeptic can show that what we had regarded as a (normally) non-dependent activity is really dependent, then he will have made out his case. He might show, for example, that whereas we had thought growing corn was a non-dependent activity; really, in central Texas, the weather being what it is, it is touch-and-go whether you make a crop. Then he will have the right to question the claim of anyone who would teach us how to raise corn in the local climate. But unless he can show dependence, his skepticism is groundless (as-

suming, as I do, that the pupil is normally attentive, sane, sober, and has the capacity to learn the skill in question).

There is a radical difference between teaching (relatively non-dependent) teleological activities and teaching formal ones; and once this difference is recognized, an ambiguity in the notion of "teaching skills" becomes apparent. To teach a teleological activity, if possible at all, is to teach how to succeed at the activity: achieve its intrinsic purpose, be it to shoe the horse, balance the account, prove the theorem, measure the distance, or repair the machine. Thus the rules, precepts, and principles that the teacher lays down are all dispensable. They apply only so far as they *help*. And the teacher is useful only so far as he is helpful—in attaining the purpose. The pupil aims to repair machines. The teacher can impart certain skills, but not skills which will inevitably, if employed, result in repaired machines. We are sometimes inclined, therefore, to deny that even relatively non-dependent teleological activities *can* be taught. In teaching Jamie how to estimate distance, the teacher might learn from Jamie: for what Jamie tries out may work. There is always the external criterion of success available against which to test what the teacher tells Jamie. The maxims, principles, etc. the teacher lays down are bound to circumstances: to the present state of technology, to the recurrence of familiar problem situations. Change the circumstances and the maxims must change.

The teacher of formal activities stands in a different relationship to his pupil. Jamie's dancing-teacher is not teaching how to succeed at dancing; so he does not claim, implicitly or explicitly, that his precepts lead to success. Hence, there are no claims for the efficacy of his precepts, which can be falsified by changes in circumstances. The point may be expanded as follows: no matter how one is taught a teleological activity, it *could* turn out that (because of the fractiousness of the horses, the introduction of computers, the increase of distances to be estimated) even though one succeeded in school, under the guidance of the teacher, one does not succeed on one's own, at the activity in question. It would then appear that one had only been taught in the non-success sense: given lessons.

But are not formal activities often (even necessarily) dependent in the same way? Are there not contingencies which invalidate the claim to have taught formal activities, just like those which arise for teleological ones? Jamie was not really taught to dance, it might be claimed, but only given lessons if he cannot waltz on a lava flow, not taught to arrange flowers if he cannot arrange crumbling flower-remnants, not taught to paint if he cannot paint with the worst quality of paint. These matters, it might be argued, are fully as much beyond the control of pupil and teacher as the fractiousness of the horses, or the introduction of computers. But the point is that Jamie's inability to waltz on a lava flow is *not evidence* that he has not been taught to waltz; and his failure to estimate great distances *is evidence* that he has not been taught to estimate distance. Not conclusive evidence, certainly, but evidence. This difference in the evidential status of subsequent failure arises from a difference in the validation of the claim that Jamie has been taught to X. If the claim is that he has been taught to dance, then it could be validated by an expert's certificate issued at the time of graduation. But the claim that Jamie had been taught to win races cannot be validated by an expert's certificate in the same way, since he might start losing races the day after graduation. Even such non-dependent activities as shoeing horses are only relatively so; only normally non-dependent. We can easily conceive of circumstances in which non-dependent activities become dependent: then the claim to have taught them may turn out false.

The teacher of formal activities is not helping Jamie achieve a purpose Jamie may be assumed to have: a purpose intrinsic to the activity. Jamie may want to learn to waltz, but the teacher himself must decide whether Jamie can waltz, or can waltz well. He must set his own standards of achievement for Jamie. When he certifies to parent or principal that Jamie is a good dancer, he is not making a prediction, but an evaluation. If Jamie fails the final recital, this is not because the teacher thinks that he will not succeed, but because he does not succeed. An examination in a flying course, on the other hand, will show whether the student is likely to succeed at flying a plane safely cross-country.

Teachers of both teleological and formal activities may wish to help the student "perfect a skill"; but the meaning of the phrase is not the same. To perfect a formal skill, one must approach closer and closer to the standards set by the practitioners of that skill. The teacher is, or claims to be, by his position, not only an aid to the achievement of perfection, but the arbiter of the degree of perfection achieved. The pupil must meet his standards of performance, and these standards may be compared with those set by other teachers and practitioners: so that a teacher may be judged by his standards. But the teacher of a teleological activity can at best make predictive judgments of the likelihood that his student will succeed. And the persons who judge that the student succeeds at a teleological activity need not be adept at the activity in question. Anyone can judge whether the aviator arrives safely home; but not everyone can judge whether the dancer dances well. Perfection in flying means (in this context) a perfect safety record; perfection in dancing cannot be so easily defined. Since there is no purpose intrinsic to dancing, the standards by which it is judged may in principle change or vary. If we say that dancing is infinitely perfectible we (should) mean not only that there is no end to improvement by a given set of standards, but also that standards can always change. It is hard, however, to get away from the ambiguity of the expression, "perfect X." We could judge a flyer, tennis player, debater, or bronco rider, on grounds of the style of his performance, rather than his success in achieving the intrinsic purpose of the activity. When we do so, we look at these activities as formal ones. But, in the last analysis, although there will be lags, good form or style tends to be the style of winners or successful performers. This is not true of dancing, painting, or acting; because there are no winners at these activities; and if contests should be set, contestants would be judged not by their success at achieving an intrinsic purpose, but by critical standards adopted by the judges.

WHAT CAN BE TAUGHT?

Formal and non-dependent teleological activities are not ruled out by the criterion of control as teachable. Dependent teleological activities are not teachable. "Teach" is used in the success sense. Of course, someone can give lessons in a dependent teleological activity. That is, he can give lessons in skills which are causally related to success in the dependent teleological activity. But he cannot teach a person how to achieve the goal of a dependent teleological activity. This is, of course, analytically true, once we accept the definitions of the relevant terms. But it does provide part of a conceptual framework for analysis of claims that this or that activity can be taught. To what extent is the teaching of geometry, for example, teaching how to do something? What kinds of activities are involved, teleological or formal? If teleological, are they dependent or non-dependent? Thus, with respect to this criterion of control, to what extent are these activities teachable? And what follows about the relationship between teacher and pupil? About the perfectability of the activities? About success at these activities?

In this paper I have made no pretense of analyzing the hoary question whether virtue can be taught. I do not mean to claim, by implication, that to teach a person a virtue is to teach him how to engage in an activity. Virtue is not, I think, something that we learn to do; virtues are, I believe, excellences of character (of a number of different types) which are exhibited in what we do. Whether a *given* virtue can be taught (and I doubt if there is a general answer to the traditional question) may turn in part on the kind of activity it is in which the virtue is typically exhibited, and on whether the activity in question can be taught, and whether in teaching it the appropriate excellences of character can be inculcated.

Good Teaching:

Overview

In this last section some educators present their notions as to what is good teaching. With this cluster of articles we come full cycle in this book, from what is to what ought to be. The selection by Marie Hughes epitomizes this movement. The article arises from a research study focusing on creating an adequate description of the teaching act. The research study was supported by the United States Office of Education and begun because of efforts to institute merit rating of teachers in Utah. Thus, an attempt to reward good teaching with merit pay led to a descriptive study of teaching, which then became the framework for presenting a model of good teaching.

Hughes and Combs present their ideas about good teaching in connection with their empirical research work. Hughes builds her model on the same seven functions she used to describe the teaching she observed.[1] The reader is asked to compare the percentages for the seven functions in her model of good teaching with the mean observed percentages for these functions based on 90 minutes' observation of 35 teachers:[2]

[1] The research is reported in Hughes' report to the U.S. Office of Education as cited in the credit line for her selection. Two summaries of the descriptive part of the report by Hughes herself are "What is Teaching? One Viewpoint," *Educational Leadership,* 19 (January 1962), 251–59, reprinted in *Teaching: Vantage Points for Study,* ed. Ronald T. Hyman (Philadelphia: J. B. Lippincott Co., 1968), pp. 271–84; and "Utah Study of the Assessment of Teaching," in *Theory and Research in Teaching,* ed. Arno A. Bellack (New York: Bureau of Publications, Teachers College, Columbia University, 1963), pp. 25–36.

[2] The observed mean percentages come from page 85 of Hughes' full report. The model of good teaching percentages come from page 223 and are reprinted in the selection in this section.

	Observed Mean %	Model of Good Teaching %
Controlling	47	20–40
Imposition	3	1–3
Facilitating	7	5–15
Content Development	16	20–40
Personal Response	5	8–20
Positive Affectivity	12	10–20
Negative Affectivity	10	3–10

Hughes' model of good teaching within the framework of the seven functions is based on "the attributes of the man we would have all children become," for example, autonomy, initiative, and openness to experience. Does the reader accept Hughes' model? Is her model realizable? Can a teacher teach these attributes to his students?

Combs, too, builds upon his research and develops his concept of the self as instrument. Given Combs' definition of the effective teacher, how does one learn to use his self as an instrument effectively? Is Combs' framework of perceptual organization in six general areas acceptable to the reader? How does Combs' idea of good teaching compare with Hughes', Herbst's, and Sprinthall's, in that they all speak of creativity as a necessary ingredient? Is Combs correct that it is fruitless to search for common-qualities among good teachers, because good teachers are unique individuals? Would Martin in Section Six agree?

On the nonempirical side of Hughes and Combs are Herbst and Dewey. Herbst presents his views of good teaching in light of his concept of the anti-school. In what ways is Herbst similar to Buber (in Scudder's article) in Section Five in his concepts and beliefs? How is he similar to Green in Section Two? Komisar in Section Two? Travers in Section Four, regarding their common attack on Bruner? Combs and Hughes in this section? How would Pincoffs respond to Herbst regarding the teachability of his concepts? How would Bruner and Dewey react to Herbst's criticism of them? And, finally, is Herbst's idea of good teaching acceptable to the reader?

Dewey's short selection is included because it is already a classic that serves as the springboard for much of the writing about teaching. (See Smith and Scheffler in Section Two.) This selection is not presented as Dewey's full or main statement on good teaching, but rather as a hint of what it might be. Note that Dewey talks about a good day's teaching. Hence, the inclusion of this selection in this section of this book.

The reader is asked to keep in mind that Dewey's paragraph is taken from the introduction of Chapter 3 in his book *How we Think,* subtitled *A Restatement of the Relation of Reflective Thinking to the Educative Process.* Dewey goes on in that chapter to treat three "tendencies or forces" (curiosity, suggestion, and orderliness) "that operate in every normal individual, forces that must be appealed to and utilized if the best methods" are to be employed. That is to say, Dewey seeks reflective thinking, a fact that is shown in greater detail in the selection by Walton in Section Five. Is the teaching for and of reflective thinking good teaching? Is this what Dewey means by the "quality of real teaching"?

The reader is asked to keep in mind the three sentences with which Dewey concludes the third chapter of his book: "It is an old saying that unity of variety marks every work of genuine art. Certainly the art of teaching bears out the saying. If one recalls his contacts with teachers who left a permanent intellectual impress, one will find that, although they may have violated in their teaching many of the set rules of pedagogy, they were persons who could maintain continuity of thought and effort even when admitting what seemed to be diversions and forays into side fields; that they were persons who introduced novelty and variety to keep attention alert and taut, but who also utilized these factors to contribute to the building up of the main problem and the enrichment of the main theme."[3]

On the empirical side is the article by Sprinthall, Whiteley, and Mosher,[4] a recent attempt to tackle empirically the issue of good teaching. These authors realize full well the dangers of such research, as pointed out in the articles in Section Six. Their research design is intended to obviate many of the pitfalls of previous empirical research. Do they succeed? Is their "cognitive flexibility" similar to Hughes' "flexible teaching," that is, teaching which is responsive to the children and the situation in which they are working? Is cognitive flexibility similar to acting in light of the dynamic aspect of teaching presented by Hyman in Section Two? Does cognitive flexibility bring about learning, the intended end of instruction?

Finally, the reader is asked for his own answer to: "What is good teaching?"

[3] John Dewey, *How We Think* (Boston: D.C. Heath, 1933), pp. 53–54.
[4] For a different approach see W. James Popham, "The Performance Test: A New Approach to the Assessment of Teaching Proficiency," *Journal of Teacher Education,* 19 (Summer 1968), 216–22.

26.

The Model of Good Teaching

MARIE M. HUGHES and Associates

Marie M. Hughes is Professor of Educational
Psychology and Director of the Arizona Center for
Early Childhood Education, University of Arizona.

We shall now present the Model of Good Teaching within the framework of interaction which we have used as our definition of teaching. We reiterate our belief that the chief impact and influence of the teacher is at the point of interaction with a child or group.

What is good teaching? The teacher-learner situation in its complexity, its flow, and its multiple relationships requires creativity on the part of the teacher. If teaching may be described as decision-making in interaction, then the product of the teacher's decision is the response he makes to the child or group with whom he is interacting.

"The Model of Good Teaching" by Marie Hughes and Associates is reprinted with permission from A Research Report: Assessment of the Quality of Teaching in Elementary Schools. Cooperative Research Project #353, U.S. Office of Education, Department of Health, Education, and Welfare. University of Utah, 1959. The Associates: F. Elena De Vaney; Ruby J. Fletcher; George L. Miller; Naoma T. Rowan; and Lawrence Welling. The selection here is from pp. 215–24.

When the response is not routine or stereotyped, it is creative. The occasion is never quite the same and won't be again. The effort made to understand and to respond within the meaning of a specific and unique child must be a creative act to be successful. The measure then of good teaching is the quality of the response the teacher makes to the child or group with whom he is interacting. It is the child who is reaching out, seeking, raising the questions, trying out his ideas.

How does the teacher respond so that he can be used as a resource by the child? To become a man of autonomy and initiative, to become a man with confidence in himself, the child needs to have opportunities to try himself out by initiating ideas and actions which are successful most of the time. This he can do only if the teacher makes the appropriate response. The responses of the teacher may include:

giving the child support by telling him

things are going along well, by assuring him that his is a good idea;

giving him a direct answer to a question that he asks, or helping him locate the answer if it is not known by the teacher;

giving him a chance to elaborate his idea by asking him more about it in a nonthreatening and nonevaluative manner;

giving him an evaluation, either positive or negative, that points up specifically what is correct or incorrect; or by

giving him a chance to relate to his own experience.

If the child is to become a man who is "open to his experience," a man who can encompass much of reality, then as a child he must relate positively to more people, things, and situations. The teacher's response to him must be such that he wants to reenter the situation. When failure is more or less continuous, one reduces his level of aspiration and oftentimes withdraws from the situation. Therefore, the teacher's response must include:

requiring from the child only that which he is capable of doing;

opening new possibilities to him without coercion;

withholding all sarcasm and ridicule;

interpreting to him the data in the situation of which he is aware.

If the child is to become a man who has positive feelings toward himself and cherishes uniqueness in others, then the teacher's response to him must respect his own individuality. Such responses may include:

giving the child some choice in what he is doing; for example, what he writes about, what he reads, the picture he paints;

expressing a belief in the child as a person;

listening to him;

accepting most of his ideas;

helping him gain competence in the things he cherishes.

If the child is to grow into a man who possesses highly developed communicative skills, he must have opportunity to talk and to listen to others. The teacher's responses must include:

seeking for his opinion and experience;

giving him an opportunity to use a variety of media of communication;

giving him a model of standard language usage;

providing him with a variety of books and other reading materials;

seeking to further his purposes in reading;

giving him opportunity to compare his reading with his new experience, to draw inferences and generalizations from his reading;

seeking the child's own idiomatic response in writing and other media of expression.

If the child is to grow into a man who acts with an attitude of social responsibility the teacher's responses must include:

setting of limits with him and for him;

clarifying standards with public criteria;

structuring the situation with clarity;

reprimanding with public criteria;

giving the child responsibility for others;

evaluating with discrimination.

Good teaching, then, requires appropriate responsiveness to the data the child and group are placing in the situation. It is in this way that the exploring and searching activities of the child or group can be rewarded properly. When their own seeking activities are rewarded, they become involved and commit themselves further to the activity. We believe: "The child's capacity to create new and challenging problems for himself is his most potent source of continuous growth and development."[1] It is his own desire for growth that makes possible the constructively creative man.

Good teaching requires a reduction in the controlling functions exercised continuously by teachers. We have shown how these controls extend to the exact wording of answers, to the minutia of a problem for attention. We have shown that the child's explorations in the way of looking ahead, of relating to his own experiences are usually crushed as the teacher restructures the child back into the narrow path laid out for him. The stereotyped and repetitive question and answer blocks children's use of higher mental processes. They recall and repeat; they do not synthesize or generalize.

The extensive and pervasive control under which children live in the classroom keeps them dependent and prevents them from full participation in the subject-matter (content) of the school.

Good teaching requires that the classroom be well managed so that the business of learning may receive full attention. This means that the teacher perform the functions of controlling with clarity and with consistency. It does mean that in the position of teacher with its superior-subordinate relationship, the power component be ameliorated through relating the direction or the command to situational factors or to the larger society.

[1] Manual Barkan, *Foundations of Art Education* (New York: Ronald Press, 1955).

It is quite probable that most teaching would be improved by the reduction of the present large number of controlling acts to one-third or one-half of what they now are.

Good teaching requires that the human environment be accepting of each individual, that in some way it tell him that he is important. This suggests that teachers not "pit" one group of children against another, but find ways to integrate the wide range of differences that are always present. It suggests a personal rapport between teacher and child. This personal rapport is built upon many little things. For example, the granting of a request other than routine says to the child, "I care for you. You count with me." Psychologists have noted that gratification in one area tends to instigate a feeling of well being that extends into other areas of an individual's life.[2]

Individual rapport is built through empathy and support from one who is a significant person in one's life. It is developed with interpretation of reality that enriches or makes the situation more for one.

Good teaching keeps the interpersonal relationships supportive within the classroom. There are common problems, concerns, and agreements because people have a chance to talk and to listen to one another. There has been time to explore the opinions and wants of the group. Out of this, a shared-problem-solving attitude develops. To maintain a supportive climate the negative acts of sarcasm and threat must be abolished. A reduction in the number of admonishments and reprimands will make those

[2] Lois Barclay Murphy, *Personality in Young Children* (New York: Basic Books, Inc., 1957), Vol. II, Chapter XIV; and Bruno Bettelheim, *Love is Not Enough* (Glencoe, Ill.: Free Press, 1950).

used more effective, especially when they are linked to clearly stated situational factors.

The concept of functions performed in the classroom by the teacher in interaction makes it possible to relate action to the objectives toward which one is working.

The effects on children of the pattern of teaching functions to which they are subjected day after day and year after year are accumulative. Whether or not the "life space" permitted them in the classroom is sufficient to allow them to explore their own ideas, to solve problems of many kinds, to have some choice as to their own activities, makes a real difference in their own involvement in the subject-matter (content) of the school, in their attitude toward learning, and in their development of autonomy. Whether or not they are respected as individuals makes a difference in their development of confidence and positive self-concept.

What teachers do in the classroom makes a difference.

Good teaching requires that the teacher be a well educated, mature person who has the insight and energy for this demanding job. Every decision made in the classroom should be a considered one. This undoubtedly means a smaller number of students in each classroom. Growth is wavering and uneven as well as forward; it goes by leaps as well as crawls. The specifics for a growing child are not entirely predictable. To provide for the differences that are the hopes of each generation requires more than a textbook and a dictionary. It requires the responsive human environment that fosters exploration and initiative.

The Model as we now present it developed from our study of the 129 records of this study and the comprehensive records, including those from

high school teachers, of the Provo Study. Through the study of these records, the functions teachers perform were identified. These functions were classified in seven categories: Controlling Functions; Imposition; Facilitating; Functions That Develop Content; Personal Responsiveness; Functions of Affectivity; and Functions of Negative Affectivity.

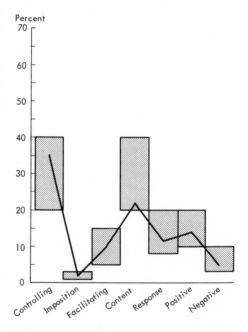

Figure 3. Model of good teaching expressed as the percentage range for each major function within which teaching acts should fall and the mean of the six thirty-minute records considered to be nearest the model.

The Model is presented in graphic form for greater ease in considering the relationship of one category to another. It will be noted in Fig. 3 that the Model is presented as a series of shaded blocks. Each block represents a category of teacher functions and suggests the range of percentage for the category that may be considered good teaching.[3] Good teaching can never be

3 The percentage scale for each category:

Category	Percentage
Controlling Functions	20–40 per cent
Imposition	1– 3 per cent
Facilitating	5–15 per cent
Content Development	20–40 per cent
Personal Response	8–20 per cent
Positive Affectivity	10–20 per cent
Negative Affectivity	3–10 per cent

considered a score or a point. If teaching is to be responsive to the children and the situation in which they are working, it must be flexible. Furthermore, teachers are people; they can be good teachers and have some differences in pattern of teaching acts.

27.

The Personal Approach
to Good Teaching

ARTHUR W. COMBS

Professor of Education,
University of Florida.

To plan effective programs for teacher education we need the very best definition of good teaching we can acquire. That seems clear enough. How to arrive at such a definition, however, has proved to be a most difficult task. Despite millions of dollars and millions of man-hours poured into research on the problem over the past 50 years, the results have continued to be frustrating and disappointing—until recently. It now appears that our failure to find useful definitions may be due to the inadequacies of the frame of reference from which we have attacked the problem.

Arthur W. Combs, "The Personal Approach to Good Teaching." Educational Leadership, 21 (6): 369–377, 399; March, 1964. Reprinted with permission of the Association for Supervision and Curriculum Development and Arthur W. Combs. Copyright © 1964 by the Association for Supervision and Curriculum Development.

THE TEACHER
AS KNOWER

The earliest conception of the good teacher was that of the scholar. It was assumed that a person who knew could teach others. Of course it is true that a teacher has to know something but, even without research, it is apparent to anyone who looks that "knowing" is simply not enough. Most of us recall out of our own experience the teacher who "knew his subject but could not put it across." In some places there can even be found good teachers whose depth of information in a particular field is woefully lacking! This is often a shocking discovery to some critics of education who still equate teaching with scholarship. One of my own studies on good teaching demonstrated that *both*, good teachers and bad ones, knew equally well what a good teaching situation *ought* to be like(Combs, 1961). Knowing is certainly important to teaching, but it is clear, good teaching involves much more.

THE "COMPETENCIES" APPROACH TO TEACHING

A second approach to defining good teaching has been in terms of teacher "competencies." The thinking goes something like this: If we know what the expert teachers do, or are like, then we can teach the beginners to be like that. This is a straightforward, uncomplicated approach to the problem and seems logically sound.

This idea has produced great quantities of research into the traits of good teachers and their methods. This has provided us with long lists of competencies supposedly characteristic of good teachers. In the beginning these lists were quite simple. Since, however, what people do is always related to the situations they are in, every situation calls for a different behavior and the more situations the researchers examine, the longer the lists of competencies have become.

The following, for example, is a list made by a conference of "Superior Teachers" in 1962:

Good teachers should:
Know their subject
Know much about related subjects
Be adaptable to new knowledge
Understand the process of becoming
Recognize individual differences
Be a good communicator
Develop an inquiring mind
Be available
Be committed
Be enthusiastic
Have a sense of humor
Have humility
Cherish his own individuality

Have convictions
Be sincere and honest
Act with integrity
Show tolerance and understanding
Be caring
Have compassion
Have courage
Have personal security
Be creative
Be versatile
Be willing to try
Be adaptable
Believe in God.

This is but a short list. There are much longer ones!

At first, attempts to discover the competencies of good teachers were highly specific. Hundreds of attempts were made to demonstrate that good teachers had this or that trait, used this or that method—all to no avail! Good teaching simply could not be defined in terms of any particular trait or method. In 1959, the American Association of School Administrators commissioned a team to review the research on the problem. Out of this the school administrators hoped to find some guidelines which might help them make the practical decisions about a high quality of teaching necessary in carrying on their jobs. Sadly, the team was forced to report that there is no specific trait or method sufficiently associated with good teaching to provide clear distinctions (Ellena, 1961).

Some investigators have thought better discriminations might be found in generic, rather than specific studies of the "teaching act." Accordingly, they have turned their attention to the *general* traits or methods used by the teacher. Approaching the problem in this way they have been able to find fairly stable distinctions in such general terms as, "good teachers are considerate," or "child centered," or "concerned about structure." The most significant of these is a study by Marie Hughes (1959) under a grant from the U. S. Office of Education, Cooperative Research Program. Dr. Hughes developed an exhaustive system for analyzing teacher behavior and applied this system to time sample observations of teachers in the classroom. She was able to demonstrate a number of general classes of behavior seemingly characteristic of good teachers. Among these were such categories as controlling, imposition, facilitating, content development, response, and positive or negative affectivity.

Similar attempts to analyze teacher behavior have been carried out by Flanders (1960), Smith (1961), Bowers (1961), Filson (1957), and Medley (1959). These attempts to examine the more global aspects of effective teaching have been somewhat more successful in discriminating between good and poor teaching than research directed at specific or detailed descriptions of behavior, or methods. But they still do not provide us with the definitive distinctions needed by the profession. Good teaching, it now seems clear, is not a direct function of general traits or methods.

SOME PRACTICAL DIFFICULTIES OF THE COMPETENCIES APPROACH

The attempt to develop a teacher education program based upon the competencies approach runs into some very knotty problems. In the first place, it is a fallacy to assume the methods of the experts either can, or should be, taught directly to the beginners. It is seldom we can determine what should be for the beginner by examining what the expert does well. I learned this some years ago when I was responsible for teaching failing university students more effec-

tive methods of study. At first glance it would seem logical to determine what should be taught to the failing students by determining the study habits of successful ones. Such an approach to curriculum construction, however, is disastrous!

Successful students study most whimsically. They operate without plan, go to the movies often, indulge in all sorts of extracurricular activities and generally behavior in ways that would be suicidal for students teetering on the brink of failure. It simply does not follow that what is good for the expert is good for the novice too! Nor is it true, that the way to become expert is to do what the expert does.

Some of the methods used by the expert can only be used *because* he is expert. Many experienced teachers have learned to deal with most classroom disturbances by ignoring them. Yet beginners cannot ignore them! The expert is able to ignore matters precisely because he *is* expert. Some methods cannot even be comprehended without adequate prior experience. One must grow to achieve them. Asking the young teacher to use methods which do not fit him may only turn him loose in the blackboard jungle to fight for his life with inappropriate weapons.

The creation of long lists of competencies is likely to be deeply discouraging and disillusioning to the young teacher for another reason. Evaluations of "goodness" or "badness" become attached to methods, and students thereafter are expected to judge their own adequacies in these terms. The net effect is to set such impossible goals of excellence that no one can ever hope to reach them. This is a terribly depressing and discouraging prospect.

Discouraging and disillusioning as the competencies approach is for the young teacher, it has equally unhappy effects on the more experienced teachers. A vast complex of competencies, all of which are demanded as criteria for good teaching leaves the individual defenseless before criticism. No matter what he does well, it is never enough! There is always so much more that he might have done, or should have done, that he can rarely find pleasure or satisfaction in what he actually has done. Add to this the fact that many of the competencies demanded do not fit his particular personality, and so could probably never be achieved anyhow, and the defeat of the individual becomes almost inevitable. In time, feeling of inadequacy produced by continual failure to meet impossible goals undermines professional pride and is likely to produce a guilt-ridden teacher suffering from a secret feeling of being "too little and too late." It should not be surprising if, after years of this kind of experience, the will to try shrivels and dies on the vine.

To use particular competencies as a measure of good teaching, irrespective of personalities, situations or purposes, leads us to the ridiculous conclusion that some of the very people who taught us most, were poor teachers. When I hear young teachers-in-training remark, "Oh, he is a lousy teacher but you sure learn a lot!" I am forced to conclude that the determination of the goodness of teaching on the basis of competencies is highly questionable.

The methods people use are highly personal. These methods cannot be judged apart from the personality they express. No one, after all, looks well, feels well, or behaves well, in another person's clothing. Methods, like the clothes we wear, must fit the people we are. Good teaching is a highly personal matter.

THE PERSONAL CHARACTER OF GOOD TEACHING

Is there a better approach? I think there is. As we have seen, the research on good teaching is unable to isolate any common trait or practice of good teachers. Yet these unanimous results, themselves, represent a most important commonality. They demonstrate the uniqueness and individuality of good teachers! The very failure of research to define common factors is, itself, a demonstration that a good teacher is primarily a personality. If good teachers are unique individuals we could predict from the start that the attempt to find *common uniqueness* would be unfruitful!

A good teacher is first and foremost a person. He has competence, to be sure, but not a *common* set of competencies like anyone else. Like the students he teachers, he is infinitely unique and becoming more so all the time. The fact of his personness is the most important and determining thing about him. The personal character of good teaching can be documented by almost any of us from our own experience. If one thinks back to his own school days he will probably discover that the good teachers he had in his own lifetime did not all behave alike or, even, with great similarity. Rather, each stands out as a person, an individual, some for one reason, some for another.

Apparently, there can be no such thing as a "good" or "bad" method of teaching. The terms "good" and "bad" can be applied to results, outcomes, purposes or ends. The methods we use to achieve these ends, however, only derive their value from the goals and purposes for which they are used. The good teacher is not one who behaves in a "given" way. He is an artist, skillful in producing a desirable result. The result may be considered "good" or "bad," but not the method.

THE "SELF AS INSTRUMENT" CONCEPT

This shift in our thinking from a mechanistic to a personal view of teaching is by no means confined to our profession alone. In fact, most other professions dealing with human problems have preceded us in this direction. The effective professional worker, in medicine, social work, clinical psychology, guidance or nursing is no longer seen as a technician applying methods in more or less mechanical fashion the way he has been taught. We now understand him as an intelligent human being using himself, his knowledge and the resources at hand to solve the problems for which he is responsible. He is a person who has learned to use himself as an effective instrument (Combs, 1961).

If we adapt this "self as instrument" concept of the professional worker to teaching, it means that teachers colleges must concern themselves with *persons* rather than competencies. It means the individualization of instruction we have sought for the public school must be applied to the teachers colleges as well. It calls for the production of creative individuals, capable of shifting and changing to meet the demands and opportunities afforded in daily tasks. Such a teacher will not behave in a set way. His behavior will change from moment to moment, from day to day, rapidly adjusting to the needs of his students, the situations he is in, the purposes he seeks to fulfill and the methods and materials he has at hand.

The good teacher is no carbon copy but stands out as a unique and effective personality, sometimes for one reason, sometimes for another, but always for something intensely and personally his own. He has found ways of using himself, his talents and his environment in a fashion that aids both his students and himself to achieve satisfaction—their own and society's too. Artists sometimes refer to "the discovery of one's personal idiom" and the expression seems very apt applied to teaching as well. We may define the effective teacher *as a unique human being who has learned to use his self effectively and efficiently for carrying out his own and society's purposes.*

The production of this kind of person is not a question of teaching him what to do. Modern perceptual psychology tells us that a person's behavior is the direct result of his perceptions, how things seem to him at the moment of his behaving. To change an individual's behavior, it is necessary to help him see himself and his world differently. It is here that teacher education must direct its effort. The modern giant computer is able to provide "best answers" to vast quantities of data depending upon the formulas built into the machine. In a similar fashion, the effectiveness of the teacher is dependent upon the internal "formulas" which select and control his behavior as he is confronted with changing situations. These human formulas are the perceptions he holds of himself, his purposes and the world in which he must live and operate.

Whether an individual can behave effectively and efficiently in a given situation, according to the perceptual psychologists, will depend upon how he is perceiving at the time. To change his behavior, furthermore, it will be necessary to produce a change in his perception of himself and his world. This means for teacher education, we need first to know how good teachers perceive. Knowing that, we may then be able to help teachers perceive themselves and their tasks in those ways.

A PERCEPTUAL VIEW OF GOOD TEACHING

What kinds of beliefs, understandings, values and concepts make up the perceptual organization of good teachers?

This way of looking at teacher education is so new that we do not yet have the precise research we need to guide us. This need not deter us, however, for there is evidence enough at least to start us thinking on new tracks, designing new techniques and planning for the research we need. To this point we have the following sources of information to draw upon for defining the probable dimensions of good teaching in perceptual terms:

1. Perceptual psychological theory, especially that having to do with the nature of the self and fully functioning behavior

2. Research on the perceptions of good practitioners in other helping professions (Combs and Soper, 1963)

3. The research already existing in our profession

4. The experiences accumulated by thousands of teachers engaged in day to day "action research" in the classroom.

Drawing upon these four sources it would appear that a good teacher is characterized by typical perceptual organizations in six general areas:

A. His knowledge of his subject
B. His frame of reference for approaching his problems
C. His perceptions of others
D. His perceptions of self
E. His perceptions of the purpose and process of learning
F. His perceptions of appropriate methods.

Under each of these major headings a series of hypotheses can be drawn concerning the teacher's characteristic perceptual organization in that area. The following is a list developed at the University of Florida by the author and his colleagues over the past five years. These were originally drawn up to serve as suggestions for future research. The list is presented here both as an amplification of the "self as instrument" concept and as possible propositions for further research by others who may be interested in the problem. The list is by no means a complete one but it serves as a point of departure for consideration of the self as instrument approach. It is presented as a promising series of leads which may excite other researchers, as it has my colleagues and me, to explore these matters further. Some of the following hypotheses (marked by *) we have already corroborated in research on good and poor counselors (Combs, 1963). Others (marked by †) are currently being explored in several researches on the perceptual organization of good teachers. Each hypothesis is stated as the two ends of a continuum with the perceptions presumed characteristic of the good teacher at the left and those of the poor teacher at the right. Those hypotheses already studied or currently under investigation include more extensive definitions. Several items, not yet subjected to research test, do not have definitions included.

HYPOTHESES REGARDING THE PERCEPTUAL ORGANIZATION OF EFFECTIVE TEACHERS

A. *A Good Teacher Has Rich Perceptions About His Subject:* The good teacher will need to be well informed about the subject matter he is responsible for teaching. That is to say, he must have a rich and extensive field of perceptions about his subject upon which he can call as required. The good teacher is not stupid. This aspect of good teaching provides us with nothing new. It is the aspect of the teaching function we have known best and developed most fully in the past.

B. *The Good Teacher's Frame of Reference:* The good teacher is always keenly aware of how things seem from the point of view of those with whom he works. His frame of reference for approaching problems and people is humanistic rather than mechanistic. He is deeply sensitive to the private worlds of his students and colleagues and accepts their feelings, attitudes, beliefs and understandings as legitimate and important data in human interaction.

Hypothesis 1*† — Internal-External frame of reference: The teacher's general frame of reference can be described as internal rather than external; that is to say, he seems sensitive to and concerned with how things look to others with whom he interacts and uses this as a basis for his own behavior.
Hypothesis 2*†—People-Things orientation: Central to the thinking of the teacher is a concern with people and their reactions rather than with things and events.
Hypothesis 3*†—Meanings-Facts orientation: The teacher is more concerned with the perceptual experience of people than with the objective events. He is sensitive to how things seem to peo-

ple rather than being exclusively concerned with concrete events.
Hypothesis 4*†—Immediate-Historical causation: The teacher seeks the causes of people's behavior in their current thinking, feeling, beliefs and understandings rather than in objective descriptions of the forces exerted upon them now or in the past.
Hypothesis 5—Hopeful-Despairing.

C. *Perceptions About What People Are Like and How They Behave:* Teaching is a human relationship. To behave effectively good teachers must possess the most accurate understandings about people and their behavior available in our generation. Each of us can only behave in terms of what we believe is so. What a teacher believes, therefore, about the nature of his students will have a most important effect on how he behaves toward them. Let us take a simple example to illustrate this point.

If a teacher believes his students have the capacity to learn, he will behave quite differently from the teacher who has serious doubts about the capacities of his charges. The teacher who believes his students *can,* begins his task with hope and assurance that both he and his students may be successful. He can place confidence and trust in his students and be certain that, if he is successful in facilitating and encouraging the learning process, they can, they will learn.

The teacher, on the other hand, who does not believe his students are capable approaches his task with two strikes against him. He is licked before he starts. If you do not believe that children *can,* then it is certainly not safe to trust them. False beliefs about the nature of people can only result in the selection of inappropriate ways of dealing with them. A prime function of the teachers college must be to assist its students to clear and accurate understandings of the nature of people and their behavior.

Hypothesis 6*† — Able-Unable. The teacher perceives others as having the capacities to deal with their problems. He believes that they can find adequate solutions to events as opposed to doubting the capacity of people to handle themselves and their lives.

Hypothesis 7*†—Friendly-Unfriendly: The teacher sees others as being friendly and enhancing. He does not regard them as threatening to himself but rather sees them as essentially well intentioned rather than evil intentioned.

Hypothesis 8*†—Worthy-Unworthy: The teacher tends to see other people as being of worth rather than unworthy. He sees them as possessing a dignity and integrity which must be respected and maintained rather than seeing people as unimportant, whose integrity may be violated or treated as of little account.

Hypothesis 9†—Internally-Externally motivated: The teacher sees people and their behavior as essentially developing from within rather than as a product of external events to be molded, directed; sees people as creative, dynamic rather than passive or inert.

Hypothesis 10*†—Dependable-Undependable: The teacher sees people as essentially trustworthy and dependable in the sense of behaving in a lawful way. He regards their behavior as understandable rather than capricious, unpredictable or negative.

Hypothesis 11† — Helpful-Hindering. The teacher sees people as being potentially fulfilling and enhancing to self rather than impeding or threatening. He regards people as important sources of satisfaction rather than sources of frustration and suspicion.

Hypothesis 12—Unthreatening-Threatening.

Hypothesis 13—Respectable-Of no account.

D. *The Teacher's Perception of Self:* Perceptual psychology indicates that the behavior of the individual at any moment is a function of how he sees his situation and himself. In recent years we have come to understand the crucial importance of the self concept in affecting every aspect of a person's life. It makes a vast difference what people believe about themselves.

The behavior of a teacher, like that of everyone else, is a function of his concepts of self. Teacher who believe they are able will try. Teachers who do not think they are able will avoid responsibilities. Teachers who feel they are liked by their students will behave quite differently from those who feel they are unliked. Teachers who feel they are acceptable to the administration can behave quite differently from those who have serious doubts about their acceptability. Teachers who feel their profession has dignity and integrity can themselves behave with dignity and integrity. Teachers who have grave doubts about the importance and value of their profession may behave apologetically or overly aggressively with their students and with their colleagues. It is apparent that, if the self concept is a fundamental in producing the behavior of an individual as has been suggested by modern psychology, then teacher education programs must give it a vital place in the production of new teachers.

Hypothesis 14*†—Identified with-Apart from: The teacher tends to see himself as a part of all mankind; he sees himself as identified with people rather than as withdrawn, removed, apart or alienated from others.

Hypothesis 15*†—Adequate-Inadequate: The teacher generally sees himself as enough; as having what is needed to deal with his problems. He does not see himself as lacking and as unable to cope with problems.

Hypothesis 16*† — Trustworthy-Untrustworthy: The teacher has trust in his own organism. He sees himself as essentially dependable, reliable, as having the potentiality for coping with events as opposed to seeing self in a tentative fashion with doubts about the potentiality and reliability of the organism.

Hypothesis 17*†—Worthy-Unworthy: The teacher sees himself as a person of consequence, dignity, integrity and worthy of respect; as opposed to being a person of little consequence who can be overlooked, discounted, whose dignity and integrity do not matter.

Hypothesis 18*†—Wanted-Unwanted: The teacher sees himself as essentially likable, attractive (in personal, not physical appearance sense), wanted, and in general capable of bringing forth a warm response from those people important to him; as opposed to feeling ignored, unwanted, or rejected by others.

Hypothesis 19—Accepted-Not accepted.
Hypothesis 20—Certain, sure-Doubting.
Hypothesis 21—Feels aware-Unaware.

E. *The Purpose and Process of Learning:* Behavior always has direction. Whatever we do is always determined by the purposes we have in mind at the time of our behaving or misbehaving. What teachers perceive to be their own and society's purposes makes a great deal of difference in their behavior. The teacher who believes schools exist only for the able and that "it is a waste of time to fool with the poorer students," behaves quite differently from the teacher who perceives society's purpose as that of helping *all* children become the best they can. Similarly, what the

teacher believes about how students learn will markedly affect his behavior. One teacher, believing children must be molded, teaches loyalty to country by carefully censoring what students read and hear about democracy and communism. Another teacher, believing children learn best when confronted with all kinds of evidence, takes a different tack in teaching his class. The clarity and accuracy of perceptions about the purposes and processes of learning will have profound effects on the behavior of teachers.

How the teacher sees the task of teaching, in the immediate sense, as it applies to moment to moment operations in the classroom, or in the broadest sense, of society's needs and purposes, will determine the way he behaves on the job. The teachers college must help him find these understanding and make them a part of his very being. Only the best and most accurate perceptions will suffice.

Hypothesis 22*†—Freeing-Controlling: The teacher perceives the purpose of the helping task as one of freeing, assisting, releasing, facilitating rather than a matter of controlling, manipulating, coercing, blocking, inhibiting.

Hypothesis 23*†—Large-Smaller perceptions: The teacher tends to view events in a broad rather than narrow perspective. He is concerned with larger connotations of events, with large, more extensive implications than the immediate and specific. He is not exclusively concerned with details but can perceive beyond the immediate to future and larger meanings.

Hypothesis 24*†—Self revealing-Self concealing: The teacher sees his appropriate role as self revealing rather than self concealing; that is, he appears to be willing to disclose himself. He can treat his feelings and shortcomings as important and significant rather than hiding them or covering them up. He seems willing to be himself.

Hypothesis 25†—Self involved-Self withheld: The teacher sees his appropriate role as one of commitment to the helping interaction, as opposed to being inert or remaining aloof or remote from interaction.

Hypothesis 26†—Furthering process-Achieving goals: The teacher sees his appropriate role as one of encouraging and facilitating the process of search and discovery, as opposed to promoting, or working for a personal goal or preconceived solution.

Hypothesis 27—Helping-Dominating.
Hypothesis 28 — Understanding-Condemning.
Hypothesis 29—Accepting-Rejecting.
Hypothesis 30—Valuing integrity-Violating integrity.
Hypothesis 31—Positive-Negative.
Hypothesis 32—Open-Closed to experience.
Hypothesis 33—Tolerant of ambiguity-Intolerant.

F. *Perception of Appropriate Methods:* The methods teachers use must fit the kinds of people they are. An effective teacher must have an armamentarium of methods upon which he may call as these are needed to carry out his teaching duties. These may vary widely from teacher to teacher and even from moment to moment. Whatever their nature they must fit the situations and purposes of the teacher and be appropriate for the students with whom they are used.

The teacher education program must help each student find the methods best suited to him, to his purposes, his task and the peculiar populations and problems with which he must deal on the job. This is not so much a matter of *teaching* methods as one of helping students *discover* methods.

While methods must always be highly personal, certain perceptions about appropriate methods may be characteristic of good teaching. Among the hypotheses we hope to explore in this area are the following:

Hypothesis 34—Helping methods seen as superior to manipulating methods.
Hypothesis 35—Cooperation superior to competition.

REFERENCES

N. D. Bowers and R. S. Soar. *Studies in Human Relations in the Teaching Learning Process* V. Final Report, Cooperative Research Project No. 469, 1961.

A. W. Combs. "A Perceptual View of the Nature of 'Helpers,' in Personality Theory and Counseling Practice." Papers of First Annual Conference on Personality Theory and Counseling Practice. Gainesville, Florida: University of Florida, 1961, p. 53–58.

A. W. Combs and D. W. Soper, "The Perceptual Organization of Effective Counselors." *Journal of Counseling Psychology* 10:222–26; 1963.

W. J. Ellena, M. Stevenson and H. V. Webb. *Who's a Good Teacher?* Washington, D. C.: American Association of School Administrators, NEA, 1961.

T. N. Filson. "Factors Influencing the Level of Dependence in the Classroom." Unpublished Ph.D. Thesis. Minneapolis: University of Minnesota, 1957.

N. A. Flanders. *Teacher Influence, Pupil Attitudes and Achievement: Studies in Interaction Analysis.* Final Report, Cooperative Research Project No. 397, U.S. Office of Education, 1960.

Marie M. Hughes. *Development of the Means for Assessing the Quality of*

Teaching in Elementary Schools. Report of Research, Cooperative Research Program, U.S. Office of Education Project No. 353, 1959.

Donald M. Medley and Harold E. Mitzel. "A Technique for Measuring Classroom Behavior." *Journal of Educational Psychology* 49: 86–92; 1958.

B. Othanel Smith. "A Concept of Teaching." *Language and Concepts in Education.* Chicago: Rand McNally & Company, 1961.

28.

The Anti-School—Some Reflections On Teaching

JURGEN HERBST
Professor of Educational Policy
Studies and of History, University of Wisconsin.

In teaching, as in everything that is important to us, nothing matters as much as our attitudes and our disposition. It is the frame of mind, the direction in which our mental as well as our emotional compass is set, that ultimately sustains us in our efforts and determines the effectiveness of our work. It is our deep-seated orientation towards life in all its aspects, intellectual and emotional, social and individual; an orientation that is revealed in a man's responses to the question: What is teaching to you? An opportunity to meet your needs and gratify your desires? A burden to be shouldered? A job you drifted into, or a profession freely chosen? A way to earn a living, or a way of life that commits you and your family with all your hopes for the future? In whatever answer a man may give—he reveals himself, his values, and his choice. He lets us see the things he cares for, and the intensity with which he cares for them.

"The Anti-School—Some Reflections on Teaching by Jurgen Herbst is reprinted with permission from Educational Theory, *18: 13–22, Winter, 1968.*

Although refined by thought and made explicit in words, attitudes and disposition are not formed merely through intellectual exercises. Although they are hammered out and tempered in experience and their worth established and proved for us in daily tests and trials, they are not only reflex and habit. Attitudes and disposition arise from the thoughtful appraisal of experience, and indicates our conscious and personal acceptance of a way of life. Such acceptance is the result of the transmutation of experience through rational reflection and emotional consent. What the discipline of education and the profession of teaching need today is neither more experience nor better definitions, but the reflective mastery of experience and its willed conversion into personal commitment. For the practical needs and concerns of teaching pure experience is as worthless as the most refined learning, either singly or combined. It is when both experience and thought are charged with the energy of personal commitment, and when they thus nourish a man's attitudes and disposition that teaching achieves its fullest potentialities for teachers and their students alike.

This view of teaching, I am afraid, does not prevail in our schools and institutions of teacher training throughout the country. Much talk and many manifestos to the contrary, American teachers as a group do not impress the observer as constituting a profession conscious of its self-chosen objectives, standards, and aspirations, and committed to uphold and improve these. Rather, teachers resemble more what was once called "the hired clergy," a corps of specialists, ready to sell their talents, know-how, and skill to the highest or least demanding bidder, and ready, likewise, to adjust not only standards and aspirations, but also convictions and orientation to the demands of their employers. Proficiency in knowledge and skills are valued higher than the ability to judge discriminately in the choice of educational objectives, and to affirm one's choice in one's teaching. The hired teacher performs his tasks by adhering to manual or directive. He, in fact, invites these guidelines when, with no commitment of his own, he asks for and accepts the authority of others. To him teaching is a job, not a profession.

From college through graduate school future teachers are told what, supposedly, they need to know to become competent teachers. This is to say, they are told what their teachers are able to tell them; what, in other words, teachers of teachers consider teachable. This is why in teacher training we emphasize so vigorously skills and techniques,

materials and devices, doctrines and theories. We have focused our attention on that part of human experience and learning that can be transferred from man to man and handed down from generation to generation. Since such transfer obviously does take place, since its techniques can be acquired and transmitted, we have capitalized on this phenomenon, have called it education, and pronounced it to be a good thing. Our current national love-affair with it is about to drown us all in a flood of unexamined assumptions concerning teaching. It matters little whether we think of parents initiating their children into the mysteries of acceptable behavior, or of teachers in the classroom. In either case we think of adults telling children what to do. For the most part this telling consists of the indoctrination of various sorts of rules and laws, and it is judged to have been successful once the students know the rules and know how to apply them or live by them.

Education, in fact, has often been defined as the transmission of culture. Past knowledge and past experience is what one generation transfers to its successors. We may ask with Thoreau whether we have anything worth transmitting, anything that is worthy of transmission in its own right; and we may wonder, too, whether a thing that was once "useful and ornamental" (to use Benjamin Franklin's phrase), will be so for our children. We are all too keenly aware how much our desire to live forever spurs on our attempts at transmitting culture, how much our wish to have our children build monuments for us inspires our actions. When we as teachers allow our ambition to be stirred by this desire, we fasten the hold of the past over the future. We use teaching to fashion the young in the image of their elders, and we neglect to ask whether the perpetuation of this image is desirable. What right do we have to tell our children how to live? The earth belongs to the living, said Jefferson, yet we in our schools labor mightily to enshrine the past and deny the present. Is it any surprise when we learn from our historians that education nearly always has been a force that conserves, nay embalms, the past?

We all have learned in school or college that it was John Dewey and his disciples who broke the grip of the past over the present, who taught that each generation defines the world anew, just as it creates its own culture and rewrites history. Seen thus, education is not merely the transmission of past culture, but the continuing creation of present culture as well. It is, in its specific pedagogic function, the initiation of the young into the culture of the present. This kind of educational progressivism, we know, was a liberating force in its time; a great, welcome and effective challenge to the thoughtless reiteration of statements and practices that no longer reflected current reality. John Dewey's reconstruction in education meant, in practice, education's attempted effort to reconstruct society and culture in and through the schools. Whatever one might think of such a program, it challenged teachers and children to forego the hand-me-down of rote learning, and to take an active part in the reconstruction of the world they lived in. It made science and the scientific method the chosen tools of this reconstruction, and shored up the reliance on science by asserting that science and democracy were born twins. The schools were to be the agents of cultural and social progress.

Unfortunately, progressivism fared no better than the traditionalism it re-placed. It, too, succumbed rather quickly to its own orthodoxy and enshrined its dogmas and definitions. Teaching and instruction were exchanged for doing and activities; education meant learning how to live with others. Not the traditions of the past, but the incessant and ubiquitous voices of the present were accepted as authorities, and children were told—as one hapless educational philosopher put it recently —to see life patternwise. In David Riesman's apt phrase, we traded in our gyroscope for a radarscope. From an initial concern with the development of individuals, progressive education moved to the assimilation and integration of these individuals into society. What had started out as a promise of a new life in school and society ended up in the mindless worship of life adjustment. Where the traditionalist teacher of the late nineteenth century had been the spokesman for the respectability of the genteel tradition, the latter-day progressive adapted his students to the conformist style of middle class suburbia. Where the nineteenth century had believed that academies, high schools, and colleges were to educate society's leaders and pacesetters, the twentieth century, being suspicious of claims to leadership, interpreted democracy to mean the homogeneity of the lonely crowd, and believed that schools should reflect this faceless society rather than challenge and reshape it. Thus the progressive reformer gave way to the other-directed man.

The latest phase of educational thought and practice reflects our current disillusionment with the progressivism of the life-adjusters and the traditionalism of advocates of memory learning. As set forth in Jerome Bruner's *Process of Education,* it represents an attempt to make respectable and respected again the academically oriented school by fashioning education in the image of scientific discovery, scholarly investigation, and theoretical understanding. The objective is neither the adjustment of individuals to their neighbors, nor the acquisition of factual information or technical skills, but the ability to think conceptually, to manipulate symbols, and to relate scientific theories to natural as well as social phenomena. Where once the more scientifically-inclined among the progressives held that "to know something thoroughly involves knowing its quantity as well as its quality," their Brunerian successors maintain that knowledge is the "general understanding of the structure of subject matter." Such knowledge, to be sure, is the scientist's or the scholar's knowledge, and it has reference to the abstractions and symbol-systems we call theories. The aim of Bruner's process is to turn students into scientists, i.e., to teach them how through intellectual abstraction they may comprehend efficiently and comprehensively the varieties of human experiences, and how to translate such theoretical understanding into purposeful action. The way in which this objective is pursued leads through the laboratory or workshop where students are asked to rediscover for themselves what others have found before them, and through the lecture hall and library where students are asked to familiarize themselves with the "structures of subject matter" previously proposed, invented, or imagined.

Education as proposed by the Brunerians was a healthy corrective to the absurdities of life-adjustment. Yet we must realize that it aims to acquaint students with the scientists' representation of the world, not with the world itself. It is concerned with science, not with nature or man. The Brunerian theory of instruction rests squarely on the assumption that the scientific way of confronting and evaluating life is the most desirable one for all who live in the twentieth century. In our schools budding scientists and intellectuals of all persuasions readily respond, and we fare best in the college-preparatory validation of hypotheses, with inductive classroom. Those of our students, however, who are less concerned with the methodologies and scientific theories; who do not feel the urge or the necessity to dissect and analyze reality according to some scientific prescription; who are much more concerned with responding to reality in concrete situations rather than with knowing its structure; those students, I maintain, are ill served by the educational theory I have been discussing. They doubt that they can afford to learn and to know before they must act. In fact they know that action precedes knowing, and that the knowledge of structures is not more than a *post facto* rationalization of experience. They ask for experience, and the Brunerians give them definitions. The methodology of science, for all we know, may be a dead-end street for them. Who is to say that for them there are not other equally valid roads? School should provide the opportunity for the young to find their own way, not push them along the scientific super-highway we happen to prefer for ourselves.

The scientist's understanding of the structure of subject matter is an effective way of knowing if one's aim is the manipulation and exploitation of the world. But, fortunately, men differ legitimately in their aims and aspirations, and not all of us either need or want to be scientists or scholars. This is a cheering thought when one considers how science is beset with its own orthodoxies and dogmas, and how salutary our skepticism towards scientific gospels may become. The Brunerians are already well on their way to endear to the interest of pedagogues words rather than things, concepts and theories rather than the realities of life. They teach subject matter rather than subjects, promise knowledge of life as interpreted in subject matter rather than the ability to lead happy lives. William James once expressed the matter well: "Knowledge of life is one thing; effective occupation of a place in life...is another." Life is too rich to be captured in subject matter, and the content of an academic curriculum too limited to represent the *raison d'etre* of a school. The Brunerians, in short, are out to shape students in their own image, mistaking themselves as part of the universe for the whole of it.

Finally, one might point out that the notion of the structure of subject matter and its teachability does not touch on the structure of reality. The structure of subject matter is our inherited abstract of reality, and we find it easy to teach that which we ourselves have created by abstraction. Vico may be our guide who wrote: "And history cannot be more certain than when he who creates the things also describes them." Are we then to conclude that since we did not create nature but only science, and since we did not create man but only wrote down his history, we cannot teach concerning nature and man, but only concerning science and history? The Brunerians, it appears, subscribe to this argument, since it is the structure of science and the structure of recorded history that they want to have taught in the schools. What is the structure of nature and of human events? Professor Bruner evades this question by referring us, not to history as events that happened, but to history

as subject matter or to the social sciences. Recently he told us that history could not be studied for an understanding of structure—presumably he discovered that it had none—but "for the end of developing style." This admission undercuts his proud boast that through an understanding of structure any subject could be taught "in some intellectually honest form to any child at any stage of development." To school children who must live in the real world of history and to their teachers, the Brunerian doctrine with its emphasis on subject matter is of little help.

> I a stranger and afraid
> in a world I never made

What of the world and the history in which I live? This, it seems to me, is the real question asked by our children today, one which Professor Bruner leaves unanswered.

When I thus reject the definitions and aims of traditionalists, progressives, and Brunerians, what, you may ask, are we left with? What are the irreducible and undeniable elements of a situation in which human beings learn from one another, and in which this learning is neither the transmission of factual information nor the largely unconscious process of socialization or "growing up," nor indoctrination in the scientific methodology of structuring reality? How can teaching be free of social and conceptual constraints? How, on the teacher's part, may it again become the personal expression of informed commitment to the nurture of curious and creative minds in meaningful encounter with one another and with their surroundings? What happens, in other words, when mere experiencing and ratiocination give way to learning that is at once spontaneous and purposeful? Under what conditions can such teaching occur, and what are its chief characteristics?

All education begins with a question asked by one eager to learn. Learning then takes place when he who responds enables the questioner to arrive at the answer for himself. Teaching thus means to free people from their dependence on others, to stand them on their own feet, and to encourage them to walk for themselves. In other words: No more baby-carriages, no more crutches, no more holding hands— Walk! Education beings with a question. If in their classroom students do not ask questions, it is not teachers we need, but drill sergeants or prison guards. A student is one who demands of his teacher: Show me how! Tell me why! Say what this is for! When teachers cease to hear and respond to these questions, when they no longer succeed in eliciting them, then their lectures and demonstrations have come to resemble those of salesmen and propagandists. It matters little whether teachers attempt to sell the facts of ancient history, the fashions of acceptable behavior, or the theories of nuclear physics. They are not responding to questions in the hope and with the intent that eventually the response becomes unnecessary and the student is able to answer his own questions. The objective of teaching is neither information, socialization, nor techniques, but the achievement of personal autonomy.

If one reflects on teaching in this manner, it quickly becomes apparent that neither traditionalists nor progressives and Brunerians view the teacher as one who responds to his students' questions. Rather they see him as the representative of society or as the scientific expert who tells his students what the authority of either society or science demands. Students who, for many and various reasons, are disposed to question this authority and who receive no hearing for their questions in the classroom, find schooling highly irrelevant and, sooner or later, rebel against it openly or covertly. In Darien where high school kids do as their elders do, they get killed or wind up in jail. In New York where they avoid doing as their elders do, they also get killed or wind up in jail. It is as Huck Finn observed: "What's the use you learning to do right, when it's troublesome to do right and ain't no trouble to do wrong, and the wages is just the same?" Authority no longer makes sense to him who is forced to grow up absurd.

Do those who cannot accept the authorities of society and science speak for today's students? Do the rebels represent fairly the American student of the mid-sixties? Do the teachers who sympathize with them and share their basic convictions express that which is vital and liberating in American education today? It is obvious, it seems to me, that the rebellious critics do not speak for the majority of either students or teachers. They do not now, as they have never done so in the past. They do, however, give shape and impetus to movements and styles in education, just as the more articulate spokesmen of the progressives and the Brunerians have done before them. Today's rebels, however, differ in one essential and decisive respect. They are leaving the schools rather than reforming them from within. High school students disappear before graduation, and college students, protesting the irrelevancy of much of their required course work, move out and set up their own "free universities," or get their education in Alabama, Vietnam, or the

Peace Corps. They all turn their back on education as it is carried on and—as they believe—stifled in our institutions of learning, and they seek its essence in new surroundings. To the anti-hero of the anti-novel we can add, without unduly straining our metaphors, the anti-student of the anti-school: the drop-out in Vietnam, the civil rights worker in Mississippi, the so-called beatnik in the Village loft.

What, you may ask, is the anti-school? Where might we find it? The answer is clear: Wherever youths find relevance in their activities (whether registering Negro voters or discussing the ethics of love), wherever they face reality (whether among migrant workers, office secretaries, or inmates of prisons and mental hospitals), and wherever they must confront themselves (whether in the rice-paddies of South-East Asia or on the picket line around the ammunitions plant), there is the anti-school. Wherever they are free to incorporate these and many similar experiences, either actual or vicarious ones, into their thoughts, emotions, and purposes without having to accept the structures and interpretations sanctioned by society or scholarship, there do they find their opportunities for an education that makes for personal autonomy. Is it too much to ask that the anti-school may be found even in the classrooms of some of our schools? Is it too preposterous to suggest that perhaps, in time, the rebels among students and teachers will move back into the schools because they may find there what they had been searching for outside?

The aim of the anti-school is the fullest understanding of man's experience of the world. It is because experience is so freely and easily available, so overwhelming, diverse, and compelling,

that the anti-school is not likely to suffer from lack of subjects. Students flock to it driven by a desperate need to master this experience, and mastery for them consists in ordering experience through structures and interpretations created by themselves. "Chaos is the law of nature, order is the dream of man," wrote Henry Adams, and in this sense, the students of the anti-school are dreamers. What they insist on is that they be allowed to dream their own dreams, not be forced to accept the dreams of their elders; to confront their own problems and order them in their own fashion, and not to be told to reshuffle the interpretations and structures of the past in the problem-solving exercises of so-called inductive teaching. The anti-school is not the swamp of anti-intellectualism as traditionalists and Brunerians try to make out. There are standards in the anti-school; standards that, it is true, are not upheld by the authority of the past, but by relevance to present and future needs, and, above all, by a concern for personal honesty, integrity, and consistency in the application of criteria for judgment. The anti-school teaches respect for subject, subject matter, and the man who beholds the subject and fashions the structure of the subject matter. It takes account of facts as they appear to the naked eye, as they are related by the probing intellect, and as they are then incorporated in a man's purposes and actions. The anti-school's contempt for purely academic knowledge of the world matches Jonathan Edwards' disdain of the merely notional knowledge of salvation, and the anti-school's insistence on personal commitment echoes Edwards' call for salvation's experimental and consenting knowledge. No one, as far as I know, has ever accused Edwards of anti-intellectualism. For the anti-school the fullest understanding of the world means objective, scientific knowledge of facts and relations, as well as personal, subjective commitment to these facts and relations. To know does not by itself mean either to accept or to reject. To know means to oblige the knower to do either. The anti-school, then, teaches its students to know the world as both observer and actor, both outsider and participant. It teaches that to live fully means to be both.

It is this quest for the fullest understanding of human experience, for the relevance of experience and knowledge to purposeful living that distinguishes the anti-school from the institutions we call schools today. We may decide, and I hope we will, that our schools might profit from the anti-schools, and we may feel that the anti-schools will provide the impetus for the revitalization of our schools. If so, we shall have to appreciate the lesson that real learning begins with the students' questions, rather than with the teacher's answers. We shall have to accept the idea that a teacher's answers are not for students to accept and memorize or even properly—i.e. with due respect for the niceties of parliamentary procedure or scientific logic—to debate, but to serve as examples not of what they assert, but of how assertions made, how they may be improved, how they may assume relevance and meaning. How many of our so academically trained teachers have yet to learn that answers to questions or statements made by teachers are not always to be taken as challenges to verbal duel, factual fault-finding, or logic-chopping, but as invitations or inspirations for the students to formulate their own answers and statements? I am afraid that the premium placed in our schools on the facility with which a student juggles the structures and interpretations of subject matter has contributed to the students' mistaking notional knowledge for the knowledge of the world, and has produced the subsequent inevitable disillusionment that has fed the anti-schools. Students, we should remember, do not want answers from their teachers, but examples of how one goes about answering, and of how one's answers are made part of one's life. They do not want indoctrination in either facts, theories, or modes of behavior, but models of reality, interpretations, and styles, in order that they may have the opportunity of choosing among them discriminately, and of creating for their own needs the reality, structures, and attitudes that will enable them to live fully. Today's students know the fraud and dishonesty of so-called authoritative answers. They know too, the brutality of honest questions, and they appreciate these questions, not because they are brutal, but because they are honest. Will we in our schools recognize the anguished cry for honesty, and will we be capable of responding to it?

I, for one, hope that the spirit of the anti-school might come alive in our classrooms to sweep out the vestiges of the progressives' other-directedness and the Brunerians' neo-traditionalism. I thus express my belief that, despite all I said, schools have a function and teachers a task. I believe that this function and task is to provide the conditions under which personal autonomy may emerge and be sustained, protected, and nurtured. I am convinced, however, that our schools today do not perform this function, and far too many teachers do not recognize their task, let alone carry it out. This is why so many of our youths search for themselves and their autonomy in the jungles of Vietnam and New York, drop out of suburbia and join up in Alabama, Nigeria, or Columbia. The schools have failed our youths, but they are thereby not doomed to persist in their failure. In this world of ever-increasing social pressures on children and adolescents, schools can be asylums for youths to grow into autonomous adults. As we have learned to protect our youngsters from economic exploitation in sweatshops and coal mines, we now must learn to protect them from the insidious pressures that demand grades, club memberships, and athletic records. In our schools we should have the golden opportunity of fostering the spirit of the anti-school in an environment that eliminates the intolerably high and cruel risks that are so much a part of the actual anti-school. It is a perverse sort of romanticism that argues that only the threat of bombs and bullets, and the kick of drugs and drink will teach autonomy. Once we allow the spirit of the anti-school to enter our classrooms, once we become aware of the ritualistic nature of the claims of past scholarship and the equally ritualistic pressure of present-day social conventions, we may be in a position, as John Holt puts it, "to clear a space for honesty and openness and self-awareness in the lives of growing children." That, I should think, is a beginning if we are to restore our schools to meaning and relevance.

The dedication of our schools to their task of fostering and nurturing the growth of autonomous individuals depends for its success on the kind of teachers we shall find in them. This revitalization of which I have spoken is not a matter of administrative reform, but of pedagogical conviction on the part of the teacher. Administrators cannot order it, although they can stimulate and encourage it. What counts are the attitudes and the disposition of the

teacher. Teachers must practice what they preach. If teachers want their students to bring their questions into the classroom, and if they urge their students to question and requestion the answers they receive, then the teachers themselves must be the first to insist on further questions, and to refuse to accept or to propose answers in such a manner as forecloses further questioning. If teachers want students to rely on the evidence of their own experience, then they must do so themselves. Teachers must not allow theories of education, of human nature, and of subject matter to stand between them and what they see. They must have the courage to trust their own eyes and ears, rely on their own thinking, and follow their own insights to their results, instead of citing the authorities of, say, Karl Marx, Sigmund Freud, or John Dewey. They must take theories for what they are: Aids to our understanding, not substitutes for it, designed to simplify reality and to present it to our view one-dimensionally, as a map represents a landscape. Let not teachers mistake the map for the landscape, and their students' ability to read a map for their skill in finding their way. Let them be autonomous themselves to be able to distinguish that which is real from that which is its copy or representation. If we want autonomous students, we must first have autonomous teachers.

This brings me back to my initial concern with a teacher's attitudes and disposition. A teacher teaches as he is, that is to say, he teaches by his personal example. It should give us pause to note how dullness breeds dullness, and enthusiasm inspires the love of learning. Think of the second-grade teacher whom John Holt quotes as saying: "But my children *like* to have questions for which there is only one answer." "They did," adds Holt, "and by a mysterious coincidence, so did she." Teachers must live their teaching in order that their attitudes and disposition do the teaching that needs to be done. If creativity is the constructive response to situations, and this response be creative rather than imitative, then it is not to models, theories, and structures that we must look, but to the energies, styles, and orientations that produced these models, theories and structures in the first place. We do not need schools today to teach people how to perform jobs. We need schools to enable people to create jobs, and to endow their existence with meaning.

For teachers all of this insists on one commandment: Be honest, genuine, and real; speak for yourself. Once your students perceive that you practice the autonomy you preach, that you refuse to be society's or scholarship's mouthpiece, they will let you teach them. Affirm and protect your autonomy and know that once you have lost it, you have lost your ability to teach, whatever your certificate, your title, or your reputation. Remember, too, that autonomy does not mean the principled rejection of authority, but rather the ability to accept or reject in the light of your own consistent standards. Once your students know your commitment to autonomy, they will accept your teaching of the authorities of society, scholarship, and science, because they will know by your example that honest men can be committed to traditional and shared values critically and sincerely. They will have learned that the flaming No of adolescent rebellion is not the same as the committed No of principled autonomy. And, judging by so many of our adolescent escapists from both suburbia and slum, this may be a lesson well worth learning or, in your case, teaching.

Let me close, then, by emphasizing the real as opposed to the academic character of meaningful education. If we have in the past largely seen schooling as preparation, and children as miniature adults; as, with the progressives, we have forced them into the accepted modes of adult behavior; and as, with the Brunerians, we regard them all as future scientists and intellectuals, we deny them the reality of their actual existence. It has taken open rebellion and violent protest to open our eyes to facts which should have been obvious; namely, that teenagers, whether black or white, in city slums or country homes will not eagerly and positively respond to an education that is designed to prepare them for a life they will never lead. They know it, their teachers know it; yet their teachers keep on teaching "by the book." That kind of book-education, let me assure you, is absurd. What's worse, the absurdity transfers itself onto both students and teachers. The students, to their credit, rebel and quit; the teachers complain and carry on—a difference that does not speak well for the teaching profession. But there you are again. When will teachers trust their own eyes and sense? When will they take a theory or a textbook for what it is, namely an aid that disqualifies itself the very minute it no longer aids? When will they speak for themselves? When will they quite transmitting a culture they cannot live with, quit accepting an authority they cannot but question, and when will they begin consciously and willingly to participate in the creation of a culture that all of us can live in?

29.

Teaching is Like Selling

JOHN DEWEY

Professor of Philosophy, Columbia
University.

Teaching may be compared to selling commodities. No one can sell unless someone buys. We should ridicule a merchant who said that he had sold a great many goods although no one had bought any. But perhaps there are teachers who think that they have done a good day's teaching irrespective of what pupils have learned. There is the same exact equation between teaching and learning that there is between selling and buying. The only way to increase the learning of pupils is to augment the quantity and quality of real teaching. Since learning is some-

From How We Think *by John Dewey. Copyright © 1933 by John Dewey. Published by D. C. Heath and Co., Boston, Mass. Reprinted by permission of the publisher. The selection here is from pp. 35–36.*

thing that the pupil has to do himself and for himself, the initiative lies with the learner. The teacher is a guide and director; he steers the boat, but the energy that propels it must come from those who are learning. The more a teacher is aware of the past experiences of students of their hopes, desires, chief interests, the better will he understand the forces at work that need to be directed and utilized for the formation of reflective habits. The number and quality of these factors vary from person to person. They cannot therefore be categorically enumerated in a book. But there are some tendencies and forces that operate in every normal individual, forces that must be appealed to and utilized if the best methods for the development of good habits of thought are to be employed.

30

A Study of Teacher Effectiveness[1]

NORMAN A. SPRINTHALL/JOHN M. WHITELEY/RALPH L. MOSHER

N. A. Sprinthall and J. M. Mosher are Associate Professors of Education, Harvard Graduate School of Education, Harvard University. R. L. Whiteley is Assistant Vice Chancellor for Student Personnel Service and Chairman, Program in Counseling at Washington University, St. Louis.

INTRODUCTION

The field of education has proved remarkably resistant both to the application of scientific knowledge and to the development of truly professional personnel (12). Nowhere is this more in evidence than in the general area of research in teaching, and more specifically, in teacher effectiveness. Existing research has a long but disappointing history. The literature on teacher effectiveness is extensive, indeed almost unmanageably so (5, 17). There is little conclusive research, however, as to the conceptual issue of what (effective) teaching is and the empirical problems of how effective teaching can be reliably predicted or measured. With few exceptions, research attempts to correlate measures of teacher attitudes or values, adjustment, needs, personality factors, intelligence, etc., with ratings of teaching effectiveness have not produced significant results (10). The same is true for correlations of the teacher's cultural background, socioeconomic status, sex, marital status, etc., with ratings of effectiveness (7). In short, "we do not know how to define, prepare for, or measure teacher competence" (2; p. 3).

Instead of proliferating research based on the above procedures, the present investigation has been designed to change the focus of research from attempts to relate static personality or social status variables to an outcome

"A Study of Teacher Effectiveness" by Norman A. Sprinthall, John M. Whiteley, and Ralph L. Mosher is reprinted with permission from the Journal of Teacher Education, 17: 93–106, Spring, 1966.

[1] The research reported in this paper was supported by the Cooperative Research Program of the Office of Education, U. S. Department of Health, Education, and Welfare. Cooperative Research Project No. S-143.

measure such as pupil gain.[2] We have selected a more proximate criterion than pupil learning and a more dynamic set of variables than personality traits or social status indicators. Our approach has been to specify a proximate criterion, teacher competence/effectiveness, in terms of a set of behaviors in the classroom as an important dependent variable.

Concurrently we have attempted to derive from and relate these behaviors to a set of concepts which appear specifically pertinent to effective/ineffective teaching, namely, cognitive flexibility-rigidity. By this is meant, very simply, the teacher's ability to think on his feet, to adapt teaching objectives, content and method in process (i.e., response to the reaction, learning difficulties, and needs of the pupils). More broadly, cognitive flexibility refers to dimensions of openmindedness, adaptability, a resistance to premature perceptual closure.

It is recognized that at present there is no evidence that "cognitively flexible" teaching is more effective in producing pupil learning. Among teacher educators, however, there is support for the general notion that flexibility or conceptual openness is both a desirable and differentiating quality in teaching. For example, Goodlad has suggested that flexible teacher behavior is most relevant to effective classroom performance. "The right decision at the right moments is the essence of good teaching. . . . [The

teacher] must decide when to begin an activity and when to bring it to a close; when to use a student interest and when to pass it by; when to insist on exactness and when to sacrifice exactness to feeling. All these things and more the teacher must take into account in timing and pacing students' learning" (11: p. 39).

Yet this definition leaves flexible teaching entirely at the operational level without relation to concepts or theories which may help explain and predict an admittedly complex phenomenon. The present study, then, attempts to (1) develop a set of concepts denoted as cognitive flexibility/rigidity, (2) relate these concepts to a proximate criterion of teacher effectiveness—teacher performance in the classroom, (3) devise a method for the assessment of flexibility/rigidity prior to teaching experience, and (4) predict and test out the predictions to actual classroom behavior by teachers in training.

This research is oriented toward providing a viable conceptual framework for prediction and evaluation of secondary school teaching, based on teacher behavior which is observable in the classroom and not dependent on static personal traits which cannot be made operational.

Although the research is centered on one variable, we do not imply that cognitive flexibility/rigidity is "the single mediating process," the unitary mechanism, or the only relevant variable for effective teaching. In fact, there are most certainly other important dimensions and significant relationships in such a complex set of interactions as occur in the teaching-learning process. As an initial step toward increasing our understanding of effective teaching, however, we have selected this one variable

---

[2] As surprising as it may be, research has yet to establish that teachers do significantly influence student learning. Research in such a complex area is easily confounded. Thus Howsam suggests: "Since it is not presently feasible to rely on the ultimate criterion of teacher effectiveness, it becomes necessary to attempt to develop intermediate or proximate criteria." (12; p. 15)

because of its logical relationship both in construct and operation to teacher behavior.

COGNITIVE FLEXIBILITY- RIGIDITY IN TEACHING

In a general sense, cognitive flexibility implies an ability or capacity to think and act simultaneously and appropriately in a given situation. Rigidity assumes the opposite, an intolerance of ambiguity or excessive need for structure, a difficulty in adaptation. In our view, classroom teaching specifically requires an efficient cog-wheeling of thinking and acting while in the situation. It is postulated in the research that apprentice teachers with open, flexible cognitive systems will perceive, think, and act effectively in the classroom. We would predict the opposite for teachers identified as cognitively rigid. Cognitive, in this sense, is admittedly quite broad; more inclusive, for example, than either intellectual capacities or a trait such as creativity. The former imples sets of factors which add up to "brightness"; creativity, or divergent thinking, implies atypical problem solving. Neither specifically includes nor predicts a person's action in a real situation, e.g., as a classroom teacher.

In terms of actual teaching behavior, cognitive flexibility-rigidity necessarily would be inferred largely from the teacher's verbal behavior in interaction with the pupil(s). Nonverbal aspects of this interaction—subtle affective cues such as voice tone, frowing, etc., would be excluded as much as possible since the relation of cognitive flexibility to such clearly noncognitive variables would be tenuous at best. In this way, limits were

placed on the focus for the concept, at least at the operational level.[3]

The major formulations for the general construct were derived from studies of political and religious beliefs, prejudices, and authoritarianism. The particular contributions of Rokeach (18, 19) have provided an important step toward conceptual clarity. Rokeach focuses on the "openness" or "closedness" of belief systems. Our interest, for research in teaching, is parallel to the extent that it is openness and closedness in terms of relating to one's world that seems critical. It is the open, flexible teacher who is aware of the subtleties and nuances of changing circumstaance in the classroom; it is the flexible teacher who uses a variety of methods in implementing plans instead of one or two formats used in all situations regardless of circumstance.

From the studies of the authoritarian personality, Adorno and others note the relevance of a person's method of cognitively structuring his world in terms of his own frame of reference instead of integrating the varied aspects of the objective situation. Dogmatism, as Rokeach (19) develops the concept, is relevant for the same reason as an example of cognitive rigidity.

For the purposes of this research, teaching in an operational sense is approached from three perspectives: the

[3] There is some research support for the study of cognitive variables in teaching. Ryans (20) suggests that certain patterns of effective teaching are significantly weighted by rather general cognitive abilities and attitudinal correlates. Also, Knoell (15) found that educational fluency—"the ability to call up many ideas"—bore a significant relation to ratings of teacher effectiveness. Even though these relationships were by no means conclusive, the results do indicate that this research focus holds some promise.

teacher's personal cognitive characteristics (planning), the teacher's cognitive attitude toward the pupil, and the teacher's cognitive attitude toward the communication of subject matter. The three dimensions were created somewhat arbitrarily as a means of classifying aspects of flexibility and rigidity which seem logically related. There are the cognitive style when planning, the approach to the pupils, and the method of conveying subject content.

PERSONAL COGNITIVE CHARACTERISTICS
(*Planning Behavior Under Stress*)

Planning, especially under stress, represents an important aspect of the first dimension. The flexible-rigid descriptions are as follows:

Flexible	*Rigid*
Intern shows open-ended lesson planning. Considers alternate ways to communicate content and/ or relate to pupils. Can plan for unexpected under stress. Cognitive process appears fluid and unconstrained.	Intern appears dominated by lesson plan, poor plan and use of time, gets trapped in digressions. Cannot handle the unexpected, especially under stress. Cognitive process appears constrained and inhibited.

The intern's ability to plan and modify the plan while teaching was, of course, crucial. At the same time it is necessary to underscore the stressful nature of the classroom situation. The interns found themselves, especially at the outset, unfamiliar with teaching skills, with age and ability differences of secondary school pupils, and with translating their college major subject in ways understandable to, for example,

twelve-to-fourteen-year-olds.   Another aspect of the stress was the model of emulation represented by the master teacher responsible for a rigorous analysis and continuing evaluation of the intern's performance. Stress also derives from an emphasis on self- and peer evaluation by interns. In such a circumstance, the relation between planning and cognitive flexibility-rigidity should be most apparent. Under stress, the tendencies toward one or the other extreme should be magnified.

Rokeach (19) is helpful in understanding the relationship between such stress or anxiety and the operational concepts of flexibility and rigidity.

> If a person feels strongly threatened or anxious in a given situation, he should above all be motivated to act so that the threat is reduced and the anxiety allayed. It is precisely because he is so motivated that the relatively closed person becomes highly attuned to irrelevant internal and external pressures and, accordingly, unable to evaluate information independent of source. (p. 62)

Stress produces, for the person with a closed system, a reliance on irrelevant factors in determining what course of action is to be taken.

Thus, the cognitively rigid person is very likely to act maladaptively. Rokeach (19) is again helpful in understanding how this stress-anxiety-rigidity system operates. He assumes that there are certain characteristics of a given situation that point to acting appropriately in it. By responding to relevant characteristics, the person's response should be appropriate. Any situation, however, will contain irrelevant factors which, if they determined a person's response, would lead to inappropriate action.

Every person, then, must be able to evaluate adequately both the relevant and irrelevant information he receives from every situation. This leads us to suggest a basic characteristic that defines the extent to which a person's system is open or closed; namely, the extent to which the person can receive, evaluate, and act on relevant information received from the outside on its own intrinsic merits, unencumbered by irrelevant factors in the situation arising from within the person or from the outside. (p. 57)

In the classroom, the competing stimuli are numerous. The choice of appropriate teaching content and method (planning) depends on careful assessment of these stimuli. In our view, it is the cognitively flexible teacher who can do this with accuracy, especially when under the stress of classroom teaching.

Cognitive Attitude to the Pupil (Responsiveness to the Class). The amount level of responsiveness to the class is an important factor in assessing the teacher's cognitive attitude toward the pupil. The flexible-rigid dimension was conceptualized as follows:

Flexible	*Rigid*
Intern is responsive to the class; sees, listens, and responds to discipline problems, inattention, learning difficulties, students' need for new knowledge, and creativity.	Intern doesn't register "cues"; children's problems are turned out. Calls on bright students too often and doesn't recognize when to call on the slow child.

Previous research seems to indicate that the flexible-rigid dimension is highly relevant to assessing responsiveness to individual differences. Bieri (3) and Kelly (14) have found, for example, that people with a more flexible structure as opposed to those with a more rigid structure of constructs are able to differentiate better among objects or situations. Jones (13) and Scodel and Mussen (21) both found that authoritarians are more insensitive than nonauthoritarians to the personality characteristics of others and more insensitive to individual differences. These joint findings emphasize the disadvantage at which a cognitively rigid person is placed in attempting to be responsive to individual differences, especially in a class; the obverse is implied for the flexible teacher.

Cognitive Attitude Toward Subject Matter and Teaching Method (Communication). The use of teaching methods was a central dimension in the assessment of a teacher's cognitive attitude toward the communication of subject matter. The flexible-rigid dimension was conceptualized in the following manner:

Flexible	*Rigid*
Intern uses a variety of methods, shows flexibility in implementation of plans, and employs inquiry for effective teaching.	Uses few teaching methods, adheres to one or two formats in planning lessons, and employs a prescriptive rather than problematic teaching approach.

Gardner and others (9) have found that subjects classified as constricted/rigid seem particularly resistive to change, "preferring to maintain sets long after they were appropriate, another indication that they could not take advantage of available cues" (p. 53). Translated to the classroom, this would result in the employment of one teaching method until well after its particular contribution has been utilized effectively. The cognitively rigid teacher would miss the cues that another approach was indicated. A constricted perceptual set followed by action in accord with those filtered perceptions would also tend to promote a mechanical presentation of subject matter or a rather prescriptive lecture *at* pupils long after attention and participation by the pupils had waned.

With the above considerations, then, as determinants, a teacher-rating scale was developed which linked operational examples to the concepts of flexibility and rigidity. Cognitive rigidity was conceptualized as an inappropriate response keyed to an excessive need for closure, structure, and an intolerance of ambiguity. This would tend to promote a prescriptive rather than problematic style in class, identifiable by the limited range of behaviors available to the teacher. At the other end of the hypothetical continuum, cognitive flexibility was viewed as promoting open evaluation and exploration, the disposition to think on one's feet and to consider the value of competing alternative teaching methods rather than accepting a single approach by default.[4]

RESEARCH OBJECTIVES AND PROCEDURES

The objective of the research were: (1) to derive from the concept of cognitive flexibility operational translations

[4] It is an open question whether cognitive flexibility can be acquired. The weight of theoretical evidence tends to indicate that a disposition to the flexibility/rigidity is rooted rather early in the personality. Researchers have found consistent clusters over time associated with flexible or rigid thinkers and relationships to child-rearing methods (22, 8). Other theorists (26, 1) have summarized descriptions of flexible and rigid personalities which indicate both stability over time and relative permanency as a life "style."

of specific teacher behavior which may serve as a criterion measure and (2) within this framework, to investigate the utility of projective instruments as a means of predicting teacher performance. The basic assumption was that certain indicators of cognitive flexibility-rigidity derived from the psychological tests would relate consistently to the observed teacher behavior in the classroom.

The sample of 28 subjects (15 male and 13 female) was randomly selected from the population of intern teachers in the Harvard-Newton summer program 1964. The subject areas represented were English, social studies, mathematics, and science.

The program from which our sample was drawn involves one full year of study. The summer segment of the program provides intensive supervised practice teaching for seven weeks. At the end of the summer program, the intern teachers spend half the following academic year as full-time graduate students in residence, and the other half as paid intern teachers, under supervision, in local school systems.

The admission standards to the program are rigorous. The average Graduate Record Examination score for admitted candidates in 1964 was 660 verbal (94 percent) and 590 math (82 percent). Over half of the accepted applicants in the master of arts in teaching program in 1962 were honor graduates in their major field of study (23).

The psychological tests used as predictors were the Rorschach and the Visual Impression Test (V.I.T.), administered before the intern teachers began practice teaching.[5] These tests provided the data for predictions on

[5] The V.I.T. is a written form of the Thematic Apperception Test.

each dimesion of the Teacher Rating Scale.

The procedures followed in scoring the Rorschach and the V.I.T. were developed for a prior study of elementary school interns (6).

In this study, the Rorschach was used in such a manner as to develop a construct of the subject in the form, "He seems like the sort of person who——." This method is based on McArthur's (16) description of the approach of clinicians who were able to make the best predictions about an individual's behavior. Translated to predicting how an individual would teach, the construct would take the form, "He seems like the sort of person who would teach——." This approach, using the Rorschach data, was applied to each flexible-rigid dimension in the rating scale. A similar approach was employed in analyzing the V.I.T. stories.

Quite obviously, certain aspects of the Rorschach and V.I.T. protocols were of more relevance in considering predictions on specific scales. The weight of each element was determined, however, by its relation to the total test protocols.

To illustrate scoring for personal cognitive characteristics, two examples are offered as illustration. The following was considered a flexible response:

Performance Proper	*Inquiry*
It is two natives beating on a drum, with monkeys and a butterfly in the background.	Those things at the top are monkeys hanging from trees and that is a butterfly in the middle, a red butterfly. It must be a jungle scene.
W + M, FC, FM H, A, Obj. P	

The subject was able to integrate the disparate parts of the blot into an integral whole response, as well as to utilize a variety of determinants content. Compare a mediocre response such as:

Performance Proper	*Inquiry*
Two men with something there in the center.	It looks like a table or something, with the men on both sides.
W F+ H, Obj. P	

Although this subject was able to see the popular figures, he was unable to breathe any life into his perception or to utilize the other aspects of the blot. The illustrative nature of these examples must be underscored. No single Rorschach response was a major determinant by itself.[6]

The second section in the rating scale concerns the teacher's cognitive attitude toward the pupil. This was assessed from the interaction of the characters in the Rorschach human movement responses and from the interaction of the heroes in the V.I.T. stories. The following V.I.T. story was judged rigid.

Here we have one of those very rare representations of the young Beethoven. The picture is entitled "Young Beethoven Contemplating the Violin of Igor." In case the reader is not familiar with the story, I shall give a brief sketch to outline the legend that accompanies the picture.

Igor, as you may or may not know, was

[6] The major elements of the Rorschach test used in the predictions of personal cognitive characteristics were as follows: Flexible indicators—Response total greater than 25, F percent less than 50, F+ percent between 70 and 90, "Whole" percepts as W+ or W++, Vista, varied content, m less than 3, shading present as F(Ch), and determinants including FC, CF, M, and FM. Rigid indicators generally were the obverse, that is, response total less than 25, F percent greater than 50, etc.

the twelve-year-old friend of Ludwig who lived next door to the composer in Vienna. At the time, Beethoven was several years younger than Igor and had no knowledge of the power of music. Igor, however, had been taking music lessons for several years and had attained no little proficiency at the violin. Unfortunately, the young virtuoso was an insufferable person and a pompous braggart who took every opportunity that presented itself to lord it over Ludwig, ignorant as he was at the time. The latter, however, was no slouch so to speak, and after listening to the fulminations of Igor for a sufficient amount of time, he decided to compose a violin concerto himself to spite his snooty friend.

This picture then shows the boy Beethoven contemplating what has come to be known as the First Violin Concerto in D. It is most likely scholars are not in total agreement that the boy is probably thinking something like this: "That Igor is nothing short of an absolute boor. Purely for the sake of grinning down my short-sleeved shirt at him, I shall compose a concerto on his very own violin. Maybe then all the other *kinder* on the *strasse* will believe me when I tell them what a show-off Igor really is."

TABLE 1

Rorschach and VIT Elements Associated with the Flexible-Rigid Dimension for Cognitive Attitude Toward the Pupil

Flexible	Rigid
M interactions are on an equal basis	M interactions condescending
VIT heroes responsive to others	VIT hero "cues" others out
VIT hero sees others as equal human beings	VIT heroes look down on others

The story itself was rendered in a condescending manner, as is evident from the remarks "in case the reader is not familiar" and "as you may not know." The relationship between Igor and Beethoven was used as a major basis for the rigid rating: there was little responsiveness to the other's feelings in the story, e.g., the young virtuoso "took every opportunity that presented itself to lord it over Ludwig, ignorant as he was at the time."

The following story was told by an intern teacher rated as having a very flexible cognitive attitude toward the student.

The son has come to tell his mother that he is engaged to marry a girl he loves very much but who is of another religion. He is troubled because he knows that this will hurt his mother, but he has resolved to marry the girl and he tells his mother this. She is not completely surprised, for she has met the girl and has expected such an announcement, but she is still taken aback. She wants to fight this prejudice within her but cannot free herself of it completely. She does like the girl and thinks her a fine girl for her son— and yet...

Mother understands son's feelings and gives her "approval."

This story is remarkable for its sensitivity to the feelings of another person: it was this characteristic that in major part determined the flexible rating. The hero in the story was able to respond to a variety of feelings, to anticipate those of the mother and to assess his own introspectively. It was felt that someone with this capacity for sensitivity, as inferred from the V.I.T., would be very responsive to students in the classroom.

Table 1 summarizes the Rorschach and V.I.T. elements associated with cognitive attitude toward the pupil.

The final variable assessed by the rating scale involves the cognitive attitude toward the communication of subject matter. Emphasis was placed on the manner in which the responses were communicated to the examiner and on how the subject viewed the open-ended Rorschach as a behavioral task. The following Rorschach response and inquiry are cited as an example of a rigid cognitive attitude:

Performance Proper	Inquiry
S. The thing in the middle is a slimy worm.	E. What about the blot made it seem like a slimy worm?
D F+ A	S. It looks like it.
	E. Why slimy?
	S. It is a slimy worm, and slimy worms are slimy.

TABLE 2

Rorschach and VIT Elements Associated with the Flexible-Rigid Dimension for Cognitive Attitude Toward the communication of Subject Matter

Flexible	Rigid
Rorschach is seen as an open-ended task	Rorschach is a given, cut and dried
Capacity for fantasy	No or little fantasy
Will "take a chance" in responding	Reports only the "facts"
Creative use of the blot	Stereotyped reasoning
Flexible sequence	Stereotyped sequence
P present but balance by O and varied concepts	P overdeveloped with banal content

The subject could not dissociate himself sufficiently from the concreteness of his perception to analyze what it was about the inkblot that made him respond as he did. The Rorschach was seen as a "given," with what he saw as a response

being so cut and dried as to be too obvious to require analysis.

The following response to the Rorschach was thought to be indicative of a flexible approach:

Performance Proper	Inquiry
It is springtime in Paris, with all the colors.	Of course you have to stretch your imagination a bit, but the Eiffel Tower is at the top, and in the center is a pool leading up to the tower. There are flower beds on the side with bright-colored flowers.
W+ CF Bot, ld, arch	

In this response, the subject was able to respond with a variety of contents logically elaborated into a meaningful whole response. In addition, the subject was able to "take a chance," to go beyond the obvious characteristics of the situation.

TABLE 3

Rank Order Correlations (Three Sub-Scales of Cognitive Flexibility-Rigidity) (Predicted and Observed Ratings N = 28)

Sub-scale Dimension	Rank Order r	
Personal Cognitive Characteristics	+ .54	(p < .01)
Cognitive Attitude Toward the Pupil	+ .49	(p < .01)
Cognitive Attitude Toward Subject Matter	+ .39	(p < .05)

Table 2 presents the Rorschach and V.I.T. elements associated with the flexible-rigid dimension for the variable of cognitive attitude toward the communication of subject matter.

The scoring system outlined above is an attempt to use the Rorschach and TAT in a manner to avoid the pitfalls of a completely objective sign approach (for a comprehensive attempt to use the Rorschach in this way see Cooley (4)). At the same time we have attempted to specify the particular elements of the protocols which we did use in deriving our predictions to avoid a completely intuitive and subjective method. Super and Crites (24) note that the Rorschach does have wide appeal as a research instrument but..."at the same time, the enthusiasm of its proponents and the extent to which it has been based on clinical intuition and subjectively rather than quantitatively analyzed experience have antagonized many more scientifically minded psychologists" (pp. 560-61).

The teacher rating scale was designed to categorize and rate certain cognitive behaviors characteristic of teaching. The categories are broad: (1) the way in which intellectual process is applied in the teaching (i.e., the cognitive "style" of the teacher); (2) the cognitive attitude adopted toward the pupil; (3) the cognitive attitude characterizing the definition of the teaching objectives, the planning of content, and the teaching method selected. Subscales are included under each category. Each subscale and the category overall are rated on a 5-point cognitive flexibility scale. Thus a score of 1 on any scale would indicate a high adjudged order of cognitive flexibility in teaching; a score of 5, a high adjudged order of cognitive rigidity. Descriptions of both flexible and rigid teaching behavior are provided for each of the subscales.

Two steps were entailed in rating: (1) the selection and specification of several categories of teaching behavior which appeared primarily cognitive in character, and (2) brief descriptions for each subscale of (cognitive) teaching behavior that could be regarded as relatively flexible and as relatively rigid. The examples of cognitively flexible and rigid teaching behaviors provided for the guidance of the rater were both modified and amplified as a result.[7]

The ratings were based on a complete period (i.e., a 50-60-minute sample) of the intern's teaching. The rater also observed the subject during the supervisory-planning conference which followed the teaching. Neither the subjects nor the supervisory personnel were informed as to the rater's purpose.

Ratings of teaching behavior obviously involve an inferential and evaluative process on the part of the rater. In the instrument employed in this study, examples of specific flexible and rigid teaching behaviors are provided for each subscale. The purpose was to focus the process of inference and evaluation on certain aspects of teaching behavior hypothesized as indices of the organizing construct. Hopefully, this would serve, too, to reduce intuitive ratings and increase the possibility of replication.[8]

---

[7] The complete teacher rating scale can be found in the full Office of Education report. Any formal control for interjudge reliability in the use of the instrument was thought to be premature at this stage of the research.

[8] The inclusion of critical incidents or excerpts of teacher-pupil verbal behavior illustrative of cognitive flexibility-rigidity is beyond the scope of the study. Such a scoring guide for raters, however, will be developed in manual form. Attempts to apply the rating scale to typescripts of teacher-pupil dialogue is another potentially useful dimension to be examined. Research along these lines would be a starting point to answer the rater reliability questions.

ANALYSIS OF DATA AND FINDINGS

To test the relationship between predicted and observed flexibility-rigidity, three analyses were made: (1) an overall rank order correlation for all intern teachers; (2) a rank order correlation for each of the cognitive subscales: (a) personal characteristic, (b) attitude toward the pupil, and (c) attitude toward subject matter; (3) a chi-square test to examine in particular the efficiency of prediction for the extreme ratings (the top and bottom 25 percent of the sample).

Overall Rank Order Correlations. The psychological tests provided the basis for the predicted ratings along each dimension of the teacher rating scale. The observed ratings of teacher behavior were made during the summer training program. The scores for the subscales were totaled for each intern teacher to derive a summary predicted and observed score on the flexibility-rigidity continuum. A rank order was derived on the basis of the predicted and observed scores for each intern. From this a Spearman Rank Correlation Coefficient was computed. The result was an $r = +.53$ between the predicted and observed ranks (sig$<.01$). This indicates a substantial and significant relationship between the predicted and observed scores.

Rank Order Correlations for Each Subscale. The next step was to test the relationship of the observed and predicted scores for each of the three scales. By taking each scale separately, a rank order correlation was computed for the three demensions. The results are presented in Table 3.

Table 3 indicates that the correlations of the first two subscales, personal cognitive characteristics and cognitive attitude toward the pupil, represent the major areas of agreement between the observed and predicted ratings. Our method for rating cognitive attitude toward subject matter was the least indicative of agreement. Although the overall findings and the relationship of actual and predicted position of the first two subscales are satisfactory, a revision of method is needed before the third subscale system can be considered adequate. The particular aspects of the Rorschach and Visual Impression Test which we hypothesized as relating to cognitive attitude toward subject matter are apparently not sufficiently differentiating without further refinement.

TABLE 4

Chi-Square Test

Predicted Performance	Observed Performance			
	Flexible	Moderate	Rigid	
Rigid	0	1	6	7
Moderate	2	11	1	14
Flexible	5	2	0	7
N	7	14	7	
				N = 28

($x^2 = 25.99$, Ndf = 4, sig $< .001$)

The Chi-Square Test. To examine the efficiency of prediction for each intern, particularly at the extremes of the flexibility-rigidity continuum, we divided the sample into three groups: (1) the seven most flexible (the top quartile, N = 7); (2) the middle group (N = 14); and (3) the seven least flexible (the bottom quartile, N = 7). We compared the predicted and observed rating through a chi-square test. The results are presented in Table 4.

From reading along the diagonal, it can be seen that accurate predictions were made for five or seven apprentices rated most flexible. At the other extreme, accurate predictions were achieved for six or seven rated most rigid. In no instance was a false positive recorded, i.e., a "most flexible" predicted as "most rigid," or vice versa.

These results are encouraging and indicate that the systems for prediction may have relevance to effective and ineffective teaching. The overall correlation was subtsantial, especially when compared with the results of previous research. Similarly the classification of teachers into extremes of flexibility and rigidity within the sample provides important information for the accuracy of individual predictions.[9]

CONCLUSION

The research findings indicate support for the basic hypothesis that effective teaching and cognitive flexibility are related. The overall findings were: (1) The dimension of cognitive flexibility-rigidity may represent a critical and differentiating factor in teaching. (2) The research method for prediction along this dimension was found accurate, using particular aspects of the Rorschach and TAT administered prior

[9] Complete follow-up information was not available to cross-validate the criterion measure of effective/ineffective teaching, i.e., how all the intern teachers performed subsequent to the completion of the summer program. Partial information did indicate, however, that the criterion may have validity. Three of the 28 interns were dropped from the program because of ineffective performance, a judgment rendered independent of the research. All three had been rated and predicted most rigid. Also reports from school supervisors, again an independent judgment, indicate consistent agreement with both our predictions and ratings. A complete follow-up is, of course, essential.

to entry into the teacher-training program. (3) The method for prediction of teacher behavior for the first two subscales of cognitive flexibility-rigidity (personal cognitive characteristics, or cognitive "style," and cognitive attitude toward the pupils) was most significantly related to observed performance. (4) Partial follow-up data indicate some cross-validation for the predictions of effective and ineffective teacher behavior, particularly for the group predicted as most rigid. (5) Finally the results from the present study are highly congruent with those from an earlier study using elementary school intern teachers.

Perhaps the most serious implication from this study was the lack of behavior change within the group of apprentice teachers identified as most rigid and hence predicted to be most ineffective in the classroom. All of these students received intensive supervision by highly skilled master teachers during the summer program, yet showed little capacity to upset our predictions. Three of the seven predicted as most rigid were dropped from the program at the end of the summer. Two who continued as intern teachers during the full semester received pessimistic evaluations; again, in spite of further efforts under supervision to promote more effective performance.

Before any firm conclusions can be drawn, there may be a need to develop special supervision and training techniques which go beyond the usual procedures presently available. It may be crucial to examine under what circumstances a change is possible or when alternative careers to teaching should be considered. It is apparent that under the present system for training and supervision the cognitively rigid student teacher is unable significantly to modify his behavior.

Because of the relatively small sample size and the pilot nature of this project, additional research is necessary. Refinements are needed for the prediction methods. It may be possible to develop less cumbersome and time-consuming assessment procedures which may be effective indicators of flexible-rigid performance; also, research is necessary for further development of the Teacher Behavior Rating Scale. Then it would be possible to draw up a training manual as a guide for use by teacher-supervisors. In this way, the problem of evaluation and reliability could be directly studied. Finally, further evidence is definitely needed to establish the degree to which a cognitively rigid apprentice teacher can change from ineffective to effective behavior in the classroom. At a time when selective admission procedures are becoming possible in teacher training, this has practical implications. Even more important, however, may be the conceptual implication of the stability of cognitive rigidity and flexibility as personality parameters.

Although the above limitations are explicit, the research investigation does suggest that the organizing construct, the predictive system, and the rating procedure are consistent and linked to a generic and recognizable conception of teaching.

BIBLIOGRAPHY

1. Allport, G. *Pattern and Growth in Personality.* New York: Holt, Rinehart and Winston, 1961.

2. Biddle, Bruce J. "The Integration of Teacher Effectiveness Research." *Contemporary Research on Teacher Effectiveness.* (Edited by Bruce J. Biddle and William J. Ellena.) New York: Holt,

Rinehart and Winston, 1964. pp. 1–40.

3. Bieri, J. "Cognitive Complexity-Simplicity and Predictive Behavior." *Journal of Abnormal and Social Psychology* 51: 263–68; 1955.

4. Cooley, William W. *Career Development of Scientists: An Overlapping Longitudinal Study.* U.S. Department of Health, Education, and Welfare, Cooperative Research Project No. 436. Harvard, Mass.: Graduate School of Education, Harvard University, 1963.

5. Domas, S. J., and Tiedeman, D. V., compilers. "Teacher Competence: An Annotated Bibliography." *Journal of Experimental Education* 19:101–218; December 1950.

6. Emlaw, R., and others. "Teacher Effectiveness: A Method for Prediction and Evaluation." *National Elementary Principal* 43: 38–49; November 1963.

7. Fattu, Nicholas A. "Research on Teacher Evaluation." *National Elementary Principal* 43: 19–27; November 1963.

8. Frenkel-Brunswik, Else. "Patterns of Social and Cognitive Outlook in Children and Parents." *American Journal of Orthopsychiatry* 21: 543–58; 1951.

9. Gardner, R., and others. "Cognitive Control: A Study of Individual Consistencies in Cognitive Behavior." *Psychological Issues* I, No. 4. New York: International Universities Press, 1959.

10. Getzels, J. W., and Jackson, P. W. "The Teacher's Personality and Characteristics." *Handbook of Research on Teaching.* (Edited by N. L. Gage.) Chicago: Rand McNally and Co., 1963. pp. 506–82.

11. Goodlad, John I. "The Teacher Selects, Plans, Organizes." *Learning and the Teacher.* 1959 Yearbook. Washington, D. C.: The Association for Supervision and Curriculum Development, 1959.

12. Howsam, Robert B. "Teacher Evalua-

tion: Facts and Folklore." *National Elementary Principal* 43: 7–18; November 1963.

13. Jones, E. E. "Authoritarianism As a Determinant of First-Impression Formation." *Journal of Personality* 23: 107–27; 1955.

14. Kelly, G. *The Psychology of Personal Constructs.* New York: W. W. Norton & Co., 1955.

15. Knoell, D. M. "Prediction of Teaching Success from Word Fluency Data." *Journal of Educational Research* 46: 673–83; May 1953.

16. McArthur, C. "Analyzing the Clinical Process." *Journal of Counseling Psychology* 4: 203–06; 1954.

17. Morsh, J. E., and Wilder, Eleanor W. *Identifying the Effective Instructor: A Review of the Quantitative Studies 1900–1952.* USAF Personnel Training Research Center Research Bulletin No. AFPTRC-TR-54-44, 1954.

18. Rokeach, M. "The Nature and Meaning of Dogmatism." *Psychological Review* 61: 194–204; May 1954.

19. ——. *The Open and Closed Mind.* New York: Basic Books, 1960.

20. Ryans, D. G. *Characteristics of Teachers.* Washington, D. C.: American Council on Education, 1960.

21. Scodel, A., and Mussen, P. "Social Perceptions of Authoritarians and Nonauthoritarians." *Journal of Abnormal and Social Psychology* 48: 181–84; 1953.

22. Shaffer, J.; Mednick, S.; and Seder, Judith. "Some Development Factors Related to Field-Independence in Children." Paper presented at American Psychological Association Convention, Division 7, New York; September 1, 1957.

23. Sizer, Theodore R. *Master of Arts in Teaching, Harvard's First Twenty-Five Years, 1936–1961.* A Report to the Administrative Board, Master of Arts in Teaching Program. Cambridge, Mass.: Harvard University, 1962.

24. Super, D. E., and Crites, J. O. *Appraising Vocational Fitness by Means of Psychological Tests.* Revised edition. New York: Harper and Brothers, 1962.

25. Symonds, P., and Dudek, S. "Use of the Rorschach in the Diagnosis of Teacher Effectiveness." *Journal of Projective Techniques* 20: 227–34; 1956.

26. Witkin, H., and others. *Personality Through Perception.* New York: Harper and Brothers, 1954.

27. Zubin, J. "Failures of the Rorschach Technique." *Journal of Projective Techniques* 18: 303–15; 1954.

Date Due